ENGAGING BUDDHISM

# ENGAGING BUDDHISM

## Why It Matters to Philosophy

Jay L. Garfield

OXFORD
UNIVERSITY PRESS

OXFORD
UNIVERSITY PRESS

Oxford University Press is a department of the University of Oxford. It furthers the University's objective of excellence in research, scholarship, and education by publishing worldwide.

Oxford New York
Auckland Cape Town Dar es Salaam Hong Kong Karachi
Kuala Lumpur Madrid Melbourne Mexico City Nairobi
New Delhi Shanghai Taipei Toronto

With offices in
Argentina Austria Brazil Chile Czech Republic France Greece
Guatemala Hungary Italy Japan Poland Portugal Singapore
South Korea Switzerland Thailand Turkey Ukraine Vietnam

Oxford is a registered trademark of Oxford University Press in the UK and certain other countries.

Published in the United States of America by
Oxford University Press
198 Madison Avenue, New York, NY 10016



Cataloging-in-Publication Data is on file at the Library of Congress.

ISBN 978–0–19–020434–1 (pbk.)
ISBN 978–0–19–020433–4 (hpk.)

9 8 7 6 5 4 3 2 1
Printed in the United States of America
on acid-free paper

བཤེས་གཉེན་ཆེན་པོ་དགེ་བཤེས་ཡེ་ཤེས་ཐབས་མཁས་མཆོག།
གང་གི་ཉེ་རིང་བྲལ་བའི་བྱམས་དང་བརྩེ་བའི་ཐུགས།
གང་ཉིད་ཡང་དག་གསལ་བར་འབྱེད་པའི་སློབ་དཔོན་ཉིད།
གང་གི་རྣམ་དཔྱོད་ཟབ་ཅིང་བརྙིང་བའི་ཆོས་འབྲེལ་ལས།
བདག་གཞན་སྐྱེ་བོར་སྩོལ་བའི་ཟབ་གནས་དམ་པའི་ཆོས།
དོན་ལྡན་སྙིང་པོ་ཐོབ་པར་བཀྲིན་རྗེས་དྲན་ཞུ།།

For the ven Prof Geshe Yeshes Thabkhas
Whose extraordinary kindness,
Whose perfect clarity as a teacher
And whose profound insight Into the meaning of the Buddhadharma
Has made it possible for me, and for so many others
To approach and to benefit from the ocean of Buddhist philosophy.

# CONTENTS

*Preface* *ix*

*Acknowledgments* *xxi*

1. What Is "Buddhist Philosophy"? 1
2. The Metaphysical Perspective I: Interdependence and Impermanence 24
3. The Metaphysical Perspective II: Emptiness 56
4. The Self 91
5. Consciousness 122
6. Phenomenology 175
7. Epistemology 214
8. Logic and the Philosophy of Language 242
9. Ethics 278
10. Methodological Postscript 318

*References* *337*

*Index* *359*

# PREFACE

The Western philosophical tradition is, of course, part and parcel of Western culture, entangled as much with Western politics and history as it is with Western religion and science. And these political and historical threads, like the more conceptual threads deriving from religion and science, determine, often in ways of which philosophers are but dimly aware, the character of the discipline.

While philosophy is, among contemporary academic disciplines, unique in containing its own history as a subspeciality, that history is too often focused on the history of specifically philosophical texts and their immediate intellectual context. The larger political history of the discipline is often occluded, and our self-understanding is thereby impaired. Unfortunately, that impairment is not a merely intellectual disability; it has a moral dimension as well. For the Western colonial enterprise, and the racism and blindness to non-Western ideas it enshrines, is as much a part of our intellectual heritage as are Plato, Augustine and Galileo. As a consequence, we are accustomed to regarding "philosophy" as denoting *Western* philosophy, "metaphysics" as denoting *Western* metaphysics, "ancient philosophy" as denoting *Greek* philosophy, and so on. And to the extent that in our professional practice, either in scholarship, the organization of professional meetings and journals, or in curriculum, we recognize non-Western philosophy at all, it is marked: *Asian* philosophy; *Indian* Philosophy; *African* philosophy, or the like. European philosophy is just "philosophy," the unmarked, privileged case, the "core" as it is sometimes put.

That phrase "the core" is revealing. When we use it we re-affirm the position of the European tradition at the center of human history, as the most important intellectual tradition the world has ever known, as that around which all others revolve. In the wake of colonialism and in the context of racism, this is both intellectually and morally indefensible. Indeed, the entire conduct of philosophy as a discipline—from the way our curriculum is structured to the way we run our professional organizations and journals—looks to anyone not already socialized into it like an extension of a British club in India, celebrating European intellectual hegemony and excluding the "natives."

To take the West as the unique locus of philosophical activity was never a good idea. For one thing, it is obviously and demonstrably false. For another, to do so deprives us of valuable philosophical insights. For yet another, in the context of centuries of racism and colonialism, it is to perpetuate at least a passive deprecation of non-Western cultures and people. All of this is a problem for us. And, as Eldridge Cleaver put it so eloquently, "You're either part of the solution or you're part of the problem" (Scheer 1968, xxxii).

This book is not devoted to making that case. Indeed, I don't think that anything but ostension is needed to make that case. Instead, it is meant as a step towards remediating the problem. For recognition of transgression is not sufficient to enable redemption. One needs to begin to see routes to a better way of living, and most contemporary Western philosophers, through no fault of their own, have been educated in so parochial a fashion that they cannot even imagine an alternative to their own philosophical practice.

To take the Buddhist tradition seriously in in the way I do here is one of the many first steps we might take in the way of solving the problem of Western parochialism. It is not the only possible first step, and it had better not be the last. The Buddhist tradition is but one of many non-Western philosophical traditions, and one way to gain access to them is to peruse a truly comprehensive history of philosophy, such as Ben-Ami Scharfstein's (1998) or one of the many handbooks of world philosophy, or introductions to such traditions as Asian Philosophy, Buddhist Philosophy, Indian Philosophy, Chinese Philosophy, African Philosophy, Native American Philosophy (Garfield and Edelglass 2011, Koller 2012, Laumakis 2008, Lai 2008, Bartley 2011, Imbo 1998, Carpenter 2014). Or one might choose a great non-Western text and dive in. Or retrain entirely. Any of these approaches work. A truly global philosophy must attend to non-Buddhist Indian philosophy, to Daoist and Confucian philosophy, to the many schools of Africana philosophical thought, to Native American philosophical thought and to a range of other less well-known intellectual traditions. But Buddhist philosophy is what I can offer, and I offer it here in the hope that attention to these ideas will advance the goal of a truly global philosophical engagement.

For those philosophers whose preoccupations are more systematic, and less historical or cultural in nature, I suspect that such engagement is best facilitated by attention to how some particular non-Western tradition can enable one to think through philosophical problems with which one is already preoccupied, or to see how non-Western voices can participate in current discussions. That is what I propose to do here, using the Buddhist tradition as a case study. I choose the Buddhist tradition for two reasons. First, and most important, it is the one with which I am most familiar. Someone else might, and should, write a similar book on Daoist philosophy or on Native American philosophy. But I am not competent to do so.

Second, and perhaps less arbitrarily, my study of Buddhist philosophy and my work with colleagues in which we have integrated Buddhist and Western approaches and ideas, convinces me that this is a living tradition that benefits from engagement with the West, and from engagement with which Western philosophy benefits. An important precondition for genuine conversation—mutual interest—is hence satisfied. Another precondition for successful conversation is also satisfied, and in part motivates this book: The concerns and methods of Buddhist philosophy and Western philosophy are sufficiently proximate to each other, sharing sufficient horizons, that they are easily mutually intelligible, but sufficiently distant from one another that each has something to learn from the other. Conversation can hence be productive.

My hope is that by taking a number of examples of important current philosophical issues and showing how Buddhist voices can contribute, I can show Western philosophers both *that* the Buddhist tradition matters to them, and *how* to engage that tradition. I am not interested in defending a Buddhist position here, much less in trying to demonstrate the superiority of either tradition over the other. Instead, I want to argue, through a series of examples, that ignoring the insights and arguments that tradition has to offer is irrational for anyone seriously interested in any of a number of philosophical problems. If anyone takes from this the hunch that the same is true, *mutatis mutandis*, with respect to many of the world's philosophical traditions, so much the better.

In this respect, the present volume is a kind of mirror image of my earlier book, *Western Idealism and Its Critics* (2011), in which I strove to demonstrate to Tibetan Buddhist philosophers the claim—frankly incredible to many of them—that Western philosophy could deliver any significant arguments or insights to discussions of idealism. I am pleased to say that many of my Tibetan colleagues took the point. I hope that I encounter minds as open in the Western academy.

There are many things that this book is not. It is not an introduction to Buddhist philosophy. There are several very good books on the market that do that already (Kalupahana 1976, Gethin 1998, Guenther 1976, Laumakis 2008, Siderits 2007, Emmanuel 2013, Carpenter 2014). Nor is it a brief for treating the Buddhist tradition as a philosophical tradition, as opposed to a purely devotional tradition. Mark Siderits (2007) and Paul Williams (2009) have already done that job admirably. Nor is it a deep exploration of some single important issue in Buddhist philosophy, or examination of a single core text. There are books aplenty that do this, and many are cited in these pages. Finally, it is not an anthology of Buddhist texts. Edelglass and Garfield (2009) have already done that.

Instead, it is a demonstration for Western philosophers of the value of engaging with the Buddhist tradition over a wide range of topics, and of the value of that engagement for contemporary philosophical practice. I would measure its success by subsequent decisions to read Buddhist texts, to take Buddhist positions seriously and to reconfigure curriculum to attend to Buddhist texts. I would be even happier if Buddhism was not alone in this reconfiguration, if the prefix "Western" or "European" became de rigeur when the topic under discussion was purely Western, and if our professional meetings and journals became a bit less like colonial relics.

There is no common structure to the chapters in the volume. Some, particularly the earlier chapters, introduce Buddhist ideas systematically and then apply them to some topic or literature of interest in the contemporary West. Others begin with a problem, and then introduce a Buddhist voice. Others take hybrid approaches. My aim is to focus on ideas, and not on comparison. And the choice of texts and ideas to which I pay attention will perforce be idiosyncratic. The chapters are arranged topically, not historically, or according to Buddhist traditions. So they move freely between Western and Buddhist ideas, and among Buddhist ideas from quite diverse traditions. I have tried to represent the range of domains in which I see fruitful dialogue emerging. There is one significant lacuna, however, and that is aesthetics. The Buddhist tradition in which by far the most sophisticated aesthetic theory has developed is that of Japan. But most of the important work in Japanese aesthetics is only available in the Japanese language, which I do not read. So, I feel a bit of an amateur in that domain, and leave it to somebody more qualified to fill that important gap.

I spend much of my professional life with Indian and Tibetan Madhyamaka and Yogācāra treatises, and so I probably give these texts more prominence than some might think they deserve. I do so not because I think that they are disproportionately representative or important in the Buddhist traditions, but rather because they are the ones that come to my mind most often when I work in Buddhist philosophy. I have tried to salt the book with texts from other traditions as well, and I hope that my readers will attend to the Buddhist tradition broadly, not only to the corner I find so absorbing. I also confess that at times my reading of parts of the Buddhist tradition may seem a bit tendentious or idiosyncratic. I present Buddhist texts as I read them, Buddhist doctrines and ideas as I understand them. I see no other way to come at this. This is a rich tradition in which canonical figures and modern scholars alike dispute with one another regarding the proper readings of texts and interpretation of doctrine. At times those disputes are central to my presentation. But I do not pretend to neutrality, or to completeness in these matters. Instead, I present my take on these matters, in the hope that it is of interest to others, and with reasonable confidence that it is a reasonable reading.

A word about the title is in order. When I use the word *Engaging*, I do so with the Sanskrit and Tibetan terms most often translated by this term in mind. In Sanskrit the term is *avatāra;* in Tibetan *'jug pa*. These terms have nice semantic ranges. They can mean *engaging with*, or *engaging in*, as in engaging with a body of literature or an object, or in an activity; they could equally well be translated as *descending*, as in coming down from a mountain into the real world; or as *manifesting*, as in being the manifestation of a deity or a realized being; they can also mean *proceeding*, as in proceeding on a journey. And they can mean *an introduction*, as in *Introduction to Buddhist Philosophy*. I like these terms, and I bring all of these senses to mind when I invite the reader to Engage with Buddhism—to take it seriously; to take up thinking through the point of view of this tradition; to come down from the mountain of Eurocentric isolation into a multicultural philosophical marketplace; to manifest as a cosmopolitan intellectual; to take up a new journey; and to be introduced to the Buddhist world.

There are many to whom I owe enormous debts of gratitude. Thanks are first due to Smith College for sabbatical leave and to the John Templeton Foundation for generous research support. Without this support and the encouragement that the College and the Templeton Foundation provided, this book would have been impossible. I also thank the Australian Research Council for research support that facilitated much of the work represented in this volume and the National Endowment for the Humanities for a summer institute in the context of which many of these ideas germinated. Thanks also to Yale-NUS College for a generous research grant that made the completion of this project a lot easier.

This book has been a long time in the making, and many have contributed to my thinking about these matters. Reflecting on their contributions only increases my confidence in the importance of dependent origination, and my sense that I deserve very little credit for the ideas I express.

I recognize the ancestry of some of these thoughts in what I was taught when I was an undergraduate at Oberlin College, first by Norman S. Care, who introduced me to Hume and Kant and then by Robert Grimm, with whom I studied Wittgenstein. I also owe an enormous debt to Annette Baier and to Wilfrid Sellars who taught me in my graduate studies. Their stamp on my own thinking about the history of Western philosophy and the philosophy of mind is indelible.

I was introduced to Buddhist philosophy by Robert A.F. Thurman, who also kindled my fascination with Tsongkhapa's thinking and directed my attention to the affinities between Hume's and Wittgenstein's thought and that of Candrakīrti. Bob has been a source of inspiration and a mentor as I have worked to develop an understanding of the Indian and Tibetan Buddhist tradition. David Kalupahana, Steve Odin and Guy Newland taught me Nāgārjuna, and Guy first directed my attention to Tsongkhapa's *Ocean of Reasoning (rTsa she tik chen rigs pa'i rgya mtsho)* as a way into Madhyamaka thought. Since that time, he has taught me much about Madhyamaka, and still more about how compassion can be embodied in life and in the academic profession. His translations and his expositions of Buddhist doctrine are models of lucidity, and his comportment itself teaches Buddhist ethics. The ven Khenpo Lobsang Tsetan Rinpoche was my first Tibetan language teacher, and the first to introduce me to the reading of Tibetan philosophical texts. I always remember him with respect and gratitude.

I thank my principal teachers of Buddhist philosophy. I have no words to express my gratitude to the ven Geshe Yeshe Thabkhas of the Central University of Tibetan Studies to whom this book is dedicated and to the late ven Gen Lobsang Gyatso of the Institute of Buddhist Dialectics. Their patient and erudite exposition of text, doctrine and method have shaped my understanding of this tradition. Their kindness and compassion, enthusiasm for philosophy and their encouragement of cross-cultural engagement have been a source of constant inspiration for this project. I also thank the most ven Prof Samdhong Rinpoche and my longtime teacher, friend, colleague and collaborator, the ven Prof Geshe Ngawang Samten, Padma Sri, Vice Chancellor of the Central University of Tibetan Studies. They have each not only taught me much about Buddhist philosophy and the Tibetan tradition, but have also facilitated my entry into the Tibetan scholarly world and my research in innumerable ways. Their generosity is a lesson in itself. The ven Geshe Namgyal Damdul, of Emory University, has been a valuable teacher and collaborator. Our work together on *Western Idealism and Its Critics* shaped many of the ideas I develop here. I also thank the ven Geshe Dorje Damdul of Tibet House for many useful discussions from which I have learned a great deal, and the ven Prof Tashi Tsering and the ven Prof Sonam Gyatso, both of the Central University of Tibetan Studies, for many productive conversations.

The Smith College Philosophy Department and the Five College Buddhist Studies Faculty Seminar have provided a rich and supportive environment for this research. In the philosophy department, I particularly acknowledge my colleague and collaborator Nalini Bhushan, from whom have learned so much about how to do philosophy across cultures and about the enterprise of Indian philosophy, and John Connolly, from whose reflections on the relationship between philosophical and religious traditions, and from whose insights into Wittgenstein's philosophy, hermeneutics, and Buddhist philosophy I have profited. I am also grateful to my colleagues in the Five College Buddhist Studies program. Peter Gregory and Jamie Hubbard have shaped my thinking about Buddhist Studies and in particular about East Asian Buddhist philosophy. Maria Heim has taught me a lot about the Pāli tradition and about how to approach Buddhist Ethics; and Georges Dreyfus has been an invaluable interlocutor on matters concerning Buddhist philosophy of mind, phenomenology and epistemology.

My new home at Yale-NUS College and the National University of Singapore is proving to be a wonderful research environment as well. I am blessed with generous and thoughtful colleagues from whom I have learned much and whose serious commitment to cross-cultural philosophy in research and pedagogy is a real inspiration. I note in particular Neil Mehta, Sandra Field, Simon Duffy, Nico Silins, Matt Walker, Taran Kang, Cathay Liu, Amber Carpenter, Andrew Bailey, Neil Sinhababu, Ben Blumson and Saranindra Nath Tagore who have all contributed to my thinking about these issues and who have contributed to the collegial environment since I have arrived here. I thank Michael Pelczar, Pericles Lewis, Charles Bailyn, Casey Nagey, Jenifer Raver and Grace Kwan Chi-En for creating an environment in which such research is possible.

My association with the University of New Mexico and with the Bodhi Manda Zen Center has been rewarding. Richard Hayes and John Taber have taught me a great deal, about Dignāga and Dharmakīrti to be sure, but also about the nature of Buddhist thought and practice in the West. The ven Joshu Sasaki Roshi has no doubt influenced my thinking in ways that I may never understand. Through this association, I was also fortunate enough to encounter Sandy Gentei Stewart Roshi, one of the most lucid and inspiring Western Buddhist teachers I have ever encountered, and one to whose formulations I often turn when perplexed. The folks at Bodhi Manda and Sandy have shown me how to integrate Zen thought with Indian and Tibetan Madhyamaka.

At Bodhi Manda I also met Prof. Shoryu Katsura, one of the titans of contemporary Buddhist Studies. Prof. Katsura's work on Buddhist epistemology and philosophy of mind and the relationship between Buddhist epistemology and Madhyamaka has been invaluable to me, and I have always profited from and enjoyed our philosophical discussions. His combination of philological erudition and philosophical acumen is rare indeed.

My life in Buddhist and cross-cultural philosophy has been immensely enriched by my association with the Hamburg Buddhist Studies community. I acknowledge in particular Prof. Michael Zimmermann, the ven Prof Jampa Tsedron (Carola Roloff), Mr. Christoph Spitz and Ms. Birgit Stratmann. I have benefitted enormously from philosophical interchange with this wonderful group in Hamburg, as well as from their generous hospitality.

My dear friend and collaborator Graham Priest deserves special mention. We have been working together on the interface of Buddhist and Western philosophy for a decade and a half. All of my recent thought about these matters has developed in the context of this conversation and co-authorship. It is truly a gift to have such a colleague and friend, and an even greater gift to have had the benefit of such a sustained philosophical friendship. I owe virtually all of what I write here in some way to our work together, and I am very grateful indeed.

This brings me to the Cowherds, the collective of which Graham is also a member. Working with the Cowherds, first on *Moonshadows* and now on *Moonpaths*, has been a source of great philosophical pleasure and real insight. This collective, also comprising Koji Tanaka, Bronwyn Finnigan, Georges Dreyfus, Tom Tillemans, Mark Siderits, Jan Westerhoff, Sonam Thakchöe, Guy Newland, Amber Carpenter, Charles Goodman and Steve Jenkins, has shown how to engage Buddhism philosophically, integrating the methodologies of Buddhist Studies and contemporary philosophical analysis. The present work is but an extension of the Cowherds' project, and I thank each Cowherd for helping me to think through problems in Buddhist philosophy and to think about the relationship between Buddhist and Western philosophy.

I do want to single out four other Cowherds for special thanks. First, I thank Tom Tillemans, whose rare combination of unparalleled philological skills and encyclopedic knowledge of the Buddhist tradition, superb philosophical skills and appreciation of contemporary Western philosophical literature, and absolute intellectual rigor made him an anchor of the first Cowherds project. Second, Jan Westerhoff deserves thanks for extended discussions of Madhyamaka and Yogācāra. We share obsessions, and Jan's clear and rigorous thinking about these matters has clearly improved mine. Sonam Thakchöe has been a colleague for decades. Every time I work with Sonam-la I learn something, and almost always I discover that something I have never considered is actually central to something about which I have been puzzled. I am always grateful for his insight and his joy in philosophical exploration. Mark Siderits and I rarely agree. But we often talk, and because of our disagreements, and because of the clarity of his thought and expression, I always learn from those talks. I am grateful for his willingness to continue these arguments.

I have also had the great pleasure and good fortune to work for years on a number of projects with John Powers, from whom I have learned a lot, especially about Yogācāra. John has been very generous to me and to a generation of younger scholars. Our most recent project on Yogācāra has brought me into closer philosophical collaboration with Dan Lusthaus, David Eckel and Douglas Duckworth. Translating and talking philosophy with this team has been richly rewarding.

In the summer of 2012, Christian Coseru, Evan Thompson and I co-directed an NEH institute on consciousness in a cross-cultural perspective. This was an extraordinary experience in which a group of scholars from Buddhist Studies, Western analytic philosophy and Western phenomenology talked all day for two weeks about consciousness. The quality of these discussions was very high, and I learned a lot from each person in that room. There are too many to name individually.

But a few deserve special thanks. First, Christian and Evan. From each, over the years, in conversation and in print, I have learned a lot. Each has devoted his professional life to the project of integrating Buddhist and Western philosophy, and each has done so with great skill and intellectual generosity. Sheridan Hough has taught me the relevance of Kierkegaard's thought to this project. Laura Guerrero has shown me new ways to think about Dharmakīrti. Special thanks to Dan Arnold, from whom I have learned so much over the years, and whose books have demonstrated the value of serious philosophical engagement with the Buddhist tradition. Dave Chalmers, Charles Siewert, Shaun Gallagher, Jonardon Ganeri, Bob Sharf, Jake Davis, Emily McRae and Jennifer McWeeny each contributed importantly to my understanding of the issues I explore here. I thank them all.

There are many other colleagues of whose contributions I am conscious and to whom I am grateful as I write here. Among them are Paul Harrison with whom I worked on Śāntideva; Charlie Hallisey whose insights into Buddhist ethics have influenced my thinking and whose encouragement in this project I value; Sara McClintock, for many useful conversations over the years; John Dunne, for spirited exchanges in which remarkable scholarship is put to good philosophical use, and from which I always learn; Jonathan Gold, with whom I started out in Buddhist Studies, and who has taught me much about Yogācāra; and Yasuo Deguchi, with whom I have recently been collaborating, and whose work on the interface of logic and Buddhist philosophy is remarkable.

As a teacher, I am also keenly aware that I owe much to my students, many of whom are now my colleagues. There are so many I could name, but I single out for thanks among those now working in the academic profession

Constance Kassor, Karin Meyers, Dan McNamara, Joel Feldman and Andrew Quintman. I learned from each of them in the classroom, and now I have the joy of learning from their published work and contributions to conferences.

I have benefited enormously from the comments and critique of the members of my graduate seminar at the National University of Singapore. Ms. Chua Wei Lin has caught important omissions. Martin Kovacic has offered very insightful comments that have improved this book. I am extremely grateful to Nico Silins, Neil Sinhababu, Ryo Tanaka and Ben Blumson, who have read with great care and generosity, and have forced me to rethink many issues and to correct many errors. Ben and Neil have been particularly assiduous in calling me out on obscurity, confusion, illicit presupposition and just simple errors, and so many of their suggestions have been taken on board that to note each one would issue in footnotes of gratitude on virtually every page. I thank them for their generous critical support of this project. I also thank the students in Graham Priest's graduate seminar on Buddhist Philosophy at CUNY Graduate Center and those in Eyal Aviv's seminar on Buddhist Philosophy at George Washington University, both in the Spring of 2014, for lots of useful feedback.

I have learned a great deal from two more recent graduate students, Nic Bommarito and Daniel Aitken, each of whom is doing groundbreaking work on Buddhist ethics. Much of my most recent thinking about Buddhist ethics has evolved in dialogue with them, and I thank them for their contributions. Special thanks to my student research assistants, Becca Alexander at Smith College and Ling Xi Min and Rocco Hu at Yale-NUS College, without whose work this project would have never been completed. They have each chased references, edited my roughest prose, challenged my claims and have helped in so many other ways.

This book is better for the careful comments I have received from my colleagues. I thank Eyal Aviv, Lynne Rudder Baker, Eviatar Shulman, Shaun Nichols, Mitch Parsell and Sonam Thakchöe for careful reading and helpful suggestions. Special thanks to Maria Heim for a searching critical reading of the text that pulled me up on a lot of my prejudices, and forced a good deal of rethinking, and to Douglas Duckworth for extensive critique, always on target. Steve Jenkins constantly challenges my readings and has talked me out of many errors and infelicities.

Mr. Yeshi Tashi, another student from whom I have learned a great deal, and now a colleague, has kindly translated the dedication of this book into Tibetan, a gift both to me and to the teacher we share.

Finally, and most importantly, I will fail to express adequately my gratitude to Blaine Garson, without whom none of this—this book or any of my other work—or indeed any of my life as I know it, would be possible. She has traveled with me to the ends of the earth, or has kept our lives going on the homefront when I have been off alone; she has supported me, and has challenged me; she has listened critically to what I have had to say, and has taught me. She has given me a life that I would not trade for any other. Nothing I could say or do could adequately repay her kindness.

# ACKNOWLEDGMENTS

Parts of chapter 2 in *Moonshadows* ("Taking Conventional Truth Seriously") appear in chapter 6 of this volume. I thank Oxford University Press for permission to use this material.

Parts of "The Conventional Status of Reflexive Awareness: What's at Stake in a Tibetan Debate" are used in chapter 5. I am grateful to *Philosophy East and West* for permission to use this material.

Parts of chapter 6 appear in "I Am a Brain in a Vat, or Perhaps a Pile of Sticks by the Side of the Road," published in Garfield and Westerhoff, *Madhyamaka and Yogācāra: Allies or Rivals*. I thank Oxford University Press for permission to use this material.

The translations from *Alaṃbanāparikṣā*, and from Gungthang's and Dendar's commentaries in chapter 6 are joint work with Douglas Duckworth, M. David Eckel, John Powers and Sonam Thakchöe. I thank them for permission to use this material.

Parts of "What Is It Like to be a Bodhisattva? Moral Phenomenology in Śāntideva's *Bodhicāryāvatāra* appear in chapter 10. I am grateful to the *Journal of the International Association of Buddhist Studies* for permission to use this material.

Chapter 10 is to be published as "Methodology for Mādhyamikas" in Deguchi, Garfield, Tanaka and Priest, *The Moon Points Back: Buddhism, Logic and Analytic Philosophy*. I thank Oxford University Press for permission to use that material.

To study the buddha way is to study the self. To study the self is to forget the self. To forget the self is to be actualized by myriad things. When actualized by myriad things, your body and mind as well as the bodies and minds of others drop away. No trace of realization remains, and this no-trace continues endlessly.

—*Dōgen, Genjōkōan* (trans. R. Aitken and K. Tanahashi)

# 1 WHAT IS "BUDDHIST PHILOSOPHY?"

## 1. Introduction

I spend a certain amount of my professional life working with Tibetan colleagues and students in India. In the course of our collaborations, they often ask me a question like, "What do Western philosophers think the nature of mind is?" or, "What do Western philosophers think a good life is?" I have to take a long deep breath and explain that the West is a very big place, that there are a lot of Western philosophers, and that they disagree among themselves about every important question in philosophy.

This might seem odd. But I have the same experience in the West. I am often asked by Western colleagues and students, "What do Buddhists think about personal identity?" or, "What do Buddhists think about idealism?" And I have to take a long deep breath and explain that the Buddhist world is a very big place, that there are a lot of Buddhist philosophers, and that they disagree among themselves about every important question in philosophy. Just like their colleagues in the West.

But not quite. For the Buddhist tradition is but one of the great Indian traditions of philosophical reflection, and India is only one part of Asia. Within the Indian traditions, the Buddhist tradition, although vast and diverse, is unified by a coherent set of joint broad commitments that define a position as Buddhist. The precise interpretation of these commitments differs among Buddhist schools, but some allegiance to some recognizable form of them defines a position as Buddhist. When I refer to "Buddhism," or to "a Buddhist view," as opposed to the view of a particular Buddhist school or philosopher, I will have this broad picture in mind. Often it will be necessary to be more precise, and to specify the doctrine of a particular figure or group of figures, but sometimes the broad brush will do for our purposes.

These commitments can be summarized as follows:

- Suffering (*dukkha*) or discontent is ubiquitous in the world. The sense of *dukkha* is complex, and we will have occasion to spell it out in detail below, but for now think of it as a sense of the unsatisfactoriness of life.
- The origin of *dukkha* is in primal confusion about the fundamental nature of reality, and so its cure is at bottom a reorientation toward ontology and an awakening (*bodhi*) to the actual nature of existence.
- All phenomena are impermanent (*anitya*), interdependent (*pratītya-samutpāda*) and have no intrinsic nature (*śūnya*). Once again, each of these Sanskrit terms is a technical term; each has a complex semantic range that does not map easily onto that of any English philosophical term; and the sense of each is contested within the Buddhist tradition. We will return to each many times in this book. But we need to start somewhere, and these rough and ready translations will do for now.
- Fundamental confusion is to take phenomena, including preeminently oneself, to be permanent, independent and to have an essence or intrinsic nature (*svabhāva*).
- The elimination (*nirvāṇa*), or at least the substantial reduction of *dukkha* through such reorientation, is possible.
- An ethically appropriate orientation toward the world is characterized by the cultivation of *mudita* (an attitude of rejoicing in the welfare and goodness of others, of *mettā*) beneficence toward others, and especially of *karuṇā* (a commitment to act for the welfare of sentient beings).[1]

Of course the specific interpretations of these commitments differ from one Buddhist school to another, and a great deal of other variation in a range of metaphysical, epistemological, semantic, logical, hermeneutical, ethical

1. The reader who is familiar with the elements of Buddhism will recognize that I have articulated what are generally known as the "four noble (or ennobling) truths" taught by Siddhartha Gautama (the historical Buddha, or awakened one) in the *Discourse Setting in Motion the Wheel of Doctrine (Dhammacakkappavattana-sutta)*, along with some related doctrine. The four truths are generally articulated as follows:

(1) All of life is suffering;
(2) There is a cause of suffering (primal confusion, leading to attachment and aversion);
(3) There is a release from suffering (through the cessation of that attachment and aversion consequent on the termination of primal confusion);
(4) The eightfold path to the release from suffering (right view; right intention; right speech; right action; right livelihood; right effort; right mindfulness; right meditation).

I have conjoined the four noble truths with the three characteristics of reality (impermanence, selflessness and interdependence) to construct this list of basic tenets.

and aesthetic commitments follow from these, each with variations. We will have occasion to remark on some of that variety below. But surveying the range of Buddhist schools and doctrines is not my aim in this book. Instead, I wish first, to spell out my own Madhyamaka- and Yogācāra-[2] (and probably Geluk (*dGe lugs*))[3] -inflected understanding of these core commitments in a way that ties them together as a coherent perspective on reality; and second, to take particular examples of Buddhist analyses and current Western debates to show what a Buddhist voice can contribute to a contemporary conversation, and what joining that conversation can contribute to the modern Buddhist tradition.

Before returning to the broad principles noted above, a remark on methodology is in order. Philosophy is, after all, the reflexive discipline: just what it is to practice philosophy in the company of texts from multiple cultural traditions is itself a philosophical problem. One approach to that practice, initiated by the great late 19th-century Indian philosopher Brajendranath Seal, is *comparative philosophy*. We needed comparative philosophy at an earlier stage of cultural globalization when it was necessary to juxtapose different philosophical traditions in order to gain an entrée and in order to learn how to read alien traditions as philosophical. But now we can safely say, "been there; done that." I therefore take it for granted that the days when "comparative philosophy" was the task are over, and a different methodology is necessary at this stage of philosophical practice.

I have previously used the term "cross-cultural philosophy" to characterize my own enterprise, and I still like that term. Mark Siderits prefers to think in terms of "fusion philosophy" (2003, xi). I like that phrase as well, but I think that it can be misleading. I intend not to fuse philosophical traditions, but rather, while respecting their distinct heritages and horizons, to put them in dialogue with one another, recognizing enough commonality of purpose, concern and even method that conversation is possible, but still enough difference in outlook that conversation is both necessary and informative. This may well be what Siderits has in mind as well, and I have no quarrel with his project, but the term suggests a project that is not my own. I am trying to build bridges, not to merge streams.

I should also note that this book is not meant to be a comprehensive introduction to Buddhist philosophy, and still less an introduction to Buddhism

2. The middle way and the Buddhist idealist schools. We will characterize each in more detail below.

3. One of the principal schools of Tibetan Buddhism, and indeed the one in which I pursued most of my own study of Buddhist philosophy.

as a civilization or religious tradition. Nor again is it meant to be a systematic presentation of a single Buddhist tradition. There is much of importance in the Buddhist world that I will ignore, including much of its attention to soteriological, cosmological, devotional and practice concerns. For example, I do not discuss Buddhist theories of rebirth, of karma, or approaches to meditation. That is not because I take these to be unimportant, or even peripheral, to understanding Buddhist thought. It is rather because I do not see them as principal sites of engagement with Western philosophy, which is the primary intent of this volume. And there are many important Buddhist ideas that I have simply left aside, either because I don't see them as important sites of engagement at the moment, or because I don't understand them enough myself at this point.

And while I try to retain a catholic, and decidedly nonsectarian attitude to Buddhist philosophical traditions, representing quite a few of them in this book, I am not self-consciously striving for completeness, or even fairness, in coverage, only touching base with the ideas that I have found most useful in my philosophical explorations. This perhaps somewhat capricious (with the etymology of that word firmly in the mind of this once and future goatherd) approach is, despite its incompleteness, very much at odds with another way I could have gone. That is, I could have restricted my attention to a single lineage or tradition, mapping and interacting with its philosophical commitments, and striving for fidelity in conveying its view of things. I have elected not to do that for several reasons. First, I simply think that the Buddhist tradition is richer for its variety, and I would like to convey some of that—there simply is no monopoly on good ideas held by any one tradition or lineage; second, I do not want to convey the misleading impression that I am an orthodox exponent of a single tradition; third, I don't want to play the sectarian game of valorizing one tradition at the expense of others.

One further remark on my methodology is important. As a translator, I am frequently confronted with the difficulty of rendering Tibetan or Sanskrit terms into English. This difficulty, as any translator or sophisticated consumer of translations, is aware, is multidimensional. (See Gómez 1999, Bar-On 1993 and Garfield unpublished for extensive discussion of these issues.) One dimension reflects the very different philosophical and linguistic milieus in which terms in source and target languages figure. Simply because the meanings of words in any language are fixed by their relations both to other terms and to philosophical or other ideological commitments in the cultures to which those languages belong, there is bound to be slippage. There will be terms in any language whose semantic range is not shared by any term in any other language. We will discuss some terms that pose this problem in Buddhist languages below.

Another dimension reflects that fact that technical terms are often contested within a tradition, and have different meanings in the hands of different philosophers. "Idea" means one thing for Locke, and another for Hume, as does "perception." And some terms are ambiguous even in the work of a single philosopher, with different meanings in different contexts. The same kinds of ambiguities and shifts in meanings of technical terms are found in the Buddhist tradition, with terms changing their meanings for a single school over time, diverging in meaning when used by distinct schools, or simply having different meanings in different contexts.

As a consequence, while I will present and rely upon quite a few translations in this book, and will adopt some favored translations of some technical terms, I will also often discuss a term and then leave it untranslated, inviting my reader to enter the world of Buddhist philosophy in part by entering some of its language. Just as we learn an unfamiliar culture better by learning at least a bit of its language, and coming to inhabit the perspective on the world reflected in that language, we can come to appreciate a distinct philosophical framework a bit better by adopting some of its technical vocabulary and accustoming ourselves to thinking through that vocabulary. While this might seem awkward at first, I invite the reader to give it a try. It will pay off.

A word on policy regarding the rendering of personal names and of the titles of texts is in order. Sanskrit personal names will always be written in Roman script with diacriticals. This has become so standard in Buddhist Studies that I see no reason to deviate from this practice. Those interested in proper pronunciation of Sanskrit can refer to any of many good published or online guides to Romanized Sanskrit. Tibetan personal names are another matter, as the standard Wylie transliteration of Tibetan gives no real clue to pronunciation to anyone unfamiliar with that language. I will therefore spell all Tibetan personal names phonetically, but will give the Wylie transliteration on first occurrence should anyone want to know how to spell these names. The titles of all texts will be translated into English, with the original-language title in parentheses at first mention. Just as we write *Critique of Pure Reason* these days instead of *Kritik der Reinen Vernuft* we will write *Introduction to the Middle Way* instead of *Madhyamakāvatāra*. This should be easier on readers unfamiliar with Asian languages. Specialists may cringe, but they have the original at first occurrence, and they should take comfort in the fact that this is one more step toward moving these texts into the Anglophone mainstream.

One final methodological note: This is not meant to be an authoritative treatment of particular texts in the history of Buddhist philosophy, but rather an invitation to those who do not know the tradition well to take it seriously enough to approach such treatments. For this reason, I eschew the common practice of including footnotes containing the original language whenever I present a translation of a passage from a canonical text. I figure that most readers won't know the original languages, and those few who do know the languages know where to find the texts. And we philosophers don't do that when we quote Kant, Descartes or Aristotle, unless we are trying to make a point about the translation or the original terms. Unless otherwise noted, all translations from Tibetan are my own. The reader unaccustomed to Pali, Sanskrit and Tibetan terminology may find some of the names and terms used unfamiliar, confusing and hard to pronounce. When discussing specific terms, I will often include terms in several canonical languages. But I will always gloss them and will always translate text names.

## 2. The Ubiquity of *Dukkha*

*The World is a beautiful place to be born into*
*If you don't mind happiness not always being so very much fun…*

—*Lawrence Ferlinghetti (1958, 108–110)*

First, let me say why I am not translating *dukkha*, which is usually translated as *suffering, dissatisfaction, unease, stress, anxiety* or even *pain*. This term is so central to Buddhist philosophy, and its semantic range does not coincide perfectly, or even very well, with any of these perfectly adequate, but very different, English choices, each of which can function as a technical term in Western moral psychology. I am therefore worried that too quick a translation can lead to too great an assimilation of Buddhist ideas to Western ideas, or to finding what Buddhist philosophers take to be Siddhartha Gautama's most fundamental insight to be either trivially true or trivially false, depending upon the translation chosen. As we explore the senses of the ubiquity of *dukkha*, what the term means will become contextually apparent, and we will do well to use this Pali loan word.

When in the *The Discourse Setting in Motion the Wheel of the Doctrine (Dhammacakkappavattana-sutta)*[4] Siddhartha Gautama says that "all this is *dukkha*," the scope of the claim is broad, and the sense of the term is rich. First of all, "all this" means everything: every aspect of human life, both on

4. The Pāli term *sutta* and the Sanksrit *sūtra* are intertranslatable. In the Buddhist context a *sutta* or a *sutra* is a text taken to be spoken by or directly approved by the historical Buddha Siddhartha Gautama. I use *sutta* when the text in question is a Pāli *sutta, sūtra* when the text is a Sanskrit *sūtra*. We will return to the relation between these bodies of literature in the final section of this chapter.

the subject and the object side, the animate and the inanimate, is either an instance of *dukkha* or a cause of *dukkha* in ordinary human experience. It is partly for this reason that we cannot use any of the standard English equivalents without careful gloss and a string of caveats. In order to see why this is the case—why *dukkha* is such a pervasive and universal aspect of experience—it is helpful to explore the three levels at which, from a Buddhist perspective, *dukkha* operates.

At the most mundane and obvious level, our lives are permeated by *dukkha* in its manifestation as straightforward physical and mental pain. We endure headaches, illnesses, the boredom of airport terminals, fatigue at the end of a long day, hunger, thirst, difficulties in interpersonal relationships, the anxiety of the dentist's waiting room, the awareness of our own mortality, the terror of immanent death. We suffer the annoyance of not having what we want ("Lord, won't you buy me a Mercedes Benz...") and dissatisfaction with what we have ("How can I miss you if you won't go away?..."). Most of us experience at least some aspect of this discomfort daily. That is the most superficial aspect of the pervasiveness of *dukkha*, and it should be obvious that just about anything and anyone in our environment can, in the right circumstances, be the occasion for *dukkha*.

If we are lucky enough to experience a day in which none of this occurs, we might say to ourselves as we settle in for a glass of good wine in the evening, "Life is good!" But even here there is *dukkha* in this first sense, even if in a subtler manifestation. For we must be aware that others are experiencing the slings and arrows of outrageous fortune that we have today avoided. We might feel sympathy for them, a sadness that they are in pain, even if we are not. ("When something is wrong with my baby, something is wrong with me...") And that emotional pain in us is *dukkha*, occasioned not only by their discomfort, but also, paradoxically, by our comfort, which we know is, in the end, a matter of chance, and not something we earned. After all, who earns the good fortune not to have been born in a war zone, or without a ghastly hereditary illness?

On the other hand, we might *not* be troubled by pangs of sympathy or guilt when we contemplate our own good fortune and the suffering of others. In that case, however, we do not avoid this subtle *dukkha*, but suffer from a deeper and subtler version of it. For none of us could contemplate a self that is utterly indifferent to the suffering of others, and utterly complacent about one's own privilege, with complete approval. ("No man is an island / Entire of itself.") None of us, that is, would want our children to grow up to be like that, or would honor a colleague for those traits. Therefore, if we notice this attitude in ourselves, we experience the *dukkha* of knowing that we are less than we would be, that we cannot reflectively endorse our own attitudes, and we experience the *dukkha* of shame.[5]

This is but the first level. The second level of pervasive *dukkha* is the *dukkha* of change. While there is a retail chain called *Forever 21,* none of us is forever 21. We are all aging, and we know that. Each moment of life is a moment closer to infirmity, pain, dementia, the loss of our loved ones and death. Each moment of life is therefore necessarily bound up with *dukkha,* and we know that. We either dwell on that fact and fret, or repress it and seethe. Everything we enjoy—all sources of happiness—are also impermanent, and so are slipping from our grasp, or at least from their status as sources of pleasure at every moment. The best bottle of wine will soon be empty; the sunset lasts only a few minutes; our children age; we tire of what was once our favorite music. This, too, is a source of *dukkha.*

The third and most profound sense of *dukkha,* and the one that gets us most directly to its pervasive character, is the *dukkha* of pervasive conditioning. We live in a world of inextricable interdependence, where most of the causal chains that impinge on our well-being are outside of our control. We cannot seize a day or our own destiny and control it; we cannot "stand on our own two feet," however much we may be exhorted to do so. Our well-being, security and success depend not only upon our own efforts, but upon our genetics, the weather, earthquakes, the presence of disease, the decisions of political leaders or university administrators, just plain luck, other drivers on the road, the skills of the pilot who flies the plane, the judgment of a doctor or the kindness of strangers.

None of us can ensure safety from misfortune on our own. We know that, and this is *dukkha,* and it is *dukkha* at its deepest and most fundamental level, for from the perspective of Buddhist metaphysics, as we shall see below, causal interdependence is the deepest and most fundamental fact about reality. Causal interdependence, in turn, is inextricably bound up with *dukkha,* both because we are subject to misfortune at any moment and because we must live in that knowledge and attendant anxiety. This is why change is a source of *dukkha,* and why, even when we are not currently suffering pain or misfortune, the presence of pain and misfortune in our past, future or fellows is nonetheless our *dukkha.*

We can now see why *dukkha* is so pervasive, and so why the term *dukkha* does not admit of easy translation into a language that does not encode this

5. It is interesting to note (and we will return to this in our discussion of ethics toward the end of this book) that a sense of shame (*hiri*) is regarded as an important human virtue in Buddhist ethical theory. See Heim (2013) for an excellent discussion.

view of reality. Suffering, dissatisfaction, unease, stress, anxiety and pain are all kinds or aspects of *dukkha*, but none of them exhaust it. Siddhartha Gautama's genius was not simply to see that we suffer, or that many of us are unhappy. That has been noted many times by philosophers in many traditions. His genius was instead to see that *dukkha* is the fundamental structure of our lives, what Heidegger would have called our *existentiale*. To be human is to live in *dukkha*.

And his genius was to see that this is a *problem*, indeed *the* problem of human life. For *dukkha* is universally undesirable, or at least it is undesirable to most of us. And this means that our lives and the worlds we inhabit, which are the most desirable of all things, are in fact, as they are lived, undesirable. If our lives are to be worth living, and if they are to be sources of happiness and legitimate motivation, this puzzle demands solution. This is the absolute foundation of the Buddhist view of the nature of human life. (See Carpenter 2014, c. 1 for a more detailed discussion of *dukkha*.)

## 3. Primal Confusion

*Dust in our eyes our own boots kicked up...*

—*The Indigo Girls*

Siddhartha Gautama argued that *dukkha* is caused by what I think is best rendered in English as primal confusion. This confusion, as the great 14th–15th-century Tibetan philosopher Tsongkhapa (Tsong kha pa) felicitously puts it, is not mere ignorance, but the positive superimposition of a characteristic on reality that it lacks. He writes,

> [Ignorance] is not just *not* seeing the way things really are, nor just any old thing. Instead it is the diametrical opposite of that, maintaining the antithetical mode of apprehension. Therefore it grasps its object as really existent. (2006, 34)

Tsongkhapa's point is that, in a kind of cognitive reflex—one that in contemporary terms seems to be part of our evolutionary endowment—we take the objects we encounter and ourselves to be independent entities, to be permanent, and to have intrinsic characteristics. From a Buddhist perspective, this is the diametrical opposite of the fundamental mode of existence of all things.

This primal confusion is not, on a Buddhist view, the *consequence*, but rather the *source* of bad philosophy. We take the world to be like this despite the fact that we know better. It is not news to any of us that all phenomena are impermanent and constantly changing; that things come into existence in dependence on causes and conditions and pass away when the conditions on which their existence depends no longer prevail. It may take a bit more reflection—reflection in which we will engage in subsequent chapters—to convince ourselves that for these reasons it makes no sense to take things to have intrinsic natures, that the notion of an intrinsic nature makes no sense at all. But this reflection, a Madhyamaka philosopher like Tsongkhapa would argue, is possible. And as we will see, this reflection is at least prima facie cogent.

Primal confusion is then more like optical illusion than like misguided reflective metaphysics. Even though we know, and can even *see*, that the lines in the Müller-Lyer illusion are of equal length, they still irresistibly appear to be of different lengths; even though we know, and even come to take it to be *obvious*, that all phenomena are interdependent, impermanent and empty of intrinsic nature, they nonetheless irresistibly appear to be independent, permanent, and to have intrinsic identities.

A special case of this primal confusion emerges in the experience of the world as structured by subject–object duality. We will go deeper into this topic when we turn to phenomenology, below. For now we just note that one way to take oneself to be an independent entity and to have an intrinsic identity that persists through time is to take oneself as radically distinct as a subject from all of the other entities one experiences. From this perspective, our objects exist only in relation to our own subjectivity. They are object; the experiencer is subject; objects are known indirectly; the self is known directly.

To take up with the world this way is to see oneself—in Kant's metaphor—as subject at the center of a phenomenal universe, or perhaps better, as Wittgenstein put it, as the eye with respect to the visual field. It is to see the world as *my* world. This standpoint, as Schopenhauer noted in *On the Basis of Morality*, is the root of egoism. But it is also, from a Buddhist point of view, on reflection, crazy. For this attitude is available to every potential subject. And not *every* subject can be the center of the universe. The world does not partition itself into a single subject and a field of objects, and to take it to do so is to confuse my own particular standpoint with ontology. Nonetheless, to take up with the world this way is a reflex. It is the reflex of taking oneself to be an ontological, epistemological and moral singularity.

This appearance and this way of taking up with the world, Buddhist philosophers argue, is the origin of *dukkha*. It is referred to canonically as "the twofold self-grasping." There are a couple of ways to parse this. But the most basic one is this: to grasp oneself as a privileged subject in this way is to assign special ontological and moral importance of the referent of 'I'. That is the first grasping.

The second, which follows from the first, is to see everything else as existing in relation to the self, as "mine": *my* friends, and those who are *not* my friends; *my* possessions and those that are *not* mine; *my* field of interest, and those that are *not* mine; *my* location, and *other* places, and so on. Once again, the idea that the fundamental nature of reality is reflected in this structure is mad, but the tendency to take up with and to experience reality through this structure is irresistible, perhaps an essential character of human phenomenology. It is the view that takes us each to live at the center of a universe most naturally mapped in a polar coordinate system, and is the view reflected in the indexical system of every natural language.

On this view the pain and irritation of life goes beyond being mere pain or irritation and becomes *dukkha* as a result of the mismatch between the illusion we project and the reality in which we live. A headache might hurt, but it becomes *dukkha* when I identify the pain as a state of the center of the universe, as the way things are, as opposed to being a transient sensation experienced in one cognitive continuum. My aging and mortality might be inescapable facts, but they become *dukkha* only when I take them to be the wrong alternative to remaining forever 21. And the fact that I have no absolute control over my life might be reality, but it is *dukkha* only if I thought that such control even made sense. Pain, impermanence and interdependence are facts; to take them as existential failures is to experience *dukkha*; and to take them in this way is the inevitable consequence of primal confusion.

## 4. Reorientation

On what I am calling a Buddhist view, a cessation (*nirvāṇa*) of *dukkha* is possible through awakening (*bodhi*) to the nature of reality, involving a direct apprehension and engagement with reality—including both our objects and ourselves as subjects—as impermanent, interdependent and lacking any intrinsic reality. This distinctive epistemological orientation is coupled closely with an ethical orientation to the world characterized by sympathetic joy (*mudita*), beneficence (*mettā*) and care, or a commitment to act for the welfare of all (*karuṇā*). Once again, we will explore each of these issues in depth in subsequent chapters. For now, we are trying only to sketch the outlines of the orientation.

Epistemologically, the idea is this: *dukkha* is caused by a misperception of reality—the cognitive superimposition of permanence, independence and intrinsic nature on things that lack it that we noted above. Therefore, *dukkha* can be alleviated by, and only by, the cessation of this superimposition. And note that this is a cessation (*nirodha*), in particular, that consummate cessation denoted by *nirvāṇa* (Pāli: *nibbāna*). The term *nibbāna/nirvāṇa* is chosen carefully, and is often misunderstood by Western consumers of Buddhist literature. It is essentially a negative term, and figures in an elaborate fire-based metaphor (Gombrich 2009). Let us spend a moment on that metaphor, as often an appreciation of the metaphors through which a philosophical framework structures a view of the world can be useful in working one's way into the way of seeing things that framework encodes. This metaphor is particularly important for understanding the broad Buddhist perspective on reality and our experience of it.

When Buddhists think about the human being analytically it is in terms of five *skandhas*, or *piles* of phenomena. For now we can enumerate these as the physical (*rūpa*); the sensory/hedonic (*vedanā*); the perceptual/discriminative (*samjñā*); the dispositional (cognitive and affective traits) (*samskāra*); and the conscious (*vijñāna*).[6] The details of this analysis need not detain us here. The important point is the complex metaphor encoded in the term *skandha* and its relationship to that encoded in *nirvāṇa*.

First, it is important to see that the term is chosen as a technical term in this context not despite, but because of its imprecision. A pile is not a precise thing. In a pile of sand, for instance, there may be considerable indeterminacy both with regard to how much sand is needed to constitute a pile, and whether particular grains are in the pile or not. There may be similar indeterminacy regarding how many piles are in a particular spot. And big piles decompose into smaller piles. Just so regarding the person. Our constituents and boundaries are indeterminate, and there may well be no canonical account of our constitution. What constitutes us may in part depend on how we count, on our explanatory interests, and so forth.

But there is a deeper point, one that connects directly to the idea of cessation mooted above. The term *khanda* (Pali for *skandha*) refers originally to a very specific kind of pile—a pile of firewood on a funeral pyre. *Skandhas*, therefore, are conceived as burning, and as being consumed. And this is an important soteriological metaphor. In the *Fire Sutta (Additapairyaya-sutta)*, Siddhartha Gautama is represented as saying that our life is led as though we are on fire. We are burned by *dukkha*, consumed by forces out of our control, and we are being depleted all the time by those forces. *Nibānna* is also a term

6. I should note that there are many ways of translating these Sanskrit terms, which do not map easily onto English. Nothing here hangs on the translation choice, and I omit the Pali and Tibetan equivalents here as they are not relevant to the present discussion.

with a very specific core meaning—the extinction of a flame, as in blowing out a candle or a lamp. *Nibānna*, or *nirvāṇa*, then, is not a positive attainment or state of being. Nor is it a state of complete non-being, of annihilation. Instead it is the state of no longer being driven, consumed and tormented (however unconsciously) by *dukkha*.

*Dukkha*, is caused by a *perceptual* process. It is not that we engage with the world, or contemplate our selves, and *infer* or decide that we or the things around us are permanent, independent and have identifiable intrinsic natures. Rather, we take the world and ourselves to be like that in our immediate perceptual engagement—we *see* the world *as* constituted by entities with that nature. Perception itself is therefore shot through with reification.

Tsongkhapa distinguishes two kinds of reification (Thurman 1984, 231). The first, or most obvious, he argues, is that caused by bad philosophy. That is the reification of self and phenomena that is articulated theoretically as a sophisticated refinement and justification of our commonsense tendency to reify. The second is what he calls "innate reification," the cognitive reflex of seeing things as permanent, independent, substantially existent. The first kind of reification, he argues, can be cured by good philosophical argument. We will see whether he is right about this as we work through these issues in this book. The second kind, he argues, because of its "innate" character—what we might characterize as its deep embedding in our cognitive architecture—can only be eradicated by a fundamental transformation of our perceptual and affective response to the world.

Tsongkhapa, like many other Buddhist philosophers, believe that this requires sustained meditative effort. The important point for our purposes is not the specific method by means of which one might effect that transformation, or even whether that transformation is possible, but rather that this transformation is not superficial, but is a deep reform of our most fundamental engagement with, or comportment to, the world. And this transformation is a cessation—the cessation of a reflex superimposition. But it is also the cessation of a reflex that distinguishes ourselves as subjects from everything else, and that takes us to be isolated, persistent, and deserving of special attention. The ontological self-grasping we considered above has its affective and ethical image in a grasping of ourselves as primary objects of concern. Egoism is therefore the ethical face of reification and subject—object dualism. It is hence the moral aspect of superimposition, and so also requires elimination.

From a Buddhist moral point of view, as we will see in our discussion of ethics below, the cessation of this form of self-grasping, and hence of egoism, leads immediately to an impersonal, non-self-centered view of pain, *dukkha*, and of happiness. This leads us to take pleasure in happiness per se, to be moved by *dukkha*, per se, and to commit ourselves to the promotion of well-being whosever it is. Hence, from this point of view, the arising of sympathetic joy, benificence and care are not positive phenomena consequent upon awakening and *nirvāṇa*. These moral attitudes, instead, are themselves negations; they constitute the way that the cessation of self-grasping, which is inextricably bound up with the cessation of reification, is experienced in ethical engagement. Epistemology, ontology, morality and soteriology are hence, on this way of thinking of the world, tightly bound to one another. (See Carpenter 2014, c. 3 for an extended discussion of the relationship between epistemology, psychology and ethics in the Indian Buddhist landscape.)

## 5. What I Am Up To

When I use the term "Buddhist philosophy," it will be to this broad orientation that I refer. It is an orientation that involves a broad metaphysical account of reality, a diagnosis of the fundamental human condition that rests on that account, and a soteriological and ethical framework resting on that diagnosis. My intention in the remainder of this book is to show that this broad framework and the many specific philosophical analyses that have developed within the tradition it inspires provide ideas and arguments that contemporary philosophy can and should take seriously, and that this framework can be usefully articulated in part through a productive engagement with the Western philosophical tradition. As I make this case, I will draw on texts and analyses from a range of sources in the Buddhist tradition, and will show how the philosophers who work within this tradition can be taken as partners in the conversation that constitutes the Western tradition. In doing so, I am emphatically not engaging in an exercise in the history of philosophy. And that is so in two senses.

First, as I noted above, I am not attempting to present a comprehensive—or even a limited—history of Buddhist philosophy. That is an important task, to be sure, but it is not mine. Much of that tradition will be ignored, and my selections will reflect not the historical importance of particular figures, doctrines or texts, but rather their relevance to contemporary Western philosophical discussions. My presentation will hence often appear—especially to scholars of Buddhist Studies—to be seriously decontextualized.

Second, I am less concerned with *lectio* (exegesis) than with *applicatio* (deployment). A historian of Western philosophy may legitimately care a great deal about precisely how a passage or doctrine in the *Nicomachean Ethics* should be read. An ethicist, on the other hand, may take the same passage, engage in creative rational reconstruction, and deploy the insights gained from reading it for her own ends. Each application is legitimate, and each has a role in our philosophical tradition.

But while *applicatio* may require *lectio*, it need not be completely constrained by it. What makes the *Nicomachean Ethics* an eminent text, to use Gadamer's term, is the fact that it commands our attention *now*, not merely as a part of our history, but as a part of our contemporary practice. To engage with Aristotle philosophically is to take him as a conversation partner, not as a topic of conversation; to talk with him, not about him.

My intention in this volume is to show that we in the West can talk with, not about, philosophers and texts in the Buddhist tradition. I will hence be concerned not with the context in which the texts I address were composed, or how we can understand those contexts, but rather with the contemporary philosophical context in the West, and what we can learn by taking these texts seriously in our own intellectual lives.

## 6. A *Very* Brief Survey of the History of Buddhist Schools

The audience I intend for this book includes people who know very little about Buddhism and its long and complex history. Those who do know something about the history of Buddhism can skip this section. Those who want more than the very brief overview I offer here are invited to consult Gethin (1998), Lopez (2002) or Skilton (1997) for a general survey, Williams (2009) for a detailed history of the Mahāyāna or Carpenter (2014) for a fine history of Indian Buddhist philosophy. Those who read on should be aware that the level of detail I am providing would be roughly that one would provide in a history of Western philosophy of this brevity, and the attempt to provide a useful overview may be equally futile. Still, I think that it is nice for those new to the terrain to have a broad map into which to locate the detail that will be coming later.

In the beginning was the Buddha, Siddhartha Gautama. There is not complete consensus about his dates, but most scholars agree that he was born in the mid-6th century BCE and died early in the 5th century BCE. Upon his death the First Buddhist Council was held at Rajgir in present-day Bihar, at which time, according to tradition, the canon of discourses of the Buddha was established. These were passed down orally and were not committed to writing in the Pāli language (itself neither a scholarly nor a vernacular language, but a language of commerce used across language groups in India) until the Third Council in the 1st century CE in Sri Lanka. When we speak of the Pāli canon we speak of the discourses of the Buddha that were committed to writing at that time, as well as the Vinaya, or monastic code and the body of commentarial literature (Abhidhamma/higher doctrine) also composed in that language and fixed in writing at that time. When scholars speak of Pāli Buddhism, pre-Mahāyāna Buddhism, (pejoratively) Hīnayāna Buddhism or (more politically correctly) Śrāvakayāna Buddhism, or sometimes Theravāda Buddhism, it is the Buddhism that evolved between the time of the Buddha and the Third Council that they have in mind.[7]

Already in this period there was a schism. The first schism reported in the tradition is said to have occurred at the Second Council, held between 50 and 100 years after the Buddha's death. It, like most such schisms, was grounded in questions of Vinaya, or monastic discipline, not in questions of philosophy or doctrine. Nonetheless, the schools that emerged from these schisms did develop some doctrinal differences. In the end it is said that 18 distinct schools emerged before the rise of the Mahāyāna, only one of which, the Theravāda (Way of the Elders) still exists. It is the dominant tradition in Sri Lanka, Burma/Myanmar, Thailand/Siam, Cambodia and Laos. It takes its doctrinal foundation to be the Pāli Suttas and the Pāli Abhidhamma.

Common to the Śrāvakayāna schools is a commitment to a broadly reductionist understanding of persons and other macroscopic objects as resolving into sequences of momentary property-instantiations called *dharmas*, a sense of the soteriological goal of Buddhist practice as *nibbāna*, or the complete cessation of *dukkha*, and as a moral ideal the *arhat*, or *accomplished one*, who has eliminated all sources of suffering in his or her own continuum. Practice and study in these schools was (and this is only changing in modernity) restricted to monastics. The role of the laity was to support the monastic community in its scholarly and soteriological venture; the monastic community in turn performed rituals for the laity and offered a route to education and salvation for their progeny.

At about the turn of the millennium, the movement in Buddhism known as the *Mahāyāna* or *Great Vehicle* took hold in India. There is a great deal of

7. Each of these terms is problematic in its own way. *Pāli* suggests that the Buddha actually spoke in Pāli and that all Buddhist discourse and scholarship in the tradition in question is conducted in that language, which is not true; *pre-Mahāyāna* suggests that the tradition in question existed only before the rise of the Mahāyāna, or even that its canon was written down before that movement began, both of which are false; *Hinayāna* means *inferior vehicle*, a term of derision used by some Mahāyāna practitioners, but understandably rejected by those to whom it refers; *Śrāvakayāna*, which has been introduced recently and means *disciples' vehicle*, suggests that there are no disciples in the Mahāyāna; *Theravāda* is the name of only one of the eighteen schools in this tradition, the only one to survive today. None of these terms are coextensive with any of the others; all are regularly used in the literature for one or more of the others. I will try to be both as minimally misleading and as minimally pedantic as possible when I use any of them.

scholarly controversy regarding its precise origins. Some take it to have originated in a lay movement to reclaim spiritual practice; others in devotional cults; still others in philosophical evolution within monastic communities. These issues need not concern us. (For details see Hirakawa 1963, Schopen 1999, Williams 2009.) We do know from the reports of Chinese pilgrims that many monasteries housed both Śrāvakayāna and Mahāyāna monks, and we also know from documents such as Nāgārjuna's *Jewel Rosary of Advice to the King (Ratnāvalī)* that there was competition for resources among these communities (Walser 2005). There is no sense that early on either regarded the other as especially heterodox. After some time, however, the split between these two broad traditions grew, and now most Theravāda practitioners regard Mahāyāna texts, doctrines and practices as heterodox, or even non-Buddhist, while many Mahāyāna practitioners regard Theravāda texts and practices as suitable only for beginners. Once again, the historical and social details need not detain us.

Buddhist schools seek foundations in *Buddhavacana*, the speech of the Buddha. It is the word of the Buddha himself, or at least words spoken in his presence and approved by him, that ultimately validate doctrine from a religious point of view as Buddhist. In the Pāli tradition, that is achieved by grounding texts ultimately in the *suttas*, which are represented as reporting the discourses given by the Buddha himself. Mahāyāna texts are composed in India in Sanskrit, the language of scholarship. The Sanskrit term for a *sutta* is *sūtra*. And Mahāyāna Buddhism appeals to a large set of Mahāyāna *sūtras* for its legitimization.

The Mahāyāna *sūtras* are regarded within the Mahāyāna tradition as having been spoken by (or in the presence of) the historical Buddha; most non-Mahāyāna Buddhists regard them as spurious fakes composed over 500 years after his death. Of course there is the problem about their provenance, and there is a canonical story to account for their appearance so long after the death of the Buddha. Briefly, worried that the doctrines they articulated were too profound for most people to understand, the Buddha, after teaching them to a small group of carefully selected disciples (many of whom were celestial beings) and telling them that if they fell into the wrong hands, they might be misunderstood and actually cause harm to those who misunderstood them, the Buddha did what most of us would do in such a circumstance—he entrusted them to a band of sea serpents (*nāgas*) for safekeeping, instructing them to hold them at the bottom of the ocean for about 500 years until a monk named Nāgārjuna came for them. Alternatively, one can suppose that these *sūtras* were composed by inspired monks in roughly the 1st century BCE through 3rd century CE and became accepted as canonical, ushering in a new, more open sense of canonicity.

Philosophically, several doctrines distinguish Mahāyāna Buddhism. Let us note the two most salient doctrines common to all Mahāyāna schools. The first is the doctrine of *śūnyatā* or emptiness. Whereas according to the *abhidharma* doctrine of most northern Indian Śrāvakayāna schools (although interestingly, not according to Pāli sources, which focus almost entirely on phenomenology, as opposed to ontology), macroscopic entities, such as jars and people, are empty of intrinsic identity, they resolve into fundamental *dharmas*, spatio-temporally atomic constituents, which do exist intrinsically with unique, essential characteristics. These *dharmas* are not empty of intrinsic identity or essential characteristics, and so exist substantially (*dravyasat*), while macroscopic objects only exist conventionally (*prajñāptisāt*).[8] Mahāyāna doctrine, on the other hand, asserts emptiness all the way down: everything, including the *dharmas*, is empty of intrinsic nature, and essenceless. There is no ontological foundation. We will be exploring these doctrines in detail in chapters 2 and 3.

From the ethical standpoint, the salient innovation in Mahāyāna Buddhism is the institution of the ideal of the *bodhisattva* in place of the Śrāvakayāna ideal of the *arhat*, one who has attained liberation from *dukkha*. The bodhisattva is one who has cultivated a special moral motivation, called *bodhicitta*, which is defined as an altruistic aspiration to attain full awakening not in order to alleviate his or her own *dukkha*, but rather to liberate all sentient beings from *dukkha* and rebirth. This aspiration to full awakening, and the altruism it involves, is grounded in what becomes the central character ideal in the Mahāyāna ethical system, *karuṇā*, often translated as *compassion*, but better rendered as *care*,[9] a commitment to act for the benefit of all sentient beings. We will return to this moral ideal in chapter 10.

Among the early Mahāyāna *sūtras* are the *Discourse of Vimalakīrti* (*Vimalakīrti-nirdeśa-sūtra*; that is, a *sūtra* that later becomes among the most popular and influential in East Asia, and one to which we will return in chapter 3), in which the hero is a layperson, and, most importantly, a body of *sūtras* known as the *Perfection of Wisdom Sūtras (Prajñāparamitā sūtras)* the oldest of which is the *The Perfection of Wisdom Sūtra in 8,000 Verses (Astahaṣrika-prajñāparamitā-sūtra)*. The others are either extensions or condensations of this one. The most popular condensation is the *Heart of Wisdom Sūtra (Prajñāparamitā-hṛdāya-sūtra)*, memorized and recited regularly by Buddhists all over central and East Asia. These *sūtras* become the foundation for the earliest Mahāyāna school—the *Madhyamaka* or *Middle Way* school.

8. See Siderits (2007) for a fine exposition of this position.

9. Thanks to Amber Carpenter for this felicitous translation suggestion.

The philosophical architect of Madhyamaka is the 2nd-century[10] CE monk-scholar Nāgārjuna, who develops the doctrine of emptiness and of the bodhisattva ideal in a set of profound, albeit sometimes rather cryptic, verse texts. Central to Madhyamaka is a particular doctrine of the two truths, or two realities, to which we will return in chapter 2. Briefly, these are conventional and ultimate reality. Conventional reality is the everyday world, with its own standards of truth and knowledge—the world of dependently originated phenomena we inhabit. Ultimate reality is emptiness. They sound entirely different. Nāgārjuna argues that they are entirely different, but also that they are identical. More of this anon.

In India, two schools of Madhyamaka develop, grounded in different commentaries on Nāgārjuna's *magnum opus, Fundamental Verses on the Middle Way (Mūlamadhyamakakārikā)*. It is important to remember, however, that the distinction between these schools was never thematized in India. It is a Tibetan doxographical construction. Nonetheless, like the distinction in Western philosophy between rationalists and empiricists, thematized by none of those so described, it is a useful rubric. One school (*thal 'gyur pa [telgyur pa]*—back-translated into Sanskrit as *prāsaṅgika*—or *reductio-wielders*) follows the commentaries of the 5th-century philosopher Buddhapālita and the 6th-century philosopher Candrakīrti, who first notes the two distinct approaches. The other (the *rang rgyud pa [rangyu pa]*—back-translated into Sanskrit as *svatantrika*—or *those who advance their own position*) follow the commentary of the 6th-century philosopher Bhāviveka. The literature on the differences between these schools is vast and subtle. Those who are interested are referred to Dreyfus and McClintock (2003) for a fine set of essays, or to Tsongkhapa (2000, 2002, 2004) for a canonical exposition.

Briefly, from a methodological point of view, the *reductio-wielders* rely on demonstrations that their opponents' positions reduce to absurdity as a philosophical strategy, with no pretence to positively establishing a philosophical position of their own. *Those who advance their own positions*, on the other hand, develop formal arguments of their own from premises they take to be acceptable to their opponents as well as themselves to conclusions they embrace and expect their opponents to embrace as well. Tibetan doxographers, following Tsongkhapa (14th–15th century), argue that this reflects a deeper ontological difference—that while *those who advance their own position* take it to be possible to provide a philosophical analysis of the character of conventional

10. Approximately—estimates of his dates vary from the 1st to the 3rd centuries. See Walser (2005) for an excellent discussion of this issue.

reality, *reductio-wielders* take that to be impossible, and think that *any* ontological account of reality is bound to fail. More of this below.

The second major Mahāyāna school in India is the Yogācāra (Masters of Practice) school, also known as the *Cittamātra* (Mind Only), *Vijñānavāda* (Way of Consciousness) and the *Vijñaptimātra* (Consciousness Only) school. This school takes as its *sūtra* foundation a collection of a somewhat later group of *sūtras*, prominently including the *Discourse Unravelling the Thought (Saṃdhinirmocana sūtra), the Flower Garland Sūtra (Avatamsika Sūtra, Hua yan* [華嚴]) and the *The Entry into Lanka Sūtra (Lankāvatāra sūtra)*. The philosophical foundations of this school are laid by the two 4th-century half-brothers Asaṅga and Vasubandhu. This school has a strongly idealist streak, with many of its texts privileging, both ontologically and epistemically, mind over the material world. But it also has a strong phenomenological bent, with an emphasis on a close understanding of the nature of experience. Much of what we know as Buddhist logic also derives from Yogācāra thinkers such as Dignāga (4th–5th centuries) and his eminent and highly influential commentator Dharmakīrti (5th century), who initiates the Pramāṇavāda tradition of epistemology and logic, to which we turn in chapters 8 and 9.[11]

The Mahāyāna moves out of India in two directions. First, it heads to China, in fact as early as the 1st century CE, as the Mahāyāna is just getting underway. While at first Buddhism was a small presence in the Chinese scene, by the 3rd and 4th centuries, in part through interaction with neo-Daoists, Buddhism was acquiring both a presence and a distinctively Chinese flavor. Over the next millennium waves of missionaries from India and pilgrims from China bring texts and ordination lineages to China, establishing a number of distinct schools. As in India, Chinese schools were grounded in *sūtras*. The principal schools of China are the *Hua yan* (華嚴) school, grounded in the *The Flower Garland Sūtra*, the *Tiantai* (天台) school, grounded in the *Lotus Sūtra* (*Saddharma-puṇḍarīka-sūtra*) and the *Chan* (禪) school, a school that paradoxically repudiates reliance on *sūtras* in favor of direct psychological transmission and realization, but which owes a great deal to the *Discourse of Vimalakīrti* among others, and which generates such indigenous Chinese *sūtras* as *The Platform Sūtra of the Sixth Patriarch (Liuzu Tanjing* / 六祖壇經).

China was hardly a philosophical tabula rasa when Buddhism arrived. It already had flourishing Confucian and Daoist philosophical traditions and a

11. There is considerable debate between Madhyamaka and Yogācāra thinkers in the history of Indian Buddhism, and this debate generates some fascinating texts. But there are also synthetic thinkers, prominently including the 9th-century figure Śāntarakṣita, who attempt to reconcile these approaches. We will encounter this literature below.

rich philosophical vocabulary. As Buddhist scriptures and philosophical ideas were translated into Chinese—by a number of translators, over an extended period, with no single translation method—Buddhist ideas became inflected in particular with Daoist ideas (and vice versa), as much of the philosophical vocabulary came from that tradition. Some ideas central to Indian Buddhism, such as rebirth and the centrality of logic to philosophy, dropped by the wayside, at least in some schools; some that had been more marginal, such as the idea of an innate Buddha-nature, or potential for awakening, came to center stage. Emphases on spontaneity and a suspicion of discursive thought permeate Chinese Buddhist traditions.

Hua yan, in the hands of philosophers such as Fazang (法藏) (7th century), develops a vision of the universe in which all phenomena mutually interpenetrate, using the metaphor of the jeweled net of Indra, comprising infinitely many jewels, each reflecting all others, as a model for the infinite interdependence of phenomena. The Tiantai school is best known for its emphasis on the *Lotus Sūtra* itself as the supreme teaching of Buddhism, with the doctrine of Buddha-nature, understood to be the primordially awakened nature of the mind, a nature that only has to be disclosed, as its central teaching. Chan takes over this emphasis on primordial awakening, taking discursive thought to be the principal means of occlusion of this mode of taking up with the world. Its emphasis on sitting meditation and the stilling of conceptual thought derives from this idea. All three of these schools migrate from China through Korea to Japan where Hua yan becomes Kegon, Tiantai becomes Tendai and Chan becomes Zen.

The transmission of Buddhism to Tibet follows a very different trajectory. Beginning in the 7th century, and culminating in the 9th century, Tibetan kings invited Indian monastic scholars, including such luminaries as Atīśa and Śāntarakṣita from Nālandā University, then the largest university in the world, to establish Buddhism in Tibet. The establishment of Buddhism in Tibet was deliberate and careful, involving a kind of national commitment to the preservation of the Nālandā University system of Buddhist practice and study and as much of the culture of the medieval Indian Buddhist world as possible in Tibet, including medical, artistic and archaeological traditions as well as academic and religious traditions. Much of this preservation has been astonishingly successful, though not to the degree that Tibetans themselves represent it.

Royal patronage was lavish and the transmission was highly systematic, including the establishment of ordination lineages and the constitution of translation commissions charged with standardizing translations from Sanskrit to Tibetan. These commissions oversaw the skilled translation—by teams each comprising both Tibetan scholars who had studied Sanskrit and Indian Sanskrit pandits who knew Tibetan, supervised by committees charged with maintaining lexical and grammatical consistency across translation teams—of virtually the entire Indian Sanskrit Buddhist canon, including not only religious and philosophical material, but also treatises on medicine, literature, and a host of other subjects. It is to this massive and precise effort, unparalleled in world history, that we owe the survival of much of Indian Buddhist literature, a great deal of which was lost in the original when the great Buddhist libraries were burned by Islamic invaders shortly after Buddhism was established in Tibet.

Despite its relatively systematic character, the development of Buddhism in Tibet is far from simple, and we will eschew the details here. (See Powers 2007, Kapstein 2002 and van Schaik 2011 for those details.) A number of distinct Buddhist schools develop in Tibet between the 9th and 15th centuries, representing significant differences in approaches to religious practice, philosophical doctrine and institutional culture.

There are five schools that deserve particular mention. The oldest is the *Jonang (Jo nang)*, which emphasizes a synthesis of Madhyamaka and Yogācāra doctrine, and a distinctive view of emptiness, called *gzhan stong (shentong)*, or *emptiness-of-other*, according to which conventional phenomena are empty of instrinsic nature, but ultimate reality is non-empty. The *Nyingma (sNying ma)* school, deriving from the teachings of Padmasambhāva, who brought tantra to Tibet, emphasizes tantric practice, with the idea that direct non-conceptual insight through nondiscursive practices is the only way to attain awakening. The *Kagyu ('bkad brgyud)* or *oral lineage* school owes a great deal philosophically to Yogācāra, and emphasizes prolonged meditation and devotional practice.

The Sakya and Geluk traditions develop in the 14th and 15th centuries and are far more scholastic and analytical in their approach. These schools reflect to the greatest degree the analytic, scholastic approach to philosophy pursued in universities like Nālandā, Vikramśīla and Takṣaśīla in India. And it is these schools that produce some of the most astute and erudite scholars, such as Gorampa (Go rams pa bsod nams seng ge), Ngog Loden Sherab (rNgog lo ts'a ba blo ldan shes rab), Sakya Chokden (Sha skya mchog ldan) and Sakya Paṇḍita (Chos rje sa skya pan di ta kun dga' rgyal mtshan) from the Sakya lineage, and Tsongkhapa, Gyeltsab (rGyal tshab dar ma rin chen), Khaydrup (mKhas grub dge legs dpal bzang), Panchen Chokyi Nyima (Thub bstan chos kyi nyi ma), Jangya (lCang bya) and Jamyang Shepa ('Jam dbyangs bzhad pa ngag dbang brtson 'grus) in the Geluk tradition. These traditions were noteworthy for the establishment not only of monasteries, but of comprehensive monastic universities that became centers of study and scholarship, and remain so to the present day. While it would be a gross exaggeration to say that the Indian and Tibetan traditions are identical, there is a clear line of continuity between them, and we owe an enormous debt of gratitude to Tibetan culture and scholarship for preserving a living tradition of Indic Buddhist philosophy. (For a much more detailed discussion of the history of Tibetan Buddhism see Powers 2007 and Williams 2009.)

The sectarianism of Tibetan Buddhism was always a mixed blessing. Politically it was often disastrous as sects jockeyed for political and economic advantage. But the philosophical and doctrinal rivalries often generated sharp debate and a honing of arguments and positions. While sometimes we find closed-minded sectarians among Tibetan philosophers, we also find eminent scholars who proudly meld ideas from distinct lineages to generate new syntheses. In the late 19th and early 20th centuries, in Eastern Tibet, a new movement, called Ri-meh (*Ris med*), or nonsectarianism, arises, specifically aimed at synthesis, rather than debate, of ideas from the major lineages. Under the influence of philosophers such as Ju Mipham Rinpoche (Mi pham 'jam dbyangs rnam rgyal rgyam tso), many scholars sought to study in the monasteries and colleges of multiple lineages. In this period, often referred to as the "Tibetan Renaissance," a great deal of very sophisticated philosophy emerged, much of which is influential today.

And of course, now Buddhism is moving west, and as it does so it will transform and will be transformed by Western culture, just as Buddhism has transformed and been transformed by every culture into which it has moved. It is too soon to predict the contours of this transformation. (But see Bhushan, Garfield and Zablocki 2009 for a set of discussions of this process.) Our students and grand-students will write the next chapters in its history. I hope that this brief and very broad sketch helps to locate some of the ideas and figures we will encounter in the next chapters.

# 2 THE METAPHYSICAL PERSPECTIVE I: INTERDEPENDENCE AND IMPERMANENCE

Before addressing specific topics in the philosophy of mind, epistemology, philosophy of language and ethics, it will be useful to bring the broad Buddhist metaphysical perspective into greater focus. To do so, we begin with three central, tightly linked theses regarding the nature of reality: all phenomena are dependently originated, impermanent and empty of intrinsic identity. We will explore these theses and their relationship to one another in some detail, with attention to the variety of ways in which they are understood in Buddhist traditions.

Second, we will address the complex doctrine of the two truths. Early in the development of Buddhist philosophy we see a distinction drawn between conventional and ultimate truth, introduced as a hermeneutical device to distinguish between claims asserted or authorized by the Buddha that are to be taken as literally true and those that are mere pedagogical devices or *façons de parler*. This doctrine, as we shall see, undergoes significant transformation in the history of Buddhist thought and becomes highly metaphysically charged with the development first of Abhidharma theory and later with the rise of the Mahāyāna. Its interpretation has been a matter of considerable contestation, both within Buddhist canonical literature and in recent scholarship in Buddhist Studies. The mature doctrine—which will concern us in chapter 3 and following—is grounded on the analysis of the relationship between emptiness and dependent origination, and so these discussions are deeply intertwined.

Finally, we will turn to one of the principal contributions I think that this broad Buddhist metaphysical analysis can make to contemporary metaphysics. If this perspective is even worth taking seriously—and I believe that it is—it may shift our thinking regarding the use of intuitions in our own metaphysical thought, and that regarding the nature of modality itself.

## 1. Dependent Origination

Let us begin with a discussion of dependent origination, a doctrine to which the Dalai Lama XIV has referred as "the entirety of Buddhist teaching." (See, for instance Dalai Lama 2001, 2005.) The standard formulation of this doctrine, occurring frequently in the Pāli canon and quoted countless times in canonical literature, is "when this arises, that arises; when this does not occur, that does not occur."[1] This is, of course, a rather laconic expression of a complex metaphysical thesis, and we will elaborate that thesis in company with the Buddhist canon at some length.

But even on its surface, it indicates that to which we in the modern West have come to refer as a "Humean" understanding of causation.[2] That is, dependent origination is spelled out as a kind of brute regularity, and brute regularity is taken to characterize reality quite generally. The world is not random; it can be characterized by laws, but those laws are not grounded in anything more than the fact of the regularity of the world. Hume was at pains to argue that not only is there no evidence of a necessary connection obtaining between regularly associated events, but that we do not even have an *idea* of any such relation, even though we have words that appear to express such an idea. According to Hume the only idea we have in the metaphysical ballpark denoted by the term *causation* is that of regular association between events and an idea of reflection of our tendency to associate them. The events themselves are merely independent occurrences, whose classification as being of the same type itself is merely nominal. Even regularity, on Hume's view, depends upon the linguistic conventions that allow us to establish sortals whose instances are regularly associated (Baier 1991, Coventry 2007, 2008, Fogelin 1985, Garfield 1994, Kripke 1982; but see Garrett 2002 and Strawson 1992b, 2011a for alternative readings).

1. This formulation may seem to prejudice the ontology of dependent origination in the direction of event causation. But while we could read *arises* as *occurs*, it could also mean *exists*, allowing the relation to obtain between entities.

2. I leave aside all of the complex debates about Hume exegesis and in particular the question of whether the position here described as "Humean" was in fact Hume's. It is also worth noting that for Hume the relata of the causal relation are "distinct existences," that is, they are entirely independent from one another. (See Bliss 2015.) That is not so on many Buddhist accounts. More of this below.

Buddhist philosophers, including Siddhartha Gautama himself, and such later systematic exponents of his views such as Nāgārjuna (2nd–3rd century CE) anticipated Hume's analysis in many respects. Necessary causal connections play no role in Siddhartha Gautama's account of dependent origination and are explicitly rejected by Nāgārjuna (Garfield 1994, 1995, 2001). Buddhists, too, are nominalists and regard sortals as merely conventional, dependent upon cognitive and linguistic conventions. And the formula of dependent origination enshrines the regularities we posit as the sole structure of reality.

Despite these similarities, there are interesting differences to note. First of all, while Hume is interested not in causality, or regularity itself, but rather in the content and source of the *idea* of causality, Buddhists are unanimous in regarding interdependence as a fundamental feature of reality. Now, we will have cause to nuance this a bit below as we encounter the doctrine of the two truths, and it will turn out that interdependence is a fundamental feature only of *conventional* reality; nonetheless, as we will see, in many Buddhist schools, conventional reality is *reality*, while in those in which it is treated merely fictionally, there is still a standard of truth and falsity to be observed with respect to it. With Hume, then, Buddhists see causal relations as merely conventional, but unlike Hume, they take this to be a principal way of being *real*, not an *alternative* to reality (Cowherds 2011). Moreover, while Hume regards events as "independent existences," for Buddhists, dependent origination guarantees that *nothing* is an independent existent. The only account we can give of anything adverts to its relations to everything else (Garfield 1995, and see Bliss 2015 for a different perspective). More of this below.

As the doctrine of dependent origination is elaborated, three kinds of relevant dependence are identified. Together they constitute a complex web of interdependence on multiple dimensions. It is important to keep all three in focus as each plays an important role in Buddhist thought more broadly. Often the phrase "dependent origination" is used to refer to the entire complex, but more often a specific instance is relevant, but not explicitly identified. In a short text called *Instructions on the Profound Middle Path of the Prāsaṅgika Madhyamaka Tradition (dBu ma thal 'gyur pa'i lugs kyi zab lam dbu ma'i lta khrid)* (1991a), Tsongkhapa writes that dependent origination is to be understood as "dependent arising, dependent existence and dependent designation" (Collected Works, *Sha* 578:3).

The first kind of dependence is that to which we have already referred—causal dependence. This is the central dimension of dependent origination and is that which receives the most attention in early Buddhist texts. All events in time, all Buddhist philosophers agree, occur in dependence on prior causes and conditions, and all states of affairs cease when the causes and conditions that are necessary for their occurrence cease.

The second dimension is mereological dependence. This dimension plays a large role in Buddhist accounts of the two truths, and of personal and object identity. On this dimension, all wholes depend upon their parts, and all parts depend for their existence as parts on the wholes in which they figure. My body only exists because all of its parts exist. Take those away, and I have no body. But my heart only exists because of the rest of my body. Take away the body, and that mass of muscle is no heart.

The most abstract and contentious form of dependent origination is the third—dependence on conceptual imputation. Divergent interpretations of this form of dependence are presented in different Buddhist schools, with some, such as Yogācāra, emphasizing fundamental cognitive processes as the mechanism for identity determination, and others, such as Madhyamaka, emphasizing language and social convention. How this kind of dependence is understood in part determines whether Buddhist ontological doctrine is conventionalist, idealist, antirealist or whether Buddhism is an ontologically neutral phenomenological doctrine. Most neutrally, we can start from this broad understanding: all phenomena are dependent for their identity as the kinds of objects they are on the conceptual structure that contributes to our experience. For something to be a single thing, or to be a thing of a particular kind, is for us to take it as falling under a sortal, and sortals are our conceptual constructions. We will interrogate this further below.[3]

## *1.1 Causal Dependency*

As we noted above, causal dependency figures in Buddhist metaphysics from its outset. In what is taken to be Siddhartha Gautama's first public discourse after his awakening, the *Discourse Setting in Motion the Wheel of the Doctrine*, he asserts that everything that occurs is caused to occur and specifically takes this to encompass both the psychological realm, through the so-called twelve links of dependent origination, and the material realm. Indeed, it is clear from

3. In what follows I will be ignoring questions regarding whether Buddhist doctrines of karma or of non-physical psychological causation require a distinct metaphysics of causality. I will simply presume that they do not, and questions about whether there are specifically moral causal laws, or whether laws governing relations between psychological events are different in form from physical laws, are simply empirical questions about how the world works, not disputes about the fundamental metaphysics.

the presentation of the twelve links that he takes these realms themselves to be causally interconnected. It is part of the Buddhist platform for human perfectibility that our unsatisfactory life is caused by primal confusion, and that eliminating this primal confusion is necessary and sufficient for the extinction of the suffering it causes. These are causal notions.

But early on, things become more nuanced. First, let us note that early Indian discussions of causation, including Buddhist discussions, are indifferent between thinking of causal relations as relations between events, things, properties and states. This gets confusing, and it is often useful to regiment discussions for clarity in doctrinal reconstruction. So it is perfectly natural in this genre to say that the disintegration of a seed (an event) causes the arising of a sprout (another event); but it is also natural to say that the seed (a thing) is the cause of the sprout (another thing); that ignorance (a property) is the cause of suffering (another property); or that *my* ignorance (a state) is the cause of *my* remaining in *saṃsāra* (another state). We may at times have to disentangle doctrinal issues from mere *façons de parler*, but sometimes what appear to be mere *façons* are more than that.

Early Buddhist Abhidharma doctrine distinguishes *causes (hetu)* from *conditions (pratyaya)*. And four kinds of conditions are then distinguished. Let us begin with the first distinction. It is often drawn (somewhat misleadingly) in the context of the example of the seed and sprout we have just been considering: A seed is the cause of a sprout. When there is a seed, a sprout arises, and indeed a barley seed only gives rise to a barley sprout, and a rice seed to a rice sprout. The specificity is important here in determining causation. But none of this happens without the cooperation of a number of conditions. The soil must be fertile. There must be adequate rain, and sun. There must be no frost, and no mouse must eat the seed before it germinates.

The cause here is that which—in some sense to be spelled out—is the primary salient explanans of the phenomenon to be explained, and it is what explains why *that* effect, as opposed to some other, came about. The conditions are the supporting cast of phenomena that enable the cause to do its work, the stuff to which we generally refer by *ceteris paribus* clauses in causal laws. So, for instance, while fertile soil, rain and sun might help that rice sprout to grow, they do not specify that it will be *rice* that grows; that is in the seed. They are the conditions for any seed to germinate. And the sprout does not grow *from* them, but from the seed. Moreover, some conditions are *negative* (no mouse, no frost), whereas a cause in an Indian framework is always a positive phenomenon.

It should be clear that a lot of vagueness lurks here, and extending this intuitive picture of the causal process to modern science would hardly be unproblematic. On the other hand, there is a certain intuitive appeal to the picture and a revealing tie of talk about causation to talk about explanation. And as we will see, this causal contextualism sets the stage for subsequent Buddhist dialectic and refinement of the picture. We can ask, "What caused that sprout?" and be told, "A seed (with the help of cooperating conditions)." But we could also ask, "What causes seeds to sprout?" and be told, "Rain, fair weather and good soil." Relative to that question, these are causes, while the absence of mice remains but one condition. (But we might also answer that question, in a different context, by saying, "the cat finally got the mice under control; that's why the seeds sprouted this year.")

Moreover, the tie between causal discourse and explanatory discourse substitutes nicely for any talk of occult causal powers or productive forces of the kind of which Hume was to be so suspicious a couple of millennia after Siddhartha Gautama flourished. If we ask *why* we attribute causation of barley sprouts to barley seeds, the answer is simply that when we plant barley seeds we get barley sprouts. We might in turn ask why that is, and we might get a story about barley genes being carried by barley seeds, and then barley DNA encoding barley genes, and so on. But in each case, when we ask why it is that we take the relevant cause to be the cause of the relevant effect, the Buddhist theorist responds by citing a deeper, more explanatory, perhaps broader regularity, and nothing more. Regularities are explained by other regularities, and when we use causal language, we do no more than promise a regularity to which we can appeal in further explanation, and we promise in turn that these regularities will be embedded in still deeper regularities.

There is one further reason, to which we will come shortly, not to worry too much about the early Buddhist distinction between *hetu* and *pratyaya*. It is but a dialectical moment, a stepping stone to a dissolution of that distinction, and a critique of the very idea of anything privileged in the causal web as a *hetu*, as a specific cause, of anything else, as opposed to a mere condition. More of that below when we encounter the later Madhyamaka (Middle Way) analyses of dependent origination, an analysis that explicitly dispenses with any notion of causal power, or real link between causes and effects, and so with any notion of natural necessity of the kind so prevalent in Western metaphysical accounts of causation.

First, let us consider the four kinds of *pratyaya*. The first is what is called the *causal condition (hetu-pratyaya)*. It is a condition that, in the early formulation we are considering, helps get things underway, such as a good soaking rain after planting. The second, the *observed* or *supporting condition (ālambana-pratyaya)*, is a standing, simultaneous state of affairs that enables an effect to eventuate, such as fertile soil. In a more familiar case, a table is an observed support for a book, and a condition of its not falling to the floor.[4]

The third, the *immediate condition (samanantara-pratyaya)*, is the kind of condition we find on the minute dissection of the causal sequence, the proximal micro-conditions of an event taking place, such as, for instance, the softening of the skin of the seed so that the sprout can emerge, or in a more familiar example, the excitation of fluorescent atoms in a light tube as an immediate condition of luminosity, where flicking a switch was the cause of the light going on. Finally, the *dominant condition (adhipati-pratyaya)* is the *telos* of an action. The barley crop I desire is the dominant condition of the sprouts, for that is what got me to sow the seeds (or perhaps it was the *chang* I hoped to drink once the barley is fermented!).

Once again we note that in specifying these conditions, we are relying not on a metaphysics of causal productivity. (After all, the *chang* I will brew after harvest does not exert a retrocausal effect on the seeds.) Instead, we are asking what explains what, what would count as a good answer to a "why?" question. The pragmatism that underlies the distinction between different kinds of conditions is exactly the same pragmatism that underlies the distinction between causes and conditions. And therein lies the key to the Madhyamaka critique of the very distinction between causes and conditions that is so fundamental to earlier Buddhist thought about causality.[5]

So, when we say from a Madhyamaka perspective that all phenomena are dependent on causes and conditions, we mean that everything is explicable, that no event or entity is independent of other events or entities for its existence, and that explanation is nothing more than an embedding in explanatorily potent regularities, of which, for any phenomenon, there are many, and which are always interest-dependent and description-dependent.

In the work of Nāgārjuna (the founder of the Madhyamaka or Middle Way school of Buddhist philosophy and a pioneer of Mahāyāna Buddhism) this

4. In epistemological literature on perception, such as Dignāga's *Investigation of the Percept (Ālambanāparīkṣā/dMigs pa brtags pa)* the supporting condition is the *percept*, the object one perceives in the perceptual process. There are important debates (which we will not address in this volume) between Buddhist schools concerning whether that percept is an external object or an internal representation or cognitive process.

5. It is also important to note that Abhidharma accounts of causality are more explicitly realistic about the conditions and about the fixity of the list of conditions than are Madhyamaka analyses, and seem to take causal relations more seriously as fundamental aspects of reality, just as they take fundamental dharmas seriously as ultimate existents in their reductionist program. These doctrines go together, and explain why Nāgārjuna takes on the causal relation and the status of conditions as the first topic in *Fundamental Verses on the Middle Way (Mūlamadhyamakakārikā)*. See Garfield (1994, 1995, 2001).

picture is made explicit. Nāgārjuna, as we will see in chapter 3, presents an analysis of all phenomena as empty of intrinsic nature, an analysis that forms the basis of all Mahāyāna metaphysical thought. In this context, he begins his major work *Fundamental Verses on the Middle Way* with an examination of the status of the causal relation itself. He argues that the emptiness of causation—the lack of any determinate identity in the causal relation—and the emptiness of causes of causal power effectively undermine the notion of causation itself, and of a cause, and hence empty the distinction between causes and conditions of any content.

Nāgārjuna therefore argues that while we can appeal to the four kinds of conditions for explanation, that appeal is grounded always in convention, and never in any ultimate facts about things. True assertions of dependence depend themselves on the descriptions under which things are explained and hence the sortals and interests we bring to the explanatory enterprise. Regularities are only explanatory to the degree that they are explained by other regularities, in a bottomless web of explanation. The anticipation here of Wittgenstein's remarks on the status of laws of nature in the *Tractatus* is startling, and there are real affinities between Nāgārjuna's view and the kinds of antirealism in the philosophy of science recently defended by van Fraassen (1980) and Cartwright (1983). On this view, there are no causal powers, and hence nothing ever arises from anything else, although nothing arises independently. Everything, including dependence itself, is dependent on other conditions.

Tsongkhapa puts it this way in his poem "In Praise of Dependent Origination" (*rTen 'brel pa legs bshad snying po*, 2014), emphasizing both the universality of dependent origination and its deep link to a lack of intrinsic nature, and hence merely conventional existence:[6]

14. The non-contingent is like a sky-flower.
Hence there is nothing that is non-dependent.
If things exist through their essences, their dependence on
Causes and conditions for their existence is a contradiction.

15. "Therefore since no phenomena exist
Other than origination through dependence,
No phenomena exist other than
Being devoid of intrinsic existence," you taught. (trans T. Jinpa 2014)

6. See the discussion in chapter 3, below, for more on the connection between the lack of intrinsic identity and conventional existence.

Tsongkhapa emphasizes in these two verses not only the universality of dependent origination, including the dependent origination of dependent origination itself, but also the fact that dependence is the very antithesis of intrinsic existence, and hence entails that the existence of phenomena can only be conventional. We will explore this doctrine in detail in chapter 3, below.[7]

## *1.2 Part-Whole Dependence*

The second dimension of dependent origination is part-whole or mereological dependence. This dimension is simpler and more straightforward. All composite entities, from a Buddhist perspective, depend for their existence and their properties on their parts. In the Sanskrit Abhidharma Buddhism of northern India, this dependence bottoms out in impartite simple *dharmas*, the momentary, dimensionless tropes that are the fundamental building blocks of all psychological and physical phenomena. On this view, as we saw in the previous chapter, *dharmas* have a very different grade of existence than those composites they constitute. And this provides the basis for a distinction between the merely conventional, second-grade existence these early Buddhist schools assign to composite phenomena and the ultimate existence they assign to *dharmas* (Siderits 2007, 111–113).

As the Mahāyāna develops, however, and the Madhyamaka critique of the very idea of a *dharma* and the reductionism it encodes takes hold, the idea that there is an ultimately real level of phenomena to which conventional phenomena reduce ends up being rejected. Nāgārjuna argues in *Fundamental Verses on the Middle Way* that *dharmas* themselves are dependently originated and empty of intrinsic nature, and hence not ultimately existent. Moreover, he argues, the idea that any real entity can be entirely indivisible is to be rejected.[8] As a consequence of these ontological developments, the idea that conventional existence is a second-rate kind of existence also falls by the wayside. This rehabilitation of the conventional truth

7. Detailed analysis of the consequences of this doctrine for the metaphysics of events occupies a great deal of Buddhist Abhidharma thought, and the interested reader might turn to Vasubandhu's *Treasury of Abhidharma (Abhidharmakośa)*, or to chapter 7 of Tsongkhapa's *Ocean of Reasoning* to get some of the flavor of that enterprise, but these details need not detain us here.

8. This argument is developed in greater detail in Vasubandhu's *Twenty Verses (Viṃśatikā)* and Dignāga's *Examination of the Percept*. Vasubandhu and Dignāga (en route to defending an idealist position, in contradistinction to the moderate realism of Nāgārjuna) argue that the very idea of indivisible atoms is incoherent.

in virtue of the analysis of the ultimate as emptiness is central to what we might call "Nāgārjuna's revolution." (See Cowherds 2011 for an exploration of this development.) As a consequence of the rejection of the ultimate existence of infinitesimal parts, the dependence relation between parts and wholes came to be recognized as a two-way street. Given that there is no ultimate decomposition of wholes into parts, the identification of any part *as a part* came to be seen as a matter of decompositional interest, just as the identification of a condition as an explanans is seen as dependent upon explanatory interests.

For something to exist as a part of a whole, on this view, is to be dependent on the whole in two respects. First, if the whole does not exist, the part does not exist *as the kind of thing it is when it figures in the whole.* To take Wittgenstein's example in *Philosophical Investigations*, a brake lever is only a brake lever, and not simply a metal rod, in the context of a car in which it so functions (§6). A biological organ, such as a heart, depends on an entire organism to develop, to function and to be an organ at all.

Second, decomposition can be accomplished in many ways. We might say that a memory chip is a part of a computer if we are decomposing it functionally, and that the parts of the chip are circuits, and so on. On the other hand, we might decompose the computer into adjacent 1 mm cubes, in which case the chip might turn out to be involved in several different parts, and not to be a part itself. If the whole in question is a solid volume, the cubes are parts; if it is a computer, the chip is a part, and 1 mm cubes are irrelevant. So, just as wholes depend on their parts, parts depend on their wholes.

### *1.3 Dependence on Conceptual Imputation*

The third dimension of dependent origination is perhaps the most difficult to understand. Mādhyamikas and Yogācārins argue that entities are dependent for their existence on conceptual imputation. The rough idea is this: the entities and properties we experience in the world depend for their reality and identity on our minds, including our perceptual and conceptual apparatus, for their existence as the entities we encounter. But this rough idea needs immediate refinement, as it is indeterminate between a number of readings.

One straightforward way to read this thesis is as a kind of idealism, and to be sure, this reading is well attested, particularly in the Yogācāra or Cittamātra school of Buddhism. On this account, the phenomena we experience are dependent on our conceptual imputation simply because they are all really nothing more than projections of our consciousness, mere ideas and not external phenomena. This position is arguably maintained by Vasubandhu in his short treatises *Twenty Stanzas* and *Thirty Stanzas* (*Trimsikakārikā*) and is certainly how he is interpreted by his most influential commentator, Sthiramati. Vasubandhu, for instance, opens *Twenty Stanzas* as follows:

> 1. All this is merely consciousness,
> Because all apparent intentional objects are nonexistent.
> It is just as one who suffers from opthalmia
> Sees such nonexistent things as moons and hairs.

From this perspective, any entity we encounter is nothing more than a conscious projection, and so any entity is trivially dependent upon conceptual imputation. But this idealism is the most extreme end of a spectrum of understandings of this kind of dependence. Closer to the center of Buddhist ideas, and more in harmony with earlier Buddhist ideas, is the Madhyamaka interpretation: a kind of conventionalism, coupled with a subtle attention to the ways in which our interface with the world conditions the world we experience. On this view, we pay attention to the entities we *experience*, to the ontology of everyday life.

From the Madhyamaka perspective there are two dimensions to this kind of dependence. First, the world we encounter presents itself to us as a world of self-presenting particulars endowed with properties and standing in relations that are determined from the side of the entities themselves. But this is a cognitive illusion. What constitutes a rabbit, as opposed to a set of rabbit parts, or a moment in a series of rabbit stages; what constitutes a jellyfish, as opposed to a colony of cells or part of an oceanic biomass depends upon our individuation conventions and interests. Whether today's church with its parishioners and brand-new building is identical to or different from the church that existed a century ago with the same name but now long-dead parishioners and a razed building depends on who is asking and why.

We see a world of colored surfaces, marked with sounds in our audible range, with muted scents. Our dogs inhabit worlds of vivid scents, drab surfaces and hear sounds in a frequency range to which we have no access. Bees and other insects see a world through compound eyes with four color cones instead of our three; in their world objects we see as being of the same color are dramatically different in color; frequencies of light to which we are not sensitive dominate their experience. Which is the real world? Who sees it aright? Which viewpoint is unimpaired? Which is distorted?

The classic Buddhist example used to introduce and to defuse these questions, widely repeated, concerns water. We humans experience it as a clear, tasteless, thirst-quenching liquid; fish experience it as the very medium of their existence; divinities, according to Buddhist lore, experience it as ambrosia; *pretas*—often known as *hungry ghosts*, one of the unfortunate kinds of beings in the world—experience water as a disgusting mixture of pus and blood. We don't need to subscribe to the karmic mythology involving divinities, pretas and other such beings to see the point—the manifest perceptible characteristics of things are not simply features of those things themselves, but arise through the interaction of objects with the particular kind of subjectivity of the subject experiencing them.

So, what is the *right* way to see the world? To the Mādhyamika it is obvious that there is simply no answer to this question, and not because we can't determine the answer, but because the question doesn't make sense. If bees are right, everyone else is wrong; if we are right, our dogs are just mistaken about their own world. If there is indeed no fact of the matter about how the world is, we are faced with the conclusion that the world we inhabit, and the standards of truth appropriate to it, depend upon our sensory and conceptual apparatus as much as on the entities we perceive. Phenomena thus depend upon conceptual imputation—a dependence with social, cognitive and sensory dimensions. This may be one of the most radical attacks on one aspect of the Myth of the Given to have ever been advanced in world philosophy. It is not simply an argument that reality—whatever it may be—is not given to us as it is; rather, it is the claim that we can make no sense whatsoever of the very notion of reality that is presupposed by any form of that myth. This dependence, however, is not absolute, and does not yield an idealism; it is rather causal, involving an interplay between the subjective and objective aspects of the reality we enact.[9]

All of this raises an important question regarding the domain of metaphysics in a Buddhist framework. When we say that phenomena are dependently originated, and in particular, that they are dependent on conceptual imputation, are we talking about the phenomena themselves, as they are independently of how we take them—what we might naively call *the world as it is*? Or are we talking about our *lebenswelt*—what we might in the same register call *the world as we find it*? That is—especially in the context of a school like Madhyamaka, with its radical rejection of the project of fundamental ontology—are we still doing *metaphysics* at all, or have we retreated to the domain of phenomenology?

9. See Thompson 2007 and Thompson and Varela 2003 for discussions of Madhyamaka-inspired enactivism in the context of cognitive science.

It is tempting to say that when we attend to the first two kinds of dependence, it is the former, and when we attend to the last (unless we are idealists) the latter. After all, it seems to be that causal relations (even if we interpret them in the regularist way Buddhist metaphysics suggests) obtain between events whether or not we experience or categorize them; that objects depend on their parts, and their parts on the wholes even if we are not experiencing them. That is what the metaphysics of dependence seems to be all about. Dependence on conceptual imputation, on the other hand, seems to directly target the world only as we take it to be.

There is something to this, but things are not so straightforward. For if the Madhyamaka metaphysical picture we are sketching is correct, *the world as it is* is not entirely given to us independent of conceptual imputation, either. That world, and the interdependencies that obtain in it, as well as its ontology of entities and parts, comprises, inter alia, the social world we construct. Such things as nations, economies, academies and families constitute and are constituted by their parts, by the wholes in which they participate, and are subject to causal dependencies, and these are constituted in part by our conceptual imputations. And given the multiplicity of ways of taking the world scouted above, there is no reason to believe that the way that we take even the natural, non-human world, is uniquely privileged. Conceptual imputation may be at work all the way down.

Another way of putting this point concerns the close relation between identity and existence, as seen from a Buddhist metaphysical perspective. The Quinean slogan "no entity without identity" has a clear ancestor in this tradition. To say that something exists, whether it is a proton, a person or a national deficit, is to presuppose that it has an identity. If we cannot say what it is that exists, an existence claim is empty. And the force of the thoroughgoing determination of ontology from the subjective side, whether by the structure of the senses, of thought, of language or of social structures and purposes, means that assertions of identity independent of those considerations are empty. We don't even know what we mean when we assert that something exists simpliciter, what the truth conditions of such a claim might be, and there may well be no content to any such claims at all.

The Buddhist critique of the idea of independent existence encodes the intuition that since identity conditions for phenomena are determined by an interplay of subject and object, and since existence is always *existence as an entity with a particular identity*, existence is also dependent in this sense. This is another way of saying that the attempt to find a determinate reality beyond the apparently ethereal *lebenswelt* may well be doomed to failure.

## *1.4 Western Connections*

These ideas are not entirely foreign to Western metaphysical thought, of course. They resonate both with ideas articulated in the Pyrrhonian and Academic skeptical traditions, as when in chapter 10 of the *Outlines of Pyrrhonism*, Sextus says, "For example, honey appears to us to have a sweetening quality. This much we conceded, because it affects us with a sensation of sweetness. The question, however, is whether it is sweet in an absolute sense" (1964, 38). Among the ten modes of Anasedemus, the first mode, that from differences in animals, is also apposite: "According to this mode, the same objects do not produce the same impression in different animals" (ibid., 45) "But if the difference in animals is a cause of things appearing different, then we shall, it is true, be able to say what—in our view—a things is; but on the question what it really is by nature, we shall suspend judgment" (49).

While all of the modes attack the idea that we can sensibly predicate qualities of objects independent of our own perceptual apparatus, the sixth mode, that from admixtures, deserves special note. Sextus writes:

> By this mode we conclude that, since none of the external objects appears to us singly, but always in conjunction with something else, it is perhaps possible to state the nature of the mixture resulting from the conjunction of the external object and that other thing which we perceive together with it, but we are not able to say what the real nature of the external object is in its unmixed state. (64)

Sextus makes it plain in the subsequent discussion that the factors he takes to be "mixed" with external objects are our sensory and cognitive faculties, including both the physical sense organs and the cognitive processes by means of which we perceive. Now, a lot of ink has been spilled on the question of how to interpret Pyrrhonian skepticism, and I do not propose to wade once again into that river. (For my thoughts see Garfield 1990.) Here I emphasize only that the Buddhist idea that our objects of knowledge—the furniture of our *lebenswelt* are dependent on both external and internal conditions and cannot be taken to be independent in any sense—is hardly foreign to the Western tradition, although the arguments for that conclusion and the ways in which it is understood may be interestingly different.

These ideas also resonate with the intuitions of the intellectual descendants of the skeptical tradition such as Hume, in his insistence that what we can know is *human nature*, and that any metaphysics of the external world is doomed, and Wittgenstein who speaks of the spade being turned when we arrive at human practices and conventions. These ideas also resonate, not surprisingly, with ideas articulated in German and British idealism (particularly with Kant's and Schopenhauer's insight that we know only representations conditioned by the structure of our sensibility and understanding, and that even what we take to be rational is conditioned ultimately by the structure of human reason and not that of any independent reality, but also with the thought of Bradley, who took all appearance to be essentially relational).

Of course these Buddhist metaphysical ideas are not *identical* with those that emerged in the West, and the point of this discussion is neither to show that they are nor to engage in bland "compare and contrast" exercise. Nonetheless, it is sometimes easier to appreciate the perspective of an unfamiliar tradition by recognizing some of its more familiar characteristics. By seeing the ways in which this network of ideas crosscuts more familiar philosophical divides we come to see that Buddhist metaphysics is not some Western program being prosecuted by other means, but a very different way of taking up with metaphysical questions, with insights of its own that demand serious attention.

In rejecting a metaphysics of independent substances overlaid with attributes in favor of a world of essenceless insubstantial relata we see anticipations of the British empiricist critique of the idea of substance developed initially by Berkeley and sharpened considerably by Hume. Berkeley ridicules the idea of substance as a substratum for properties in the first of the *Three Dialogues Between Hylas and Philonous* when after developing a regress argument to the effect that substance can have no properties, including that of being the basis of properties, he says, "It seems then you have no idea at all, neither relative nor positive, or matter; you know neither what it is in itself nor what relation it bears to accidents?" (40). Hume echoes this claim of the incomprehensibility of the idea of substance when he says, "...[T]hese philosophers...suppose a substance supporting, which they do not understand, and an accident supported, of which they have as imperfect an idea. The whole system, therefore, is entirely incomprehensible..." (222). Hume's great advance over Berkeley, of course, is to extend this argument to an attack on *mental* substance as well as physical substance, thus completing the reprise of the critique developed originally by the Buddha.

This affinity will be more apparent when we turn to questions concerning time and identity. But we should also note that in understanding the fundamental mode of existence of all phenomena to be relational, and not intrinsic, there are also powerful anticipations of Bradley's radical ontology. These entities are hence not, as we remarked above, Hume's independent existences connected by contingent relations, but are rather insubstantial nodes in networks of insubstantial, contingent relations.

The emphasis on the role of perception, cognition and convention in the constitution of identity and the determination of existence that we see in Buddhist metaphysics anticipates Hume's analysis of identity over time, of personal identity, as well as his account of causation. But it also anticipates Kant's analysis of phenomena as co-constituted by noumena and our sensory and cognitive faculties. We can put the broad difference this way: In providing an account of a world, the ontology of which is determined by imputation, Buddhist philosophers, partly for soteriological reasons, partly for metaphysical reasons, are emphasizing that the entities and properties with which we interact are those that have significance for us, those about which we care, that stand out from and are framed by backgrounds, or that constitute the backgrounds that give significance to that which stands out.

And this makes perfect sense. Buddhist philosophy, as we said at the outset of this study, is aimed at solving a particular problem, that of the omnipresence of suffering; that suffering is created by and enacted in the world of things and properties we take to be meaningful, and in ascribing them the meanings that allow them to be sources either of suffering or its alleviation, we construct them as the properties they are for us. The choice of the *lebenswelt* as the site of metaphysics is thus not a retreat from reality, but a focus on the reality that matters to us. Its metaphysics is the metaphysics that can make a difference. While Western phenomenology may not share this soteriological concern, the insights the Buddhist analysis generates are nonetheless hard to resist.

This *lebenswelt*, especially in the Mahāyāna tradition, is a social world, a world in which conventions can be constituted. One of the central meanings of *convention (samvṛti, vyāvahāra)*, as the 6th-century Indian philosopher Candrakīrti emphasizes in his *Autocommentary to Introduction to the Middle Way (Madhyamakāvatārabhāṣya)*, is *agreement*, or *mundane* practice. For this reason, from a Mahāyāna perspective, not only are our salient social practices and linguistic meanings conventionally constituted, but so is our ontology. The connections between this perspective and the insights of the later Wittgenstein are also salient. Here I have in mind both the centrality of social conventions in the constitution of ontology and epistemic practices and the insight that the phenomena we encounter in everyday life are essenceless. Wittgenstein, like Madhyamaka philosophers, argued that such phenomena as meaning, intentionality, justification and categorization depend crucially on human purposes, forms of life and conventions.

Thurman (1980) notes the uncanny parallel between the philosophical strategy adopted by Candrakīrti and Tsongkhapa on the one hand and by Wittgenstein in his later work on the other. He refers to this strategy as "non-egocentrism," although the terms "conventionalism" or even "communitarianism" have become more popular. Candrakīrti and Tsongkhapa argue that our conventions—including both linguistic and customary practices and innate cognitive commonalities—constitute our ontology, and that the very possibility of any individual knowing anything, asserting anything or thinking anything requires participation in those conventions. (See also Thakchöe 2013.) Explanatory priority is located at the collective level, not the individual level. In a similar vein, Wittgenstein argues that meaning is constituted by collective linguistic practice enabled by shared innate propensities; that intentionality is parasitic on linguistic meaning and that knowledge depends upon epistemic practices that are in turn grounded in conventions regarding justification, doubt and so on. Once again, while there is considerable overlap in perspective, the Buddhist traditions that anticipate Western ideas are distinct enough in their approach to merit serious attention.

The very practices that constitute our world and the practices of justification and assertion are conventional through and through. And those conventions are rough, dependent and variable enough that when we try to specify essences—sets of non-trivial necessary and sufficient conditions—for things, we almost always fail. Conventional reality for Wittgenstein, as for the Mādhyamika, cannot withstand too much analysis. Not *despite*, but *because* of that fact, it works for us. And for Wittgenstein, like the Mādhyamika, who and what *I* am, and what *I* can think and talk about depends upon who and what *we are*, and what *we* can think and talk about. Convention runs deep. And the conventional status of reality is deeply connected to the impermanence of all things, a topic to which we now turn.

## 2. Impermanence

All Buddhist philosophers, of all schools, argue that all phenomena (with the exception of *nirvāṇa*, and of space in certain schools) are impermanent. The details vary, of course, with varying accounts of the nature of time, and of the temporal extent of the processes of arising, endurance and cessation. But in general, the existence of phenomena is regarded as momentary. There are two general senses of impermanence in Buddhist metaphysical theory, generally referred to as "gross" and "subtle" impermanence. To say that phenomena are impermanent in the first sense is to say that everything changes over time, at least in minor ways, and over larger periods of time, often in substantial ways; over great stretches of time, in dramatic ways. To say that phenomena are impermanent in the second sense is to say that at every moment, everything is changing, if only in imperceptible, minute ways.[10] Because of these kinds of change, all identity over time, from a Buddhist point of view, is a fiction, albeit often a very useful fiction.

Nāgārjuna makes this point in chapter XIII of *Fundamental Verses on the Middle Way*. He begins the discussion by anticipating a plausible objection to the view that impermanence entails essencelessness and lack of intrinsic identity:

> 4.cd If there were no nature,
> How could there be transformation?

He replies as follows:

> 5. A thing itself is without transformation.
> Nor is transformation in something else,
> Because a young man does not age,
> And because an aged man does not age either.
>
> 6. If a thing itself transformed,
> Milk itself would become yoghurt.
> But what other than milk
> Could become the entity that is yoghurt?

Impermanence then is neither the gross nor the subtle change of any entity that retains its identity through change. While we might say that a person gradually grows old, and so that the person must endure through the change, that is not literally true. Instead this is a way of saying that there is a continuum to which we refer with a single name comprising both youthful and elderly stages that are causally connected. The point is driven home by the milk to yoghurt example. The fact that we say that milk became yoghurt does not mean that there is a single entity that was once milk and is now yoghurt, but rather that there is a causal continuum in which earlier stages were milk and later stages are yoghurt. There can be no identity between the two.

The ramifications of this insight are significant. Gross impermanence is reasonably straightforward. We are born very small. We grow and mature.

10. This distinction between gross and subtle impermanence can be drawn in terms of the two Buddhist *pramāṇas*, or instruments of knowledge, viz., perception and inference. (We will address these in detail in chapter 7.) Gross impermanence is the impermanence we can perceive; subtle impermanence is the impermanence we infer on the basis of what we perceive. Since we can see that things change over large periods of time, we can infer that they are constantly changing moment by moment.

We age and die. Mountains are raised by tectonic forces. They wear away, and their rocks become topsoil in the flood plains of rivers. Stars are assembled from interstellar dust, give rise to planets that orbit them for billions of years, supernova, cool and collapse into black holes. Universes evolve, and perhaps collapse into themselves. To deny the impermanence of things in this sense seems simply mad. To deny its significance may be more tempting, but we will come to that below. For now, let us simply note that this conception of phenomena is central to a Buddhist outlook.

From a Buddhist standpoint, gross impermanence entails subtle impermanence. Gross changes of the kind we just noted are continuous processes. This means that even though we may not notice these changes, subtle changes are occurring at every moment. Our aging is a process of continuous change. Every second we are not only (trivially, but importantly) one second older and one second closer to our death, but also older in material ways, with cells dying, some being replaced, some not, with deterioration in our tissues occurring constantly. Mountains are rising imperceptibly at each moment, and deteriorating imperceptibly at each moment, and so forth. This means that at each moment, every thing that we identify as a single entity has properties it lacked a moment before, and properties that it will lack a moment later.[11]

Buddhist metaphysicians were fans of Leibniz's law long *avant la lettre.* That is, they regard the condition of real identity as indiscernibility in all respects. To differ in any respect is to fail to be identical. The classic example here occurs in a late Śrāvakayāna text, *The Questions of King Milinda (Milindapañha)*, a text written in the form of a dialogue between a possibly fictional monk, Nāgasena, and a king modeled on a the Greek Bactrian king Menander who reigned in the 2nd century BCE. The dialogue is replete with illustrative metaphors, as will be obvious from this extract from the second

11. The Sarvastivādin school—an important Buddhist abhidharma school—argued that in fact everything that has ever or will ever exist in fact exists, and that being present is only a kind of manifestation at the present moment of entities that nonetheless exist eternally, an anticipation of the recently popular "spotlight" view of the present. (Clifton and Hogarth 1995, Skow 2009) This position was defended in part on the grounds that fundamental dharmas, being substantially existent, are independent and cannot arise or cease, but more importantly on the grounds that as objects of knowledge of an omniscient Buddha, they would have always to be present to his mind in order to be known. This position was effectively buried by Madhyamaka critiques of this position, particularly that of Nāgārjuna. But the debate between Mādhyamikas and Sarvastivādins is an interesting anticipation of recent debates between 4Dists and presentists regarding endurance vs. perdurance over time. It is intriguing that nobody in the West to my knowledge has ever defended a 4D view on the grounds that objects of knowledge are required for an omniscient god, a curious lacuna in theological metaphysics.

chapter of Book II, in which the king queries Nāgasena regarding the nature of personal identity.

> The king said, "He who is born, Nāgasena, does he remain the same or become another?"
> Neither the same nor another.
> Give me an illustration.
> Now, what do you think, O King? You were once a baby, a tender thing, and small in size, lying flat on your back. Was that the same as you who are now grown up?
> No, that child was one. I am another.
> If you are not that child, it will follow that you have had neither mother nor father! Nor teacher. You cannot have been taught either learning or behavior or wisdom.... Is the mother of the embryo of the first stage different from the mother of the embryo in the second stage, or the third, or the fourth? Is the mother of the baby a different person from the mother of the grown-up man?...
> Certainly not. But what would you, Sir, say to that?
> The Elder replied, "I should say that I am the same person, now I am grown up as I was when I was a tender tiny baby flat on my back. For all these states are included in one by means of this body."
> Give me an illustration.
> Suppose, O King, a man were to light a lamp, would it burn the night through?
> Yes, it might do so.
> Now, is it the same flame that burns in the first watch of the night Sir, and in the second?
> No.
> Or the same that burns in the second watch and the third?
> No.
> Then is there one lamp in the first watch, and another in the second and another in the third?
> No. The light comes from the same lamp all the night through.
> Just so, O King, is the continuity of a person or a thing maintained. One comes into being; another passes away; and the rebirth is, as it were, simultaneous. Thus, neither as the same, nor as another does a man go on to the last phase of his self-consciousness.
> Give me a further illustration.
> It is like milk which when once taken from the cow, turns, after a lapse of time, first to curd, and then from curd to butter, and then from

> butter to ghee. Now, would it be right to say that the milk was the same thing as the curd, or the butter, or the ghee?
> Certainly not; but they are produced out of it.
> Just so, O King, is the continuity of a person or a thing maintained. One comes into being; another passes away; and the rebirth is, as it were, simultaneous. Thus, neither as the same, nor as another does a man go on to the last phase of his self-consciousness. (Müller 2005,. 63–65)

Beyond the literary merits of this little dialogue, there are a few remarkable points to note. First, given the Buddhist doctrines of no-self and impermanence, one might have expected that the king gets it right in his opening remark, when, based on the differences between his infant self and his present self, he pronounces himself a different entity from that he was when young. And indeed, we realize when we come to the end of the dialogue that he was correct, in a fashion. Had he answered in the opposite way, it is clear that he would also have been refuted. But things are not so simple.

Nāgasena deploys two Buddhist rhetorical devices in arguing that while on the one hand he is, like the lamp, the same being at the end of his life that he was at the beginning, on the other hand, like the milk become ghee, he is a different being at every moment, dying and being reborn in every instant in an extended causal continuum. The first device is an early deployment of the rubric of the two truths. Conventionally, for all kinds of reasons, it makes sense to ascribe identity to a life or an object over time. Otherwise, we can make no sense of the idea that one is old, or has parents. But upon analysis—ultimately, from the standpoint of this early Buddhist position—nothing persists for more than a moment. To say simply that one persists through time is incorrect; to say simply that one exists only for a moment is equally incorrect. Each statement must be parameterized. (Braddon-Mitchell and Miller make much the same point in their defense of perdurantism in 2006).

The second device is the denial that we can say anything definitive about the self. For there is no self. Were there one, the king's adult self would have to be either identical to or distinct from his infant self. But since neither can be asserted, the fiction of the self is to be abandoned. In its place, we get two entities: a conventional person, constituted by our conventions of individuation and discourse; and a continuum of momentary entities that constitute its basis of designation,[12] the causal ground that makes sense of the conventions.

12. Some Buddhist philosophers go even further. Tsongkhapa, for instance, argues that there is no intrinsically identifiable basis of designation for any conventional entities whatsoever, but only designations, which themselves require no basis. The spade on Tsongkhapa's view, is simply turned when we note what we do and say.

The conventional person is neither identical to nor different from that continuum. It is in part constituted by it, but only given a set of human interests and practices. The failure of the preservation of indiscernibility over time precludes genuine identity.

It follows from this, as Nāgasena notes at the close, that since *no entity* retains all of its properties from one moment to the next, no entity endures from one moment to the next. Even were the only changes in an entity to be relational, these are changes. Even if the only changes in an entity were to be its age, these are changes. And as we know, there are far more central changes than this in every entity from moment to moment. Any identity over time is hence a fiction, at best a continuum of states and processes that are similar to one another and causally connected. Impermanence hence has profound implications for ontology.

## *2.1 Conventional Identity*

What then does a Buddhist metaphysician say about the apparent identity over time of persons, mountains, planets and institutions? Given the obvious utility of discursive and other practices that take identity over time for granted, not only of persons but of all of the middle-sized dry goods around us; and among these discursive practices are specifically *Buddhist* discourse about personal development, about the composite nature of entities, and even about gross impermanence, we need some account of why we can talk about continuants in our world.

The Buddhist reply to this demand is to argue that what we usually take to be things that *endure* over time are in fact continua of momentary, causally interacting events, or as they have come to be called in contemporary metaphysics, *tropes*. These continua are temporally extended, and are causally coherent enough, with successive stages that are similar enough to one another, that it is practically useful, *for many, though not for all purposes*, to refer to them with single terms, and to treat them as though they were endurants. This utility is often confused with reality. The anticipations of Hume are remarkable, and to see Hume's positions on these matters as Buddhist is quite reasonable.[13]

Continua, then, may be regarded as *conventionally real*, in that we have reasonable conventions for referring to and interacting socially and otherwise

13. Indeed Parfit (1984) notes the affinities of his own neo-Humean views regarding the nonexistence of continuing selves to Buddhist views. See also Gopnik (2009) for interesting speculations on possible historical connections between the Buddhist tradition and Hume.

with them. They are not, however, *ultimately* real; that is, there is nothing in any causal or similarity continuum itself that demands recognition from us as an entity independent of our conventions and interests. After all, a distributed mass of air and water together with some nutrients in the soil, a tree, an acorn, another tree, a pile of logs, some ash, and a flower fertilized with that ash are indeed a continuum, but not one we recognize as a single entity, while a caterpillar, a chrysalis and a butterfly might well be.

Buddhist philosophers often draw the distinction between ultimate and conventional reality in terms of the distinction between being *dravyasat*, or substantially real, and being *prajñaptisāt*, or merely conceived as real. And this indeed is the kind of distinction in the background of the dialogue from *The Questions of King Milinda* we discussed above. In this Sanskrit Abhidharma Buddhism, momentary *dharmas* are regarded as *dravyasat*, and continua or collections of them—enduring complexes—are regarded as merely *prajñaptisāt*.[14] In later Madhyamaka, nothing at all is regarded as *dravyasat*, and only the emptiness of that substantiality is regarded as ultimate truth. More of this later.

This ascription of conventional reality, but not ultimate reality, to most of what Western philosophers would regard as unitary entities is one sense in which Buddhist metaphysicians take themselves to be hewing to a middle path between nihilism (the denial that these things exist in *any* sense, or that they ground truth in any sense) and reification (the view that because they exist and can serve as truthmakers in *some sense*, that they exist ultimately). Tsongkhapa, glossing Candrakīrti, puts the point this way:

> [The statement that conventional truth is obscurational] means that conventional truth is that which is true from the perspective of

14. It is important to remember that, despite a widespread tendency among scholars in Buddhist Studies to assimilate the Pāli Abhidhamma tradition to the later north Indian Sanskrit Abhidharma tradition, this understanding of the distinction between ultimate (*paramārtha*) and conventional (*saṃvṛti*) truth/reality in terms of *dravyasat* and *prajñaptisāt* develops *only* in the latter tradition. Pāli scholars, on the other hand, never gloss this distinction in ontological terms, but only with regard to the nature of the language the Buddha used in teaching, and the level of technical precision vs. the colloquial nature of that language. Moreover, the sense of *saṃvṛti* as *deceptive* or *concealing* that figures so prominently in the Sanskrit literature is entirely foreign to the Pāli *sammuti*, which is never understood in this sense. Pāli Buddhist theorists do not, therefore, distinguish (or then identify) different levels of reality or truth, but rather different languages for describing human experience. The ontological turn, and with it, the distinction between these levels of reality is a Sanskrit innovation. I thank Maria Heim for drawing my attention to this point and for emphasizing its importance in understanding both the diversity and the development of Buddhist thought in India.

> ignorance—obscuration—but not that it is truly existent from the standpoint of nominal convention. Otherwise, this would be inconsistent with the system according to which nothing exists through its own characteristic even conventionally. Since the refutation of true existence and the proof of the absence of true existence are presented through nominal convention, it is not tenable that their true existence is posited through nominal convention. If they were not so presented, they could not be presented ultimately, either and it would follow that no framework would be coherent. (2006, 482)

There is a lot of technical language here, and a few technical dialectical moves, but Tsongkhapa's central point is this: Even though Mādhyamikas argue that nothing exists truly—that is, ultimately, or independently—we must accept that things exist conventionally, for otherwise, we would not even be able to say that they do not exist ultimately. And when we say this, we do so truly, and so conventional existence, or conventional truth, must ground truth. If it couldn't, nothing could. Note the intriguing parallel to Wittgenstein's analysis of knowledge in *On Certainty*: Our epistemic conventions are just that, conventions; nonetheless, they underlie our justificatory and critical practices; if they could not, nothing could. The Mādhyamika anticipates this form of argument, but delivers it at the register of truth and existence, as opposed to knowledge, playing for slightly higher stakes, as it were.

There is another, closely related middle path here. Another version of nihilism—a more temporalized version—is to take continua as nonexistent because there is nothing that persists—no common fiber in the thread—from moment to moment, and so no bearer of the identity as a whole. And another, temporalized, version of reification—often referred to as *eternalism* in Buddhist literature—is to assert that there *is something* that persists in a temporally extended continuum; that is, the continuum itself which endures despite having no part that endures. In another passage of *The Questions of King Milinda*, Nāgasena deploys the analogy of a flame transferred from lamp to lamp as an analogy for a continuum across rebirths, stressing the role of causation, without any identity, and the fact that to talk about a flame that is transferred is nothing but a *façon de parler*. There is no flame, only a sequence of causally related things that serve as the basis of designation for what appears to be a referring expression. But for all that, the flame is not *nothing*. Tsongkhapa puts it like this:

> In all of these cases [of temporally extended personal continua] in general—without specifying the identity of the self in terms of time

> and place—the self, because it desires to obtain happiness and to avoid suffering, does such things. The mere self is taken to persist through these times as well. Thus it is not erroneous for these people to take the mere self as the referent of 'I'. Therefore, the person who uses the expression "I am," and the basis of the use of that expression should not be taken to be coextensive; instead, the person should be understood as a segment of that self. (2006, 272)

Tsongkhapa here is emphasizing that we must distinguish three putative entities here: a continuing self; a mere self; the basis of designation of the mere self. The continuing self is simply an illusion. There is no such thing at all. The mere self is just whatever we mean when we use a pronoun or a name—a conventionally designated cluster of phenomena with no clear identity conditions. Its basis of designation is a causal continuum. That is, that continuum is causally responsible for the utility of pronouns and names and is the basis for our thinking of ourselves as continuing entities. But it is not the *referent* of the name. When I use the pronoun 'I', or the name *Jay*, I do not refer to a continuum of causal processes that stretches indefinitely, and which has no clear identity conditions. I take myself to be referring to a self; in fact, I am referring to a *mere self*, just whatever *now* causally grounds the use of that term.

The Buddhist middle path here consists in rejecting nihilism on the grounds that continua, like threads, have perfectly good, albeit merely conventional and rough-and-ready identity conditions that are not undermined by change—a view supported by common sense and empirical science—and to reject reification in virtue of its patent circularity and ontological gratuity. An endurant where nothing retains identity is what is to be proven, not a mere redescription, and to posit a super-entity that exists non-conventionally in order to explain the conventional identity of a continuum is unnecessary when conventions themselves can do all the work.

## 2.2 Apoha: *A First Pass*

This metaphysics of impermanence, together with the commitment to causal interdependence of all phenomena, also underlies Buddhist nominalism with regard to properties. Since universals are abstracta, and hence both causally inert and permanent, they fail to satisfy the most fundamental Buddhist criteria for reality—causal interdependence and spatio-temporal locality. It is for this reason that all Buddhist philosophers regard universals of all kinds as conceptual projections, and as entirely unreal. This rejection of universals of course requires not only an ontological account of a world of pure particularity, but also an alternate theory of predication, of word meaning, of concepts and of inference. The most prominent Buddhist response to this set of demands is the construct of *apoha*.

This idea is introduced by Dignāga in the early sixth century and is ramified by a series of subsequent Indian commentators and interlocutors—prominently including his immediate commentator Dharmakīrti—until the demise of Buddhism in India in the 11th century, with a final Indian account in the work of Ratnakīrti. *Apoha* theory was very influential in Tibet and is debated in the Tibetan academy to the present day. *Apoha* is a hard word to translate, and the fact that there is such a bewildering variety of *apoha* theories on offer makes it even harder, for an apt translation of the term as it is used by one philosopher runs afoul of the interpretation of another, even though they take themselves to be arguing about the same thing. *Apoha* is often translated as *exclusion* or *elimination*. But it can also be read as *discrimination* or *distinction*.

Here is the general idea: To use the stock example, when I say that Daisy is a cow, it *appears* that I am saying that the particular *Daisy* (give or take a bit of ontology, given that she is a composite, a continuum, etc., but let us leave that aside) participates in or is saturated with the universal *cowness*, something that also permeates Marigold, Bossie and Daisy's other barnmates. Daisy is impermanent and localized; *cowness* is permanent and non-local. But that appearance is an error. For there is no such thing as *cowness*. What I am really saying, on *apoha* theory is, to a first—and startlingly unilluminating—approximation, that Daisy is not a non-cow. The double negation is the *apoha*. The hope is that there is a way of understanding this device that explains the meaning and truth conditions of the assertion, the possession of the concept that enables it and explains what it is that instances of cows have in common.

Dignāga, in his *Encyclopedia of Epistemology* (*Pramāṇasammucāya*), explains it roughly this way: We are able to distinguish cows from non-cows using some cognitive mechanism. All that mechanism does is distinguish things from one another, eliminating (*apoha*) those that are not similar to an exemplar from those that are. (See Hayes 2009.) This is what Tillemans (2011b) calls a top-down *apoha* theory. On this view, the meaning of the word *cow* just is the ability to draw this distinction; to possess the concept is to be able to draw that distinction, and what cows have in common is that the mind distinguishes them from non-cows. *They* do not share a property that inheres in *them*, but instead *a capacity in us* to assort particulars leads us to sort them into the same pile.

Dharmakīrti, Dignāga's commentator (or wholesale reviser, depending on one's perspective) adopts what Tillemans (op. cit.) calls a bottom-up version of *apoha* theory. On this view, although in perception we immediately encounter particulars, these particulars elicit in the mind a representation. (Dharmakīrti is silent about the specific cognitive mechanisms and adverts simply to tendencies in the mind that are the results of past karma. But we can imagine a modern cognitive account here, as does Chatterjee 2011). So, when I take myself to see Daisy,[15] a representation (*ākara/rnam pa*) of Daisy arises in my mind. The representation is suitably general in that it could easily represent Marigold and Bossie as well. It just could not represent anything that is not a cow; it represents everything that is *not a non-cow*. It is an *apoha*. I easily mistake the representation I have constructed for the particular it represents, thinking that because it equally represents all cows I have apprehended something that all cows share. I have confused an *apoha*, which is a particular representation, with a universal. On this view, the meaning of the word *cow* is determined by the ability to draw the relevant distinction between those things we call cows and those we don't; mastery of the concept consists in the generation of the appropriate representation when in contact with the relevant particular.

Just as in the case of Dignāga, we eliminate universals in a psychologistic account of verbal and conceptual capacities. And, like all iterations of *apoha* theory, we see a presumption of a brute psychological capacity to respond to and to recognize similarities on certain dimensions. This capacity is meant to do the heavy lifting, as opposed to any universal in the objects classified. The anticipations of Hume and Quine are obvious. It is not surprising that many non-Buddhist critiques anticipate Armstrong's (1984) response in the service of a realistic account of universals: similarity in *what respect?* Much of the debate between Buddhist and non-Buddhist philosophers regarding the status of universals in fact turns on this question. I note this not to resolve the debate, which we will leave aside here, but once again to highlight an unfamiliar path into familiar terrain.

Dharmakīrti's commentators are legion, and the study of *apoha* theory is a major subspecialty in Buddhist philosophy. The theory raises enough difficulties to engender both a vigorous debate between Buddhist and non-Buddhist philosophers on the status of universals and the nature of meaning, and a vigorous debate within the Buddhist world on the best way to formulate *apoha* theory. It would be impossible in this context to do justice to this rich tradition.[16]

15. In fact, I can only *take myself* to see her, on Dharmakīrti's view, since what I *actually* see can only be a momentary particular. One way to think about the primal illusion at the basis of *saṃsāra* in this tradition is the pervasive confusion of perception with conceptual activity.

16. See Dreyfus 1997, 2011b; Dunne 2004, 2006, 2011; Katsura 1969, 1991; Kellner 2003; Patil 2009; and Siderits, Tillemans and Chakarabarti 2011 for excellent discussions of Indian and Tibetan *apoha* theory; the latter is particularly useful for the many connections the essays it collects draw to contemporary philosophical concerns.

Ratnakīrti is the last figure in the Indian Buddhist tradition to address this matter, and his position deserves mention. Ratnakīrti takes up Dharmakīrti's view that *apoha* involves a representation and a distinction and gives it a novel twist. He argues that *apoha* provides an analysis of concepts and meaning as follows: a concept is a pair, consisting in a representation and a capacity for distinguishing between what is similar to it and what is not. To possess the concept *cow* on this view is to have the prototype representation and to be able to draw the relevant distinction. The meaning of the word cow is its use in drawing that distinction. The anticipations of Wittgenstein and Rosch are striking.

We got ourselves into *apoha* theory for metaphysical reasons. Buddhist commitments to interdependence and impermanence entail nominalism with respect to universals, and nominalism with respect to universals requires some fancy footwork in semantics and the theory of cognition. *Apoha* is that tango. The metaphysical payoff is that instead of appealing to the universal *cowness* to explain the truth of *Daisy is a Cow*, the meaning of *cow*, or the grasp of the concept *cow*, Buddhist theorists appeal to our ability to recognize similarities, to draw distinctions and to classify particulars in terms of the way we respond to them and in terms of our purposes. Psychologically, this involves a model of our contact with reality as mediated by representations, generated by sub-personal, brute tendencies to respond to particulars in certain ways, which in turn enable us to draw these distinctions, and a semantics that accounts for word meaning in terms of our use of words, and not in terms of reference to properties. (See Thakchöe 2012b.)

To the extent that we take universals seriously, on this understanding, we are driven to hypostasize an underlying ground that justifies a convention for using a predicate. This hypostatization, Buddhist theorists argue, leads in turn to metaphysical nonsense that does not even deliver the requisite explanations—nonsense because one can make no sense of the reality of universals given that they depend on nothing and have no effects; a failure because we have no account of our cognitive access to them, which we must have if they are to explain our cognitive and linguistic capacities. Instead, from a Buddhist point of view, all that justifies, and all that is needed to justify, our use of language is a set of linguistic conventions and cognitive habits. This Humean-Wittgensteinian program is familiar to the Western philosopher, even if its mode of prosecution is different. Whether this program can succeed is another matter; but once again, there is reason to engage.

Buddhist philosophers connect this conclusion regarding universals to the Buddhist account of continua, and so tie this nominalism more deeply to the metaphysics of impermanence. For successive momentary phenomena to be regarded as identical, or even to be regarded as, on their own, parts of a single continuum, is for them to be united by a universal, what we might call a "longitudinal universal." And the same holds true, of course, for simultaneous parts taken as united into a whole. That is, for instance, for successive sets of tropes to be regarded as the same table, or the same person, is to regard them as satisfying at minimum the property "moments and parts of this table/person." But that property is already a universal, and so is unreal. There is hence *nothing* from the side of the events in the world themselves that unites them into continua or entities at all. That work is done from the side of language, convention, thought and a host of non-discursive practices of sentient beings. Thus interdependence and impermanence, thought through the problem of universals, takes Buddhist philosophy immediately back to the merely conventional status of the world we inhabit. We will return to *apoha* theory and will take up these topics in more detail in the context of a discussion of Buddhist epistemology in chapter 7.

All of this takes us back to the fundamental primal confusion that Buddhists diagnose at the root of the suffering that sets the philosophical and soteriological agenda for Buddhism. We can now see that primal confusion as operating at a deeper metaphysical plane. Primal confusion on this view is the cognitive reflex that takes sequences of momentary, interdependent phenomena to be real entities that bear their own individuation conditions. This involves the superimposition of unreal universals constructed by thought and the projection of that superimposition onto reality itself; a confusion of the construction of the conventional world with the discovery of an ontologically constituted world that we passively, and accurately, record in consciousness.

This dimension of Buddhist metaphysics is, of course, immediately relevant to contemporary debates about the metaphysics of continuants. It constitutes an important, and little noted, position in the debate between 3D and 4D accounts of object identity, one that denies the ultimate reality of continuants entirely, while preserving through an account of conventional reality the intuition that entities are real, four-dimensional phenomena. The 3D–4D debate has been hot lately. (Baker 1995, 2000, 2007; Braddon-Mitchell and Miller 2006; Donnelly 2011; Fine 2008; Miller 2005a, 2005b, 2008, 2009; Sider 2001; Simmons 2008; Yagisawa 2010 among a host of others.) Miller (2005a) felicitously sums up the principal positions as follows:

> Three-dimensionalism is the thesis that persisting objects have only spatial dimensions. Thus, since our world is a world in which there are three spatial dimensions, persisting objects are three-dimensional. Four-dimensionalism, on the other hand, is the view that persisting

> objects have both spatial dimensions and a temporal dimension. Since our world is a world with three spatial dimensions and one temporal dimension, this is the view that persisting objects are four-dimensional: they are extended in time as well as in space.
>
> The three-dimensionalist holds that all objects are wholly present whenever they exist, and persisting objects, which exist at more than one time, are wholly present at each of those times. The most common version of four-dimensionalism holds that objects persist through time by being only partly present at each moment at which they exist, that is, by having a temporal present at each time at which they exist. Thus objects persist by perduring, where an object perdures if it persists by being the mereological sum of temporal parts. (309–310)

The question then is this: what is the correct analysis of the mode of persistence of physical objects and persons? Are we wholly present at each moment of our existence, or are we mereological sums of our stages? The debate, as metaphysical debates will, quickly becomes complex and develops a series of epicycles. It is neither my aim to articulate it in detail nor to settle it. On the other hand, I do want to suggest that it rehearses the very issues about identity and time that are introduced in *The Questions of King Milinda* and picked up in subsequent literature such as Candrakīrti's *Introduction to the Middle Way*, and that it might profit by attention to those texts and the moves they make.

In fact, Braddon-Mitchell and Miller (2006) unwittingly come very close to this, and reinvent some nice old wheels in the process. They even (501) consider the example of the relation between the child and the adult, arguing that there are good reasons to say both that the child will become an adult and that it will not. After all, it will develop into an adult, but at that time there will be no more child. A bit later, they say:

> [T]here are many cases where it seems as though there is a sense in which a common sense claim is right, and another in which it is wrong. For instance, consider the following claims: "I won't have my puppy in a few years, for by then it'll have become a dog"; "the butterfly was a caterpillar' and 'the corpse was a child". In such cases it turns out that there is some analysis under which the claim is true, and some analysis under which it is false, depending on which parts of the rich four-dimensional ontology ordinary talk is about, and whether the terms in question are being used as phase sortal terms or substance sortal terms. (502)

Braddon-Mitchell and Miller, as the last remark suggests, like many of those in the Buddhist tradition, resolve this tension by reference to two levels of discourse. They distinguish substance from phase sortals, the first picking out four-dimensional objects, the second three-dimensional objects. Many ordinary language predicates, they point out, are ambiguous between these two readings. Their position sorts out a number of issues in this debate rather nicely, but we might worry about the commitment to a substance ontology and indeed to the idea that phases or substances can be picked out in non-question-begging ways.

In a rich discussion alive to these problems, Braddon-Mitchell and Miller rediscover the Buddhist idea that causal relations are insufficient to determine persistence and the identity conditions of ordinary continua, but do not resolve the conundrum of what does determine them. Perhaps a recasting of the dichotomy of phase and sortal into ultimate and conventional and a focus on the role of convention in ontology would help. Attention to the Buddhist literature would naturally take one in this direction.

Braddon-Mitchell and Miller also note the connection of the 3D–4D debate to questions about constitution and identity. One of the great virtues of their analysis is their demonstration that constitution can be understood naturally in terms of the sharing of temporal parts. On the metaphysical picture they develop, constitution, as opposed to identity, captures the relation between parts and wholes as well as that between statues and lumps.

A Buddhist analysis following *The Questions of King Milinda* and Candrakīrti's *Introduction to the Middle Way* would suggest that constitution both goes further down than that and is less metaphysically robust than it might appear in the contemporary Western literature. Indeed, it provides an analysis of the relationship not only between parts and wholes, statues and lumps, but even also between temporal stages and entities. But once we give up on the idea that these relations are relations between metaphysically fundamental entities, we might come to see that relations between that which constitutes and that which is constituted obtain not in virtue of any properties internal to the relata, but in virtue of our own cognitive, linguistic, social and behavioral conventions. Constitution, from a Buddhist point of view, is the construction of conventional reality, and given the fundamental character of impermanence, it is the only route to entities we could ever recognize, or be.

## 3. Where We Are

As we noted at the outset, interdependence and impermanence are at the heart of all Buddhist metaphysics. It is impossible to understand anything of the Buddhist approach to metaphysics, epistemology or ethics without understanding these commitments and the particular nuance they receive in the Buddhist tradition. My hope is that this aspect of Buddhist metaphysics is now coming into focus, and that this discussion will provide a foundation not only for a discussion of emptiness and the two truths in the next chapter, but also for an understanding of Buddhist approaches to epistemology, ethics and the philosophy of language later.

Moreover, I hope that it is already becoming clear that Buddhist philosophical perspectives are sufficiently different from those we find in the Western tradition that they represent genuinely new voices. I also hope that it is clear that there is enough overlap in concern and viewpoint that there is a basis for conversation. While Buddhist viewpoints may not always strike us as natural, they should strike us as reasonable, as demanding consideration, and as repaying contemplation. In the next chapter we continue this exploration of the fundamentals of Buddhist metaphysics.

# 3 THE METAPHYSICAL PERSPECTIVE II: EMPTINESS

With this backdrop of interdependence and impermanence in hand, it is much easier to articulate what is often taken to be the most obscure, if perhaps profound, doctrine in Buddhist metaphysics, that of the emptiness of all phenomena. We have already taken on step to its de-mystification in noting in chapter 1 that emptiness in the relevant sense is never, from a Buddhist point of view, emptiness of *existence*, but always emptiness of some more determinate metaphysical property. That is why in understanding Buddhist doctrines of emptiness, it is always important, as Tsongkhapa puts it, to identify the *object of negation (dgag bya [gak cha])*, that of which something is claimed to be empty.

We can sort major Buddhist schools and doctrines regarding this matter pretty neatly by attending to this advice. We will first consider a series of Buddhist doctrines concerning emptiness, following a historical order, which also helps us to make sense of their relation to one another in dialectical sequence. We will then turn to the Buddhist doctrine of the two truths, principally as it arises in the Mahāyāna schools of India, Tibet and China, and we will conclude with some remarks on the relevance of all of this for contemporary modal metaphysics as it is practiced in the roughly Anglophone West.

Much of what follows will depend on the complex doctrine—or doctrines—of the two truths, or two realities, and so a brief introduction to that doctrine here is in order. We will turn to this issue in more detail below. Let us begin with a translation issue. The Sanskrit term *satya* (Tibetan: *bden pa [den pa]*) can be used, depending on context, to refer to what we would in English call *truth* in a perfectly straightforward sense, and, depending on context, to refer to what we would call in English in a perfectly straightforward sense *reality*. This can cause some confusion. It can also sound like an ambiguity. But, in order to get a sense of an Indian perspective, it is important to realize that in Sanskrit or Tibetan this is not regarded as ambiguity, but simply as a single meaning. *Sat* means *to exist* or *to be the case. Satya* just means *that which is existent, or is the case.* When we say in Sanskrit (or Tibetan) that a sentence is *satya (bden pa)* or that a table is a *satya (bden pa)*, this sounds to a speaker of those languages like the same kind of statement, that the sentence, or the table, accords with reality. Another way of getting to this point is that the term for *false, ālika,* is often glossed as *deceptive (jālika)*. Inasmuch as a table is non-deceptive—it both is, and appears to be, a table—and inasmuch as the statement that it is a table is non-deceptive—it reports what is in fact the case—neither is false; hence both are true. When appropriate, I will use *truth* and its cognates and *reality* and its cognates to translate *satya* and its cognates in ways consistent with English usage. But it will be helpful to bear in mind that in a Buddhist tradition they amount to the same thing. (And taking this idea seriously might enrich Western thought about truth as well.)

The rubric of the two truths has its origins in hermeneutical worries about the resolution of prima facie inconsistencies in the discourses of the Buddha. In some *suttas*, for instance, the Buddha talks about the self or the person, emphasizing the fact that we are each responsible for the kinds of beings we become; in others he emphasizes that there is no self, and that persons are illusions. The hermeneutical mechanism for reconciling such statements is the device of *upāya*, or skillful means. The idea is that the Buddha adopts the language and framework of his audience in order to best communicate what those in the audience are capable of understanding and need to hear. For some, who cannot really understand the doctrine of selflessness, he speaks with the vulgar about a self; for others, whose difficulties are conditioned by their adherence to a belief in the self and who are capable of moving beyond that, he talks about selflessness. But the exegetes who deployed *upāya* in this way do not want the Buddha to be convicted of *lying*, of speaking falsely, or deceptively. So there must be a sense in which when he says something at one level of discourse, or in one context, that he disavows at a higher level of discourse, or in a more sophisticated context, he nonetheless speaks the truth in that discourse, in that context. Enter the two truths.

The first truth, in this early articulation of the doctrine is called *saṃvṛti-satya (kun rdzob bden pa/tha snyad bden pa [kundzop den pa/thanyet den pa])* or *lokavyavahāra-satya (tha snyad bden pa/'jig rten bden pa [jik ten den pa])*. The term *saṃvṛti* generally means *conventional*, as in *by agreement, everyday, ordinary*. But it can *also* mean (and this is real ambiguity) *concealing* or *occluding*. The Tibetan translations are *kun rdzob*, literally meaning *costumed*, and *tha snyad*, literally *nominal*, or *verbal. Lokavyavahāra-satya* means *truth in the everyday world*, or *transactional truth, truth in the marketplace*. The Tibetan translates this again either as *nominal truth (tha snyad bden pa)* or as *everyday truth ('jig rten bden pa)*.

The second truth is *paramartha-satya (don dam bden pa)*, or *ultimate truth, truth in the highest meaning*. This is the final account of the way things really stand. The idea then is that when the Buddha is using *upāya*, he is talking the everyday talk, the way folks talk in the marketplace, even if that talk conceals reality. It is good enough for everyday transactions. When he wants to really get to the heart of things, he speaks of things as they are ultimately. When a cabinetmaker thumps her hand on a just-finished table and says, "This table is solid," she speaks the truth; when a physicist thumps on the same table in a lecture on quantum mechanics and says, "This table, despite appearances, is not solid; it is mostly empty space," he speaks the truth as well. From an early Buddhist perspective the carpenter is speaking conventionally, the physicist ultimately,[1] and there is no contradiction between their claims.

In early Buddhist theory, the relation between the two truths is often cast as one of reduction, or at least ontological supervenience. They clearly represent different levels of reality, and different senses of assertion. The entities that are held to be conventionally real are taken to be, in the end, fictions, to be eliminated by practice and analysis from any ontology one takes seriously. One is then is left only with fundamental *dharmas*, momentary property

1. Though to be sure, no Mādhyamika would regard physics as delivering ultimate truth; instead, it would be taken to yield a deeper understanding of conventional truth. But there is another way to think about scientific discourse and the precision at which it aims from a Madhyamaka point of view. Tsongkhapa argues that for reductio-wielders, such as Candrakīrti, nothing has intrinsic identity even conventionally, and that the meanings of words and ontology are purely conventional, and always rough and ready. (Compare Wittgenstein on word meaning.)

For those who advance their own position, on the other hand, he argues, while nothing has intrinsic identity ultimately, *conventionally* things do have intrinsic identity, because, he argues, those of this school must take word meanings to be fixed precisely in debate, and so they take language to have precise, necessary and sufficient conditions of application. We might see this as an account of the meanings of the terms of precise scientific discourse, even if the meanings of ordinary language are not set that way.

Now, this also connects to the question about the status of scientific entities. Tsongkhapa distinguishes (again, following Candrakīrti) between *ultimate* and *conventional* analysis. Ultimate analysis is the attempt to find the fundamental nature of a thing; this, Tsongkhapa argues, always comes up empty: There is no fundamental nature of reality. Conventional analysis, on the other hand, is simply the use of our ordinary epistemic instruments to take us as deep as we can go into conventional reality. Science, on this view, would have to be conventional analysis, even if its language may give us entities understood as having intrinsic natures, conventionally. (Tsongkhapa holds this position to be unstable, but that is another matter. See Cowherds 2011; Dreyfus and McClintock 2003; Garfield 2002b, 2001.)

instantiations, in a complex of mutual interdependence that give rise to the deceptive appearance of macroscopic continuants.

Part of the Mahāyāna revolution, effected in the *Perfection of Wisdom sūtras* and the works of Nāgārjuna and his followers, is the re-thinking of the doctrine of the two truths. On this view, as we shall see below, *nothing* turns out to be ultimately real, *everything* is merely conventionally real, and the ultimate and conventional truths, while radically different in one respect, are in fact identical in another. That is the profound doctrine of the emptiness of emptiness.

## 1. Varieties of Emptiness

### *1.1 Pre-Mahāyāna Sanskrit Abhidharma doctrine*

Early Abhidharma doctrine identifies the object of negation as *substantial existence (dravyasat)*. It is important to note in this context that the distinction for Indian Abhidharmika scholars of the pre-Mahāyāna period between those phenomena (*dharmas*) which *do* exist substantially and those which do not, but which are merely mereological sums of *dharmas* and are reducible to them, is a serious distinction indeed. It is the distinction between that which exists *ultimately*, independent of human conventions, and that which exists merely *conventionally*. Given this distinction, not *everything* is empty on the relevant sense. Only composite phenomena (*saṃskāra*) are empty; impartite *dharmas* are non-empty. The former lack substantial existence; the latter have it. So, to take the stock example, while its most fundamental parts—*dharmas*, conceived as momentary, punctual instantiations of property-instances—are *dravyasat*, the chariot they constitute is not. It is merely *prajñāptisāt* (nominally, or conventionally, real).

On this view, then, to be empty is to be *reducible* to and to be constituted by something non-empty. The sense of reduction here is *ontological, mereological* reduction. Constitution in this sense is a relation between that which lacks reality on its own (the conventionally real, composite merely *prajñāptisāt*) and that substance of which it is constituted (the *dharmas*). And much of the metaphysics of this time consists in an attempt to enumerate the *dharmas*, to map the causal relations between them, and to analyze composite phenomena into their constituent *dharmas*. (See Siderits 2007.)

The fact that substantial identity requires partlessness entailed that these *dharmas* also lacked *temporal* parts. Hence the Buddhist doctrine of momentariness—the subtle impermanence we encountered in the previous chapter—captures the nature of these *dharmas*. They remain in existence as infinitesimal property instantiations only for an instant, conditioned by previous *dharmas*, and giving rise to subsequent *dharmas*. The conventional composite entities constituted by continua of these *dharmas* exhibit the gross impermanence of constant perceptible change in virtue of the constant minute momentary change of their constituent parts.

Real change on this view is the momentary change reflected in the rapid succession of real *dharmas*, that is, subtle impermanence. The gross impermanence of which we are aware, as the impermanence of unreal phenomena, is itself merely conventional, and unreal, but nonetheless constitutes our first evidence, or entrée into the subtle impermanence that conditions our existence. Gross change is empty, simply because the entities it characterizes are in the end unreal; subtle change is ultimately real, as it is grounded in the momentary nature of *dharmas*.

This distinction emphasizes another important feature of early Abhidharma metaphysics, one noted by Siderits (2007). Reduction can either be a way of vindicating the reality of something—as when, for instance, we show that heat is a real property of a gas by reducing it to mean molecular kinetic energy—or it can be a way of showing that something lacks the kind of reality we thought it had. That is, if one thought that heat was a primitive property of things, the reduction to mean molecular kinetic energy shows that there really is no heat. There is only mean molecular kinetic energy misleadingly called "heat," just as there is no demonic possession, only epilepsy, misleadingly called "demonic possession."

To the extent that one is pluralistic about modes of existence, one is generally tempted to the vindication model; we gain greater confidence in the reality of a phenomenon when we embed it in a larger theoretical context through a scientific reduction. To the extent that one privileges a particular theoretical level of description as uniquely real, on the other hand, taking phenomena not characterized at that level as less real, reduction looks like *elimination*. This is why contemporary eliminative materialists (e.g., Churchland 1979) sometimes take the prospect of the reduction of the mental to the physical (if possible) to entail the elimination of the mental in favor of the physical, whereas some methodological pluralists (Garfield 1988, Baker 2000, 2007) would take that very same prospect of reduction to entail the *reality* of the mental (however suspicious they might be of the prospects for such reduction).

Given the commitment of early Abhidharmikas to the substantial reality of *dharmas*, their status as ontologically and explanatorily fundamental and as constitutive of the *ultimate truth*, we can see this Abhidharma theory as *eliminativist* with regard to such macroscopic phenomena as tables and persons. In *Reality According to the Abhidhamma (Abhidhammatthavibhāvini)*, the early Śri Lankan commentator Sumaṅgala puts it this way:

> [I]t is the definition of the particular natures of ultimate *dhammas* that is taken as absolute; the explanation by way of agent and instrument should be seen as a relative manner of speaking.... The explanation of these terms should be understood as for the purpose of indicating the nonexistence of an agent, etc., apart from the particular nature of a *dhamma*. (In Edelglass and Garfield 2009, 20)

Really, macroscopic things do not exist. What exists instead is a continuum of causally interacting evanescent *dharmas*. Ultimate existence is ontological coin of the realm. Conventional existence is a counterfeit. The Buddhist project on this view is the replacement of a life in which we take the counterfeit for real with one in which we engage only with the gold standard. Needless to say, this entails a dramatic transformation in our everyday consciousness. That, on this view, is the work of prolonged meditation.

### *1.2 Madhyamaka*

The Madhyamaka revolution in Buddhist metaphysics gets its start in the emergence of the *Perfection of Wisdom sūtras* around the turn of the first millennium, but really begins to be systematized in a rigorous way by Nāgārjuna in approximately the late 2nd or early 3rd century CE. This movement is both an evolution of the Abhidharma metaphysics and a radical reaction against it. We can see this revolution as the replacement of one understanding of the relevant object of negation with another, a replacement with far-reaching and profound implications.

On the one hand, we might say that Madhyamaka and early Abhidharma agree about the fact that none of the entities we encounter in our ordinary engagement with the world have *svabhāva*. Let us pause on this term for a moment, for the respect in which they differ can profitably be understood through a re-thinking of the meaning of this term. While this term is absolutely central to understanding all Mahāyāna metaphysics, it has no perfect English equivalent. A number of terms have been used to translate it, and a survey of these terms is a good first step to triangulating its meaning. First the real English: *substance, essence, intrinsic reality, intrinsic identity, nature*. Now the Buddhist Hybrid English neologisms: *self-nature, self-being, own-nature, own-being*.

There is a clear core idea here. Lexically the term consists in a root, *bhāva*, meaning *being*, with a prefix, *sva*, meaning *self*. It is worth noting that it has a nice Sanskrit polar companion *parabhāva*, prefixing the same root *bhāva* with *para*, meaning *other*. It is also worth noting that no simple English term, such as *substance, essence* or *nature* has this feature. So when we use the term *svabhāva* we are implicitly contrasting something that has its being or nature *on its own* with something that borrows its being or nature from something else. For this reason, I prefer the term *intrinsic nature*, as we can naturally contrast it when necessary with *extrinsic nature* (though I confess to having used *essence* liberally in the past, and, I still believe, with good reason).

Now, whereas for the Abhidharmika, to have *svabhāva* is to be substantially existent, and this is the way *dharmas* (and nothing else) in fact exist, for the Mādhyamika, *svabhāva* is a property that no actual thing can ever have. And that means that the term has undergone a subtle semantic shift, reflecting a deeper philosophical analysis and rejection of the Abhidharmika position. To have *svabhāva* in the sense relevant to Madhyamaka is to have one's nature intrinsically, as the Abhidharmika believe that *dharmas* have their natures. But Mādhyamikas argued that to exist in this way would also require being *independent*. For if a *dharma* is caused by, or is the cause of, another *dharma*, as they must be, given the doctrine of dependent origination, then part of what it is to *be* a particular *dharma* is to be caused by particular predecessors, to cause successors, to be part of certain composites, and so on. That is, since it is of the very nature of all phenomena, *including putatively fundamental dharmas*, to be interdependent, then no identity conditions can be given for any phenomenon independent of others. So, since all phenomena are *interdependent*, and *svabhāva* requires *independence*, *svabhāva* is impossible, a property nothing can have.

Mādhyamikas, like their Abhidharmika predecessors and colleagues, understand *svabhāva* as independent existence, as intrinsic nature. This is what they take to be the object of negation, arguing that *svabhāva* in this sense is what we project onto the phenomena we encounter in everyday life. They also argue that *svabhāva* in this sense is what we, like the Abhidharmikas, seek when we attempt to find out reductively what things *really are*, but that nothing at all can possibly have this property. Everything lacks essence, substantiality, independence. They disagree, however, in that while the Abhidharmikas thought that *svabhāva* is a property that certain things, such as *dharmas*, can have, Mādhyamikas argued that *nothing* can have this property, simply because it is incoherent.

Here is a way to understand this doctrinal shift: The anti-realism with respect to the macroscopic, composite entities of ordinary life espoused by early Abhidharma philosophy is extended in the Madhyamaka perspective to the *dharmas* themselves. This amounts to an adoption of what Siderits (2007, 2011) has called *global anti-realism*. But when taken so globally, this amounts to more than a mere extension, since the relevant contrast with the substantially real is lost. If nothing at all is real in this sense, even the term *anti-realism* loses its meaning. For this reason, it makes sense to see Mādhyamikas, in virtue of this radical extension of anti-realism, to have recovered a robust realism regarding the ordinary, conventional world, albeit a moderate *kind* of realism.

Paradoxically, then, from an Abhidharma point of view, Madhyamaka looks to be downright nihilistic in virtue of its denial of *svabhāva* to everything, including the *dharmas*. But from a Madhyamaka point of view, Abhidharma philosophy looks nihilistic about the conventional world, in virtue of denying its reality, while it appears illicitly to reify the ultimate in virtue of assigning *svabhāva* to the *dharmas*. It is because it takes itself to find a middle path between this nihilism and reification, treating both the macroscopic and the microscopic as interdependent and therefore as lacking *svabhāva*, that this school is called the *Middle Way (Madhyamaka)* school.

The *Heart of Wisdom Sūtra*[2] says, in one of the best-known Buddhist formulae of all:

> Form is empty.
> Emptiness is form.
> Form is not other than emptiness.
> Emptiness is not other than form.

The *Heart Sūtra* emphasizes that just as all phenomena (for which *form* stands proxy, as the text itself makes clear in the next passage) are empty of intrinsic nature, their emptiness is not some distinct phenomenon, somehow more real than ordinary phenomena—ultimately, as opposed to conventionally real. Instead, the emptiness of any phenomenon simply is a property of that thing, and so is dependent upon it, and so is impermanent, and so is itself empty, and so is itself merely conventionally real. In the third and fourth lines, the text emphasizes that this is not a mere contingent fact. To be a conventional phenomenon is to be empty; to be empty is to be merely conventionally real. The ultimate reality of things (their emptiness) and the fact that they are merely conventionally real are the same thing. After all, my desk is brown, and its brownness is nothing more than the brownness of the desk. But that is a contingent fact. We would never say that to be a desk is to be brown; to be brown is to be a desk. But the relationship between the ultimate reality of emptiness and the conventional reality of dependent origination, from a Madhyamaka point of view, is an ontological identity.

This point is made elegantly in a more formal mode in the *Discourse of Vimalakīrti*. In the ninth chapter, the text addresses the nature of

2. Canonically regarded as Indian, but almost certainly Chinese in origin (Nattier 1992/1993).

nonduality. The hero of the text, the lay bodhisattva Vimalakīrti, asks an assembly of highly accomplished bodhisattvas to explain nonduality, the ultimate reality of things. After many intriguing deconstructions of apparent dualities the bodhisattva Mañjuśrī asserts that the ultimate truth of nonduality is indescribable in language. The hero, Vimalakīrti, is then asked his view and remains silent. The silence that expresses the ultimate truth, though, can do so only in this context, in which it is itself a kind of speech. We will return to this textual moment in our discussion of language in chapter 9.

Nāgārjuna makes a similar point in a more philosophical register in the twenty-fourth chapter of *Fundamental Verses on the Middle Way*:

> 8. The Buddha's teaching of the dharma
> Is based on two truths:
> A truth of worldly convention
> And an ultimate truth.
>
> 9. Those who do not understand
> The distinction between the two truths
> Do not understand
> The Buddha's profound teaching.
>
> 10. Without depending on the conventional truth,
> The meaning of the ultimate cannot be taught.
> Without understanding the meaning of the ultimate,
> Nirvana is not achieved.

In this series of verses, Nāgārjuna emphasizes the distinctness of the two truths, the necessity of each of them for a coherent ontology, and the dependence of the ultimate on the conventional. But in the following verses he undermines this duality dramatically:

> 18. That which is dependent origination
> Is explained to be emptiness.
> That, being a dependent designation,
> Is itself the middle way.
>
> 19. There does not exist anything
> That is not dependently arisen.
> Therefore there does not exist anything
> That is not empty.

In (18) Nāgārjuna identifies dependent origination with emptiness—the conventional truth with the ultimate—and explains that emptiness, dependent origination, and *even their identity* are mere dependent designations—merely conventional facts. Understanding that everything, including the most profound truths of ontology, is empty, and merely conventional, is the middle path. And in (19) he emphasizes the universality of this claim. Emptiness is empty; it is emptiness all the way down, with no ontological foundation. Nothing exists ultimately.

Nāgārjuna's Madhyamaka can hence be seen as neither a realism nor an anti-realism, but a transcendence of the realism/anti-realism distinction through a critique of the very notion of reality it presupposes. Like his rough contemporary Sextus Empiricus, Nāgārjuna navigates between the extremes of the realism/anti-realism dichotomy by suspending the debate at issue; and by doing so he rejects the very presupposition of that debate—that to be real is to be ultimately real, to have *svabhāva*. Instead, Nāgārjuna argues, the only reality anything can have is conventional reality. To be real on this understanding is hence not to *possess, but to lack, ultimate reality*. (See Garfield 1990, 2002b for more on this point.)

And this goes for emptiness as well. Not only are all composite phenomena empty of intrinsic nature, as well as all of their constituents, but emptiness, too, is empty of any intrinsic nature. This is because emptiness cannot be a real universal, as there are none. Any emptiness is only the emptiness of a particular phenomenon, and so is dependent upon that phenomenon, and so has no being of its own. Emptiness, too, is empty, as is its emptiness. This doctrine of the emptiness of emptiness is one of Nāgārjuna's most profound innovations. It is what ensures that emptiness does not amount to an absolute reality beyond a veil of illusion, but simply the fact that everything, itself included, exists interdependently, conventionally, impermanently.[3] Madhyamaka thus constitutes an effort to escape both the horns of realism and of nihilism in forging its middle path.

On the other hand, this does involve real paradox, and this paradox was evident from the very earliest strata of the *Perfection of Wisdom sūtras*, articulated clearly both in the *The Perfection of Wisdom Discourse in 8,000 Verses* and in the *Diamond Cutter (Vajrachedika)*. As Garfield and Priest (2003) have argued, emptiness is both the absence of intrinsic nature, and the intrinsic nature of all things, since anything, in virtue of existing at all, is empty of intrinsic

3. We should note, however, that not all Buddhist commentators regard emptiness as itself impermanent. Interesting debates ensue regarding its status, debates I leave aside for present purposes.

nature. As *The Perfection of Wisdom Discourse in 8,000 Verses* puts it, "all things have one nature—that is, no nature." Paradox, however, does not entail incoherence, and Nāgārjuna, like many Buddhist philosophers in subsequent generations, notes that reality is in fact profoundly paradoxical. Consider the following remarks from *Fundamental Verses on the Middle Way* XIII:

> 8. The victorious ones have said
> That emptiness is the elimination of all views.
> Anyone for whom emptiness is a view
> Is incorrigible.

In his commentary to this verse, Candrakīrti offers an example of a customer trying to buy something in an empty shop. In a paraphrase of an earlier deployment of this example by Buddhapālita, he writes:

> This is similar to a case where someone says, "I have no goods to give you." And the other person says, "Give me what you call 'no goods'"! (*Lucid Exposition [Prasannapadā]* 83b, quoted in Tsongkhapa 2006, 299.)

Emptiness is the lack of any intrinsic nature, not another intrinsic nature instead of those we naively superimpose on entities. If one misreads Madhyamaka as the replacement of one intrinsic nature with another—emptiness—one is like the customer who wants to purchase the nothing on the shelves. As Candrakīrti asks in the next sentence, "How would he get hold of anything?" That is, the Madhyamaka program is not one of fundamental ontology in the ordinary sense, but rather a critique of the very enterprise of fundamental ontology, anticipating those of Heidegger and Wittgenstein.

This critique and the way it is prosecuted raises important questions about how to understand *svabhāva*, the object of negation; and so about the relation between classical Indian metaphysical concerns and those of the West; and finally about how to translate these central terms. As we noted above, *svabhāva* has connotations of intrinsic nature, of essence and of independence. These ideas are unified in the Sanskrit term, but come apart a bit in English and in Western thought more generally, and so a bit of precision is necessary here. In particular, in modern Western metaphysical discourse, it is common to consider relational properties to be candidates for essences. For instance, Kripke (1980) argues that it is essential to me that I have the parents I indeed have. The sentence *I could have had different parents* is on this view necessarily false. I do not want to worry about the correctness or incorrectness of that particular position. The important point for present purposes is that such a property is *extrinsic*, and so the property regarded as part of my essence on this view would not count as a *svabhāva* in the Sanskrit sense. In Sanskrit, this would be a *parabhāva*, an extrinsic property.

Nāgārjuna considers in *Fundamental Verses on the Middle Way* I:3 the coherence of the very idea of such extrinsic natures and rejects it. Candrakīrti and Tsongkhapa argue that this is because in the absence of *svabhāva* there is no determinate otherness, and so no way of identifying the other on which one's nature depends as really other. The point is that if the idea of extrinsic essences can be made coherent, then essence and intrinsic nature come apart, and we need to be clear about what the target of the Madhyamaka analysis is. The answer is that it would have to be intrinsic nature, at least initially. Nonetheless, as we have noted, there is an argument present in the tradition that if there is no intrinsic nature, there can be no extrinsic nature either. And that is not entirely implausible. After all, if we follow Nāgārjuna's reasoning, specifying an extrinsic essence—such as, to take the example at hand, mine as comprising, at least inter alia, the property of being Learita and Sam's offspring (once again, leaving aside the plausibility of this particular account)—requires us to specify the relata in a determinate way. If we can't do that, the putative extrinsic essences are not precise enough. So, in my case, we need to know who my mom is, and who my dad is, and since they also have only extrinsic nature, this gets us off on a regress.

Now, one might argue that that regress is benign. It just amounts to a kind of structuralism. The essence of everything is given by its place in a structure of relations. But then nothing bottoms out, and everything exists only in relation to everything else. That itself is the Hua yan vision we will discuss in the next section, and amounts to a deep kind of essencelessness: if the identity of all that exists is dependent on other things, the Buddhist position is simply right. And here we see the work done by the idea of groundlessness. One way to specify an essence is this: it is what we come to at the end of the analysis of what it is to be a particular thing—an ontological analytical ground. The Madhyamaka idea is simply this: Analysis, as Freud was to note much later in a very different context, never ends. There is no ground.

If the project of fundamental ontology is to find the final nature of things, this means that fundamental ontology is quixotic. The quest for the fundamental nature of things issues in the insight that there is no fundamental nature of things, no final metaphysical account of reality. In the previous chapter we asked whether this critique of fundamental ontology necessarily involves a retreat from metaphysics into phenomenology. While, as we will see in chapter 7, certain Yogācāra philosophers take this route, it is not inevitable. Nāgārjuna is rather, at least as read by commentators such as Candrakīrti and Tsongkhapa—perhaps, more like Wittgenstein than Heidegger—developing a metaphysical theory, albeit one that in virtue of rejecting the idea of a fundamental nature of reality, is deeply paradoxical, seeming to provide an account of the fundamental nature of reality while rejecting the very coherence of that notion. For all that, it is not incoherent. And indeed, here we see a significant contribution that the Buddhist tradition can offer to contemporary Western metaphysics. Taking Madhyamaka seriously—whether in its Indo-Tibetan or Chinese guise—is to take seriously the possibility that metaphysics is directed not at a deeper analysis of reality, but at extirpating the need for such a deeper analysis.

Since on a Madhyamaka analysis to exist is to be empty, emptiness—the lack of any intrinsic nature—is the intrinsic nature of all things. Here is another way to put this: to attack the enterprise of fundamental ontology where that is taken to be the project of finding the ultimate nature of reality, is nonetheless to do fundamental ontology. The fact that Madhyamaka doctrine is paradoxical is hence no accident of expression. Emptiness, on this view, reveals a fundamental paradox at the heart of reality. Nāgārjuna returns to this theme in chapter XXII:

> 11. We do not assert "Empty."
> We do not assert "Nonempty."
> We assert neither both nor neither.
> They are asserted only for the purpose of designation.

Here the paradox is expressed in the formal, rather than the material mode. In a remark recalling the passage in the *Discourse of Vimalakīrti* we discussed above, Nāgārjuna makes it plain that even the statement that phenomena are empty of intrinsic nature is itself a merely conventional truth, which, in virtue of the necessary involvement of language with conceptualization, cannot capture the nonconceptualizable nature of reality. Nothing can be literally true, including this statement. Nonetheless, language—designation—is indispensible for expressing that inexpressible truth. This is not an irrational mysticism, but rather a rational, analytically grounded embrace of inconsistency. The drive for consistency that many philosophers take as mandatory, the Mādhyamika argues, is simply one more aspect of primal confusion, a superimposition of a property on reality that it in fact lacks. An important implication of Madhyamaka metaphysics is hence that paraconsistent logics may be the only logics adequate to reality. This, too, would be a valuable insight to take on board.[4]

4. See chapter 8 for more discussion of paraconsistency in Buddhist logic.

The 14th-century Japanese Zen scholar Dōgen returns to this point in a memorable passage in *Actualizing the Fundamental Point (Genjōkōan)*:

1. All things are buddha-dharma. There is delusion and realization, practice, and birth and death, and there are buddhas and sentient beings.

   As the myriad beings are without an abiding self, there is no delusion, no realization, no buddha, no sentient being, no birth and death.

   The buddha way is, basically, leaping clear of the many and the one; thus there are birth and death; delusion and realization; sentient beings and buddhas.

   Yet in attachment blossoms fall, and in aversion, weeds spread.

2. To carry yourself forward and experience myriad things is delusion. That myriad things come forth and experience themselves is awakening.

   Those who have great realization of delusion are buddhas; those who are greatly deluded about realization are sentient beings. Further, there are those who continue realizing beyond realization, who are in delusion beyond delusion.

   When buddhas are truly buddhas they do not necessarily notice that they are buddhas. However, they are actualized buddhas, who go on actualizing buddhas.

   . . .

4. To study the buddha way is to study the self. To study the self is to forget the self. To forget the self is to be actualized by myriad things. When actualized by myriad things, your body and mind as well as the bodies and minds of others drop away. No trace of realization remains, and this no-trace continues endlessly. (Dōgen 1985, 69–70)

Philosophers approaching Dōgen's cryptic mode of expression for the first time often have difficulty unpacking his insights and dismiss him as an oracular mystic. In fact he is a subtle thinker who expresses himself through a complex mixture of intertextual allusion and metaphor, and careful reading reveals him to be rigorously analytical. Nonetheless, Dōgen does not shy away from paradox. Let us pause to unpack this passage. Learning to read these texts is part of learning to engage. (And let us not forget that many Western texts demand that we learn new ways of reading as well. Recall the first time you read Augustine, Heidegger, or Wittgenstein!)

In (1) Dōgen begins with what might seem deeply paradoxical: the claim that both delusion, realization, and the other such pairs exist, and that there are none of these things. But there is no real paradox here. He is simply repeating the trope of the two truths, both comprised under "buddha-dharma." Conventionally, these things are present, but because of selflessness (emptiness) they do not exist ultimately. Paradox first emerges when Dōgen comments on this verse in terms of "leaping clear of the many and the one," abandoning not only duality, as in the *Discourse of Vimalakīrti*, but also in abandoning nonduality, as in Nāgārjuna's XIII:8 in *Fundamental Verses on the Middle Way*. Here he asks the reader to take the rubric of the two truths itself as merely nominal (echoing Nāgārjuna again at XXIV:18) and then, more radically, stating that only because of this deeply paradoxical nature of reality are things such as birth and death, delusion and realization, sentient beings and buddhas—that is, the world in which we live—possible. Each of these things is possible only because of the primordial emptiness of all phenomena. That emptiness is their absence of any nature, and they must have that emptiness as their nature. And then he immediately urges us not to take this too seriously either, lest blossoms fall and weeds spread. The roots of cyclic existence—attachment and aversion—are present in philosophy as well, in the form of a conviction that our words and thoughts capture reality just as it is!

Passage (2) is largely a gloss on (1) and it is a nice one. The trick to living with this paradox, Dōgen urges, is to work to drop the habit of objectification—of reification—and to work toward a radically different subjectivity, one of participation in manifestation that takes one beyond experiencing oneself as a subject standing over and against an object. This idea comes directly from Yogācāra thought, and will, I hope, become clearer after reading the next section of this chapter and chapter 7. The closing lines are important: Buddhahood itself—awakening—is a transformation of a mode of experience, not a thing to be experienced; it is in fact a transformation that dispenses with *things* as objects of experience.

For a first pass, think of the transformation of subjectivity that occurs in expert sport or musical performance. In the midst of play on a football (soccer) field, an expert footballer does not *experience* herself making a cross to a striker; she *actualizes* being an expert footballer making a cross to a striker; as any good sport psychologist knows, one who in the moment of play objectifies that situation inevitably fails to actualize that expertise in virtue of that transformation of subjectivity. The virtuoso violinist does not notice his own virtuosity as he performs, or indeed the notes themselves; instead he manifests that virtuosity in a mode of subjectivity that goes beyond awareness of self and other. It is that virtuoso life that Dōgen recommends here.

Passage (4) is perhaps one of Dōgen's most famous remarks, and is a gloss on the sense of virtuosity articulated in (2). Self, or intrinsic identity, is the fundamental object of study—as it is put in the Tibetan tradition following Tsongkhapa, the object of negation. But it is studied only to be negated. That negation, however, does not result in a nihilism regarding oneself, but an actualization of the only kind of existence one could ever have in interaction, in interdependence. That very actualization is not itself something to be taken as the object of some higher-order awareness, but is rather the objectless form of awareness that is the goal of cultivation.

### *1.3 Yogācāra*

Yogācāra, or *Practice Mastery* (also known as *Cittamātra* [Mind Only], *Vijñāptimatra* [Consciousness Only] and *Vijñānavāda* [The Way of Consciousness]) arises in the 4th century CE. Grounded in *The Discourse Unravelling the Thought (Saṃdhinirmocana-sūtra)* and the *Entry into Lanka Sūtra (Lankāvatāra-sūtra)*, and articulated philosophically by the half-brothers Asaṅga and Vasubandhu (c. 4th century CE) and through the commentaries on their work by Sthiramati (6th century CE), Yogācāra involves both idealistic and phenomenological strains of thought. While Madhyamaka–Yogācāra polemics in India and some Tibetan and Chinese doxography, following Sthiramati and Candrakīrti, tend to emphasize the idealistic side of the school, Śāntarakṣita, Kamalaśīla and some important Tibetan traditions—in particular the modernist *Rimeh*, or non-sectarian tradition, represented principally in the work of Mipham—emphasize the phenomenology.

Historically, both strands are important. While there is no firm consensus regarding how to read each important Yogācāra text (Anacker 1984, Lusthaus 2003, Nagao 1991, Wood 1991, Schmithausen 2014), it is reasonable to say that Vasubandhu explicitly articulates an idealistic perspective in his *Twenty Stanzas* and *Thirty Stanzas* and that this view is adopted by the influential epistemologists Dignāga and Dharmakīrti. It is also reasonable to read Asaṅga, particularly in *The Bodhisattva Stages (Bodhisattvabhūmi)* and Vasubandhu in his final work *Treatise on the Three Natures (Trisvabhāvanirdeśa)* as developing a phenomenology. We might also say that the *Entry into Lanka* grounds the idealism in this school, whereas the *Discourse Unravelling the Thought*, particularly the *Paramārthasamutgtāta* chapter (the chapter structured around the questions of the bodhisattva Pramārthasamutgata), grounds the phenomenology. From a modern standpoint, the phenomenological strand of thought is more important and interesting. Few in the West today, and even few contemporary traditional Buddhists, take radical idealism seriously, but phenomenology is a central concern of contemporary philosophy of mind and cognitive science. As we shall see, Yogācāra phenomenology can be an important resource for contemporary thought.

Central to Yogācāra metaphysics and to the understanding of emptiness in this school is the doctrine of the three natures and corresponding three naturelessnesses, or three aspects of emptiness. Three-nature (*trisvabhāva*) theory regards all objects of awareness as having three distinct, but interdependent natures, or modes of existence. I will try to articulate these in a way neutral between the idealistic and phenomenological understanding of the doctrine, and then turn to their relationship to emptiness, as articulated in the *Discourse Unravelling the Thought*. Here is a central portion of the dialogue between the Buddha and Paraṃārthasamudgata in which the doctrine of the three natures and the three naturelessnesses is introduced:

> Paraṃārthasamudgata, thinking of the three types of essencelessness of phenomena—essenceless in terms of characteristics; essenceless in terms of production; and ultimate essencelesseness—I taught that all phenomena are essenceless.
>
> Paraṃārthasamudgata, what is essencelessness in terms of characteristics? It is the imagined nature. Why? Things have the characteristic of being posited through words and symbols, but do not exist with that characteristic. Therefore they are essenceless in terms of characteristic.
>
> Paraṃārthasamudgata, what is essencelessness in terms of production? It is the other-dependent nature. Why? Things arise through the power of other conditions and not on their own. Therefore they are essenceless terms of production.
>
> Paraṃārthasamudgata, what is ultimate essencelessness? Dependently originated phenomena . . . are essenceless in virtue of being ultimately essenceless. Why? Paraṃārthasamudgata, I teach that the ultimate is an object of observation for purification. Since the other-dependent nature is not an object of observation for purification, it is ultimately essenceless. (trans Power 1995, 100)

First, every object has an *imagined nature (parikalpita/kun brtags [kuntak])*. This is the way an object is taken to exist in naïve consciousness—existing as external, as given to the mind in veridical awareness, as independent, as substantial, etc, to exist as presented by our sensory faculties. Second, every object has a *dependent nature (paratantra/gzhan dbang [shenwang])*. This is the fact that every object of experience is dependent on causes and conditions for its existence, but more specifically, in the context of Yogācāra, dependent for its appearance to consciousness on our cognitive and perceptual apparatus. The objects we experience are not passively received, but constructed by our subjectivity as the objects they are, even if they are not *experienced* this way (hence the *imagined nature*).

Third, every object has a *consummate nature (pariniṣpanna/yongs su grub pa [yongdup])*. This is perhaps the most difficult to explain. A brief grammatical remark may help, though. While *paratantra* in Sanskrit is a purely nominal construction, both *parikalpita* and *pariniṣpanna* are past participles. And this is important. Objects of awareness, according to Yogācārins, are in fact constructed by our perceptual and cognitive faculties. (Again, this for now can be taken as neutral between an idealistic and a phenomenological or psychological point.) But they are *imagined* to exist independently, as items we *discover*, as opposed to those we *construct*. Understanding this allows us to see that they are devoid of the imagined nature, and this is their consummate nature—the fact that they do not exist as they are imagined; this is the nature they are ascribed when we do not impute independence to them. They are, in this sense, empty of the nature they are imagined to have. The grammatical difference between *parikalpita* and *pariniṣpanna* on the one hand and *paratantra* on the other indicates that while the dependent nature may be more or less ontologically neutral, referring only to the causal role of our cognitive activity in experience, when we construct objects of experience, we actively imagine them to exist in a certain way. As a consequence, to understand their reality, their mode of being independent of that construction, we must empty them of that we imaginatively attribute to them.

Every object, on this view, has these three natures. When I consider my coffee cup, for instance, it appears to me to be an independently existing external object that possesses all of the properties I naturally ascribe to it, including a color, feel, or some other property, that I simply register through veridical perception and cognition. This is its imagined nature. In fact, the object *as I experience it* is represented in my brain as a result of a complex set of perceptual and cognitive processes, and may be experienced quite differently by beings with very different kinds of minds, for instance an insect or a dog. The fact that as an object of consciousness it is dependent on my cognitive architecture is its dependent nature. And seeing this leads me to see that as an object of experience, while it exists in one way (as dependent) but appears in another (as imagined), it is devoid of existence in the way that it is imagined, and this is its consummate nature.

Now, to each of these natures corresponds a sense of naturelessness, or emptiness. And here we begin to see the Yogācāra understanding of emptiness. Emptiness with respect to characteristic *(lakṣana-niḥsvabhāvataḥ/ mtshan nyid ngo bo nyid med pa [tsenyi ngobo nyi mehpa])* corresponds to the imagined nature. Objects are empty of the characteristics we naively impute to them. When I see ordinary physical objects around me, for instance, I take my sensory faculties to deliver them to consciousness as they are. But I know that that is crazy. My visual awareness, for instance, is a result of the interaction of external objects with my eyes, my nervous system, etc., creating a state of consciousness to which—as Berkeley pointed out—resemblance of an external object makes no sense at all. Objects are empty of the characteristics I take them to have.

Emptiness with respect to production (*upadāna-niḥsvabhāvataḥ /skye ba ngo on yid med pa [kyaywa ngobo byi mehpa]*) corresponds to the dependent nature. That is, these phenomena are empty of independence on our cognitive and perceptual processes, despite the fact that we naively take the objects of our perception to be independent. And emptiness with respect to the ultimate (*paramārtha-niḥsvabhāvataḥ /don dam pa'i ngo bo nyid med pa [dündam peh ngobo nyi mehpa]*) corresponds to the consummate nature. That is, ultimately, they have none of the characteristics we take them to have.

This is one way of understanding the reconfiguration of the concept of emptiness in Yogācāra thought. But there is another that emerges from this. We can think of these three senses of *emptiness* or *naturelessness* as resolving into a simple emptiness of subject–object duality, or of the externality of objects to subjectivity. On this view, primal confusion consists simply in taking our experience and the objects it presents us in a deceptive way: we partition our experience, and reality itself into ourselves, as passive, experiencing subjects, who confront our objects, objects that constitute a fully and independently constituted reality of which we are aware just as it is.

Emptiness is the emptiness of everything we experience, including our own minds as we are aware of them in introspection, of that duality. Instead, experience consists in a complex, opaque, causally determined construction of objects. This emptiness of subject–object duality, or of the externality of our objects to our subjectivity, is the most common way of representing the Yogācāra understanding of emptiness.

This is, to be sure, a different understanding of emptiness than is the Madhyamaka understanding in terms of essenceless and interdependence. When Yogācāra is read idealistically, the metaphysics represent a stark contrast. While the Mādhyamika, on this reading, takes all phenomena, including mind and the external world, to be conventionally real but ultimately empty, and to be interdependent, the Yogācārin takes external objects to be mere appearances to mind, to be utterly non-existent, and takes mind to be the substantially real subjective substrate of those representations. So, in *Autocommentary to Examination of the Percept (Ālambanāparīkṣā svavṛtti)*, for instance, Dignāga argues that what we take to be external objects in perceptual consciousness are nothing but the cognitive processes that emerge from the ripening of potentials in our foundation consciousness, and that while these processes are real, there are no external objects corresponding to them. A similar position is defended by Vasubandhu in *Twenty Verses*.

This ontological distinction in status between mind and its objects is what constitutes an idealist Yogācāra position as idealist. Yogācāra certainly was read this way in India, and debates between Yogācārins and Mādhyamikas turn on the question of the identity or difference in the ontological status of mind and its objects, and on the object of negation of emptiness—intrinsic identity or externality, which in turn resolves into a kind of subject–object duality. On the other hand, when we adopt a phenomenological reading of Yogācāra, there is no contrast to be drawn with Madhyamaka. On this view, Madhyamaka gives us an account of the ontology of phenomena—of their interdependence and lack of any intrinsic nature. Yogācāra then gives us an account not of the emptiness of phenomena, but of the nature of our subjectivity—of the way we experience empty phenomena and project a kind of reality they lack. While Madhyamaka treats emptiness from the standpoint of the object, Yogācāra treats it from the standpoint of the subject, and provides an analysis of our erroneous experience of our own subjectivity.

If we take this seriously, we find yet another very deep Buddhist critique of the idea of givenness, suggesting not only that the objects we experience are not given to us as they are, but also that our own experience, often taken for granted as immediate and transparent, is as opaque to us and as deceptive as are the objects we encounter. We construct ourselves and our awareness just as surely as we construct the objects we posit, and we confuse our experience of ourselves and our inner states with their nature just as surely as we do our experience of external objects and their nature. There is, on this reading, no firm ground or horizon that can be taken for granted. Once again, this anticipation of the attack on the Myth of the Given in Wittgenstein's *Philosophical Investigations* and Sellars's *Empiricism and the Philosophy of Mind* are striking. But the approach to that attack is very different, itself anticipating a trajectory more associated with Heidegger in *Being and Time*. This may be one key to seeing, through a Buddhist lens, the deep affinities between these strands of

Western thought often taken to be in tension with one another. It turns out that sometimes one understands one's own tradition better when one views it from a bit of hermeneutical distance. We will see a number of instances of this phenomenon as we move forward.

## *1.4 Hua Yan*

The Chinese Hua yan tradition, grounded in the *Flower Garland Sūtra*, is perhaps the most striking development of the idea of the unity of emptiness and interpenetration. Through a series of apt metaphors, principally that of the net of Indra and that of the golden lion, Fazang, the Chinese patriarch of this tradition, develops an account of infinite interdependence of all phenomena, and in the end of the unity and non-difference of all phenomena. Hua yan synthesizes ideas drawn from Madhyamaka and Yogācāra and takes them to a grand and dizzying metaphysical conclusion.

The metaphor of the net of Indra—an infinite network, at each node of which is a jewel that perfectly reflects all other jewels in the net—illustrates the Hua yan view of interdependence. Just as each jewel owes its characteristics to every other, and participates in the characteristics of every other, each phenomenon in the universe, in virtue of bearing some relation to every other phenomenon, owes part of its nature to everything else. Part of who I am is constituted by my distance from some speck of stardust in a distant galaxy, and to you who now read these words; part of who you are is determined by your reading these words now, and your ever-so-slightly different relation to that speck, and its nature is determined by our relation to it, and so on. In short, everything is related to everything else, and, in virtue of the fact that we are constituted by our relations, everything is constituted by everything else in a non-well-founded hierarchy of mutual interdependence.

What does this mean for emptiness? Emptiness here, just as in Indian Madhyamaka, is a lack of independent existence. But it is more than that. It is a lack of *difference* between entities. For on the Hua yan account, since the identity of everything is constituted by everything else, that which constitutes the identity of any one thing is the same as that which constitutes the identity of every other thing. (See Priest 2014a, 2014b.) There is therefore no substantial difference between any two things in the universe. In this framework, all is one.

But things get even more interesting. For emptiness (the lack of any independent existence) and existence (the positive reality as an entity) also interpenetrate one another. Fazang interprets this as the unity of characteristic and characterized, or of form and substance. Here are a few signal passages from the *The Treatise on the Golden Lion (Jin Shi Zi Zhang)*. The nature of the Madhyamaka-Yogācāra synthesis in a Chinese voice will be apparent. Fazang asks us to consider a golden lion.

> 1. *Clarifying the Fact that Things Arise through Causation*
>
> It means that gold has no nature of its own. As a result of the conditioning of the skillful craftsman, the character of the lion consequently arises. This arising is purely due to causes...

The golden lion we apprehend, Fazang asserts, appears to have the nature of being a lion. But this is not part of its nature. It is, after all, just a lump of gold, and its appearance as a lion is the result of causes and conditions utterly extraneous to the statue itself. Just so, when we instinctively take things around us to have the characteristics they do by their very nature, we forget that these are the consequences of countless extraneous causes and conditions.

> 2. *Distinguishing Matter and Emptiness*
>
> It means that the character of the lion is unreal: there is only real gold. The lion is not existent, but the substance of the gold is not non-existent. Therefore they are called matter and emptiness. Furthermore, emptiness has no character of its own; it shows itself by means of matter. This does not obstruct its illusory existence....

The lion, Fazang says, is hence empty of being a lion. It does not exist apart from a set of causes and conditions, including the gold, which is its supporting condition. So, he claims, the lion stands to the gold as form does to emptiness, as the way in which emptiness is manifest at a particular moment. But, while this might appear to privilege the gold (emptiness) over the lion (form) it should be noted that the gold must appear in some form, and cannot simply exist with no character whatsoever. The gold is only the gold of the lion, just as emptiness is only the emptiness of form. Here we see Fazang following very closely the *Heart Sūtra*, which as one of the *Perfection of Wisdom sūtras* is foundational to Madhyamaka. But he now abruptly switches to a discussion of categories coming from the *Discourse Unraveling the Thought*, a founding text of the Yogācāra school, whose insights he fuses with those of the Madhyamaka tradition:

> 3. *Simply Stating the Three Natures*
>
> The lion exists because of our feelings. This is called the nature arising from vast imagination. The lion seems to exist. This is called dependence

> on others. The nature of the gold does not change. This is therefore called perfect reality.

This is Fazang's analogy for the three natures. We imagine the golden lion as a lion; it seems to exist as a lion, but only in dependence on our cognitive imputation of lionhood onto a lump of gold; it is really only gold, and its appearance as a lion is the result of something foreign to it. So, Fazang says, we see in this simile the imagined, the dependent and the consummate nature. He now turns to the three naturelessnesses.

> 4. *Showing the Nonexistence of Characters*
>
> It means that the gold takes in the lion in its totality; apart from the gold there is no character of the lion to be found. Therefore it is called the nonexistence of characters.

Fazang begins with naturelessness in terms of characteristic. The lion simply is just a lump of gold. There is nothing in its nature that makes it a lion.

> 5. *Explaining Non-coming into Existence*
>
> It means that at the moment when we see the lion come into existence, it is only the gold that comes into existence. There is nothing apart from the gold. Although the lion comes into existence and goes out of existence, the substance of the gold at bottom neither increases nor decreases.... (Chan 1963, 409–410)

The lion also illustrates naturelessness in terms of causal dependence. It comes into existence as a result of causes and conditions, including the craftsman and our recognition of its shape, and ultimate naturelessness. Ultimately, it has none of the characteristics of a lion, only those of gold.

Later in the text, Fazang poses a number of ontological questions that draw these ideas together: Is the lion the same as or different from its gold? Is the lion the same as or different from its shape? Is its instantiated shape the same as or different from the gold that instantiates it? Are the manifold parts identical to or different from the unitary lion?

In each case the answer is "yes" and "no." The lion is the same, because if you hand me the gold, you hand me the lion. But it is different, for that gold could be melted down and made into the statue of a Buddha. Without the shaped gold, there is no shape; but that shape could have been instantiated in another material, or the gold could take another shape. And so on. In each case, characteristic and characterized interpenetrate one another. While they are different, they are also identical.

For this reason, in the Hua yan tradition, the fact that there is no difference between distinct phenomena, despite their distinctness—just as despite the distinctness of the infinitely many jewels in Indra's net there is no difference between them—is just the beginning of ontological vertigo. For on the one hand there is all the difference in the world between emptiness and existence. For anything to exist is for it to have an identity, and to stand out as the thing that it is. On the other hand, for anything to exist is to be thoroughly ontologically interpenetrated with everything else, and to be empty of any such independent identity. And an object's existence and its emptiness are nonetheless identical.

Hua yan presents perhaps the most radical Buddhist ontological vision, one we might regard as verging on a kind of mysticism. Nonetheless, it represents an important voice in ontological debates. It is often assumed that we can take the existence and nature of individuals for granted and then ask about their relations to others. It is also often assumed that we can talk about entities and their characteristics as independent and take the framework of particulars and universals for granted. Hua yan calls all of that into question. Ontology on this view can never be an account of the nature of anything, but at best a reminder that there is no nature of anything, and that what we see depends not so much upon where our gaze falls but about the nature of that gaze.

## 2. The Development of the Doctrine of the Two Truths in the Mahāyāna Traditions

We can now draw much of this discussion together by placing the doctrine of the two truths at center stage. We have been talking extensively about various understandings of emptiness and of the relation between emptiness and conventional existence, and it is clear that in these Mahāyāna analyses of emptiness the Abhidharma rubric of the two truths as a hermeneutic device has come to have major ontological significance. In early Buddhism, as we have seen, this framework indicates the difference between that which exists ultimately, the fundamental *dharmas*, and that which merely exists conventionally, those fictional extended composites that are regarded as real, but are in fact nonexistent entities that are posited as a consequence of the mistaken perception of a reality of momentary interdependent property instantiations. While this specific framework is discarded in the move to Mahāyāna metaphysics, the idea that to exist ultimately is to exist independently of convention, and to be what is found to be substantially real through metaphysical analysis is retained. It is just that nothing ends up satisfying that description. The idea that there are two truths—a conventional and an ultimate truth—but that nothing is ultimately real or true is, as we have seen, both powerful, and paradoxical.

We have seen Madhyamaka philosophers, such as Nāgārjuna and Candrakīrti, emphasize the paradoxical relation between the two truths, that they are distinct and yet identical. Let us first explore the sense in which conventional truth and ultimate truth are necessarily distinct. Conventional truth is merely nominal, determined by and characterizable through discursive practices; it is truth as taken for granted by ordinary people, in conformity with mundane practices; and it is always deceptive, appearing to be more than merely conventional when it is not. Ultimate truth, on the other hand, transcends description, since all descriptions implicate a conventional ontology of objects and properties, none of which exist ultimately; it is independent of mundane practices as the primordial mode of being of all things, and is not directly apprehended by ordinary modes of consciousness; and it is non-deceptive—when emptiness is apprehended, that is a correct apprehension of the absence of any intrinsic nature. So, in all of these senses, conventional and ultimate truth are an exhaustive, mutually exclusive partition of the modes of existence of things.

Nonetheless, conventional and ultimate truth are, as we have seen in our reading of the *Heart Sūtra* and of *Fundamental Verses on the Middle Way*, identical. The ultimate truth is emptiness, and emptiness is dependent origination, which is the fundamental nature of the conventional world; the ultimate truth is that there is no intrinsic nature to things, only their conventional nature, and so there is nothing other than that nature; and emptiness is dependent on empty things, and so only conventionally real anyway. Since the only way that anything can exist is conventionally, and that is the ultimate truth, the ultimate truth is the conventional truth.

It is this paradoxical identity and non-identity of the conventional and ultimate that saves Madhyamaka from collapsing into another version of an appearance–reality distinction of the kind so central to other Indian philosophical traditions, such as Vedānta. It is also this paradoxical identity that saves Madhyamaka from reifying emptiness as a non-apparent absolute and from deprecating the conventional world as unimportant. Madhyamaka thus makes it possible, for instance, to take epistemic and moral practices in ordinary life seriously (Cowherds 2011, 2015). But it is also the insight that this is what is required to avoid an unacceptable duality of an inaccessible reality and a pointless mundane world that leads Madhyamaka to the insight that the heart of being is deeply paradoxical.

Indeed, as I have been emphasizing, one of the more profound insights of this Buddhist tradition may be that paradox is different from incoherence (Garfield and Priest 2009, Deguchi, Garfield and Priest 2013a, 2013b, 2013c, 2013d). A great deal of Western philosophical thought since Aristotle (with a few notable exceptions, such as Hegel and Bradley) up until very recent developments in paraconsistent logic (Priest 2002, 2006) has been predicated on the idea that any true account of reality must be consistent, simply because no contradictions can be true. But this may simply be a logical prejudice born of too little formal and ontological imagination. Reflection on the semantic and set theoretic paradoxes is one way to come to see that a logic that can tolerate contradictions may be a better way to understand an inconsistent formal reality. Reflection on emptiness may be the best way to come to see that a philosophical perspective that can tolerate contradictions is a better way to understand the inconsistent reality we inhabit. After all, who ever said that a particular, and rather arbitrary, human approach to logic must constrain the nature of the universe?[5]

The Yogācāra account of the relation between the two truths, despite its later emergence, is perhaps a bit more prosaic and owes more to pre-Mahāyāna perspectives on this distinction. It is not for nothing that some Mādhyamikas regard Yogācāra as the Mahāyāna school for those not yet ready for Madhyamaka. The conventional truth is the imagined nature. That is, from this perspective, conventional reality is a nonexistent reality of things imagined to be external to and dually related to the mind. Ultimate reality is, on this view, the consummate nature, that is, the absence or complete nonexistence of that superimposed externality and duality. On this view, of course, the two truths are as different as night and day: the conventional is completely imaginary, and the ultimate is its unreality.

The pivot point that defines the relation between these truths in the Yogācāra system is the dependent nature. This Janus-faced character of things forms the basis for both the conventional and the ultimate truth. When externality, independence and duality are superimposed, it is the conventional; when they are removed, it is the ultimate. While this does not unify the two natures, as in

5. Tsongkhapa expresses this point in *Lam rim chen mo (Great Exposition of the Stages of the Path)* by saying that ultimate and conventional truth are extensionally equivalent, but intensionally distinct (*ngo bo lcig ldog pa tha' dad*). There is no ontological distinction to be drawn between them, but rather a conceptual distinction. This is a strategy for defusing apparent paradox (something that Tsongkhapa, a philosopher very much committed to consistency, is always concerned to do in his Madhyamaka exegesis). Maintaining this view, however, requires a great deal of systematic re-reading of a lot of Madhyamaka literature, with the interpolation of allegedly suppressed terms ("qualifying phrases" as Tsongkhapa puts it). See Jinpa (2002) and Thakchöe (2007) for detailed explorations of this strategy.

Madhyamaka, it does indicate a close ontological relationship between them. Note that while we have insisted that a phenomenological understanding of Yogācāra is possible, one to which we will return in a moment, in the context of purely Yogācāra accounts of the two truths, it is hard to read this doctrine as anything but idealist: it privileges the reality of mind and the mental, and ascribes to the external world a merely imaginary existence.

Śāntarakṣita, an important 9th-century Buddhist philosopher central to the dissemination of Buddhism from Nālandā University in Bihar—where he taught and served as abbot—to Tibet, where he established the Buddhist monastic order and educational system, famously synthesized Madhyamaka and Yogācāra through the rubric of the two truths in his verse treatise *Ornament of the Middle Way (Madhyamakālaṃkāra)* and its autocommentary. Śāntarakṣita argues that Yogācāra provides a correct account of conventional truth and that Madhyamaka provides the correct account of ultimate truth.

Conventional truth is, as Nāgārjuna notes in *Fundamental Verses on the Middle Way* XXIV:10, the necessary stepping stone to ultimate truth. And, as Candrakīrti notes, conventional truth is always deceptive. Now, if Madhyamaka is taken to be the authoritative doctrine regarding ultimate truth, and if the doxographic framework in which Śāntarakṣita worked, in which Yogācāra as the penultimate doctrine on the way to Madhyamaka is taken for granted, then it is natural to take Yogācāra as the (albeit deceptive) conventional truth that is the stepping stone to the ultimate truth revealed in Madhyamaka. And this, indeed, is how many canonical and contemporary Tibetan scholars take matters to go.

In the following verses toward the end of *Ornament of the Middle Way*, Śāntarakṣita invites such a reading:

> 92. On the basis of Yogācāra,
> One should understand the absence of external objects.
> On the basis of our system,
> One should understand that there is also a complete absence of self.
>
> 93. Whoever rides the chariot of these two systems.
> Guiding them with the reins of logic,
> Will thereby attain the goal,
> The realization of the Mahāyāna itself.[6]

This apparently irenic reading has one important hermeneutical virtue. It explains the continuity between Yogācāra thought when read as a kind of

6. Tibetan text in Blumenthal (2004). All translations are my own.

idealism with the more realistic Madhyamaka, and does so, paradoxically, by showing how the more thoroughgoing antirealism of Madhyamaka in the end undermines the view that mind has a special ontological status.

This reading, for all of its virtues, nonetheless faces a massive hermeneutical problem. Conventional truth, on a Geluk reading of Madhyamaka—a reading that is faithful to Candrakīrti's exposition (Cowherds 2011)—is supposed to be truth as *ordinary* people take it to be, the world as we naively take up with it. So, on this reading of Śāntarakṣita's synthesis, ordinary people are *idealists*, and experience the world as illusory. Only when they become Mādhyamikas on this view do they come to accept the reality of external objects. As a piece of philosophical anthropology, this seems simply insane. If we are to take Śāntarakṣita's claim that Yogācāra captures conventional truth seriously, and if we understand conventional truth as, say, Candrakīrti understands it, we cannot also take him, as the 15th-century Tibetan philosopher Gyeltsap and other Geluk commentators do, to read Yogācāra idealistically. But ironically, Gyeltsap's own (rGyal tshab dar ma rin chen 1999) incisive comments on these verses suggest a much more interesting, more radical possibility:

> Consider all phenomena comprised under causes and effects. They are not substantially different from consciousness. This is because they exist in virtue of being experienced through authoritative perception. This entailment is valid because given this premise, they necessarily exist substantially as consciousness. These phenomena should be understood conventionally in this way as merely mind, in virtue of lacking any external realty. But ultimately, even mind does not exist. For ultimately, it has neither a singular nor a manifold nature. (599)[7]

We can clarify Śāntarakṣita's argument by attention to the 19th-century Tibetan philosopher Mipham's commentary on the verses of *Ornament of the Middle*

7. Gyeltsap rejects the inconsistency of Yogācāra—at least as it is deployed by Śāntarakṣita—with Madhyamaka on surprisingly different grounds from those one might expect if he were defending the graded reading we first considered. The former, he indicates, gives us an analysis of our experience of the natural world ("all phenomena comprised under causes and effects") as known to us only through consciousness; the latter shows us that neither object nor subject exists ultimately; there is no contrast possible between their ontological status.

This is an apposite development of Śāntarakṣita's insight. Inasmuch as *the world we experience* is only a world delivered by our consciousness, nothing *we immediately experience* can be substantially different from that consciousness. But that non-difference from consciousness does not *in the end* give consciousness a privileged position; both the subject and object side are ultimately known in the same way (through perceptual and conceptual mediation) and exist in the same way—as empty of intrinsic identity.

*Way* in which Śāntarakṣita articulates the sense in which Yogācāra delivers conventional truth. I focus on verses 63–64 and then turn to the summary in verse 78.

> 63. Therefore, these things
> Only have conventional characteristics.
> If one were to maintain that they exist ultimately,
> What can I do?

Here Śāntarakṣita asserts that despite the fact that Yogācāra focuses on cognitive states in its analysis of reality, those states are not asserted to exist ultimately. Everything that is said of them is said merely conventionally. Mipham immediately glosses conventional (*saṃvṛti/kun rdzob [kundzop]*) as *deceptive*, or as *false*, one of the three glosses offered by Candrakīrti in his analysis in *Lucid Exposition:*

> . . . Here, "conventional" means that, with respect to the dichotomy between real and unreal, they are unreal, having a false nature. They never have the nature of being real—of being truly existent; this reality is what is denied.[8] (Mipham 2004, 422)

Importantly, Mipham immediately, once again following Candrakīrti, clarifies the sense of *false* at issue: it is *not* to be nonexistent, but rather to exist in one way and to appear in another:

> . . . Here, to be mere appearance, and to be truly empty is the nature of the conventional. If it existed in the way it appears, it would not be conventional. In that case, it would not even exist ultimately. Here, since it does not exist in the way it appears, it is conventional. In *that* case, it would have to exist ultimately. But all phenomena lack ultimate essence that transcends unity and multiplicity. Therefore, these mere appearances have the characteristics of the conventional. Therefore, these two truths clarify each other, and could never be inconsistent with one another. . . . (Ibid., 426)

On this reading, the sense in which the mind and its immediate objects exist merely conventionally is this: the mind, mental states and objects appear to

8. In what follows I rely on the Tibetan text as reproduced in Mipham (2004). The translations, however, are my own.

exist in a way that withstands analysis; they appear to have a definite nature. But they do not. Ultimately they are empty of the nature they appear to have.

Mipham's reading distances him from an idealist or ontological understanding of Yogācāra according to which the mind and appearances are taken to be truly existent, while external objects are taken to be nonexistent. But most dramatically, and most revelatory of Śāntarakṣita's philosophical originality, it also distances him from any view according to which the mind is self-revealing, and immediately available to consciousness. For if it were self-revealing, if it existed in the way it appears, if introspection were inherently veridical, the mind, according to Mipham, would be non-deceptive, and would exist ultimately. Mipham is thus taking Śāntarakṣita's account of Yogācāra as conventional truth as a platform for an analysis of the mind as what is referred to in Buddhist epistemology as "a hidden object," one not directly observable, but knowable only from inference. We see here a 19th-century reading of a 9th-century text as developing yet another attack on the Myth of the Given much as it is developed by Sellars in the 20th century. Śāntarakṣita continues:

> 64. Apparent[9] only when not analyzed,
> Subject to arising and cessation,
> And capable of performing functions,
> Their nature is understood to be to exist conventionally.

Here we encounter yet another gloss on conventional existence, one that emphatically affirms conventional truth as a kind of truth, and hence the Madhyamaka background of this analysis. To exist conventionally is to be dependently originated, to be functional in the everyday world, and to be taken for granted without analysis. Mipham emphasizes this realism, contrasting the nature of conventional existents with that of illusions:

> ... This conventional reality does not consist in such things as the horns of a rabbit, which are only expressed by words, are never seen, and cannot perform any function. Rather when we examine dependently arisen

9. Here I read *rnam dgya'* as meaning *apparent*, not *delightful* as it is often read in English translations. (See Blumenthal 2004, Miphan 2004, trans. Doctor). This reading is attested in other contexts, and is supported by Mipham's own gloss on this term:

> The phrase "apparent only when not analyzed" (*ma brtags nyams dga'*) should be understood to mean to remain content to take something such as an illusory experience for granted as long as it is not analyzed. This does not mean that to say that illusions are pleasant (*nyams dga'*) for frightening appearances can obviously occur.... Hence this term does not refer to physical or sensual delight.

> phenomena, although they are taken for granted when not examined—*only when not* analyzed—they thus *are apparent* to perception. These objects that are causes and effects—*subject* to instantaneous *arising and cessation*, that are seen, and that are *capable of performing* desired and non-deceptive *functions*, the *nature* of these objects *is understood* to be denoted by the word *conventional*. Here, the characteristic of the conventional is presented in three ways in terms of elimination, and in one way in terms of determination. (They appear, they are momentary, and they perform functions; and they are *conventionally real*.) (Ibid., 428)
>
> . . .

Now things get interesting and startlingly contemporary, for anyone paying attention to current literature on consciousness. Mipham turns to a consideration of the mode of appearance and the mode of existence of the cognitive. He explicitly takes as his example the *appearance* of a double moon, as when one gazes at the moon and simultaneously presses one's eyeball, not the *appearing double moon*. And he argues that the appearance itself—the cognitive phenomenon—exists in one way, but appears in another. That is to say, it is a conventional existent, but as conventional, it is deceptive; it does not bear analysis; our awareness of the *appearance itself* is not awareness of it *as it is*, but only *as it appears*:

> Consider a mistakenly grasped appearance such as a double moon: in this case, the *appearance* is merely consciousness itself appearing to itself. Therefore, one should not commit the error of not including it in the conventional. However, when we consider whether or not these apparent objects exist in the same way that they appear, they are just non-existent in that way. (Ibid., 438)

That is, even the appearance does not exist as we take it to be. While we take our access to our own inner states to be infallible and immediate, it is not. Our access to our own cognitive states, in virtue of being mediated through opaque cognitive processes, is only indirect and fallible.[10] On Mipham's reading, building on Gyeltsap's, Śāntarakṣita takes the relation between Madhyamaka and Yogācāra not to be one of rival ontologies, but of complementary parts of a single ontology, and one that demonstrates a very deep degree to which

10. This idea is also developed elegantly by the 18th-century Tibetan philosopher Gungthang (Gung thang dkon mchog bstan pa'i sgron me) in his *Ornament for Dignāga's Thought Regarding the Investigation of the Percept (dMigs pa brtag pa'i 'grel pa phyogs glang dgongs rgyan)*.

reality—not only on the subject side, but also on the object side—is opaque to our ordinary consciousness.[11]

As we will see in chapter 6, below, this reading harmonizes very nicely with an understanding of the phenomenological theory of the Yogācāra philosopher Vasubandhu. This is because the task of limning truth as it is understood by ordinary consciousness, and the basis of our ordinary social, discursive and epistemic practices is the task of phenomenology. Yogācāra does precisely that. It explains how we take the world to be, and how we come to so take it. But while that enterprise is important as a sketch of our *lebenswelt*, and is essential to providing a clear view of how we live, act, justify and interact, it can never pretend to be fundamental metaphysics, or to provide an account of the final nature of reality. That is the task of Madhyamaka, which, Śāntarakṣita agrees, delivers the verdict that *there is no fundamental nature of reality*. Madhyamaka metaphysics and Yogācāra phenomenology are hence reconciled in a remarkable feat of metaphilosophical synthesis.

## 3. Madhyamaka and Yogācāra in the 21st Century

The rubric of the two truths, even in India (we have not, after all, considered all of the complexities that emerge when this doctrine is adumbrated and elaborated in Tibet and China) is hence understood in a variety of ways. It is clear that there is a significant difference between the way that doctrine is read in pre-Mahāyāna Buddhist philosophy and the way(s) it comes to be understood in the Mahāyāna traditions. On one dominant reading, within the Mahāyāna tradition we have two contrasting readings, with Madhyamaka defending a reading that affirms the reality of the conventional and identifies the truths and Yogācāra denying the reality of the conventional and drawing a sharp distinction between them. On this reading, Yogācāra may appear to be but a historical curiosity, like the Berkeleyan idealism to which it is often compared. But we have seen that there is an alternative to this picture: a Madhyamaka understanding of ontology wedded to a Yogācārin approach to phenomenology provides a remarkably rich approach to metaphysics, to phenomenology and to the philosophical project broadly conceived. It also suggests a number of interventions into contemporary discussions.

For one thing, Madhyamaka, understood as Candakīrti and Śāntarakṣita take it, suggests that debates between metaphysical realists and metaphysical antirealists may be hollow. If Nāgārjuna is correct, a realism that takes

11. For a subtle treatment of the use of the idea of illusion as a vehicle for understanding reality, see Westerhoff (2010b).

there to be a convention-independent ontological ground of our practices, of knowledge, of truth and reference, is a fantasy. But to conclude from this that our lives float completely free is to go too far as well. For even if there are no foundations, reality never presupposed them, and if conventional reality is all there is, there is plenty of it. Conventional truth may not be ultimate truth, but it is all the truth there is, and all the truth we could ever need.

Madhyamaka also suggests that in thinking about the nature of composite, three- or four-dimensional entities, we can get beyond taking their reality and nature to depend upon their having strict identity conditions, or being reducible or not to something more fundamental. Ontology is not going to deliver us a final account of the nature of things, simply because the very idea of a final account, or a nature of things, may be just plain incoherent. Instead, to the extent that we are interested in the nature of the world in which we live, a metaphysically modest inventory of what we find, together with a psychologically sophisticated account of the manner in which we present the world and ourselves to ourselves, and of the sources of distortion that inevitably involves, including the sources of distortion of any account of any sources of distortion can yield a modicum of understanding and a modicum of humility regarding that understanding. This may be all philosophy can or should deliver.

This is not a recommendation to give up on truth, or on the world. We can also learn from these Buddhist interventions that we can take truth and the world very seriously without taking them so seriously through metaphysical reification that we place them beyond any cognitive or practical access. Taking *conventional* truth seriously is how to take *truth* seriously; taking the world we collectively constitute seriously is how to take ourselves and the world around us seriously. To decide that only an ontology beyond convention and only a world that exists independently of our apprehension of it is real is to cut ourselves off from any reality at all.

Modern modal metaphysics and modal logic have been preoccupied with understanding essences and necessity as features of the world around us. Essences are often understood as qualities that an individual has in any world in which that individual exists, and necessity is often understood in terms of truth in possible worlds. Possible worlds, and often domains of individuals and sets of properties, are then often taken in these investigations as primitives. And our intuitions regarding individual identity, criteria for property attribution, and truth or falsity in other worlds are taken as evidence for modal claims.

So, for instance, we might fight about whether I am possibly a goldfish. If our intuitions are that humanity is essential to me, there are no worlds in which I am a goldfish. If, however, we think that philosophically active goldfish are possible, and that a world in which the thing most like me is a goldfish preoccupied with Madhyamaka and modern Western philosophy, and that Lewisian counterpart theory is true, we think that I might be. We might think that since contradictions are obviously not possible, there are no possible worlds in which they are true; or we might think that since there are, they are possible. And so it goes.

From a Mahāyāna Buddhist perspective, this is all nonsense, or at least needs a great deal of fundamental defense. The entire enterprise of taking our intuitions as serious evidence is called into question in a framework in which our intuitions typically reflect primal confusion rather than insight; the enterprise of searching for the essences of things, or of reasoning based on claims about them, makes no sense in a framework in which the very idea of an essence is regarded as incoherent. Much of modal metaphysics as it is currently practiced may be little more than an exploration and systematization of intuitions that deserve dismissal, not reification; an elaboration of illusion of the kind that Buddhists call *prapañca,* or conceptual fabrication—an idle but deceptive spinning of conceptual wheels.

If we take Madhyamaka metaphysics, Yogācāra phenomenology and Śāntarakṣita's synthesis of these perspectives seriously, we take seriously a philosophical framework in which our intuitions about the nature of reality and even about our own experience of reality are likely to be profoundly wrong, and we take seriously a philosophical framework in which an attempt to discover a reality beyond the world of appearance is to be seduced by an illusion that there is reality greater than what we find in front of us. What we have on this view is the world we inhabit. Our task is to understand and to improve it, not to search behind it for something better.

These first two chapters present a mere sketch of the outlines of Buddhist metaphysics, primarily as articulated through the Indian and Tibetan Mahāyāna tradition, albeit with some attention to antecedent Indian ideas and a few Chinese developments. I hope that this picture accomplishes two goals. First, it should provide the foundation for the more specific discussions of the self, of knowledge, phenomenology, ethics and the philosophy of language to follow. I fear that none of this would be intelligible without this metaphysical framework in the background.

Second, I hope that it is apparent that the Buddhist tradition takes up metaphysics in a way worthy of attention by contemporary Western philosophers, even if they are not interested in what follows in the present volume. As I have emphasized, many of the topics central to current concerns were and are central to the concerns of Buddhist philosophers. Often the conclusions to which Buddhist scholars have arrived are recognizable positions in Western debates. Sometimes they are novel positions or suggest new ways of thinking about those debates. Often the arguments and the starting points are intriguingly different, allowing us to see those debates and the positions they define in new light. If philosophy is, in Sellars's memorable phrase, "the attempt to understand how things—in the broadest sense of that term—hang together—in the broadest sense of that term" (1963, 1), taking this philosophical tradition seriously is good philosophy. We now turn to a more specific topic, that is, the status of the self and the person.

# 4 THE SELF

There is a lot to say about the self, and a wide range of debates regarding the self. I do not aim to provide a comprehensive view either of Western or of Buddhist views about the self. But I do want to focus on some of the central debates that dominate current Western thought about the self to see what a Buddhist perspective can contribute. And I want to begin with debates regarding the very existence of anything that deserves to be called a self. Let us begin by asking just what is at stake in debates about the existence of a self, as that will aid us in achieving the requisite focus.

There are four principal issues to which I will draw attention: diachronic identity; synchronic identity; personal essence; and minimal conceptions of self. I take them in this order as each successive worry seems to replace its predecessor in the philosophical dialectic once the predecessor is seen to be intractable. Let us first get clear about each issue, not with an intention to resolve it, but rather to bring the debates they inspire into sharp relief, and only then turn to the Buddhist tradition to see what it might contribute.

## 1. Some Contemporary Western Positions

The problem of diachronic personal identity is easy to state, and it is easy to get a feel for the perplexity and anxiety it generates, both phenomenological and theoretical. What is it, if anything, that makes me now the same person I was yesterday, or that I will be tomorrow? We have an overpowering sense of our own strict numerical identity over time. My memories are memories of *my* life, not of someone rather *like* me, or of someone to whom I bear some philosophically recherché relation; my plans are plans for what *I* will do, not plans for the future actions of some similar fellow; my attitudes such as pride or shame reflect my views regarding what *I* have done, or who *I* am, and so forth. Or so it seems.

In virtue of the intimate connection between memory, intention, agency and responsibility to personhood, to fail to recognize myself as an enduring agent and subject would be to fail to recognize myself as a person.

And much of our social life and our shared theory of such practices as census, taxation, reward and punishment, education and the rest seem to depend centrally on the fact of our diachronic identity. We assign birthdates, social security numbers and passports to individuals, not to successions thereof; I pay taxes on what the government takes *me* to have earned *last year*; we punish a criminal long after the commission of a crime because we take *her*—the one in the dock *now*—to be the perpetrator of what was done *then*, not just her nominal heir. To fail to identify others over time would hence be to fail to recognize others as persons—as beings worthy of rational interpretation, of the attribution of rights, of respect. Strict numerical identity hence seems built into our very conception of ourselves and to the social practices that constitute the environments in which we become, live and treat not only ourselves, but also others as *persons*.

On the other hand, as Leibniz and Hume pointed out, numerical identity requires indiscernibility. Two things that differ in properties can't be the same thing. And every moment I am growing older. Not only that, my composition is constantly changing in subtle ways from moment to moment, and in more dramatic ways over time, as are my character, my beliefs and my memories. Hence no two stages of me are literally identical to one another. They may be very similar to one another, *specifically* identical, as Hume felicitously put it, but *not* numerically identical.[1]

Specific identity—identity in *kind*, despite numerical diversity—is, as Hume also argued convincingly, *conferred*, not *discovered*. The relevant dimensions of similarity and the degrees of similarity along those dimensions that two distinct entities must bear in order to count as identical depends upon our purposes and the grain of our judgment. Identical twins are similar to one another in many respects, but not in all. So, too, are "identical" copies of a single type of coin, car or cloned sheep. But these are also different in many respects. For some purposes they count as identical, for others not.[2] To decide

1. There are, of course, important contemporary responses to this position, including 4D positions, according to which properties of any thing are time-indexed, and so that distinct temporal slices are parts of a numerically identical continuant. We will consider these issues below.

2. Not all metaphysicians would agree, of course. There are those such as Armstrong (1978, 1989) who argue for a small, fixed stock of universals and for the claim that reality itself determines what kinds things really belong to. This is not the place to debate these issues, however, and I set those positions aside in favor of a broadly acceptable view that whether things count as instances of the same kind in a context depends upon our classificatory

between identity and difference in a particular context depends as much on the purposes of the actors in the context as on an examination of the entities themselves.

It hence appears on reflection that while I might be very similar to earlier and later stages of what I think of as "myself," I am not identical to them in any sense that could be merely *discovered*, although plenty of *decisions* come down in favor of treating my current self as specifically identical to those stages.[3] But if a self is an entity that grounds from its own side those judgments and determines that whatever purposes one might have, one *must* regard those stages as stages of *that self*, there is no such *self* that persists as one and the same thing over time.

Now, at this stage, of course, many metaphysical moves can be made. We can appeal to causal connectedness, or to memory, for instance, to constitute special relations between person-stages that are determinative of identity. But if it is strict identity grounded in fundamental metaphysics that is at issue—as opposed to explanations of conventions of individuation—there are decisive countermoves to each of these in the form of fanciful counterexamples of personal fission and fusion; of memory insertion and brain transplants; and of reduction to software.

Derek Parfit is the best known and most systematic purveyor of such examples. He asks us to consider, among other possibilities, the case in which a molecule-for-molecule duplicate is created of ourselves on a distant planet through teleportation. At the moment of the creation of this duplicate—assuming even the weakest supervenience of the mental on the physical—the two copies of me (the one here and the newly created one) are psychologically identical. Over time, they diverge. Any relation determining diachronic identity determines equally that successive stages of each of these duplicates is diachronically identical to pre-fission me. But they are distinct from one another, violating the transitivity of numerical identity.

interests. On this view, there are many kinds, many of them uninteresting, to be sure, but still many of interest, and when we say that two things are specifically identical, the truth conditions of that claim depend on the kinds we have in mind at the time. Those with a more robust sense of the determinacy of universals may balk. Buddhists, moreover, are nominalists about universals (more of this in chapters 7 and 8). Most Buddhist philosophers are hence happy to countenance a plethora of potential classificatory kinds, but to deny any of them an interest-free or mind-independent reality.

3. And once again, if we countenance Kripkean essences of origin, we might say that the fact that each of these states shares the essential feature of being a descendant of my parents, this might provide a convention-independent ground for identity. But we are better off eschewing such essences for reasons scouted in the previous chapter.

Once again, there is an extensive dialectic of replies and more fanciful examples deployed in this literature, and the interested reader is invited to explore it, beginning with Parfit (1986). But whatever these examples may or may not show about our actual conventions of personal individuation, they do demonstrate rather convincingly that there is nothing to be found in the person that by itself, absent a network of such conventions and purposes, determines diachronic identity.

When we ask what it is to be a self—to be a person—we are asking is, in part, what it is to exist as the same person in the relevant sense over time. And that requires first that we determine what that relevant sense is. It is of course ludicrous to claim that nobody has ever lived for more than a moment. But it may be untenable to maintain that the grounds of that fact can be found by careful metaphysical dissection revealing the basis of that endurance. This understanding of our extension in time is part of what is at stake in understanding what it is to be a person, and the broadly Humean considerations scouted above suggest that that understanding is not grounded in fundamental metaphysics, but in social convention.

But this is not all that is at stake. One might concede that there is no convention-independent fact of the matter regarding diachronic identity, taking our existence to be like that of a string of beads, or of a spun thread—both popular Buddhist metaphors, by the way—with no single entity persisting over time. Nonetheless, one might insist that such a picture does identify a specific sequence of individually identifiable entities, each of which has determinate identity conditions, and that we can get some kind of metaphysical determinacy for a sequence of metaphysically determinate constituents. So, while a rosary may exist only by convention, each bead exists on its own, independent of our aggregation of them into a single conventionally constituted ritual object.[4] Following the metaphor, one might then suggest that while diachronic personal identity is conventional, or even fictional—to be constructed rather than to be discovered—our synchronic identity may well be determinate. After all, even if there is nothing that constitutes my being identical with my previous avatars, there must be something that constitutes my present difference from the present *you*!

Once again, both phenomenology and metaphysics seem to be on the side of determinacy. On the phenomenological side, when we say 'I,' or when we

4. Now one might press the rosary metaphor and point out that the beads are joined by a thread. Well, yes. But if that thread is spun from many fibers it doesn't really help much. On the other hand, one can switch metaphors and save the point. Think about constellations. It is surely a matter of interest and decision whether any group of stars constitutes a constellation, and it matters a whole lot from which point in the universe one views those stars!

introspect, there seems to be no question about who the referent of that pronoun is, no question about the object of introspective awareness. I seem to be unable to mistake myself for anyone else, and it seems that I know immediately who I am and what my subjective states are. Some might argue that I can be wrong about some of my mental states, or certainly about the state of my body, but those errors, one might urge, only show that those states are not themselves *me*. About my identity, there can be no error. This intuition has spawned the extensive literature on immunity to error through misidentification (Shoemaker 1968; Perry 1993, Pryor 1999, Campbell 2004, Evans 1982, Bermúdez 1998, Cassam 1997, Prosser and Recanati 2012).[5]

Moreover, such human phenomena as agency, rationality and responsibility seem to demand at the very least synchronic determinacy of identity. If I am to act, as opposed to move, to take reasons as motivators and to be author of my life, there must be some *me* who takes those reasons seriously, for *whom* they are motives, and who *acts* on them. An indeterminate swarm of events and processes is the wrong kind of thing to do this. And if I am even to take myself to be rational, to be an epistemic agent, I must take myself to endorse beliefs for reasons, to reflect on my epistemic processes and to draw appropriate inferences. If these are not integrated, the very idea of rationality comes apart.

This is what Kant had in mind when he identified the transcendental unity of apperception as a condition of genuine subjectivity, of rationality and agency. If the "I think" cannot accompany all of our representations, he argues, representations could not constitute human experience, as human experience is necessarily the synthesis and integration of multiple representations—we might add, in a more contemporary vocabulary inflected by cognitive science, multiple modalities of representation—into a single, systematic manifold that constitutes an objective world of which we can take ourselves to be subjects, about which we take ourselves to reason, and toward which we take ourselves to act and to adopt evaluative attitudes. Subjectivity, agency and rationality are not committee phenomena, but individual phenomena, and individuation requires determinacy. Kant's powerful analysis is not a matter of mere historical curiosity; it grounds our modern way of thinking about subjectivity.

Nonetheless, there are powerful considerations going the other way. Just as individuation seems to demand determinacy, determinacy seems to demand

5. Actually, this idea has an older lineage. G. E. M. Anscombe raised similar ideas in (1975). But the issue is explored even earlier with considerable ingenuity by K. C. Bhattacharyya (1930).

individuation. Quine's dictum "no entity without identity" (1969, 23) can be converted: "no identity without an entity." And it is hard to see how we are to individuate the self synchronically and informatively.

Bodies are notoriously inadequate. First of all there are all of the transplant and teleportation thought experiments to consider. These are problems not only for diachronic but synchronic identity as a body inasmuch as the fact—if it is a fact—that I could undergo a body transplant and remain *me* shows that *what it is to be me* is not to be this body. And if I am teleported—if my body here is disintegrated and reassembled in a galaxy far, away, where I happily resume my life—then once again, it seems that my identity is not that of my body. Then there are the facts on the ground regarding the dispensability of any part of my body—if we take parts to be small enough, say even cells—to my identity. And finally there is the fact that I experience myself not as *a body*, but as *embodied*. I take myself to be uniquely associated with my body, but available to myself in a particularly intimate way; even my body fails to be available in *that way*.[6] One way to put this point is to say that if my identity is immune to misidentification error, it cannot be bodily identity in which it consists.

But if I am not constituted even at a time, simply by a body, by what am I constituted? To say that it is my mind instead introduces new problems. First, it suggests an implausible dualism that is so at odds with contemporary science that it can hardly be taken seriously. But even if we did take a body-independent mind seriously, figuring out just how to identify *it* in a way that yields enough determinacy to provide an internal identity condition is far from simple. And that is simply because on any plausible account, the mind itself is far from simple. So many aspects of our psychology are unconscious; our psychology is so dynamic, so intertwined with our physiology and environment, that to find some kernel that constitutes the self would appear to be impossible. As Hume noted, it is hard to introspect and to find anything more than a flux of cognitive and affective states and processes. And a self we can never experience seems little better than no self at all. So, when we ask what is at stake in historical and contemporary debates about the self, we have to add synchronic identity to diachronic identity. When we ask what the self is, and whether there is one at all, we are asking not only what unifies us over time, but also what constitutes the unity we experience at a single time.

While it might seem natural to think about our identity in terms of the primitive identity of a soul or pure subject/agent, this is on the one hand very culturally specific and religiously grounded (note, for instance, that it is not even recognizably classically *Greek*—while Plato and Aristotle, for instance,

6. See Bhattacharyya (1930) for an elegant exploration of this phenomenon.

recognized a *psyche*, this was a composite affair, and not a simple, primitive identity) and on the other hand does not so much *solve* the problem of identity, but transforms it into two problems: first, in what does the identity of the soul consist, and second, how is it connected to the selves we *know*, our psycho-physical selves on whose identity we are to give up?

When I say that this way of thinking is culturally and religiously specific, I do not mean to say that it is unique to European philosophical thought. Similar ideas emerge in the religious and philosophical matrix of classical India, for example in the schools that posit an *ātman*, or substantial self, and indeed that is the view that is the explicit target of Buddhist *anātman* theory. (See Siderits, Thompson 2014, Thompson and Zahavi 2013.) But it is worth noting that many philosophical and religious traditions reject any basis for such a primitive identity. These include not only the Buddhist tradition with which I am concerned in this volume, but also the Daoist and Confucian traditions of China and the Cārvaka tradition of classical India.[7] Classical Greece certainly did not take a soul with primitive identity conditions for granted either.

I emphasize this fact because much philosophical reflection about the self begins with the presupposition that we are in some metaphysical sense substances with identity conditions. The task then is to locate that substance, and to articulate those identity conditions. But that presupposition reflects more the fact that we imbibe certain religious prejudices with our mother's milk, and that philosophical reflection—however much it pretends to antagonism regarding faith—is often little more than a rational reconstruction of and apology for uncritically accepted prejudices whose religious and cultural origins are unacknowledged. One of the signal benefits of pursuing philosophy cross-culturally is the hermeneutic power of such engagement to foreground and to allow us to interrogate these prejudices. (See also Garfield 2002d, 2014a.)

The questions we ask about our diachronic and synchronic identity are each ways at getting at a deeper question about who we are, the question of our essence. We take it for granted that most of our ordinary properties are *accidental*. This includes our physical properties such as our height, hair color, and even the particular neurons that constitute our central nervous systems. Any of these could have been otherwise. It also includes our mental properties, such as our intelligence, personality, values, emotional state, beliefs, etc... Any of these could have been otherwise, and we would still be ourselves.

7. The latter defended an eliminativism with regard to the self and to the mental, a position even more radical than the Buddhist no-self view, akin to that suggested by Churchland (1979).

And living in cultures saturated both by a generically Greek outlook and a generically Abrahamic outlook, we take a distinction between essence and accident for granted, and even take such tests as conceivability by us to be reliable ways of distinguishing between essence and accident. This is a further cultural prejudice in need of interrogation.

We will problematize this metaphysical distinction and the epistemology of modality it involves below. But for now, let us take it for granted as setting the context that determines, once again, what we care about when we ask in the context of the Western philosophical tradition about the nature of the self. It is clear that we are asking what our *essence* is. And this is why the diachronic and synchronic identity questions are so tightly linked to one another. Each is in the end a way of getting at what it is that constitutes the necessary and sufficient conditions of *being me*, that with which I am me, whatever changes in my accidental properties may occur, and that without which I would cease to me be, no matter how many of my accidental properties remained constant.[8] Given the critique of *svabhāva* mounted in the previous chapter, we should already be suspicious of this enterprise.

The Abrahamic soul is meant to be just that thing that answers the question about personal essence. But it is not the only candidate, and contemporary Western philosophers have sought alternative conceptions of personal essence. We will examine some of these in due course. But for now I just want to note one more thing that is at stake, perhaps the most fundamental issue at stake when we ask about our identity, that is, whether there *is* anything that constitutes our *essence*.

I venture to say that central to a premodern and modern Western approach to the self is a presupposition that the question of our essence makes sense in the first place. Of course the postmodern turn initiated by Nietzsche in *Twilight of the Idols* and carried forward by Heidegger and de Beauvoir problematizes this question in profound ways. But as we will see, even those who take much of this phenomenological and anti-Cartesian perspective on board have difficulty jettisoning a reflex essentialism,[9] and essentialism is still very much at the mainstream of Anglo-American-Australasian metaphysics.

These considerations are not meant to suggest a crude genetic fallacy: the fact that the doctrine that there is a self has its origins in the West in these religious traditions hardly entails that it is false, no more than does the fact that in

8. There are always lots of trivial, uninformative identity conditions that can be patched together, and even trivial essential conditions, such as being such that 2+2=4 and being in this place and time but none satisfies the demand for determinacy.

9. See Spelman 1988 for an excellent study of this problem in the domain of feminist theory.

India it has its origins in Vedic traditions. And the fact that the idea that there is no self has its origins in a Buddhist tradition hardly entails that it is true. That is not the point. Rather, the point is that noticing that divergent traditions embody such radically different presuppositions, or horizons against which questions can be raised, suggests that when we encounter a position that seem simply obvious, or a question that seems to make sense, it is always worth interrogating the presuppositions and roots of that position or question to find out whether things are as obvious as they appear to be. (Garfield 2014a)

One might think that this claim is belied by the plethora of recent proposals for "minimalist" conceptions of the self (Strawson 1999, 2011a, Gallagher 2000, Thompson 2007, 2014, Zahavi 2005, 2009). These are interesting and important in their own right, and will demand our attention, but, as we shall see, they do not in general represent a retreat from essentialism about the self so much as a more modest version of that presupposition. Each takes it for granted that there is a self of which an account—however minimal—must be provided; none take seriously the idea that there might be no such thing.

Minimal conceptions come in several forms. Some, such as Strawson's (1997, 2009, 2011a), "reduce" the self from a diachronic continuant to a series of momentary entities, each of which is nonetheless an integrated subject of experience and agent of reasoning and action, emphasizing a kind of *synchronic* unity at the expense of diachronic unity. This is an interesting move, but one that should raise suspicions from the start. As Kant emphasizes in the *Schematism* section of the first *Critique* and as Husserl argues in *The Phenomenology of Internal Time Consciousness*, even synchronic identity may demand diachronic identity, inasmuch as an identity devoid of retention and protension is no human identity at all, and perhaps not even a kind of consciousness.

Others reduce the self to a "point of view," or a perspective, emphasizing not its *diachronic* continuity but its synchronic status as a kind of vanishing point, the Tractarian eye in the visual field (Hutto 2007, 2008, Damasio 1999, Dennett 1991, Schechtman 1996, Gallagher 2003). Still others, such as Zahavi (2005), take the self to be nothing but a kind of pure subjectivity, a self-consciousness that accompanies all consciousness, a sort of mine-ness, with no substantial owner, either synchronically or diachronically. With regard to a position such as this, we will have to ask two questions (to which we return below, both in this chapter and in the next): first, is there indeed such a pervasive sense, and second, if there is, would it constitute an analysis of selfhood at all, or an abandonment of that very idea?[10]

10. Someone might argue as follows: Gettier problems show that it may be impossible to provide any set of necessary and sufficient conditions for knowledge; Wittgenstein shows

But some offer more robust notions of selfhood—recognizably minimalist, but nonetheless presenting that minimalist, constructed self as grounded in more fundamental processes with a claim to a more substantial level of reality. Ganeri (2012), in explicit dialogue with Buddhist and orthodox Indian accounts, defends a position according to which the self is an emergent phenomenon supervening on more basic non-personal psychological events. On this account the self, albeit a real phenomenon, is not fundamental. Thompson (2007) defends a neurobiologically grounded conception of a *constructed* self along these lines. He begins by arguing that any account of embodied agency for biological organisms like us requires a conception of selfhood, on pain of positing knowledge, agency and experience without any subject for those phenomena:

> The dynamic sensorimotor approach needs a notion of autonomous selfhood or agency because to explain perceptual experience it appeals to sensorimotor knowledge. Knowledge implies a knower or agent or self that embodies this knowledge.... (2007, 260)

Thompson then characterizes this self as an "invariant topological pattern that is recursively produced by the [nervous system]":

> The nervous system establishes and maintains a sensorimotor cycle, whereby what one senses depends directly on how one moves, and how one moves depends directly on what one senses. Whereas biological selfhood in its core cellular form is brought forth by the operational closure of autopoietic network, sensorimotor selfhood results from the operational closure of the nervous system. In either case, it is

that it is impossible to provide necessary and sufficient conditions for being a game. And so on. But nobody takes Gettier to have shown that there is no knowledge, and nobody takes Wittgenstein to show that nobody has ever played a game. And so the failure to find the essence of a thing or a kind cannot be taken to demonstrate that there is nothing of that kind. And so, in particular, the failure to be able to say what it is to be a self does not mean that there is no self.

But this objection misses the point in the present case. In these cases, we have an ordinary kind whose instances we recognize when we see them, and terms with fairly non-controversial conditions of application, despite our inability to articulate those conditions. These are manifest image phenomena, to use Sellarsian language, not theoretical posits. The self under examination here is not like that. It is not something we observe; it is not a theoretical posit of any science; it is a philosophical posit meant to explain a range of first-person phenomena, and it is not clear that it explains any of them. In order to do so, it would have to be made determinate, and it can't be.

> legitimate to invoke the notion of "self" because the dynamics of the system is characterized by an invariant topological pattern that is recursively produced by the system and that defines an outside to which the system is actively and normatively related. (260)

As we proceed, we will have to ask whether theorists like Ganeri and Thompson have in fact simply provided an argument not for the reality of the self, but for its elimination in favor of a kind of no-self account of personhood; and whether such a pattern of activity is what we grasp when we grasp ourselves *as selves*. Perhaps the maximally minimalist account is Hutto's (2008) or Dennett's (1991) "narrative self," a self constructed as the principal character in a story we tell about ourselves, a protagonist in a useful fiction. Each of these approaches has some claim on the minimalist title, as each takes what we might call an inflated view of the self, as a continuing substantial entity, and deflates it along one or more dimensions; each, on the other hand, might be seen as a strategy for arguing *against* the reality of the self.

It is easy to see what drives minimalism as something like a movement. On the one hand, we have the strong intuition that we are selves in some sense—subjects, agents, centers of consciousness and referents of personal pronouns—and philosophical commitments in domains as diverse as metaphysics, epistemology and ethics to some kind of unified subject if agency, choice, rational justification and moral assessment is to be possible. On the other hand, the clear naturalistic light of reason tells us that over and above a complex organism in a rich social matrix there seems to be nothing that fits the bill of a continuing, integrated entity that subserves these functions.

Minimalism presents itself as the middle path, providing a self that does all of the requisite philosophical work and satisfies at least most of our pretheoretical intuitions, but without the objectionable ghostly substance or suspect empirical claims that more maximal theories involve. Buddhists love to valorize their positions as middle paths; after all, in the *Discourse Setting in Motion the Wheel of the Doctrine* the Buddha presented his doctrine as the middle path. Nonetheless, we must always beware of claims to the middle; they can end up being little more than Solomonic compromises, giving to neither side anything it could ever want. In any case, this seems to be the final major issue at stake in Western debates about the self: Is a minimal conception of the self viable, and if so, which minimal conception is in the end acceptable? Let us turn to the Buddhist world to see what light its debates concerning the self might throw on Western discussions.

## 2. The Buddhist Landscape

Somewhat different, but importantly related issues are at stake in Indian Buddhist debates. To get a feel for these debates (explored in great depth and with great subtlety by Ganeri 2012) it is important to remember that Buddhism first and foremost emerges as an Indian philosophical system in dialogue with other Indian philosophical systems, both orthodox and heterodox. Buddhism in particular sets itself apart in this dialectical context as a doctrine of no-self (*anātman*) against most orthodox systems, but as non-nihilistic about persons against the eliminative materialist *Cārvaka* system. In its characteristic trope of representing itself as a middle path between extremes, Buddhists argue that the self posited by most of the orthodox does not exist, but that this denial of existence does not amount to a denial that persons exist at *some* level of description. It permits us to say that a person exists *conventionally*, even if a *self*, appearances to the contrary notwithstanding, does not exist *in any sense*. So, once again, the rubric of the two truths will be important as we talk about a conventional person who turns out, yet, not to be a *self*.

Orthodox Indian philosophers offer a range of reasons—most of which are familiar in structural terms at least, to Western philosophers—for the necessity of a substantially real, continuing self.[11] For one thing, philosophers such as Kumārila and Gangeśa argue that the possibility of retention and protention require a self that retains its identity over time. Without such a self, they argue, there would be no account of the relation between past experience and present memory, or present intention and future action.

Second, they argue, the unity of consciousness requires a self. After all, consciousness is multi-modal, but integrated. If the multiple features of a single object are to be synthesized into a single representation, and if different experiences are to be experienced in relation to one another, there must be a single central locus at which these are all experienced in relation to one another. A particularly striking version of this is the argument of the 6th-century Nyāya philosopher Uddyotakara, whose position is represented by the 9th-century Buddhist philosopher Śāntarakṣita in his *Encyclopedia of Ontology (Tattvasaṃgraha)* as follows:

> Uddyotakara argues as follows: "Devadatta's cognitions of visible form, flavor, odor, and texture bear the mark of one and many; for they are

11. In this discussion I am collapsing a number of very different orthodox Indian schools. These schools diverge dramatically from one another on a number of important metaphysical issues, but they do share a broad commitment to the reality of *ātman*. For an excellent treatment of Indian views about the self, see Ganeri (2007, 2012) and Carpenter (2014).

> unified together by the cognition 'I'. Similarly, the cognitions of many persons, who have previously entered agreement, are linked together during the single instant when the dancing girl raises her brow.
>
> His meaning is this: Just as man might enter into an agreement, saying, "As soon as the dancing girl raises her brow let us all throw fine fabric onto the stage...," so that the many agents and the many cognitions "I have seen her raise her brow" are unified because of the singularity of the sign, the raising of the brow; so, too, in the present case, cognitions with many different objects should be unified owing to the singularity of a sign, and that single sign is the self. The unification, moreover, is of many cognitions, such as "I have heard," which are linked together by the characteristic of having a single knower. (In Edelglass and Garfield 2009, 325)

It is worth noting the anticipation of Kant's argument for the transcendental unity of apperception in judgment. Uddyotakara's point is straightforward: When we have a unified experience of the sights, smells, sounds, tastes and textures in experiencing a night of entertainment (in a brothel, in this case!) that is not the experience of a committee, but of a single consciousness. The principle of unity when we all agree on the moment at which to hurl our token of appreciation may be in the *object* of experience, but the principle of unity of the total experience for each of us lies in our *subjectivity*. That, Uddyotakara argues, can only be explained by the presence of a self—in his sense, a permanent, purely subjective level of consciousness that is the substratum of all psychological processes and that unifies perceptual and conceptual experience.

Śāntarakṣita responds that such a self is a gratuitous and explanatorily impotent posit—that higher-order cognition can do all of the work. He argues first that there is a genuine multiplicity of sensory cognitions at work in a complex sensory experience such as our night with the dancing girl, and that these indeed need to be unified. But, he argues, the mechanism of unification is simply psychological. He appeals to the introspective or mental sense faculty (*manas-vijñana/yid dbang shes [yi wang sheh]*) and asserts that it takes as its object all of the input from all of the external sensory faculties (ibid., 329–330).[12]

12. Note that Śāntarakṣita's proposal is not far off from that of Thompson, noted above. But Śāntarakṣita takes himself to be arguing *against* the reality of a self, and explaining an *illusion* that there is a self, whereas Thompson takes himself to be explaining the construction of a real, but minimal, self.

Now, in one sense, this seems to be an explanatory standoff and a begging of the question. Uddyotakara says that the self does the experiential integration, and doesn't say how; Śāntarakṣita says that a cognitive process does it, and doesn't say how. But in another sense, Śāntarakṣita wins the day. For even though he can't specify *how* a higher-order cognitive process can do the work, he does point out that in order to do psychology, we don't need to go transcendental—we shift instead to empirical ground; moreover, he is *right*. To solve the "binding problem" in perception—and that is the problem that Uddyotakara and his Nyāya colleagues are properly raising for their Buddhist interlocutors—we need to talk about higher-order cognitive processes, and that is what is happening in contemporary cognitive neuroscience; *pace* Uddyotakara and Kant, we don't posit a transcendental subject to do the work. Śāntarakṣita was just a millennium or so too early to have the requisite science at his disposal.

Third, it is urged by orthodox proponents of a self that many of the properties that attach to the self cannot attach to a physical body, such as cognitive or affective properties, even if they may require a body in order to be realized. That thing to which they attach must therefore be a self that is distinct from a body. Furthermore, many advocates of the reality of what is called in the orthodox Indian traditions *ātman* (usually translated as *soul*, but really just *self*)—a continuing, substantially existent self—argue, the very phenomenon of consciousness demands a self. For when we are conscious, they argue, we are always conscious of both a subjective and an objective aspect of our experience. The subjective aspect consists in a certain perspective on or ownership of the experience. Where there is perspective or ownership, there must be something whose perspective it is, or an owner, and that is a self.

Finally, it is argued, personal individuation and immunity from misidentification require selves. For me to be distinct from you, and for it to be impossible for me to confuse my cognitive or affective states with yours, there must be a real difference between us and a special kind of access we have to ourselves distinct from any access to our bodies or to the states of other selves. There must be an object of this distinctive kind of access and objects of this important individuation relation. Bodies won't do the trick as we can commit errors regarding their identity, so there must be selves.

These of course are at this stage the very sketchiest accounts of the relevant arguments. (See Ganeri 2007 for details.) But they are sufficient to indicate what is at stake between Buddhists, who deny that there is any self of the kind posited by their orthodox opponents, and those orthodox philosophers themselves. The self posited by the orthodox, whether it is a distinct substance or not, regardless of its precise relation to the body, is posited as a continuing entity with an important degree of ontological autonomy (where this could range from substantial identity to non-reductive supervenience) that is the subject and integrator of experience, the continuing basis of memory and intention, and the self-conscious basis of personal individuation and continuity. The Buddhist denies that any such entity exists, and indeed that any such entity is needed to explain, or even could explain, the putative phenomena it is called upon to explain. The arguments, as we will see, are various, some denying the reality of proffered explananda, some offering explanations that do not advert to the self.

On the other hand, no Buddhist philosopher wants to reject the fact that such linguistic devices as names and personal pronouns make sense, or that there are distinctions between individuals, or that there is memory, agency, cognition, and other such phenomena. There must therefore, even on a Buddhist view, be *some sense* in which persons are real. In just what that reality of persons consists, and how it prevents Buddhism from sinking into an implausible nihilism, is not straightforward and animates most of the important intra-Buddhist debates about the self (*ātman/bdag [dak]*), the person (*pudgala/gang zag [gangzak]*) and consciousness (*vijñāna/shes pa [shehpa]*).

The doctrine of *anātman* is fundamental to Buddhist philosophy and is articulated in the very earliest strata of the Pāli canon. In the *The Discourse on the Characteristic of No-Self (Anatta-lakkhaṇa-sutta)* we read:

> Material form, monks, is not-self. Now, were this material form self, it would not lead to affliction, and one would be able to effectively say, "Let my material form be like this, or not like this." But inasmuch as material form is not-self, therefore it leads to affliction, and one cannot effectively say, "Let my material form be like this, or not like this." [The same is then said of feeling, perception, dispositions and consciousness.]
>
> What do you think about this, monks? Is material form permanent or impermanent? "Impermanent, venerable sir." But is that which is impermanent painful or pleasant? "Painful, venerable sir." But is it fitting to regard that which is impermanent, painful, and of a nature to change as "This is mind, this am I, this is my self?" "No, venerable sir." [The same is then said of feeling, perception, dispositions and consciousness.]
>
> Therefore, monks, whatever is material form: past, future or present; internal or external; gross or subtle; low or excellent; far or near; all material form should be seen as it really is by right wisdom thus: "This

> is not mine; this I am not; this is not my self." [The same is then said of feeling, perception, dispositions and consciousness.] (Edelglass and Garfield 2009, 269)

Here we see the historical Buddha reported as first decomposing the person into the five aggregates (*skandhas*) of material form, feeling, perception, disposition and consciousness, and then arguing that none of these can constitute the self on the grounds that we in fact do not identify with any of them. The self for the sake of this critical argument is taken to be that self we posit as the referent of the first-person pronoun when we use it. We take that thing to endure, and to possess, but not to *be* the aggregates. That is, when I think about the body, we think of it not as *me*, but as *my* body. I can imagine a body transplant; in that case, I think, I would still be *me*, but I would have a new body.

Even when I think of my mental constituents, the Buddha argues, I do not identify any of them as *me*. I can dream, for instance, of a mind transplant. So, I can say to myself—regardless of the metaphysical coherence of the reverie—"I wish—if only for a day or so—that I could have the mind of Stephen Hawking. It would be so much fun to understand general relativity so clearly." When I do so, I imagine *me*, Jay, having *his* mind. And this shows that I at least take myself not to be identical to my mind, or to any particular mental faculty, but rather to take myself to be a fundamental *possessor* of my mind. All of this is a way of saying that from a Buddhist perspective when we identify the self that is the subject of critique—the self we mistakenly grasp as the basis of our identity—that is in fact none of the constituents of the person; and beyond those constituents there is nothing to grasp. Therefore, there is no self.

This is made more explicit in another simile from *The Questions of King Milinda*, the simile of the chariot, adapted in the 6th century CE to a Mahāyāna analysis of the self by Candrakīrti in his influential *Introduction to the Middle Way*. Here is the simile as it occurs in *The Questions of King Milinda*. We begin with the challenge posed by the king:

> ...If you say, "Fellows in the holy life, address me, sire, as Nāgasena," what here is Nāgasena? Is it, venerable sir, that the hairs of the head are Nāgasena? "Oh no, sire." "That the hairs on the body are Nāgasena?" "Oh no, sire." "That the nails...the teeth, the skin, the flesh, the sinews, the marrow, the kidneys, the heart, the liver, the membranes, the spleen, the lungs, the intestines, the mesentery, the stomach, the excrement, the bile, the phlegm, the pus, the blood, the sweat, the fat, the

> tears, the serum, the saliva, the mucous, the synovic fluid, the urine, or the brain in the head" are any of them Nāgasena?" "Oh no, sire."
>
> "Is Nāgasena material form, venerable sir?" "Oh no, sire." "Is Nāgasena feeling... perception... dispositions or consciousness?" "Oh no, sire."
>
> "But then, venerable sir, is Nāgasena form-feeling-perception-dispositions-and-consciousness?" "Oh no, sire." "But then, venerable sir, is there Nāgasena apart from form-feeling-perception-dispositions-and-consciousness?" "Oh no, sire." "Though I, venerable sir, am asking you repeatedly, I do not see this Nāgasena. Nāgasena is only a sound, venerable sir. For who here is Nāgasena? You sir, are speaking an untruth, a lying word. There is no Nāgasena."

There are a few noteworthy aspects to the king's challenge. The important thing to note is that this is *not* an orthodox, or *ātamavādin*, position. In fact, the king gives voice to what one might call a "near miss" to a Buddhist position, a pretty good, but not excellent, student's presentation of the Buddhist position. The text is thus aiming not at a simple reply to a non-Buddhist opponent, but rather a careful refinement of the proper way to express a Buddhist position on the self. The king begins with a kind of parody of an Abhidharma reductive analysis, asking whether the self can be identified with any specific constituent of the psychophysical continuum or of any of the five aggregates. Of course it cannot; this merely recapitulates the kind of analysis we have already encountered in the *sutta* discussed above.

In the second sally, the king offers what one might think is the obviously correct analysis—that Nāgasena is in fact the combination of all of these entities. Nāgasena rejects that out of hand. This might bring us up short. But it makes sense. For as Hume was to point out nearly two millennia later using his analogy of the church in the *Treatise*, this combination is constantly changing, but the referent of *Nāgasena* must continue if our conventions for individuation is to make sense. Our hair grows or is cut, our perceptions and personalities change, but our nominal identity does not. The person, the referent of the name, hence cannot be the combination, any more than the church can literally *be* such things as the building, current parishoners or the corpses in the graveyard. The relation between the conventional person—the referent of the name or pronoun—cannot be this assemblage; nor can it be something other than them, for when they are all removed, nothing remains. Hence the puzzle.

> Then the venerable Nāgasena spoke thus to King Milinda: "You, sire, are…noble…Now, did you come on foot, or in a conveyance?" "I, venerable sir, did not come on foot. I came in a chariot." "If, sire, you came in my chariot, show me the chariot. Is the pole the chariot, sire?" "Oh no, venerable sir." "Is the axle the chariot?" "Oh no, venerable sir." "Are the wheels…the body of the chariot, the flagstaff, the reins, or the goad the chariot?" "Oh no, venerable sir." "But then sire, is the chariot the pole-axle-wheels-body-flagstaff-yoke-reins-and-goad?" "Oh no, venerable sir." "But then, sire, is there a chariot apart from the pole-a xle-wheels-body-flagstaff-yoke-reins-and-goad?" "Oh no, venerable sir."
>
> "Though I, sire, am asking you repeatedly, I do not see the chariot. Chariot is only a sound, sire. For what here is the chariot? You, sire, are speaking an untruth, a lying word. There is no chariot. You, sire are the chief king of the whole of India. Of whom are you afraid that you speak a lie?"
>
> "I, venerable Nāgasena, am not telling a lie, for it is dependent on the pole, dependent on the axles….That *chariot* exists as a denotation, appellation, designation, conventional usage, a name."

This introduction of a *dependent designation*, a term we encountered when discussing Nāgārjuna in the previous chapter, is the crux of the analysis. Here the claim is that apparently referring terms, like names, pronouns and nouns, which lead us to believe in discrete entities that serve as their referents, in fact have no such referents. Instead, they are useful conventions that enable ordinary transactions. Their apparent denotations are fictional. They are neither core parts or substrata of complex phenomena, nor aggregations, nor anything apart from them. But they are related to such aggregations. Those aggregations are the *bases of designation*. They are causally responsible for the conventions that enable these terms to be used and hence that constitute the fictions that are their referents.

Nāgasena draws this conclusion explicitly: Conventionally, there is a person, but ultimately there is none; just as conventionally, Ahab is the captain of the *Pequod*, but ultimately there is no such person. Just as literary criticism would be impossible without a discussion of Ahab, copyright law would not work if *Jay Garfield* was not used as it is; just as the captain in *Moby Dick* is the husband of the protagonist in *Ahab's Wife* (Neslund 1997), despite the century-odd lapse between their composition and the difference in authors, the child who grew up in Pittsburgh is the elderly author of this text, despite the differences between them. Nāgasena now draws attention to another difference: that between the conventions that establish the utility of a name and the fictional denotation of the name.

> "It is well: you, sire, understand a chariot. Even so is it for me, sire, it is dependent on the hair of the head, and on the hair of the body...and dependent on the brain in the head, and dependent on material form, and on feeling, perception, dispositions and dependent on consciousness that *Nāgasena* exists as a denotation, appellation, designation, as a conventional usage, merely a name. But according to the highest meaning (ultimately) a person is not apprehended here." (Edelglass and Garfield 2009, 272–273)

But this analysis by no means settles the question, even within the Buddhist philosophical world. While no Buddhist school would acknowledge that it posits a self in the orthodox sense of that term, there is an early Buddhist line of thought called the *personalist* or *pudgalavāda*[13] school that does argue that while there is no self, there is a real, continuing *person* that is distinct from, but related in a very particular way to, the sub-personal *skandhas*. This school constitutes a kind of metaphysical waystation between early Abhidharmika views and later Mahāyāna views and flourished in the waning centuries of the last millennium BCE and the first few centuries of the Common Era. Pudgalavādins argued that there is a person whose nature and precise relation to the underlying psychophysical aggregates is inexpressible; that it is only present when they are, but is neither strictly identical to, nor strictly distinct from them. In modern terms, we would describe this position this way: that there is a self that supervenes narrowly upon the psychophysical aggregates and which, although they are constantly changing, is a stable entity not identical to them, but nonetheless constituted by them.

Other Buddhist schools criticized this view savagely as a retreat to a view of a self, and in fact this school of thought disappeared from the Buddhist tradition under the pressure of these attacks. Abhidharmika Buddhists argued instead for a reduction of the self to impersonal cognitive processes and events as a way of eliminating its privileged ontological status. While the Abhidharmikas concur with earlier Buddhist analyses such as that of *The Questions of King Milinda* that the conventional self is a nonexistent fiction in need of elimination in a final ontology, they held that the final ontology of *dharmas* provides a reduction of that self to an ultimately real continuum of those evanescent *dharmas*.

13. The term *pudgalavāda* is actually an epithet attached to the proponents of this view, who called themseles the *Vātsiputrīya* or *inexpressibilists*.

Mādhyamikas, in particular Candrakīrti in his *Introduction to the Middle Way* and *Lucid Exposition*, criticized this view trenchantly from the other side. First, they argued that a self about which so little could be said was hardly explanatory of anything at all, and so not worth the metaphysical effort. Second, they argued that if the self is to be the object of self-grasping, and so the foundation of egoism and suffering, it can't be such an intangible, abstract object. The (nonexistent) self we grasp is grasped as a concrete, perceptible entity, not supervenient epiphenomenon.

Third, and most importantly, however, they argued that the Pudgalavādins got the supervenience base wrong, and this issue is central to Candrakīrti's construction of Madhyamaka. The Pudgalavādins take the aggregates to determine the person, and take the ultimate reality of the aggregates to give the supervenient person its reality. Candrakīrti, as we will see below, takes social and verbal conventions, and the utility of collecting the stages of certain psychophysical continua and denoting them by proper names or personal pronouns, to be all that gives the person its conventional reality. One way to put this is that Candrakīrti argues for a broad supervenience base for the person, comprising not only the psychophysical aggregates themselves, but also the network of social conventions and dispositions that together constitute our common practices of personal discourse.

Now it might seem at first glance that this third critique falls afoul of the second: if supervenience on a narrow base sinks the Pudgalavādin position in part on the grounds that nothing that abstract could be the object of self-grasping, how could a broadly supervenient entity do any better? Answering this question enables us to see the real space between Madhyamaka and Pudgalavāda. Pudgalavāda, like some minimalist views of the self, by analyzing the self as narrowly supervenient, is an attempt to save the self; the entity they posit is meant to be independent of verbal conventions, for instance. But Candrakīrti, by broadening the supervenience base, does not intend to provide an analysis of a self, or of the object of self-grasping; to the contrary, he is arguing that there is none. Instead, he is offering an account of a conventional person and arguing that the person, while conventionally real, is not the object of self-grasping. That object, while grasped, is entirely unreal. The person as it exists could never be that object. While it is often hard to see the metaphysical distance between Pudgalavāda and Madhyamaka—which, after all, accepts a conventionally real person—when we put it in terms of this distinction between supervenience bases, and so in terms of the direction of determination between ontology and convention, the difference appears stark, as it did to Buddhist philosophers in India.

While this critique of Pudgalavāda is important, Madhyamaka arose primarily as a reaction against the Abhidharma project, and it is to that critique that we now turn. Mādhyamikas targeted the reductive eliminativism of Abhidharma metaphysics. They argued that reduction is not elimination and that the very processes to which the Abhidharmikas reduced the self were real enough to preserve everything that Buddhism aimed at rejecting. That is, they argued that the real object of negation in an analysis of the self is intrinsic identity. The Abhidharmikas, in reducing the self to a series of *dharmas* that themselves have intrinsic identity, thus failed to eliminate the most important object of negation. Moreover, to the degree to which the members of such a continuum are taken to be ultimately real, that continuum is itself ultimately real, and the claim that the self is merely that continuum retains too much reality for Buddhist comfort.

Mādhyamikas therefore argued instead that there is no self at all. Instead, the linguistic conventions and cognitive capacities the self is meant to underwrite—to the extent that they are justified or real—are *mere* conventions, with their reality and truth amounting only to conventional truth. The entities to which they appear to refer are at best mere fictions, or deceptive cognitive constructions. And this is the space, for instance, between a Mādhyamika such as Śāntarakṣita and contemporary minimalists, despite the appearance of a close kinship between them. While minimalists are minimalists about a self, Mādhyamikas are eliminativists about the self, while realists about persons.

In *Introduction to the Middle Way*, the locus classicus for this discussion, Candrakīrti, after an interesting reprise of the chariot analogy and a systematic reply to a number of Buddhist and non-Buddhist conceptions of the self (see Huntington and Wangchen 1987 and Mipham 2005 for good English translations) summarizes his Madhyamaka analysis as follows (I include the most crucial root verses and some of Candrakīrti's autocommentary):

150. Therefore, the basis of self-grasping is not an entity.
It is neither identical to nor different from the aggregates.
The aggregates are neither its basis nor does it possess them.
It exists insofar as it is established on the basis of the aggregates.

How is it that it is said here merely to arise in dependence on the aggregates? We maintain that it exists insofar as it is not analyzed, within the framework of conventional truth. Just as even though we say such things as "neither without a cause, nor arising from self..." in the context of dependent designation, we say that this arises from that in order

> to avoid error, we say that the self is merely designated on the basis of the aggregates in the context of mundane convention. That is, the self is seen only in the context of convention.

Here Candrakīrti employs the framework of the two truths from a Madhyamaka perspective. Note that he takes conventional existence to depend on ordinary, everyday verbal and other conventions, not on any analysis—not on a developed ontology. (Compare Wittgenstein on games or on standing "roughly there." (*Philosophical Investigations* §70–71)) To reject those conventions would not be to be more precise; it would be to be in error. But the consequence of this is that an entity that exists in this way does not have clear identity conditions, and does not stand in fundamental explanatory relationships. It is merely conventional.

> 151. Like a chariot, the self is not different from its parts.
> Nor is it non-different, nor does it possess them.
> It is neither in the parts nor are the parts in it.
> It is neither the mere collection of the parts, nor their configuration.

Here Candrakīrti is summing up what is known as "the sevenfold analysis," his partition of the space of possible relations a thing can have to its parts. This analytical strategy is a central part of his own appropriation of the chariot example from *The Questions of King Milinda*. A thing can be identical to it parts or different from them; it can possess them; it can contain them or be contained by them; it can be the collection of the parts, or the parts configured.

So, as Candrakīrti discusses the chariot in the preceding verses, he argues that the chariot can't be identical to its parts (for then even a heap of unassembled parts would be a chariot); can't be different from them (because if you take them all away it vanishes); can't possess them (because then it would be a distinct entity over and above them—that is, even though we can say correctly in Sanskrit, Tibetan or in English that the chariot *has* two wheels, an axle, and other such parts, this should not be taken to mean that there is an entity, distinct *from* those parts, that possesses them, as for instance the Nyāya argued); doesn't contain them (for the same reason); is not contained by them (since when you have the parts, you just have the parts, not some other thing); isn't the mere collection (since you could replace parts but have what would count conventionally as the same chariot, and you would still face the problem that the chariot would be identical with the heap of chariot parts on the ground); and it isn't the parts in configuration, since the configuration changes as the chariot moves, and once again, parts can be replaced.

> 158. Even though in the context of everyday life
> Its existence cannot be established through sevenfold analysis,
> In everyday life, without any analysis at all
> It is accepted that it exists in dependence on its parts.

> ...In this context, on the basis of what is accepted in ordinary life, it is obvious that they exist, because one can refer to chariots, and that is all there is to it. Even though they are nothing but nominal referents, since, without any analysis they are accepted in everyday life, we maintain that they exist.

> 159. This very thing has parts and pieces;
> This very chariot is called the agent.
> According to ordinary people it is the appropriator.
> Don't forsake the conventions of ordinary life!

> The opposite of ordinary life is reality. Even though the conventional phenomena of ordinary life when analyzed are found not to exist, when not analyzed they are accepted, and therefore exist in that sense....

In these verses and the commentary on them Candrakīrti is once again emphasizing that conventional existence is indeed a *mode of existence*, not an *alternative* to existence. Since nothing actually exists in any other way, this is the only way things can exist. Nonetheless, to exist in this way is not to have the definite and precise ontological status that one might expect from something for which one could provide a final conceptual analysis.

> 162. In the same way, since they are accepted in ordinary life,
> We even accept the self as the appropriator
> In dependence on the aggregates, the elements
> And the six sense faculties.

> 163. Nonetheless, since there is no such entity,
> It is neither dependent nor independent;
> Neither momentary nor permanent; neither arisen nor ceased.
> It is neither existent nor non-existent; neither identical nor different.

Even though we have a set of conventions for talking about ourselves and others, it does not follow that there are entities that correspond to the pronouns and nouns we use. These terms function like those in fictional discourse, and so when we ask certain questions—particularly philosophical questions—about them, there are no answers that can satisfy us.

> 164. The self is that to which beings constantly
> Develop the attitude of grasping to 'I' and 'mine'.
> The self arises from the grasping to 'I' and 'mine'
> Taken for granted without analysis it exists only as a result of confusion. (2009, 252–257 passim.)

Here Candrakīrti closes by connecting the self both as effect and as cause to the self-grasping that is part of primal confusion, and hence to soteriological concerns. It is taking the bases of designation of our nouns and pronouns to be more than that—to be such things as selves—that gives rise to the reification that leads us to worry about the nature of the self in the first place. And that reification in turn leads to a more rigid sense of the reality of the self, and a way of taking up with the world that distinguishes between self and other, and that relates to everything—from our own bodies and thoughts to our friends, homelands and possessions and to those of others—as *ours*: I take this body to be *mine*; I take some people as *my* acquaintances; others as strangers to *me*; there are places *I* have been, and those *I* have not. An odd way to think that reality is structured, on reflection, but one that becomes instinctive, Candrakīrti thinks, once we enter the framework of a real self.

This Madhyamaka view, on the other hand, was regarded itself as too extreme, too nihilistic and too explanatorily impotent by many Yogācārins. They argued that while the self posited by the orthodox schools is certainly nonexistent, an evolving, constantly changing series of interdependent processes cannot explain the continuity, specificity and lucid nature of consciousness. They posited instead a primal foundation consciousness (*ālaya-vijñāna/kun gzhi [kunshi]*) as the basis of the evolving mental stream, and as the locus of the causal potencies that give rise to it. Philosophers such as Asaṅga and Vasubandhu developed rich phenomenological accounts of perception, affect and consciousness according to which virtually all of our cognitive life is afflicted by illusion, including the sense that the self we project is the real, continuing, substantial self. We will consider this illusion further in the next two chapters.

On the other hand, they argued, even those illusions require a basis in something real. That underlying reality, or foundation consciousness, they argue, provides the perspective from which those illusions are experienced, as well as the continuity and individuation so hard to recover from causal streams alone. The theory of the foundation consciousness—which we might conceive as a Buddhist unconscious—posited a set of potentials imprinted in that level of consciousness. When these potentials are triggered by sensation, they result in the production of such things as full-fledged perceptions, desires, intentions, and so on.

It is important to see that the foundation consciousness is not held to be a self in this tradition (though Madhyamaka critics of Yogācāra such as Candrakīrti argued that it might as well be one), but rather a continuum of unconscious processes and a repository of causal chains linking past to present and future that underlie conventional personal identity and that gives rise to experience. That experience is structured by the framework of subject and object, and the projected subjectivity in turn gives rise to the illusion of self. We will return to this framework in much more detail in chapter 6, below. Even this tradition, while demanding a more robust account of the basis of imputation of self, regards the self as an illusion.

We might therefore say that within the Buddhist tradition, debates surrounding the self all concern the limits of minimality, and the precise object of negation of the phrase "no self." All parties agree that no robust sense of self answers to anything real (and note that minimalists such as Hutto or Thompson would agree); all agree that we are *in some sense* nothing but streams of causally connected psychophysical events and processes (and again, many contemporary minimalists would agree). But all also agree that that there is a robust, persuasive and well-entrenched illusion that we are more than that. All agree that that illusion must be dispelled. But all agree that some account must survive of our ordinary psychological lives, which, after all, are the basis of the problem Buddhism sets out to solve—that of suffering—and of the solution if offers: liberation from primal confusion. And here the Buddhist parts company with the minimalist, wanting not to restructure our talk about selves, but rather to dispel the illusion that anything at all answers to that term.

This sense that the illusion of self underlies all of suffering is nicely captured by the 20th-century Japanese Buddhist philosopher Nishida Kitaro:

> As individuals in this world, our selves are always thoroughly self-contradictory. Therein lie the primary and fundamental dilemmas of human existence. This also constitutes the predicament of the world. We penetrate the root of our own self-contradiction; this way we win true life from the standpoint of absolutely contradictory self-identity.... Self-cultivation constitutes...what Dōgen as the method of meditation that "casts off body and mind." (from "The Problem of Japanese Culture" in Edelglass and Garfield 2009, 363–364)

Nishida's prose is not always immediately transparent. But in the context of our exploration of earlier Buddhist approaches to the self, this statement is clear. To take ourselves as entities, as opposed to as mere conventional designations, is to plunge into incoherence. Only when we cease that process of reification—the cessation Dōgen describes as the "casting off of body and mind"—can we see ourselves as we truly are: on the one hand as nonexistent as anything can be, that is, as fictional entities; and on the other hand, as real as anything can be: as conventional entities in conventional reality.

## 3. A Dialogue

Now, if we look back at the question regarding the reality and/or nature of the self and of illusions of self with a more binocular view, bringing together the questions that are at the center of concerns in the West and those at the center of Buddhist concerns, we might identify a set of core issues, the real issues that matter when we ask what we take the self to be, whether there is such a thing, what else there might be. We must account first of all for our sense of ego-identity. That is, we must take it as a datum, that at least pre-reflectively, we take ourselves to be persistent individuals who are the subjects of our experience and the agents of our actions. That central, distinct mode of being for ourselves demands explanation, even if it is only an appearance.

We have seen that the Buddhist tradition offers approaches to this problem. We must distinguish two different senses of ego-identity. First, there is the reification of a substantial self that persists in time. To account for that sense is to account for a persistent illusion. The tradition is virtually unanimous that the origins of this illusion lie in an innate cognitive reflex of reification, homologous with that which leads us to reify external objects, and to confuse our representations with reality as it is. But second, there is the conventional reality of the persistence of conventional persons in time, and of the causal continuities that enable memory, intention, ordinary awareness and social life. That, all Buddhist philosophers insist, is also explicable, though as we have seen, there is less unanimity in the tradition regarding its possible explanation. Abhidharmikas offer a reductive explanation; Mādhyamikas offer a fictionalist account according to which our explanatory spade is turned at the level of brute convention; Yogācārins argue that the continuity is provided by a persistent flow of unconscious processes.

Second, we must explain the temporality of our existence, including the possibility of memory, of anticipation and intention, and our ability to represent the entire manifold of temporal experience as episodes in temporal relation to one another (the Kantian synthesis through schemata). That is, we must be able to explain why, instead of a sequence of experiences of moments, we experience a sequence of moments in time. Buddhist responses to this demand follow closely those to the demand for an explanation of ego-identity over time. The bases of imputation that ground the conventions for identity also provide our sense of temporality. In unifying our past and our future moments into single conventional continuants, we thereby temporalize our experience.

Third, we must explain why even at a moment, to continue the Kantian language, we experience not a manifold of intuitions, but an intuition of a manifold. We must solve the binding problem and explain why it is that we experience coherent objects and not simply qualities, even located qualities. Here, I think that the Buddhist tradition is largely silent. Not completely silent: There are words to describe the fact that we have cognitive processes that unify our experience and project representations of objects and an inter-related world. That is what the *skandha* of perception is for; that is partly what the innate predispositions posited by Yogācāra theory in the foundation consciousness are meant to explain. But Buddhist philosophy is an old tradition, and the solution to this problem is empirical, not conceptual; those experimental resources are only now available to us.

Fourth, we must explain why we are immune to error through misidentification. What is it about us that engenders the impossibility of taking our mental states to be those of another? This demand in turn raises the demand of working out what the factors are that constitute us as individuals. To put this another way, these two joint demands—on any account of what we are and of what we take ourselves to be—amount to the need to provide an account of what underpins both the ascription of identity to us by others and our own apprehension of our own identity. Even if that identity is *constructed*, or even *fictitious*, and so must be *explained away*, its apprehension is a reality that must be *explained*.

That fictitious identity, achieved through the process called *ahaṃkāra* or self-construction, is frequently characterized by Buddhist philosophers on two dimensions: *I* and *mine* (*ātman/ātmīya* or *bdag/bdag gi ba [dakgiwa]*). That is, to posit the self is not only to grasp one's own identity as that of a substantial subjective ego, but also to grasp one's intentional objects and more generally the world one inhabits, as existing in relation to that self. When I grasp myself as the substantial referent of *I*, I also grasp my body, my possessions, my friends and family, and my world in general as *mine*. These two self-graspings are taken by many Buddhists as being inextricably bound with one another. Thompson (2007) reflects this connection in his own account of selfhood and its intentional structure:

> When I pick up a bottle and grasp it with my hands, I experience the bottle as other to me, but the feeling of grasping the bottle is immediately

> and noninferentially experienced as mine. The intentional object of my tactile experienced is the bottle, but at the same time I live through my grasping feeling in a nonintentional (non-object-directed) manner. To experience the feeling as mine I do not have to identify it as mine. Rather, the feeling comes with an intrinsic "mine-ness" or "first-person givenness" or "ipseity" (I-ness) that constitutes its subjectivity. (2007, 261)

Thompson parses the correlativity these "two self-graspings" in terms of the need to posit a self if we are to experience objects around as "mine." This differs only in direction of explanation from the Buddhist account according to which once we posit the self, we necessarily regard everything else in relation to it. But he also, as a minimalist, takes it for granted that this is the primordial structure of our reality, something to be explained. From a Madhyamaka or Yogācāra point of view, however, that begs the question. For what Thompson takes as self-evidently accurate as an account of the world and our experience of it, the Mādhyamika or Yogācārin takes as an illusion, something to be explained *away*.

Here, if we follow the Mahāyāna account of innate mechanisms of reification coupled with social conventions for the aggregation of causal continua into wholes, we see the outlines of an answer to the question with which Thompson challenges us: Why do I ascribe my experiences to me, and not to someone else, or as the experiences of nobody in particular? The answer from the Mahāyāna side is simple: the mechanisms that cause me to posit a self take as their causal basis these very experiences. I do not first experience a self, and then experience experiences and wonder whether they are associated. I first *have experiences*, and use them to construct a representation of a self, and representations of objects as connected to that self as mine.

The explanation of that construction is psychological, and here there may be little distance between the metaphysical outlines of a Buddhist answer and the kind of enactivist, embodied answer Thompson's work so persuasively suggests. Other persons do the same. And our ascriptions of identity to one another rely on much broader social conventions, for we do not experience others' psychological continua. We rely on criteria of bodily and behavioral causal continuity in those cases. But in either case, what we are explaining is not the nature of a self, or the fact that the objects in its experience are *its*, but the mechanisms by which the *illusion* of a self and the illusion of that orientation are constructed in a world in which they have no fundamental existence.

In sum, when we ask about the reality and nature of the self, whether within a Western or a Buddhist tradition, we are asking the two most fundamental questions of the metaphysics of the person: what is the nature of our being, and what is its source? And Buddhist thought has a great deal to contribute to our effort to formulate and to answer these questions. To be sure, it does not deserve to be the *only* voice in this conversation, and it may not in the end prove to be the most *influential* voice, but it is an important voice.

This is so for several reasons. First, as we have seen, there is a matter of philosophical and analytical experience. Buddhists, as we have seen, simply have been thinking hard about the nature of the self and illusions of self for a long time, in dialogue with self-realists, and in an internal dialogue aimed at sorting out the most plausible form of minimalism about the self. Buddhist thought has also attended with great care to the phenomenology of subjectivity as well as its metaphysics, and the complex relationship between phenomenology and metaphysics in this domain. When we are considering the nature of subjectivity, this connection is very intimate indeed. After all, if what constitutes the self is its point of view, or subjectivity, and if what constitutes subjectivity is a certain kind of phenomenological perspective and relation to the objective world, a distinction between the metaphysics of the self and the phenomenology of selfhood may in fact be impossible to draw.

But beyond an argument from long experience, there are specific aspects of the Buddhist approach to the self that render its voice distinctive and valuable. First, Buddhist thought has emphasized more than most Western thought[14] the ethical, affective and social dimensions of the representation of the self. Positing a self, as Śāntideva (8th century CE) notes, lies at the foundation of egoism and extirpating that sense of self is the foundation for the cultivation of care.

For instance, in chapter VI, on patience (verses 22–31) of *How to Lead an Awakened Life (Bodhicaryāvatāra)*, a text to which we will return at greater length in chapter 9, Śāntideva argues that anger requires both a personal object and a representation of harm to oneself as a person. Neither of these can be justified, though, if there is no self. So, absent a self to be harmed, there is no cause for anger, and absent a self in another, there is no object at which anger can rationally be directed. Śāntideva points out that for any action taken against oneself that is a putative justification of anger, the body of the perpetrator and indeed the intentions are simply caused by countless prior causes and conditions. One might, he argues, with equal justification be angry with the stick with which one is beaten as the arm that wields it, or

14. The great exception here is Hume, as Annette Baier has emphasized (1991, 2008).

the intention that impels the arm, or some other causal antecendent. One will never find a core self that originates the harm.

Moreover, Śāntideva argues, the drive to posit the self has an affective ground. It is not only the basis of attraction and aversion, but the consequence of attraction and aversion as well. Inasmuch as the self is constituted through grasping both 'I' and 'mine', it is constituted not only by my sense of who I am, but also by my sense of what belongs to me, and of what does not; of what I take on board as part of myself, and what I do not. I do not first identify myself and then determine what I want and what repels me; those affective sets are causally and constitutively operative in the construction of my self in the first place.[15] And given the ineliminable role of language and social conventions, it is also constituted by what others ascribe to or withhold from me.

On a Madhyamaka account, therefore, our construction of a self, or our exaggeration of the reality, primacy or substantiality of the self, does not simply have ethical or affective *consequences*, although, to be sure, on a this view it does; more importantly, part of the *explanation* of the posit of the self is affective. For this reason, the phenomenology that underlies our determination to regard ourselves as determinate centers of experience and agency has a moral dimension. Our innate affective reflexes lead us to take ourselves as centers of experience, as independent agents, and as objects of special concern. Part of the point, then, of moral cultivation on a Buddhist view is to reduce this kind of hypostasization.

Moreover, on this view, positing the self is a matter of convention, in a number of important senses, and conventions are inevitably social. On this picture, societies do not emerge from an association of independently constituted selves; instead the constitution of selves and cultures are mutually dependent, with our conceptions of who we are and our identities depending as much on others as on ourselves. This last issue leads us to another contribution Buddhism brings to the table: a sense that the question of the reality of the self is not one that admits of a univocal answer. As a consequence, a Buddhist perspective, in which we do not presuppose the reality of a self, but in which we take for granted the conventional reality of persons, leads us to ask questions about personal identity in a very different register.

Buddhist analyses make use of the devices of the *catuṣkoti*, or four-cornered approach to semantic evaluation, and of the two truths, or two realities, as analytic approaches. And these devices are brought into effective use by philosophers in the Madhyamaka and Yogācāra traditions especially in the context

15. Once again, the comparison to Hume's account of the role of the passions in the representation of the self in Book II of the *Treatise* is apposite.

of the discussion of the self. Buddhist analyses hence offer ways to think of the self as *neither* existent nor nonexistent—as the wrong kind of thing to figure in existential questions in virtue of being merely a posit of construction. They also offer ways of seeing the self as *both* existent and nonexistent, as conventionally real, but as ultimately nonexistent. (For more on *catuṣkoti* see chapter 8.)

This range of analytical possibilities can provide a great deal more texture to discussions of the self, adding a dimension of modality as an alternative to the dimension of substantiality that seems to underlie discussions of minimality versus maximality. That is, instead of focusing on questions concerning that in which the self consists, or on its reality, a Buddhist analysis suggests that we focus on the manner in which our sense of ourselves is constructed, on the consequences of those processes and of that sense, and on how we might best conceive of the nature of our lives on rational reflection.

This suggests in turn a different direction of fit between conceptions of personhood and persons. Instead of taking it for granted that there is something in which we, or persons, consist, and then working to develop a metaphysical account of that kind of existent, a Buddhist analysis suggests that we determine what kind of conception of personhood and of human life is maximally beneficial and rational to adopt, and construct ourselves in that image. This might seem radical, but only to one in the grip of a metaphysics that takes personal substance for granted. Dropping that prejudice, and detaching the idea of a person from that of a self, might be the first step to clarity about matters of personhood.

Consideration of the metaphysics of the self is always incomplete if we do not consider the nature and status of consciousness. Indeed the self is often conceived—whether its reality is maintained or not, and regardless of its level of reality—as the seat of consciousness. It is thus to a consideration of debates about the nature of consciousness and Buddhist contributions thereto that we now turn.

# 5 CONSCIOUSNESS

Consciousness is perhaps the hottest of all hot topics in contemporary philosophy of mind. The range of accounts of consciousness on offer is breathtaking, as is the panoply of distinctions between different kinds of consciousness. To survey, let alone to adjudicate, the range of options would require a substantial volume of its own (and fortunately, there are many such substantial volumes, such as Blackmore 2004, Chalmers 2010, Block, Flanagan and Güzeldere 1997, Dennett 1991, Zelazo, Moscovitch and Thompson 2007). Since these volumes exist, I don't need to do that hard work here. Instead, I am going to rehearse what I see as the most important specific debates and alternatives, the complex set of presuppositions they involve and questions they raise.

As it is, this chapter addresses a range of issues, each of which might merit its own chapter, or indeed its own book. We will consider questions about the nature of perceptual experience, about the nature of introspection, the status of qualia and even the possibility of zombies! I don't pretend to offer the last word on any of these matters, or even the last word on the way that Buddhist philosophy can contribute to discussions about these matters. Instead, I want to draw attention to a thread that links them, and to the ways in which adding Buddhist fibers as we spin that thread can make it stronger. That thread is the understanding of what it is to say that we are conscious and what the nature of consciousness, in its various senses, might be.

## 1. Senses of *Consciousness*

There is a widely accepted distinction in the Western literature between two *senses* of the term "consciousness," that is, between what is I will call "access consciousness" and what is often called "phenomenal consciousness." By "access consciousness" I will mean *introspectibility*.[1] A psychological state or process is conscious in this sense if we are able to report on it, to take awareness of it as input into our reasoning processes. My belief that I am typing right now is access conscious in this sense. I can introspect and determine that I do believe this.

"Phenomenal consciousness," on the other hand, denotes something more like the felt character of experience, often denoted by the problematic phrase, due to Thomas Nagel, "what it is like" to be in a particular state. So, unlike my belief, which doesn't feel like anything, my typing right now is phenomenally conscious. It feels like something to be typing. At least to a first approximation, an approximation from which we may backtrack later. Phenomenal consciousness might also be called qualitative consciousness, and that of which we are phenomenally conscious is sometimes referred to as "qualitative character," or even hypostasized into *qualia*.

This distinction is already a bit too crude, however, even to capture the questions debated in this literature.[2] To these we might add two more senses. We might want a term to denote the property of being responsive to a stimulus, even if that responsiveness is not introspectible and has no phenomenal character. This might be the right way to think about low-level proprioception or our responsiveness to happenings on the road when our primary attention is on the radio news broadcast, and such things. Call this "responsive consciousness."

Finally, we might want to discuss the pre-reflective background horizon of awareness, or bare subjectivity, that many, especially in the Husserlian tradition, regard as the most basic precondition of any kind of conscious activity. This kind of consciousness might be thought of as the non-thematized awareness of ourselves as subjects of our conscious states, and of those states as *our* states. To be conscious in this sense is simply to be a subject and, at least pre-reflectively or transcendentally, to take oneself as a subject. In order not to beg any philosophical or historical questions regarding the precise character

1. It is important to note that I am using this term not in the original sense in which it was introduced by Block (1995), but in a sense that has become more common since then. Block used it to denote access to external information, as in the case of blindsighted individuals, who in *his* sense have access to information about objects in their environment despite lacking any of what he called (and what I will call) *phenomenal consciousness*. I instead use this term to denote access to one's own inner states. Below I will call that to which Block refers as *access* consciousness as *responsive* consciousness. I think that this vocabulary is more intuitive, and accords more with ordinary usage these days.

2. And of course the contemporary literature is replete with alternative classifications of kinds of consciousness.

of whatever might be denoted by "consciousness" when used in this sense, let us call this "subjective consciousness."[3]

So, when we ask what consciousness *is*, how and whether it can be explained, what its relationship is to the body, whether it is discursive or not, or even whether there is such a thing, we need to be clear in each case and each context, in which of these *four* (and more may be forthcoming) senses we are using the term. It is one thing merely to be subjectively conscious. We might experience this in the barest moment of awakening in the morning. It is another to be responsive: we orient toward a sound that we have not even registered in any introspectible awareness; the sound then acquires a qualitative existence in our mental life, as in the case of the sound of our alarm clock and we are phenomenally conscious of it. A moment later we find that we can introspect and report on our state of mind—all of this is now accessible.

It might be tempting to think of this unfolding of awareness in the first few seconds of our day as a simple increase in a single dimension—as we wake up, we simply become progressively *more* conscious. If, however, this set of distinctions among *senses* of the term "consciousness" (leaving aside the question of whether the term in any or all of these senses denotes anything at all—at this point we are simply mapping the way these terms are used in contemporary philosophical discourse) is right, then we aren't talking about the same thing when we say: first I was simply conscious, then conscious of something, I know not what, then of a sound, and then that I was waking up. Instead, new kinds of relations between subject and object (or at least kinds of states of subjects), perhaps interrelated, emerge as our engagement with our environment, inner and outer, becomes progressively more complex.

It is also worth noting that responsive and access consciousness are each characterized as explicitly *relational*. That is, when we say that we are conscious of a particular stimulus in the sense that we are responsive to it, or that we are conscious of an inner state in the sense that we can introspect and report it, we are explicitly describing relations we as subjects bear to particular objects. There is not even a whiff of an idea that we are describing a monadic or intrinsic property of subjectivity itself. And indeed, the relation we describe here is not even prima facie different from that we would describe between a thermostat and the temperature of a room in the case of responsiveness, or that between a fuel gauge and a fuel tank in a car in the case of the second.

3. This is sometimes called *creature consciousness*. But this term may beg questions regarding whether there is a common phenomenon in this neighborhood across phylogenetic types.

It is tempting to respond to this observation, as have many who are interested in the nature of consciousness, by saying that these kinds of consciousness are not what we are *really* talking about when we ask about the nature of consciousness—in the now familiar jargon due to Chalmers (2010), they do not pose the *hard problem*. Zombies might be conscious in *these senses*. The hard problem of explaining consciousness, both analytically and scientifically, this line of thinking continues, concerns phenomenal and subjective consciousness. These are the kinds of consciousness, Zombologists argue, that we have, but that Zombies—beings behaviorally and functionally identical to us, but without any genuine inner life or phenomenology—lack. There is something that it is like to be us, they urge, and that something is captured by our experience of ourselves as subjects and by the phenomenal character of our perceptual and affective experience.

This line of argument has a kind of plausibility to it, and we will return to it below, with attention both to the conceptions of consciousness at work and with respect to the possibility of zombies. But for now, it is worth registering one preliminary reason for skepticism about the wedge the argument requires between responsive and access consciousness, on the one hand, and phenomenal and subjective consciousness, on the other. That wedge, as we have seen, finds its narrow edge in the distinction between relational and non-relational senses of consciousness. If we are to take this seriously, we have to take seriously the idea of a fundamental property of our mind that is intrinsic to it, a kind of mere objectless awareness. This is not as obviously a given, a self-presenting explanandum, as it might appear to be.

In this context, it is worth considering the complex role of affect in consciousness, another matter about which we will see that Buddhism has much to say. In contemporary discussions of consciousness in the West, affect often enters into the picture as an *object* of awareness, typically of phenomenal consciousness.[4] On this view, represented perhaps most prominently by Chalmers (2010), our affective states have a phenomenal feel, and we are conscious of these much as we are conscious of sensory qualities.[5,6]

There is an immediate problem with this view, suggested by Buddhist analyses, to which we will turn below. On the one hand, we should countenance

4. The exception is that body of literature deriving from Heidegger's attention to mood as structuring subjective consciousness.

5. But see Harman (1990, 1996), for instance, for a very different view of qualia, not as direct objects of consciousness, but as aspects of a transparent relation to distal objects.

6. Of course they are also the objects of access and responsive consciousness, but that is beside the present point.

the possibility of affect that is neither accessible to introspection nor phenomenally present—what we might call in a Freudian moment, "subconscious" affect. Emotions that circulate below the radar may nonetheless determine much of our conscious life. And this leads us to the second problem: It may be more important to think of affect as a cause, rather than an effect or an object of the character of our conscious engagement with the world. As noted in passing above, this is very much part of a Heideggerian (and Freudian) picture in the West, but is in tension with views according to which we have privileged access to our affective lives, and so according to which all emotion is to some degree accessible. It is also a central part of a Buddhist understanding of the relationship between the five *skandhas* and of the nature of the origin of *dukkha*.

Buddhist discussions of consciousness feel radically different from contemporary Western discussions. Nonetheless, we will see that they can be valuable sources of viable alternatives, both with respect to positions on the topic and, more fundamentally, with respect to how questions and debates are framed in the first place. But first, we should be clear about terminological issues, as it is easy for participants in these atemporal, cross-cultural discussions either to talk past each other or to find their positions seriously distorted by misleading translation. We will have to acknowledge that to a certain extent Buddhist and contemporary Western discussions of consciousness occur in different intellectual contexts and are pursued for different reasons, in different vocabularies. But if we are clear about this, we will still find important points of contact.

## 2. The Buddhist Conceptual Landscape

It is methodologically useful to recall that our own philosophical vocabulary, as well as that of any other tradition, often structures, rather than reflects, the ontology of a domain or inquiry. This is particularly true of the psychological domain, as Wittgenstein notes in *Philosophical Investigations* and as Sellars notes in "Empiricism and the Philosophy of Mind." In this domain, we become so accustomed to the use of a language, and a way of mapping the inner domain, that we take it for granted that the language we use and in which we think carves the inner world at its joints, joints that are simply apparent to our introspective gaze. In doing so, we forget the origins of our terms, which often lie in theoretical frameworks we explicitly reject, and forget that other traditions carve the mind in radically different ways, which they equally take as obvious. Taking another tradition seriously hence requires taking its vocabulary seriously and adopting a conversation horizon that allows us to problematize our own—and their—way of taking the landscape.

Let us begin with some basic Sanskrit terminology and rough glosses to get a sense of the lexical terrain and move from there to a more conceptual overview. There is a plethora of Sanskrit terms (and Pāli, Chinese and Tibetan equivalents or rough equivalents—for the sake of convenience I will focus on the Sanskrit here) that denote phenomena in the conceptual neighborhood of the already semantically complex English "consciousness." I choose a few that are most relevant to the present discussion.

The most central term is probably *vijñāna* and the various compounds in which it figures. The term has a complex semantic range across Indian philosophical literature. We can read it as indicating *that which enables knowledge.* In Buddhist literature its most important locus for present purposes is in its denotation of the fifth *skandha*, or aggregate underlying personhood. The functions of that *skandha* are manifold, including conceptual thought, judgment, attention, reflection, etc...

We can get a sense of how *vijñāna* functions when we see it in the context of the psychology of the *skandhas*, in which we begin with the action of the physical body (*rūpa*), as in the functioning of a sense organ, leading to sensation (*vedanā*), which in turn gives rise to perception (*saṃjñā*)[7]—note again the root *jñā* (cognate with the *kn* or *gn* in terms like *knowledge* or *gnosis* in European languages, denoting awareness)—in which that which is sensed is initially, but in a sense *preconsciously*, brought to cognitive determinacy, and as a possible object of knowledge through the mediation of our affective and habitual predispositions, which, again, function *prior* to consciousness.

A second set of terms relevant to this discussion includes *saṃveda* (a term that figures prominently in the compound *svasaṃvedanā*, denoting reflexive awareness, to be discussed below) and *anubhava*. *Saṃveda* connotes perceptual awareness, the kind of consciousness of something we have when we perceive it, a consciousness that is both phenomenal and recognitional. When I am conscious of something in this sense, I both sense it and categorize it. *Anubhava* has a similar semantic range, denoting consciousness of something immediately present.

*Samprajaña*, a term often translated as *mindfulness*, is used to denote attentiveness to one's own current state, a higher-order, introspective awareness. By distinguishing *samprajaña* from *saṃveda* or *anubhava*, the Sanskrit

7. This term as well deserves comment. *Saṃjñā*, unlike *perception*, connotes a kind of discriminative awareness, and even a linguistic, or quasi-linguistic awareness, what we would call *perception-as*, as opposed to a mere undifferentiated awareness.

Buddhist tradition presupposes that it makes sense to talk about qualitatively rich perceptual consciousness, consciousness capable of guiding behavior, without presupposing that one is explicitly aware that one is having such consciousness.

One final term in this large family may be relevant for present purposes. *Cetanā* is most often translated as *intention* and figures most prominently in discussions of action and responsibility.[8] And this is fair enough. But it shares a good part of the broad philosophical semantic range of the technical English (Latin) term *intentional*, indicating as well directedness on an object. *Cetanā* can hence also refer to the state of being conscious *of* something in the barest sense of being directed toward it, of registering or being responsive to it, tracking the sense of *responsive consciousness*. (See Meyers 2010, Heim 2013.)

I belabor this range of terms because it is important to remember that simply translating a conversation or a literature from a canonical Buddhist language into English, and using the term *consciousness* to translate all of the terms it most naturally translates, can mislead the unwary into thinking that there is a single sense of "consciousness" at work in the Buddhist literature. Or, with equal infidelity to the tradition, one might simply presume that the same set of distinctions among senses of *consciousness* in English is replicated in the relevant Buddhist language or literature. We must be alert to the fact that the distinctions encoded at the outset in language serve in part to define the conceptual landscape, and that the Buddhist and Western conceptual landscapes may not be entirely commensurable.

## 3. Consciousness and the Self—Buddhist Perspectives

When consciousness is identified as one of the *skandhas*, it is, as we have noted, *vijñāna* that is meant. But one of the questions of importance in Buddhist philosophy of mind, as we saw in the previous chapter, is what constitutes the basis of designation of the self. In a Buddhist framework, as we have seen, there is no self. But this is not, of course, a simple matter. After all, from a Buddhist perspective, there is a persistent illusion of self to be explained as well as a reasonable convention of individuation permitting pronominal and nominal reference, ascription of agency and other relevant personal conventions. We must therefore ask what the role of *vijñāna* is in the propagation

8. This term can also have the sense of *volition*, or intention to act. And so it shares the ambiguity of *intention* in English. But that sense is not relevant to the present discussion. For more on the range of the term, see Meyers (2010) and Heim (2013).

of the illusion of self as well as what its role is in the establishment of these conventions.

It may seem more plausible to think that our conventions of identification that allow us to designate ourselves and others, to re-identify persons over time, to ground morality and so forth—all that constitute persons in the everyday world—take ordinary *vijñāna,* or the aggregate of conscious cognitive processes, as the basis of designation. That is, one might think that even though this *skandha* is not the illusory self against which so many Buddhist arguments and analyses are ranged, it is the conventional self left untouched by those analyses.

But that has to be wrong. After all, especially in the identification of others, but also in reference to ourselves, our bodies (*rūpa*), personalities (*saṃskāra*) and feelings (*vedanā*) play significant roles as well. The whole point of *skandha* theory in the first place is that the basis of designation of self even if it is intrapersonal, is not a single thing but a complex, interwoven set of continua. This insight raises the possibility that much of who we are is unconscious and so the possibility that our focus on the conscious in our self-conception may be unwarranted.

There is another reason to think that from any Buddhist point of view, to take the *skandha* of *vijñāna* to constitute a self, or even to be the referent of a name or personal pronoun, would be—although tempting—a serious error. The *skandha* cannot be a genuine self because of its constant change and because of its dependence on the other skandhas. Most importantly, when we posit a self in the relevant sense, we posit it not *as vijñāna,* but rather as that which *has vijñāna,* as a subject more primordial than consciousness itself, modally independent of any particular *skandha.* As we pointed out in the previous chapter, the same consideration that shows that we don't identify ourselves with our bodies—the imaginability of a body transplant—applies to our minds.[9] Just as I can wish that I had the body of Usain Bolt, I can wish to have the mind of Stephen Hawking.

Yogācāra Buddhism, as noted in the previous chapter, does suggest a way in which a particular level of consciousness could be identified with the self, namely the *alaya-vijñāna,* or foundation consciousness. On certain Yogācāra

9. It is important to remember in this context, as we noted in that context, that the mere fact that we imagine such things is no guide to fundamental metaphysics. This doesn't entail that we are something entirely distinct from our body, our mind or our aggregates, only that when we take ourselves to be selves in that sense, these reveries seem to make sense. The imagination exercise, then, tells us a great deal about what we take ourselves to be, but nothing at all about what we actually are. This does not mean, however, that considerations of these exercises are metaphysically idle. When we are interested in what a self would be, it is essential to fix on the object of negation, to make it clear, even if our purpose is to demonstrate its nonexistence.

views, this is the basis of identity over time and the unified ground of all other conscious states. It is the pre-reflective ground of experience.[10] For this reason, in part, Mādhyamika philosophers such as Candrakīrti in India and Tsongkhapa in Tibet criticize this view as a smuggling of the self back into the basement after hard analysis has kicked it out of the front door. Yogācāra philosophers typically reply that the foundation consciousness is not a self in the pernicious sense—it is not an unchanging, substantial ground of experience; it is not that which we imagine ourselves to be in the act of self-grasping or in the narratives we tell about ourselves and the world; it is not even phenomenologically accessible. The self that is the object of negation of Buddhist analysis is a self like *that*.

If this is right, though, then even if the construct of the foundation consciousness made sense, it would not constitute an identification of consciousness *of any kind* with *self*. Buddhist reflection on consciousness also suggests that we are best not focusing on consciousness—in any sense—as a singular thing. Even the *skandha* of *vijñāna* decomposes on most Buddhist analyses into a number of different faculties. For each of the six perceptual faculties (the five external senses and the introspective faculty) there is a corresponding faculty of sensory consciousness.

On a standard Buddhist model, perception first involves physical contact of the organ with the sensory object, then the registration in the sense faculty of the perceptual object, and only finally the consciousness of the object. But that consciousness is particular to the relevant sensory faculty. Visual consciousness is a different faculty from auditory consciousness. The introspective consciousness, on this picture, unifies the deliverances of the sensory consciousnesses as it takes them as its proper object. (See the discussion of Śāntarakṣita on the unity of consciousness in the previous chapter.) But importantly, consciousness is not unitary; it is present in each sense faculty prior to the action of the sixth sense.

If we accept the *alaya-vijñāna* in addition to these so-called "evolving consciousnesses" as a more fundamental level of consciousness, things get even more complex. This level of consciousness, which we might characterize as pure subjectivity, is regarded by the Yogācāra as the unifying principle that gives rise to the other forms of consciousness and in which the consequences of actions and events are stored, with the potential to give rise to future episodes of consciousness. But it is not introspectible and is not the seat of the subjectivity of any particular conscious episode, but rather stands as a transcendental condition on any awareness being conscious at all. It is more like

10. Once again, it is worth recalling the similarity of this view to that of Husserl and his more recent followers, such as Zahavi (2004, 2005) and Thompson (2007).

the horizon provided by subjective consciousness, not something of which we are aware, but that in virtue of which we are aware.

On any Buddhist account, then, consciousness is neither singular, nor a monadic property, nor something that is simply present or not. It is a many-layered set of phenomena that are principally relational. Leaving the foundation consciousness aside for the moment, to be conscious is to be conscious of something. Consciousness is always a relation between a sensory faculty and its object. To understand consciousness is to understand that complex relation, the processes and conditions that make it possible, and those it in turn enables.

Even the foundation consciousness is, according to those who posit it, in ordinary circumstances relational in character.[11] It is described as a kind of consciousness because it is the metaphysical ground of the relation to the evolving consciousnesses as objects of introspection. It can be thought of as the possibility of taking those forms of consciousness as one's own.

## 4. Buddhist Rubber Hitting the Contemporary Road

David Chalmers lists a number of conscious phenomena that pose what he calls "easy problems" (2010, 3–13):

- The ability to discriminate, categorize and react to environmental stimuli
- The integration of information by a cognitive system
- The reportability of mental states
- The focus of attention
- The deliberate control of behavior
- The difference between wakefulness and sleep. (4)

These correspond, at least roughly, and probably exactly, to the second of the senses of "consciousness" scouted at the beginning of this chapter. Explaining them, Chalmers argues, is easy, because they are functional capacities that we can understand as being subserved by physical mechanisms. They contrast with the sense of "consciousness" in which the *hard* problem is posed:

> The really hard problem of consciousness is the problem of *experience.* When we think and perceive, there is a whirl of information processing, but there is also a subjective aspect. As Nagel (1974) has put it there

11. We leave aside here the hard-to-characterize state of awakening, in which that consciousness undergoes a complete transformation and becomes an objectless awareness.

> is *something that it is like* to be a conscious organism. This subjective aspect is experience. When we see, for instance, we *experience* visual sensations: the felt quality of redness, the experience of dark and light, the quality of depth in the visual field. Other experiences go along with perception in different modalities: the sound of a clarinet, the smell of mothballs. . . . What unites all of these states is that there is something that it is like to be in them. All of them are states of experience. (Chalmers 2010, 5)

The "hard problem"—explaining how experience is possible in a physical organism—Chalmers argues, is the problem of explaining consciousness in *this* sense. Seeing the problem as "hard" requires us to acknowledge two things: first, that the sense of *experience—of there being something that it is like to be in a state*—makes clear sense. Second, that it is possible to do all of the "easy to explain" things, and yet for it to be possible to differ from those with experience just in that one has *no* experience, the possibility of zombies.

We will come back to zombies below. But let us first consider the problem of understanding phenomenal experience, that the having of which is supposed to be like something. Of course there are many different theories on offer regarding the nature of such experience. But once again, Chalmers's account can be taken as paradigmatic for present purposes. Phenomenal experience, according to those who deploy this notion (whether perceptual or not)[12] involves the formation of phenomenal beliefs, which in turn involve the deployment of phenomenal concepts, concepts not of properties, but of the supposed inner correlates of those properties. Chalmers puts the point this way:

> Phenomenal beliefs always involve *phenomenal concepts*, concepts of the phenomenal character of experience. When one believes that one is having a red experience, one deploys a phenomenal concept of a red experience. The most important phenomenal concepts are those we acquire directly from having experiences with that sort of phenomenal character. For example, when one first learns what it is like to experience an orgasm, one acquires a phenomenal concept of the experience of orgasm. (251)
>
> . . .

12. Whether there is non-perceptual phenomenal experience is another fascinating question we will leave to one side, as it has no bearing on the issues at hand here.

> I look at a red apple and visually experience its color. This experience instantiates a phenomenal quality R, which we might call phenomenal redness. It is natural to say that I am having a red experience even though experiences are not red in the same sense in which apples are red. Phenomenal redness (a property of experiences or subjects of experience) is a different property from external redness (a property of external objects), but both are respectable properties in their own right. (254)

Perhaps the most important sentence to note here is the last. If we are to take phenomenal consciousness as a special kind of consciousness, not simply the awareness of properties in the external world, but awareness of a peculiar family of inner properties, there must be a difference between these phenomenal properties and the properties of external objects. This distinction, and the consequent positing of consciousness as a special singular phenomenon characterized by properties of the second type, demanding a special theory, is driven by the idea that there is nothing "that it is like" merely to *see* a patch of blue; a non-conscious zombie might see patches of blue. But there is something "that it is like" to *experience* seeing a patch of blue. This involves special inner states that are blue in a different sense, *phenomenally blue*.

Now, the idea that inner states have such properties as blueness, redness, or other such properites, albeit in some special sense, has legs in Western philosophy, and has properly been subjected to critique before. (See Sellars 1992a, b for an elegant discussion.) Indeed, many contemporary theorists of phenomenal properties argue that such properties as *phenomenal blueness* are only contingently related to *actual blueness*, and that terms such as *phenomenal blueness* are as semantically distant from such terms as *blueness* as the term *blunderbuss* is from *buss*. On this account, phenomenal properties are simply those of our inner states that are causally connected to typical causes of the properties whose names sound like them. I don't want to take us too far into this terrain, but suffice it to say that even if these accounts avoid the Sellarsian critique, they fall from that frying pan into the Wittgensteinian fire of critiques both of private language and of the very idea of special introspectible properties of inner processes. Now, these critiques may not be decisive, but they are weighty, and indeed, as Thurman (1980) has argued, both Candrakīrti and Tsongkhapa anticipate those critiques in precisely this context.

This thought—and the debate it occasions—has ancestry in the Indian and Tibetan Buddhist traditions. Dignāga and his followers in the Yogācāra tradition argued—against the earlier Vaibhāśika school's direct realist theory of perception—that perception must be mediated by a representation (*ākāra/*

*rnam pa [nampa]*) and that this representation is the intentional object (*artha/ don [dön]*) of a perceptual state. The perception of a patch of blue, on such a model, is the immediate apprehension of a representation that is blue. Dignāga puts the point this way: "What we call an *intentional object* is what a cognition ascertains to be the entity itself. This is because its representation arises.... An object produced by self-presenting awareness is understood as a percept" (*Autocommentary to Examination of the Percept* commentary on verse 1). Perception on Dignāga's model is always the immediate awareness of a representation; the qualities perceived are qualities not of external objects—indeed in this text he argues that they cannot be—but rather of internal representations.[13] His 18th-century Tibetan commentator Gungthang (Gun thang dkon mchog bstan pa'i sgron me) comments on this as follows:

> Suppose someone asks, "...[H]ow could [a representation] appear?" The representation does not appear as it exists. For example, when an image of the moon appears in a mirror, spatiality also appears. The moon appears to be different from its action of reflecting. Although it is apprehended with an appearance of externality, the object is that which exists internally. (4)

Gungthang's principal claim here is that according to Dignāga, even though we might think of distal objects as the objects of perception, the objects of immediate awareness are always representations. To the extent that distal objects figure at all in our consciousness, it is in virtue of the indirect relation they bear to us, mediated by these representations. On the other hand, Gungthang also emphasizes that the mode of appearance of these representations is itself deceptive: just as a reflection of the moon appears to be located in space, and not to be a mere process of reflection, our own representations appear to us to exist as internal objects that we observe, when in reality they are merely cognitive processes. Ngawang Dendar (Ngag dbang bstan dar), writing later in that century, amplifies the argument that perception engages immediately with representations and only immediately with their objects:

> Regarding the way in which the Sautrāntikas and more advanced schools maintain that cognition is representational, *Introduction to the*

13. The material in this discussion related to *Alaṃbanaparikṣā* and its commentaries is from as yet unpublished joint work with John Powers, John Makeham, Sonam Thakchöe, Douglas Duckwkorth, M David Eckel and Dan Lusthaus, supported by the Australian Research Council.

> *Middle Way* states, "Whatever the mind represents is its intentional object." [VI:13] When a representation of a blue intentional object arises for a visual cognition apprehending blue, because it thereby apprehends blue, it is said that there is an apprehension and an apprehender of blue. Other than by way of subjective cognition becoming like its object, there is absolutely no way for cognition to apprehend its object.
>
> For example, when a crystal is placed on a blue cloth, all facets of the crystal turn blue. In the same way, when a visual cognition apprehending blue sees blue, the color blue is transferred to the visual perspective and so the subjective visual cognition becomes just like the blue object. The visual cognition apprehending blue is referred to as "a visual cognition that arises as a representation of blue." This is the criterion for the direct apprehension of blue. (227–228)

Dendar emphasizes here that the consequence of this view is that the qualities we perceive—those of which we are immediately aware—are qualities of appearances, not of external things. It is qualitative blue, the blueness of an experience that I perceive, not any property of any external blue object. We will see soon enough that this view comes in both for extension and for critique in the Buddhist tradition. Some of the arguments and doctrines we will encounter will anticipate some we find in contemporary Western debates about phenomenal properties and phenomenal concepts. Some are unique to the Buddhist tradition. But all are bound up in a Buddhist context with a more general worry about the nature of consciousness itself, and it will be useful to put aside worries about the nature of phenomenal properties themselves for now and to explore the questions in the philosophy of mind they engender. Many are also bound up with issues concerning the epistemology of the inner.

## 5. Reflexivity, Consciousness and Self-Knowledge

Indian and Tibetan Buddhist philosophers share with their contemporary Western colleagues a concern for the structure of self-knowledge, and roughly the same range of positions that emerge in the West are found in Indian Buddhist debates. Moreover, just as we see in contemporary Western debates, the positions regarding the structure of self-knowledge do double duty as models of consciousness itself. We hence see reflexive models of self-consciousness and self-knowledge, higher-order thought models, higher-order perception models and self-luminosity models.

Reflexive models take consciousness always to involve two aspects: a directedness toward the manifest object of consciousness and a self-directed aspect that makes possible both knowledge of the conscious state itself and its status as a conscious, as opposed to an unconscious state. Higher order thought and higher order perceptual models take states to be conscious in virtue of other states that take them—either cognitively or perceptually—as their objects, and which enable our epistemic access to them. Self-luminosity models take conscious states to be primitively conscious and self-manifesting without being intentionally directed upon themselves, and without being the intentional objects of other states, revealing their subjectivity as a primitive property.

## *5.1 Reflexivity of Awareness*

The idea that perception is, *au fond*, an engagement with phenomenal properties, Dignāga and his followers realized, issues in an intriguing dilemma. Given that it is the perceptual engagement with phenomenal properties that is meant to be constitutive of consciousness, the apprehension of these phenomenal properties must either itself have phenomenal properties apprehended by a higher-order state in order for it to be conscious, or it must be reflexively conscious—conscious of itself at the same time that it is conscious of its perceptual object (*svasaṃvedena/svasaṃvittiḥ/rang rig*). Otherwise, phenomenal properties themselves would not be apprehended, and would constitute at best a mysterious fifth wheel in the explanation of perception. The latter position (anticipating that of Husserl, a position inspiring the work of Coseru 2012 and Zahavi 2004, 2005) is adopted by all Indian Yogācāra thinkers and Śāntarakṣita, and in Tibet by eminent Sakya scholars such as Gorampa and Sakya Chokden. The former position, prescient of that of Sellars and his followers, is adopted by most Indian Mādhyamikas and in Tibet by Geluk figures such as Tsongkhapa.

There are three principal arguments for the reflexivity of awareness in the Buddhist literature, two that seem unique to that tradition, and one that anticipates Husserl's argument for reflexivity pretty directly. Dignāga advances what has become known as the "memory argument" for reflexivity. He argues that when I remember yesterday's sunshine I remember *myself seeing yesterday's sunshine*. The memory of the sunshine and the memory of my seeing it are one and the same. Moreover, he argues, one cannot remember something of which one was not conscious. Therefore, since the memory of the sunshine and my seeing the sunshine are identical, and since my memory of the sunshine presupposes that I was aware of the sunshine, my memory of my apprehension of the sunshine presupposes my consciousness of that apprehension. And, since the memory of the two phenomena is identical, the two phenomena must be identical. Hence my apprehension of the sunshine was at the same time my awareness of the apprehension of the sunshine, and perceptual consciousness is therefore reflexive.

Candrakīrti represents Dignāga's argument as follows:

> Even those who do not [mount the regress argument] will inevitably have to accept reflexive awareness. This is because otherwise, although when a memory arises at a later time of the form "...was seen," an object would thereby be remembered, when a thought of the form "I saw..." occurs, the object that was seen would not thereby be remembered. Why is this, you might ask? Since the memory is to be experienced subjectively, and since consciousness is not perceived, it can't be remembered. It follows that if there were no reflexive awareness, nothing could experience itself. And it makes no sense to say that it is experienced by another consciousness. Why is this? Because if it had to be experienced by another consciousness, an infinite regress would ensue. (Candrakīrti 2012, 166–167)

There are two arguments here. The first is the memory argument. My memory of yesterday's sunshine could come to me in the form, "I saw the sunshine yesterday" or in the form, "Yesterday was a sunny day." These seem to be the same memory, but if awareness were not reflexive—that is, if my memory of the sunshine were not identical to my memory of seeing the sunshine—the first would simply be a memory of a subjective state, and not of its object, and the second a memory of the object, and not of the experience, and they would be distinct and unrelated. They are not; so awareness must be reflexive.

At the end, the argument is reinforced by the second argument, a regress argument also proffered by Dignāga and his commentator Dharmakīrti. They argue that every conscious state must be known to its subject. Otherwise, it would not be conscious. If it is known, it must be known either reflexively, or by some higher-order state. If a cognitive state could be known only by a higher-order state, then either that higher-order state would be conscious or unconscious. If the former, we are off on a regress, requiring an infinitude of higher-order states in order for any state to be conscious; if the latter, there is no explanation of how an unconscious state could make another state conscious. Therefore, every conscious state must be reflexively aware. Dignāga offers a related argument for the necessity of reflexive awareness, one that emphasizes the need to be aware that one is aware in order to be aware, which, coupled with the regress argument, entails that any genuine awareness must involve reflexive awareness.

> Although reflexive action is not conventionally presented as the object of the sense faculties, and such things as objects and attachments are presented without reflexive thought, meditators and lamas without exception whenever they perceive or think of an object maintain that there is reflexive awareness....
>
> Superficial perception is obscured for it is involved with conceptual thought. It is the effect of epistemic engagement, and although it is said to be authoritative, it is not actually discriminative. However, reflexive awareness is its effect. As a consequence of that, its object is ascertained, for reflexive awareness is authoritative with respect to the appearance of its object, and thus one says that the object is epistemically engaged.
>
> Therefore, the appearance is the apprehended object. Epistemic authority is consequent on that. Therefore, apprehending consciousness arises from these three distinct things: the consciousness of the object; the consciousness of that consciousness; retaining these two modes of consciousness in memory. Through these two considerations we prove that awareness is reflexive. If a second consciousness was needed to perceive the first, there would be an infinite regress, and so an infinite number of distinct objects, and this is not what is observed. (*Encyclopedia of Epistemology [Pramāṇasamucccaya]* sDe dge 15b–16a)

This view is, of course, well known in the contemporary literature on consciousness as well, and is championed most notably by Kriegel (2009). Kriegel puts it this way: "[M]y conscious experience of a blue sky is the conscious experience it is in virtue of its bluishness, but it is a conscious experience at all in virtue of its for-me-ness." (1) Kriegel clarifies this notion of "for-me-ness," which he calls *subjective character* as follows:

> [T]o say that my experience has subjective character is to point to a certain *awareness* I have of my experience. Conscious experiences are not states that we may *host*, as it were, unawares.... A mental state of which one is completely unaware is not a conscious experience. In this sense, my conscious experience is not only *in me*, it is also *for me*. (8)

Continuing in his recapitulation of Dignāga, Kriegel sums up his own argument for reflexive awareness as follows:

1. C is conscious in virtue of S's being suitably aware of C.
2. For S to be suitably aware of C is for C to be suitably represented by S; therefore,
3. C is conscious in virtue of being suitably represented by S; therefore,
4. C is conscious in virtue of being suitably represented;
5. it is not the case that C is conscious of being unconsciously represented; and
6. it is not the case that C is conscious in virtue of being consciously represented by a distinct state; therefore,
7. it is not the case that C is conscious in virtue of being represented by a distinct state; therefore,
8. C is conscious of being represented by itself; that is,
9. C is conscious in virtue of suitably representing itself. (21)

The first premise is a recapitulation of Dignāga's opening move. He then recapitulates Dignāga's and Dharmakīrti's regress argument.[14]

One comment on these arguments is in order before turning to some Buddhist critiques of them. These are not arguments for a broad pre-thetic awareness of one's own subjectivity of the kind advanced by Husserl, and much later defended by Zahavi (2005) and Coseru (2012), as well as the late 19th-century to early 20th-century Tibetan philosopher, Mipham, who seems to endorse that broader reading of reflexivity. We will return to this below. Instead, these philosophers defend the claim that every conscious mental episode, in virtue of being a conscious episode, has a dual intentional content: on the one hand it is directed upon its nominal intentional object; on the other hand it is directed back upon itself, a view more like those of Gennaro (2011) and Kriegel (2009), views advanced on somewhat different grounds. This view instead is aimed at explaining how our responsiveness to the phenomena we apprehend can be conscious, and the explanation is that it is the reflexivity that makes this possible.

There are a lot of problems with these argument (as noted by contemporary proponents of Higher Order Thought [HOT] and Higher Order Perception [HOP] theories of consciousness), and its faults were pointed out by a number of Buddhist scholars. For one thing, there is a problem with the first premise. Given the enormous variety of prima facie conscious states, it is simply not true that all are known by their subjects. Much of our consciousness is

14. Kriegel, at the time he wrote this, was unaware of the Buddhist antecedents to (and critiques of) his view. I do not want to suggest, however, that he remains unaware of them. In any case, it is instructive to read his argument in the context of those antecedents.

opaque to us much of the time. And there are so many forms of consciousness to consider. In the Buddhist tradition, this is part of what motivates meditative practice: one thereby becomes increasingly aware of aspects of one's consciousness of which one is generally unaware. We do not know our own minds flawlessly, but only through fallible perceptual and inferential means (Tsongkhapa 1991a). In modern cognitive science this is simply the familiar phenomenon of the opacity of consciousness to introspection and the prevalence of illusions of consciousness (Noë 2002, Schwitzgebel 2011 and Gennaro 2011). We will return below to the importance of these phenomena for understanding a Buddhist contribution to contemporary debates.

Second, the regress-generating premise fails to generate the requisite regress. Even if a conscious state must be known by another state, it does not follow that that higher-order state must itself be conscious. Just as my perception of a blue sky does not need to be perceived in order to be a perception, my consciousness of that perception does not have to be consciously observed in order to be conscious, even if it must be the *possible* object of *some* higher order state (See Rosenthal 2005b, Gennaro 2011). At best the proponent of the argument might get the premise that it must be *possible* to become consciously aware of any conscious state through a higher-order state. That generates a regress, but a benign regress. It just means that I *can* iterate higher order states of consciousness, not that I *must*, just as the fact that every natural number has a successor means that I always *can* count higher, not that I *must*.

Candrakīrti (2012) and Śāntideva (1997) each criticize the memory argument. Candrakīrti points out that the account of memory at work in the memory argument is problematic.

> [168] Now, suppose that this is supposed to concern that which exists substantially. Then, since there is neither arising either from self or other, memory is not possible at all. So how could a non-existent memory demonstrate the existence of a non-existent reflexive awareness? On the other hand, suppose it is supposed to exist in terms of mundane conventions. Even in that case it is impossible to use memory as a reason to prove the existence of reflexive awareness.
>
> Why is this, you might ask? Suppose that, just as in the case of fire, you had to establish the existence of reflexive awareness by appeal to another cognition. If this were the case, just as the existence of fire is proven by smoke that is observed at a later time, it would have to be proven to exist by a later memory. But since the cogency of reflexive awareness hasn't been proven, how could a memory that itself is

> not reflexively aware prove the existence of reflexive awareness? In the same way, just by seeing water you can't prove the existence of a water-producing crystal; [169] nor can you prove the existence of a fire-producing crystal just by seeing fire.
>
> After all, water comes about without crystals, as a result of such things as rain, and fire comes about without crystals from such things as matches being struck. In the same way, memory can occur without reflexive awareness. Therefore, memory can never serve as a premise to prove the reflexivity of awareness. Since it has not already been proven to exist, in order to prove the existence of reflexive awareness, you would need a memory that was already proven to be reflexive, and this has not been proven to exist. (2012, 168–169)

This is, of course, not an argument against the reflexivity of awareness, but a rebuttal of the memory argument, an argument that ends up looming large—perhaps too large—in the Indian context, simply because it was one of the first arguments advanced for the reflexivity position. Subsequent theorists all feel the obligation to take it on. First, Candrakīrti notes that the domain of this debate is conventional reality, not ultimate reality; this debate is not about fundamental ontology but about psychology and the philosophy of mind. Candrakīrti then notes that the argument can't proceed just by noting that reflexivity would explain the effect in question, for all kinds of things could explain the phenomenon of memory. Moreover, if awareness is necessarily reflexive, then the memory to which one appeals should independently be taken to be reflexive. If that were the case, nothing else would need to be said; if it is not, the conclusion is false.

All that is necessary for memory, Candrakīrti argues, is that the cognition that counts as a memory is caused in the right way by a previous cognitive episode. So I might experience today's sunshine, fail to be reflexively aware that I am experiencing it, and tomorrow recall the sunshine in an episode caused (in the right way) by today's perception, but in neither case thematize my own subjectivity in the matter.

Śāntideva goes further, arguing that the illusion of reflexivity arises only in virtue of the inferential processes used in memory reconstruction, using as an analogy the fanciful example of a bear bitten by a rat while hibernating, who wakes up to discover a painful, infected wound. The bear, Śāntideva says, knows on the basis of the painful wound that he suffered a rat bite, even though at the time of the bite he was not *aware* of the bite. The point of the analogy is this: (1) One can come to be aware of a previous event through causal sequelae of that event even though one was not aware of that event at the time of its occurrence; (2) Those sequelae can induce a cognitive state intentionally directed at that previous occurrence even if one was not aware of that occurrence at the time. And we might note that contemporary cognitive science, with its reconstructive, rather than storage-and-retrieval models of memory, is on the side of Candrakīrti and Śāntideva in this debate.

It hence follows not only that one could come to remember an event of which one was not explicitly aware at the time of its occurrence, but also, and most importantly, that one could have a memory with the intentional structure "I experienced..." even if one was not aware of experiencing that event when it occurred, despite being aware of the event. Suppose, to take a more contemporary event, one was engrossed in participation in a sporting event, diving to catch a goal in a game of Ultimate. At the time of the event, one might be aware of the flight of the disk, but not aware of one's awareness of it; that is, the awareness of the disk is not accompanied by self-awareness. Nonetheless, after the game, one reports, "I remember diving for the disk, hoping I would catch it...." This later memory is caused by the previous event, and although the memory presents itself as reflexive, the event itself need not have been one involving any reflexivity. (See Garfield 2006b for an extended discussion of these arguments.)

All of this is grounded in Candrakīrti's more general concern with two issues—the importance of interdependence and the absence of any intrinsic nature in anything on the one hand, and the role of linguistic convention, and hence intersubjectivity, in constituting meaning and knowledge on the other (Thurman 1980). For Candrakīrti, reflexivity as a mechanism for self-knowledge would render cognitive states *intrinsically* known, independent of any other cognitive apparatus, and so would violate interdependence, and would amount to assigning cognitive states a kind of essence. And for the mechanism of their knowledge to be essentially inner would violate the principle that the epistemic instruments—perception, inference, testimony and analogy—are constituted as justificatory intersubjectively, by convention. The so-called knowledge that would be constituted by reflexivity, on this account, would not be knowledge in any sense at all, given its essential privacy and its isolation from the rule-governed, public epistemic practices that confer warrant on our beliefs. This view, once again, as do so many Madhyamaka analyses, nicely anticipates both Sellars's attack on the givenness of mental content and Wittgenstein's emphasis on the social dimensions of knowledge in *On Certainty*.

There is a final issue raised by Candrakīrti, and this may be the most profound, anticipating the more contemporary "rock" problem raised by Stubenberg (1998) for Western Higher Order theories, but mobilizing it against First Order theories that appeal to reflexivity. Stubenberg points out that if having a distinct conscious state directed on an object were sufficient to render it conscious, then my thinking about a rock should render the rock conscious; if it cannot, there is no reason to think that a higher-order state directed on a state not already conscious on its own could make that state conscious (185–195).

So, if there is a regress problem, reflexivity can't be the answer to it. For the regress problem suggests that a state that is merely perceptually directed on an object but not the object of another state would not itself be conscious. Grant that claim for the sake of argument. Then consider a reflexively aware perceptual state. If that state were not reflexive, it would not be conscious. But to add reflexivity is then only to add the already unconscious awareness of an unconscious state. It is hard to see how *that* could issue in consciousness if an unconscious higher order state could not. Candrakīrti replies to the regress in a Sanskrit grammatical register with a clear point:

> If one says that a conscious state knows itself then the nature of the process of knowledge would be as follows: Since there must be an agent of that action of knowledge, the account of that action would make no sense, since it would follow absurdly that the agent, action and object would be identical. Such a unity is never observed. For instance, the woodcutter, the wood and the cutting are not identical. For this reason we can see that there is no reflexive awareness, and that we do not become aware of a cognitive state through that state itself. As the *Entry into Lanka sūtra* says,
>
> A sword
> Cannot cut its own blade,
> And a finger cannot cut itself.
> Reflexive awareness is exactly the same. (2012, 171–172)

Now, this argument is cast in a classical grammatical mode, arguing that agent, action and object are necessarily distinct on the grounds of case, and in that form, the argument is hardly compelling. As many proponents of reflexive awareness in the Indian and Tibetan traditions point out, for instance, lamps do reveal themselves, and to the extent that we think of awareness as a kind of revelation of its objects—a very frequent image in Indian philosophy of mind and encapsulated in the term *svaprakaśa* (self-illumination)—that is not a bad counterexample. But Candrakīrti also makes a deeper point. If it is in virtue of reflexivity that a state is conscious, the state that is the object of the reflexive awareness must already be conscious, since it is identical with the awareness that makes it conscious. But if that is so, reflexive awareness is awareness of an *already conscious* state, and so cannot be that which makes it conscious. The very idea of reflexivity thus presupposes the very property it is meant to explain. An unconscious state directed on itself would hardly make itself conscious.

Candrakīrti's critique may have been what led the 9th-century Buddhist philosopher Śāntarakṣita to maintain that reflexivity is simply definitional of subjective consciousness as such, that it is what differentiates sentience from insentience. Here is what he has in mind. Both sentient and insentient matter is subject to effects, and indeed, we might add, many of those are information-rich effects. My footprints in the sand are indicative of the shape of my foot just as is my visual perception of my foot. So no merely relational account of the interaction between my visual faculty, my eye and the foot will distinguish between the interaction between my foot and the sand in a way that will explain why the one is conscious and the other is not. There must therefore be some intrinsic character of consciousness itself, namely its reflexivity, the fact that it presents both the object and our subjectivity of that object, that makes sentience sentience. Here is how Śāntarakṣita puts the point in his *Ornament of the Middle Way*:

> Consciousness arises as diametrically opposed
> In nature to insentient matter.
> Its nature as non-insentient
> Just is the reflexivity of awareness. [16]
>
> Since it makes no sense for that which is unitary and partless
> To have a threefold nature,
> The reflexivity of awareness
> Does not have an agent-action-structure. [17] (verses in Blumenthal 2004)

Śāntarakṣita eschews any talk of self-representation or of the explanatory force of reflexivity in favor of a brute definitional move coupled with phenomenological reflection. In (16) he simply claims that reflexivity—awareness of oneself as a subject—is constitutive of consciousness, and in (17), conceding Candrakīrti's critique, he asserts that reflexivity is non-representational and pre-thetic. This view anticipates those of Husserl and his followers, such as Zahavi (2005), Thompson (2007) and Coseru (2012), suggesting a primordial pre-thetic character to subjectivity. As we will see, it also comes in for trenchant critique by Tsongkhapa, following Candrakīrti.

## 5.2 *Implications for Self-Knowledge*

Just as in the case of the theory of consciousness, debates about reflexivity play a large role in Buddhist debates about self-knowledge. Dignāga introduces this issue in his account of *pramāṇa*, or epistemic warrant, and the nature of epistemic instruments in his *Encyclopedia of Epistemology*. There he argues that reflexive awareness is the mechanism by means of which we know our own inner states. Since this is a kind of *perception*, on Dignāga's view it gives us immediate, non-conceptualized knowledge of our inner episodes, and this, as we saw above, is why he thinks that perception, despite its ordinary fallibility, is, in the end, authoritative. While this might appear to be a classical Buddhist version of a contemporary higher-order perception model of self-knowledge (HOP) (Armstrong 1968, Lycan 1997), it is not. For the point of a reflexive model of awareness in Dignāga's framework—and in subsequent Buddhist articulations of this doctrine—is that each mental state is itself reflexive, requiring no higher-order state to make itself known.

On the other hand, there are homologies between this reflexive model of self-knowledge and contemporary HOP theories. In both accounts, self-knowledge is taken to be direct, unmediated by theory, and hence available even to those who lack the capacity for sophisticated theory, such as small children and animals. Both views recognize the spontaneous, non-reflective nature of self-report, and the fact that we seem not to theorize, when we know our own minds. A great virtue—or a great vice—of this account, depending on one's perspective, is the fact that it represents self-knowledge as very different in kind from knowledge of other minds. Whereas we know other minds only by inference, we know ourselves, on the other hand, directly. This kind of view explains both the apparent asymmetry with respect to mode of access and epistemic security between self- and other-knowledge as well as the apparent symmetry between this kind of knowledge and ordinary perceptual knowledge.

But there are also important differences between Dignāga's theory and HOP theories. For Dignāga, reflexivity is not limited to the case of explicit introspection: it is also implicated in the process of external perception becoming conscious. Reflexive awareness generating self-knowledge is indeed the means by which we know ourselves, but this same reflexive awareness is implicated in every conscious state, and explains not only self-knowledge but consciousness itself. Once again, this may constitute a theoretical virtue or a vice depending on one's perspective. On the one hand, to the extent that one thinks that there are no unknown—or at least no unknowable—conscious states, this model explains that fact; on the other hand, to the extent that one thinks that there are, this model might make the wrong prediction regarding our epistemic access to our own minds. Moreover, because reflexive awareness is not contaminated by conceptual superimposition, Dignāga is committed to the view that our awareness of our own mental states, at least until the moment that we conceptualize it in verbal judgment, is veridical. (See Yao 2005 for more detail.) He thus provides the platform for a strong doctrine of the transparency of mind to itself, although not one committed to a kind of higher-order model of cognitive access.

Now Dignāga's account is a starting point, and perhaps most interesting for its historical role as the beginning of a tradition of Buddhist reflection on the epistemology of the inner, a topic which, while central to the Buddhist soteriological project, receives surprisingly little attention prior to Dignāga's reflections. Things get more interesting as we move forward in the history of that reflection.

## *5.3 Self-Luminosity*

Dignāga's commentator and successor in the development of Buddhist epistemology, Dharmakīrti, develops Dignāga's account of reflexivity and self-knowledge in terms of self-luminosity. He argues that all consciousness is necessarily dual in aspect, incorporating both an awareness of the object of consciousness, whether external or internal, and an awareness of the act of consciousness as such. Mipham endorses this view in his commentary on Śāntarakṣita (Mipham 2004, 273).

On this model, we know our own mental states simply in virtue of being in them, for it is of the very nature of a cognitive state to present itself as the state that it is in its manifestation. While this view is very close to Dignāga's, and is presented as a gloss on that earlier view, it is slightly different. On Dignāga's account, every mental state takes itself as object, providing a representation of itself, as well as of its object, to consciousness; on Dharmakīrti's view, each state is instead internally complex, with its subjective aspect self-presenting as subjectivity, not as the object of any state, including itself. While its primary intentional content is its apparent object, it takes its own subjectivity as a secondary intentional object. This is a pre-thetic awareness of subjectivity itself, by means of which we know ourselves and our states immediately.

A similar self-luminosity position is also well represented in the West. As noted above, it has its modern origins in Husserl's account of consciousness (Zahavi 2005, Kriegel 2009). According to this position, our cognitive states are known immediately because it is of their very nature to present themselves to consciousness as the states they are. My belief that 7 + 5 = 12 is, on this view, at the same time a cognitive state directed on an arithmetic fact and a state which presents myself as subject. My knowledge that I have that belief is part and parcel of the belief itself. Kriegel, Thompson and Zahavi, each in his own way, defend just such a view.

To take a belief to be self-luminous is to take it that to be in a cognitive or affective state (or at least to be in a conscious cognitive or affective state, with the appropriate sense of conscious to be filled in, or perhaps an occurrent state) is to know that state immediately, not only without the need for any higher-order thought or perception of that state, but also without any perception of that state even by itself. This is possible, on this view, because conscious states are self-illuminating, requiring no second state in order to be known. Just as we do not need a second light bulb to see a glowing light bulb, on this view, we do not need a second state to allow us to become aware of a first state. We may need a light bulb to illuminate that which is not self-luminous, of course, like the furniture in the room, and so we may need conscious states to mediate our awareness of the world around us, but to require a higher-order state, on this view, is to invite a vicious regress. On this account, just as to be self-luminous in this sense is constitutive of and criterial for consciousness, since cognitive states are conscious states, self-luminosity is criterial for cognitive states as well (Zahavi 2005, Kriegel 2009).[15]

Debates about self-knowledge and reflexivity extend into Tibet, with its rich tradition of analytic epistemology. The 13th-century Tibetan scholar Sakya Paṇḍita argued that self-knowledge is achieved through reflexive awareness, relying heavily on Dharmakīrti's analysis of cognitive states as self-luminous. He argues, however, that since in any perceptual or cognitive apprehension, subject and object must be distinct, in the case of reflexive awareness, since there is no such distinctness, there is no object of that awareness. Such knowledge, he argues, is in fact objectless. Now, of course this raises the question of just in what sense reflexive awareness counts as knowledge at all. Dreyfus (1997, 402) compares this account to that of European phenomenologists like Sartre, who argue that all consciousness presents subjectivity pre-thematically as a precondition of any awareness. On the other hand, while this might vouchsafe the very general self-knowledge that one is aware, it would hardly

15. Expressivist views, such as those of Shoemaker 1994 and Bar-On 2004, share with the self-luminosity view the sense that self-knowledge is immediate, as opposed to being mediated by additional cognition, but these views distance the subject slightly from the state known, requiring an act of profession. One way of putting this point is that while on the self-luminosity view, it is impossible to be in a conscious mental state without knowing oneself to be in that state, on the professing view, it is possible to be in such a state, and only to come to know it when that state finds explicit inner or outer expression.

take one to knowledge of the *contents* of one's own mind, and may in the end be too thin to count as any kind of knowledge worth having, in addition to being so odd, that it is hard to see it as knowledge in the sense that anything else we count as knowledge is knowledge.

This worry about both the sui generis nature and the thinness of reflexivity was very much in the mind of Sakya Paṇḍita's 15th-century Sakya successor Gorampa. Gorampa argues from the fact that reflexive awareness is the mechanism of self-knowledge that it must therefore be intentional, and therefore *must* have an object of knowledge (Dreyfus 1997, 403). Now, Gorampa's own view is that all knowledge is mediated by representation, and this raises further difficulties for the account that reflexivity is the basis of self-knowledge. For if we grant the necessity of the mediation by representation of all knowledge, then self-knowledge must be mediated by representation as well, and if this is so, a regress looms. If we need a representation in order to know our own inner state, then presumably to know this representation a further representation is needed, and so on.

Gorampa is aware of this potential problem, and cuts the regress off by following Dharmakīrti in another respect, that is, in distinguishing two aspects of any cognitive state, a subjective and objective aspect.

> The representation is the object of apprehension. To say that the instrument of knowledge, its effect and the apprehension are three different things therefore makes no sense. With regard to the object, consciousness and the consciousness of that consciousness appear to consciousness in a twofold manner, and this how it is in memory at a later time as well. Reflexive awareness is this twofold appearance. If there were no reflexive awareness there would be no perception. And if a distinct consciousness was required to perceive it there would be an infinite regress. And memory would always be of another object. (*Elucidation of Epistemology [Tsad ma rnam 'grel]* 300). (See also an extended treatment in *Illumination of the Ascertained Object [Ngas don rab gsal]* 577–582)

A reflexive awareness, he argues, takes, in its subjective aspect, the objective aspect of the state as its object. This may cut of the regress, but once again there is a cost. Subjectivity now takes objectivity as an object, but to the degree that this is all that is involved in reflexivity, it is a thin sense of self-knowledge, sounding more like a restatement of the fact that subjective states have objects.

Geluk scholars, following Tsongkhapa, take Nāgārjuna and Candrakīrti more as touchstones in this debate than they do Dharmakīrti. Tsongkhapa

(1988) argues, following Candrakīrti, that reflexivity makes no sense in the first place.

> Suppose someone asked, "If according to your view there is no assertion of reflexive awareness, how does memory occur?" According to mundane convention, the mind does not experience itself. But the previous state of consciousness perceives a previous object, and this is the cause of the effect, which is the later memory. (289)

Here Tsongkhapa follows Candrakīrti in asserting that the simplest explanation of memory is simply a causal process, requiring no special higher-order intentionality. He now turns to a possible objection. Does the denial of reflexivity undermine the possibility of ordinary introspective knowledge? He argues that it does not, but that our ordinary understanding of introspective knowledge is in terms of higher-order perception and thought (which he does not clearly distinguish here, but which can easily be in a Buddhist framework in terms of their respective objects—particulars vs. universals).

> Suppose one thought as follows: Since it would be to deny that one experiences such things as pleasure and pain through the introspective consciousness, how could there be no reflexive awareness? We commit no such error, because the denial of reflexive awareness is consistent with the distinction between subject and object with respect to all cognitive states that are directed inward.... According to mundane nominal conventions as well, the experience of pleasure and pain occurs in this way. Since the perceiver and the perceived appear distinctly, there is no need to posit reflexive awareness as it is accepted in our opponents' position. (Ibid., 297)

Tsongkhapa now comes to the heart of the issue. He takes as his target the position recently defended by Kriegel, a self-representational model of reflexive awareness: The only cogent model of reflexivity, Tsongkhapa notes, is representational. After all, reflexive awareness has to have an intentional structure, and its intentional content must be known via a representation. Hence every cognitive state must represent itself on this view. But once we grant that representational structure, Tsongkhapa says, we can now ask about the epistemic status of that reflexive state. If it contains itself as object, it must be completely authoritative. How could it be mistaken about its own nature? But if it is authoritative, we have the consequence that we would have omniscient access to our own minds.

Now Tsongkhapa, like many contemporary philosophers, takes this to constitute a *reductio* on reflexivity. Of course any proponent of strong privileged access to our own doxastic and perceptual states—and there are such people—would take this as a *welcome* consequence. Blumson (personal communication) argues for such a view, advancing two distinct arguments, which I consider here because I think that they express exactly the intuition against which Tsongkhapa is concerned to argue. First, Blumson urges that the *Cogito* provides a clear example: If I am thinking, I know immediately and irrefutably that I am thinking. Hence, I have infallible access in this case to my own mind. Blumson may be right about the premise, but it hardly establishes the conclusion he wants. For I know that I am thinking because of the *logic* of thinking, not because of the content of any thought. It does not follow, for instance, that if I am thinking that roses are red that I know that I am thinking *that*. And that is what the strong reflexivist position requires.

The second argument is meant to respond to this point, and appeals to what one might call the *BB principle*, that is, that if one believes that *P* one believes that one believes that *P*. Leave the regress issue aside—there are ways to finesse that by talking about potential but not actual regresses. The obvious response from Tsongkhapa's perspective (and from that of much contemporary research in cognitive development—particularly that devoted to the acquisition of Theory of Mind) is simply that the principle is false. To believe something is a conceptually enriched act; to believe that one has a belief requires that one have the concept of belief, and many small children and infralingual animals don't have it. And then there is the Freudian point, at the heart of Tsongkhapa's concern: It also requires that one have a pretty good understanding of one's own cognitive life, something that even many adults fail to have. On this perspective, self-knowledge is far from immediate, far from given. And while this might appear counterintuitive from certain other perspectives, it turns out to be surprisingly well-confirmed empirically. Here is how Tsongkhapa makes this point:

> If any consciousness to which the object of that consciousness appears were also its own object, that consciousness would appear as a representation. If that consciousness were non-deceptive with respect to that, that mundane, non-deceptive consciousness just by being *known as authoritative*, would have to *be authoritative*. In that case, if the apparent object of knowledge were to be established by that consciousness, the subject would already have to have been. (Ibid., 298–299)

Knowledge, Tsongkhapa argues, is always a relationship between a subject and an object. If we know our own mental states, it is because of epistemic states that take our cognitive states as object, and moreover, states that are distinct from those that they know. Self-knowledge, on his view, if it is to mean anything, is an understanding of our own cognitive lives and perceptual experience achieved by the same mechanisms by means of which we know external events.

Moreover, the Geluk school is realist, not representationalist, about perception, taking perception to be a relation between a perceived object, a sensory system and a cognizer. Tsongkhapa's demand that apperception and self-knowledge are constituted in the first instance by higher-order perception does not, therefore, engender a vicious regress, and at worst, only a regress of potential higher-order states, corresponding to potential higher-order states of knowledge. This position does raise another issue, though. On this analysis, the introspective power is mediated by the sixth sense faculty (the introspective faculty), epistemically aligned to the external sense faculties, as a perceptual state. But perception, at least for ordinary beings, is also epistemically complex and problematic on a Buddhist account. For while it may in principle be veridical, in practice it delivers us data that are infected by the imperfections of our sensory organs and our instinctive superimposition of conceptual categories—many or all of which may be intrinsically falsifying—on the deliverances of sensation. So, while higher-order perception may be a central part of the story, it may well be that any analysis of that perception must appeal to higher-order thought as well, and on this account, unlike those of proponents of a special self-revealing nature of first-order cognitive states, self-knowledge will always be fallible. That is, on this account the mind, like external objects, always is, at least to some degree, hidden to us.

To take self-knowledge to be mediated by HOT, as one must on Tsongkhapa's view, is to see it as reflective, as theoretical. On this model we know ourselves in part by theorizing about ourselves, by inference to the best explanation. Our inner states are not perceptible, but our behavior is interpretable, and when we self-ascribe cognitive states, we engage in an act of interpretation, just as we do when we ascribe cognitive states to others in the absence of any ability to perceive them directly. This homogeneity of self-ascription and other-ascription is, depending on one's perspective, a great virtue or a great vice of this account. On the one hand, it eliminates the mystery of a sui generis access to our own mental lives and explains our fallibility with respect to the mental. On the other hand, it suggests that creatures incapable of the requisite degree of reflective capacity, such as young children and animals, do not know their own minds at all. This is an important insight, for, as I have been emphasizing, it is easy to take for granted the view that our access to our own minds is immediate. That is probably not just a part of our Cartesian legacy; it seems to have an intuitive hold on many people, and in many traditions.

The Madhaymaka view defended by Tsongkhapa is hence not just common sense. That is not to say—as I have also been at pains to emphasize—that it has no counterparts in the contemporary Western literature. Rorty (1979) as well as Churchland (1979) make similar claims, though on different, more metaphysical grounds. It is interesting to contrast Tsongkhapa's view with Lewis's otherwise similar position (1995), as it is representative of this trend. Lewis argues that qualia are inconsistent with materialism and therefore should be rejected en route to a more general rejection of immediate self-knowledge. Fair enough, but if one is not antecendently materialist, as many contemporary qualiaphiles are not, this argument may seem patently question-begging, or at least ad hoc. For this reason, the Indo-Tibetan Buddhist tradition might be a welcome voice in this debate: it provides more principled reason for treating self-knowledge in the same way as knowledge of the external world, grounded in an analysis of perception, self-knowledge and subjectivity.

## 6. Higher-Order Theories

It might appear that there is something terribly flat-footed about any insistence such as that of Śāntarakṣita's that nothing relational, nothing not already subjective, could ever differentiate conscious from unconscious phenomena. But it is a position remarkably prescient of new mysterians (those who regard the psychophysical relation as unknowable, either in principle or in practice) such as Stoljar (2006), Chalmers (2010) and McGinn (2004) and even of those who insist on some intrinsic feature of mental states that make them conscious, such as Searle (1997), Levine (2001) and Gennaro (2011). On the other hand, Śāntarakṣita raises an important issue. There is a burden of proof on the shoulders of the higher-order theorist. She must explain how some relations among subjects, their faculties and their objects constitute consciousness and why others do not. If she cannot do this, reflexivity looks like the only option, an argument taken up in a different register by Kriegel (2009).

Before turning to Madhyamaka responses to this challenge, let us spend a bit of time with contemporary higher-order theories. Peter Carruthers (1996) has offered the most extensively worked-out higher-order theory of consciousness. (There are many more, of course, most recently that of Gennaro [2011]. But to survey and address the contemporary literature on consciousness is well beyond the scope of this discussion. My aim is simply to show how Buddhist theory can inform that discussion.) Carruthers writes:

> Consider routine activities, such as driving, walking, or washing up, which we can conduct with our conscious attention elsewhere. When driving home over a route I know well, for example, I will often pay no conscious heed to what I am doing on the road . . . I *saw* the vehicle double-parked at the side of the road, since I deftly turned the wheel to avoid it. Yet I was not conscious of seeing it, either at the time or later in memory. My perception of that vehicle was not a conscious one. (135)
>
> . . .
>
> Recall just how rich and detailed an experience can be. There can be an immense amount of which we can be consciously aware at any one time. For example, imagine looking down at a city from a window high up in a tower block . . . In this case I am consciously perceiving the complex distribution of trees, roads, and buildings; the colours on the ground and in the sky above; the moving cars and pedestrians; and so on. And I am conscious of all of this simultaneously. (166–167)
>
> . . . [C]onsciousness is constituted by an accessibility-relation to occurrent thinkings, where those thinkings are conscious in turn (that is, where they are regularly made available to further occurrent thinkings). Conscious experiences, in particular, are those which are *available to acts of thinking which are reflexively available to further thinkings* . . .
>
> What makes my perception of a glass on the desk to be conscious, on this account, is the fact that perceptual information about the glass is held in a short-term memory store whose function is to make that information available to conscious thinkings—where those thinkings are conscious, too, in virtue of each one of them fed back, reflexively, to the same (or similar) short-term memory store to be available to be thought about in turn. (194)

There is a lot to be said about this discussion, but I want to focus on three points here: first, the way that *consciousness*, for all of Carruthers' philosophical care, is taken as a unitary, all-or-nothing phenomenon; second, the easy claims regarding what we are conscious of or not in perception (surveying the cityscape from the skyscraper vs. driving); and third, the implication of *thought*, and hence of *language*, in the story.

The term *consciousness* is used in this passage to denote our sensitivity to information in order to make the claim that we are conscious of the visual array when looking from the window of the skyscraper, to denote introspective availability (but *not mere sensitivity*) when denying conscious awareness of what we are doing when washing dishes or what we are seeing when driving, and conceptual availability when offering a more formal definition at the end of the passage. This easy slide is commonplace in this literature, and it is pernicious. It is pernicious not because there are many senses of *consciousness* at play; it is only appropriate that there are, as there are many cognitive phenomena denoted by this vague single term; rather, it is pernicious because the very singularity of the term and our familiarity with its use leads us both to take consciousness to be a unitary phenomenon, and one whose presence or absence is simply apparent to us.

From a Buddhist perspective, neither could be further from the truth. As we have seen, Buddhist psychology recognizes multiple kinds and levels of consciousness, including sensory and conceptual forms of consciousness; consciousness that is introspectible and consciousness that is too deep for introspection; consciousness that takes external phenomena as objects and consciousness that takes inner phenomena as objects; consciousness that is merely receptive and consciousness that is constructive and even projective. In general, the complex set of phenomena is opaque to casual introspection, and are knowable only theoretically or perhaps by highly trained meditators. Let us leave the meditators to the side, for a moment. To take seriously the idea that consciousness itself is both complex and opaque is to see that what Carruthers here takes as unproblematic data may well be nothing more than fantasy, akin to taking the flatness of the earth, so manifest to us, as a datum in astronomy.

The second point is closely connected. Carruthers blithely asserts that he is conscious simultaneously of all of the trees, cars and colors below his window, but also that when driving he is not conscious of the obstacles on the road he avoids when his mind is occupied in conversation. How on earth can he know either of these things? We already know that when surveying our visual field, or even attending voluntarily and carefully to part of it, that there is much that we do not see. We are inattentionally blind, change blind, blind to foveal gaps and to the monochromicity of our peripheral vision. Introspection is no guide to what is available to vision (Most 2010; Most et al. 2005; Mack 2003; Rensink 2001, 2002, 2004; Rensink, O'Regan and Clark 1997; Noë 2007; Noë, Pessoa and Thompson 2000; Simons 2000a, 2000b; Simons and Ambinder 2005; Fendrich, Demirel and Danziger 1999; Guirao and Artal 1999).

There is a neat dilemma here for one who wants simply to take the data of naive introspection as a starting point for inquiry in this domain: either take the term *conscious* to apply only to what is available to introspection or take it to be a complex, theoretically informed term that may well comprise a natural kind whose members are heterogeneous and whose natures are hidden from introspection. If we take the first option, all we are doing is investigating introspective awareness, something we know to be variable among subjects, prone to illusion and dependent on attentional variables. Characterizing that might be interesting as a matter of autobiography, but not as philosophy or psychology. If we take the second, casual introspective reports are irrelevant. And this is why most Buddhist theorists eschew naive introspection as a source of data for reflection on consciousness, taking it to be the report of illusion, not a veridical source of data.[16] This is an issue for almost every current philosophical account of consciousness.

Finally, it is noteworthy that Carruthers's account (like those of Rosenthal and Gennaro), as a higher-order *thought* account, implicates conceptual thought in its account of consciousness—at least in its account of what we might more precisely call introspectible conscious experience—and hence language, as the vehicle for the expression of concepts. (I leave aside the vexed question of whether there are inexpressible *phenomenal concepts* for now. We will return to phenomenal concepts and qualia below.)

Here there is real harmony with at least several important strands of Buddhist thought about apperception. Philosophers as different in perspective as Vasubandhu and Candrakīrti (the former a Yogācāra and the latter a Mādhyamika critic of the Yogācāra school) in India; Tsongkhapa and Gorampa in Tibet (the former a Geluk insistent on the importance of conventional truth and the latter a Sakya scholar insistent on its entirely deceptive character) and Dōgen in Japan (who rejects virtually all of the analytic philosophy developed in the Indian and Tibetan scholastic tradition) agree that introspective awareness is mediated by thought and therefore by language. Therefore, moreover, it is mediated by the conventions that determine linguistic meaning and the structures of our concepts, and hence is always a matter of convention, not a

16. On the other hand, some Buddhist traditions, particularly meditative or tantric traditions, do rely heavily on the introspective reports of trained and experienced meditators, taking those reports to provide compelling evidence regarding the nature of cognition. Whether this is an epistemically warranted practice is a real question, both in Buddhist epistemology and in contemporary contemplative neuroscience. On the one hand, science requires observational data, and trained observers are better than untrained observers. On the other hand, trained observers can easily find only what they seek, and in the introspective domain calibrating the observer is difficult, if not impossible. I note this issue only to set it aside for another time.

deliverance of the nature of mind to a lucid instrument observing it. But from a Buddhist perspective, *this* insight of the HOT school undermines, rather than facilitates, its more general program of developing a theory of *consciousness, per se.* At best, one could hope for a theory of our folk conception of the meaning of the word *consciousness.* Not much to write home about.

## 7. Qualia

A very different strand of thought running through contemporary theories of consciousness is the idea that *qualia* or *qualitative properties,* which are posited or said to be discovered introspectively as the inner objects of experience, constitute or explain the fact that "there is something that it is like" to have conscious experience, and given the emphasis that Buddhist ethics places on the interests of *sentient beings* (see chapter 9 below), the question of the nature of sentience, and hence of experience, is central to the Buddhist philosophical project. The idea that something like qualia are essential to sentience is common to a number of theoretical perspectives that differ among themselves in countless other ways, including Higher-Order Thought, Higher-Order Perception, Intrinsic First-Order, Phenomenological and Reflexive models. We have already encountered Chalmers's posit of phenomenal properties and concepts to go with them. Gennaro makes a similar claim:

> There is significant disagreement over the nature, or even the existence, of qualia, but they are most often understood as the felt properties or qualities of conscious states. There is something it is like to have qualia or to be in a qualitative state. Most generally, perhaps, qualia are "introspectively accessible phenomenal aspects of our mental lives." But even this can be misleading if it is taken to imply that only introspected, or introspectible, states have qualia. Surely first-order, or world-directed, conscious states also have qualia.... What it feels like, experientially, to see a red rose is different from what it feels like to see a yellow rose. (2011, 7)

There is a massive philosophical literature on qualia and related constructs. I will ignore most of it in the interest of focusing once again on what Buddhism brings to this debate. But first, a few preliminary remarks on qualia to open the field for another perspective. It is often taken for granted in recent literature on consciousness that "surely... conscious states... have qualia." But given how little clarity there is on just in what qualia are supposed to consist, we should be suspicious of this consensus. As we have seen, qualitative redness is not redness. Roses may be red, and violets may be blue; but red and blue qualia are found only in me and in you. These are inner properties, or properties of inner states. As Nida-Rümelin puts it,

> To have a particular phenomenal property is to have an experience with a specific subjective feel. If you have a phenomenal concept of a phenomenal property, then you know what it is to have an experience with that subject feel. (2007, 307)

The echoes of Dignāga are striking. Levine (2011) agrees that phenomenal properties are special properties of inner states, essentially grasped by *having them* (just as the facets of the crystal turn blue when placed on the blue paper) and that perception is characterized by the immediate awareness of these properties. So, we should ask ourselves what reason there is to posit this second layer of properties in order to understand consciousness or experience.

There are two principal kinds of reasons one might have: observational or theoretical. The only kind of observational evidence could be introspective, and, as we have already noted, introspection is a highly fallible instrument for limning the cognitive world. But suppose that, for the sake of argument, we grant its veridicality. Let us now ask what occurs when we see a red rose. In particular, what *introspective evidence* could there be for the claim that beyond the redness we perceive in the rose, there is a second *phenomenal* redness that we perceive immediately, or that permeates our perceptual experience? To have such evidence, both properties would have to be evident, and we would have to be able to distinguish them. But by the qualiaphile's own lights, only the phenomenal property is directly perceived. So, perhaps the evidence is theoretical. But then we would imagine that, somewhere in the best psychological theory of perception, qualia, qualitative properties, or qualitative concepts appear. The fact that they do not should at least give philosophers pause. I conclude that the *surely* that precedes the claim that our conscious states have qualia is the protestation that evidence and argument are not needed, albeit for a claim nobody really understands. We will see why this is below.

It might be interesting to take a whirlwind tour through the doxography of Buddhist positions on perceptual experience to get a very different take on these matters. Buddhist doxographers distinguish a number of schools of thought organized in a hierarchy of degrees of supposed sophistication. On the one hand, this doxographic enterprise helps to systematize the history of Indian Buddhist philosophy. On the other hand, it provides a dialectical map for reflection and education, motivating each successive view on the ranked list as a reply to difficulties raised by the immediately preceding view.[17]

The most straightforward account of perceptual awareness in the Buddhist world is presented by the Vaibhāṣika school. A pre-Mahāyāna school, the Vaibhāṣikas presented a non-conceptual direct realist theory of perception. On this view, perceptual awareness arises from the direct contact of sensory apparatus with perceptible objects or qualities in the environment, unmediated by any representations. We might see this as a kind of proto-Gibsonian model of perceptual consciousness: consciousness is not a kind of mental accompaniment to sensory contact, or even a downstream consequence of it; it is the very fact of sensory contact with the world. According to the Vaibhāṣika, then, consciousness is not a property, a thing, a process, but rather a simple relation between a sensory/cognitive system and the world. In this system, note, nothing answers to qualia; there are no special qualitative properties. Instead, in perceptual experience we are immediately aware of ordinary external properties. This direct realism, however, has difficulty accounting for perceptual illusion, as perception itself is taken to be veridical.

The Sautrāntika system arises as a response to the difficulty the Vaibhāṣika system has accounting for perceptual error or illusion. Sautrāntika is a representational theory of mind, interposing a representation (*ākāra/rnam pa [nampa]*)[18] as the direct object of awareness between the external object and subjectivity. While for a Vaibhāṣika, when I perceive a patch of blue, I perceive the patch directly, and the consciousness of that patch of blue just is the relation between my perceptual apparatus and the patch of blue, for a Sautrāntika, that consciousness is immediately of a *representation* of that patch of blue. The representation is itself *blue*, but in a different sense from

17. Doxography of this kind, common in India, Tibet and China, might strike the Western philosopher or historian of philosophy as a bit exotic and odd. But of course we engage in doxography as well to organize our own canon, even if we don't go in for the hierarchies that characterize Buddhist views. We have our Platonists and Aristotelians, rationalists, empiricists, Kantians, idealists, realists, and even HOT, HOP and FO theorists in the present debate. Doxographies are, of course, both useful heuristics for understanding the history of philosophy and polemical strategies for shaping it. Here we follow a fairly standard, and clearly polemical, Tibetan doxographic framework. (See Hopkins 1996 and Cabezón 1994, as well as Gregory 1991 for more on Buddhist doxography.)

18. This term has a very complex semantic range and functions in many ways as a technical term in Buddhist epistemology and philosophy of mind. In some contexts it is best translated as *aspect*; in others as *image* or *form*. (Think of the many ways in which *idea* is used in early modern philosophy as a parallel.) A complete exploration of Buddhist theories of *ākāra* would take us far afield and would require a substantial volume of its own. For a very fine exploration of the role of this term and the phenomena it denotes in Buddhist epistemology see Kellner and McClintock (2014).

that in which the patch is blue. It has *blue content*, or *resembles* the blue patch in some way.

It is here, if anywhere in the Buddhist tradition, that we come close to a doctrine of phenomenal properties. For the Sautrāntikas, like the Vaibhāṣikas to whom they respond, inner cognitive phenomena like representations cannot be *literally* blue. On the other hand, if they are the immediate objects of perception, since in perception we are conscious of blueness, they must be blue *somehow*. Here we might say that the account of perceptual consciousness on offer trades directly on the presence of blue qualia as mediators of our perception. We have encountered this view in our discussion of *Examination of the Percept* and its commentaries.

So, it might seem that the Buddhist world is friendly to an account of perceptual consciousness in terms of qualia. But not so fast. We are only on the second rung of the doxographic ladder. Yogācāra is presented as the next step in sophistication, and as a response to an intractable problem posed by the Sautrāntika representationalism, one that directly concerns the qualitative representations it posits. The problem, as Buddhist theorists see it, is two-fold: First, if the blue representation is blue in a different sense from that in which the blue patch is blue, or if it somehow resembles the blue patch, the only way that it could mediate perceptual knowledge of the blue patch would be if we were to know how it resembles the external patch, or how one sense of blue connects to the other. But the very point of the representationalism is that we are cut off from direct contact with the represented, and so have no idea what it might be like, and so no idea of what is represented, or how.[19]

This is, of course, an anticipation of Berkeley's argument against representationalism in the second *Dialogue*. And like Berkeley, the Yogācāra wield the argument in favor of idealism, arguing that since direct realism is incoherent, as is representationalism, the direct and only object of conscious experience is an inner state. A second argument deployed against the Sautrāntika position is a simple regress argument: if the only way that we can be perceptually aware of an external patch of blue is by directly perceiving something qualitatively blue, then it would seem that the only way that we could ever perceive a patch of qualitative blueness would be by perceiving something that was qualitatively qualitative blue. And so on. That is, if the mediation of the perception of a property by the perception of a second property is needed

19. Here especially (but throughout this discussion) I simplify considerably, eliding substantial disagreements among philosophers in these schools in favor of a broad brush. The reader interested in the details of these debates should refer to Coseru (2012), Dreyfus (1997) and Kellner and McClinock (2014).

in the first place, the perception of that second property should need similar mediation. If it does not, there is no reason to think that the first does, either.

The view that there are phenomenal properties corresponding to the properties of experienced objects, and that our perception of the properties of objects is mediated by those phenomenal properties is well-known in Buddhist literature as well. The eighth century Indian philosopher Dharmottara, in his *Epitome of Philosophy (Nyāyabindu)*, a sub-commentary on Dharmakīrti's *Commentary on the Encyclopedia of Philosophy*, considers and replies to a query regarding the causal basis of perceptual intentionality:

> Question: How can a single cognition have the relation of intended and intentional?
>
> Response: Since that cognition, experiencing the likeness of blue, is established as apprehending blue by a thought that is a judgment (*niácaya-pratyaya*), therefore the experienced likeness is the cause of intending. And that cognition, being established as an experience of blue by a thought that is a judgment, is what is intended. Therefore, a cognition's resemblance, which is realized by way of exclusion of what is unlike (*apoha*), is a cause of intending; and the fact of being in the form of a thought of blue, which is realized by exclusion of thoughts of nonblue, is what is to be intended. (trans. Arnold 2009, 194–195)

The interlocutor here wonders how it could be that an internal state could have both subjective and objective character, that is, to be, in this case, at once the apprehended blue of an intentional object and the apprehender of that blue. The reply is that the apprehended blue is grasped by means of a subjective aspect of the intentional state which resembles that blue, which is subjectively blue. Now, I think it is plain that this account falls prey to the same difficulties that afflict contemporary perceptual theories according to which perception is mediated by inner phenomenal properties that correspond to external properties. Nonetheless, it is better off than most of these theories in one odd respect. Because this is an idealist theory of perception, according to which there is no genuine external object to be perceived, the two occurrences of blue are both mental. It is much easier to see how one mental occurrence of blueness could be involved in the perception of another in virtue of similarity than to see how a mental occurrence of blueness could be similar enough to physical blueness to constitute the mechanism by means of which an intentional state is directed on that property, as Berkeley pointed out.

In a Yogācāra analysis of perceptual consciousness, the external object and the distinction between subject and object drop out entirely. As a response to a mediated view of consciousness, Yogācāra reinstates an immediate theory, but one in which the only terms of experience are inner. On this view, perceptual consciousness has no external object; to be conscious is just for a conscious perceptual state to arise in cognition, and the analysis of the contents and character of consciousness involves only attention to inner states. This view has certain obvious advantages: it avoids the need to posit a layer of mysterious properties that are not obviously explanatory, and it avoids what looks like a nasty explanatory regress, with the claim that conscious states simply arise as a consequence of propensities in the foundation consciousness, or, as we might put it, our fundamental psychological architecture.

On the other hand, Yogācāra is not obviously successful as an explanation of perception or consciousness, inasmuch as what looks like awareness of external objects, and what looks like a distinctive mode of engagement with the world, simply are explained away as the sui generis arising of conscious states from a foundation consciousness. What looks like explanation seems more like the positing of brute fact; while it looks like perceptual consciousness should arise from a variety of causal factors, it ends up being a kind of explanatory surd.

Madhyamaka enters as the most sophisticated view, then, as a response to this explanatory predicament. The Madhyamaka view of perceptual consciousness is simple and sophisticated. Mādhyamikas analyze consciousness, as they analyze all phenomena, as a set of relations, not as an independent phenomenon or characteristic. In this case, perceptual consciousness is simply the fact of the relations between a perceived object, a sense organ, a sensory system and the conceptual and motor systems to which that sensory system is connected. Just as the illusion of a self is resolved in favor of a network of interconnected psychophysical processes, the illusion that there is a special property or center of consciousness is resolved in favor of a network of processes.

That they constitute consciousness is simply the fact that they are perceptual, conceptual, conative and affective. The properties they deliver are simply the properties of the external objects we perceive, as they are delivered by our perceptual processes.[20] There is nothing more than that. This may feel disappointing, as deflationary accounts often do, but, from a Madhyamaka perspective, all that we lose in such an account is the illusion that there is more in conscious experience than the psychology and physiology of experience. In particular,

20. It is important to note here that despite their important differences along other dimensions, the Yogācāra and Madhyamaka traditions are united in the view that there are not *two*, but instead *one* set of such properties. Despite the fact that Yogācāra offers an idealist account of perception and Madhyamaka a realist account, neither posits both a set of empirical and a set of phenomenal properties in order to explain perceptual experience.

reference to internal representations, qualia, phenomenal properties and other such ghostly mediators of our experience drop away. Ontology becomes cleaner, perhaps more naturalistic, and certainly more public, less private.

I review this Buddhist doxography in order to point out that what is taken as *obvious* in so much of the Western discourse on perceptual consciousness—that it centrally involves something like *qualia, qualitative properties* or *qualitative concepts*—is taken in this tradition as but one unstable moment early in a dialectic, and a moment that emerges not from naive introspection, but from reflection on illusion, as did the introduction of sense data in the early 20th century. This dialectic, moreover, is not aimed at providing an analysis of a special, singular property that makes our experience come alive, or confers subjectivity to it, but at dispelling the illusion that there is any such singular property. There are many kinds and degrees of consciousness on this view, and they reflect the many kinds of ways that cognitive and perceptual processes engage their objects. It is the engagement that constitutes, rather than gives rise to, or is accompanied by, consciousness on this view.

I do not claim that this Madhyamaka view—or any Buddhist view—is obviously correct, only that it is a voice with which to be reckoned. And reckoning with this voice forces the theorist who takes something like the qualitative character of experience to be real, and to be essential to consciousness, to defend and not to presuppose that view. And the route to a defense is not at all obvious. It also forces us to ask once again just whether when we propose a theory of consciousness, we even know what we are talking about, or whether the object of our theory exists. We may be doing something akin to the biology of unicorns.

## 8. The Sense of Self in Consciousness

There is a major strand of theory in contemporary consciousness studies that we have ignored so far, the neo-Husserlian phenomenological strand left hanging in the previous chapter. On this view, consciousness is essentially bound up with self-consciousness, and to understand what it is to be conscious is in the first instance to understand what it is to be self-conscious. Dan Zahavi (2005) is a sophisticated proponent of this view. He writes:

> Although phenomenologists might disagree on important questions concerning method and focus, and even about the status and existence of the self, they are in nearly unanimous agreement when it comes to the relation between consciousness and self-consciousness. Literally all

> the major figures in phenomenology defend the view that the experiential dimension is characterized by a tacit self-consciousness. (11)

This is intriguing. Of course this is not an argument for the claim that all consciousness involves self-consciousness, but it does indicate a willingness to take this as read as a starting point for investigation. Of course to say *that* all consciousness involves self-consciousness is not yet to specify *how* it involves self-consciousness, or what the nature of that self-consciousness is. It may be, for instance, that self-consciousness is merely potential, and not actual; that it is the mere consciousness of subjectivity, as opposed to the consciousness of a self; it may be that it is the consciousness of a specific subject of experience. Let us see how Zahavi specifies the account:

> Self-consciousness is not merely something that comes about at the moment one scrutinizes one's experiences attentively... Rather, self-consciousness comes in many forms and degrees. It makes perfect sense to speak of self-consciousness whenever I am not simply conscious of an external object—a chair, a chestnut tree, or a rising sun—but acquainted with my experience of the object as well, for in such a case my consciousness reveals itself to me. Thus, the basic distinction to be made is the distinction between the case where an object is given (object-consciousness) and the case wherein consciousness itself is given (self-consciousness). In its most primitive and fundamental form, self-consciousness is taken to be a question of having first-personal access to one's own consciousness; it is a question of the first-person givenness or manifestation of experiential life. (15)

Self-consciousness, then, is being "acquainted with my experience of the object as well," or "first-person givenness or manifestation of experiential life." It may seem obvious that when I see a blue sky I am not only acquainted with the blue sky but with my experience thereof, and that I know my own life from a first-person perspective. The latter fact, however, is a tautology. How else could I know my own life? The sleight of hand that gives content to this formulation is only apparent when we ask whether when an object is "given"—that is, when I become perceptually aware of an object—my *experience* is also *given*—that is, made aware to me—as a second object of awareness. This is not at all obvious, and no argument is offered for it. For my part, when I perceive a sky, my experience is exhausted by seeing the sky. If the experience of the object is distinct from the experiencing of the object, I sense one object too many, and we are pushed back to the Sautrāntika position, and the regress problems it raises.

Zahavi insists that his theory is no higher-order theory. Like Kriegel, he argues that self-consciousness is intrinsic to consciousness, and not the result of a moment of awareness itself becoming object of another state:

> In contrast to higher-order theories, the phenomenologists explicitly deny that the self-consciousness that is present the moment I consciously experience something is to be understood in terms of some kind of reflection, or introspection, or higher-order monitoring. It does not involve an additional mental state, but is rather to be understood as an intrinsic feature of the primary experience. That is, in contrast to the higher-order account of consciousness, which claims that consciousness is an extrinsic property of those mental states that have it, a property bestowed upon them from without by some further states, the phenomenologists typically argue that the feature that makes a mental state conscious is located within the state itself; it is an intrinsic property of those states that have it. (20)

Thompson follows Zahavi closely:

> Consider visual experience, When I see the bottle of wine in front of me on the table, I experience (I am visually aware of) the wine bottle. But I also experience my seeing. In experiencing my seeing in this way, I do not need to introspect or reflect; my awareness is instead an implicit and nonreflective one. I experience my seeing by living it nonreflectively. (2007, 285)

From a Madhyamaka perspective, this is seriously problematic stuff. When we say that a state is intrinsically conscious, we are stating that its being conscious is independent of its relation to any object, to any perceptual system, to any other psychological processes. Even philosophers like Dharmakīrti and Śāntarakṣita, with their respective accounts of the primitive manifestation of subjectivity in conscious states, took that subjectivity to be parasitic on their intentionality and directedness to an objective content. Zahavi's and Thompson's view, on the contrary, like Husserl's, raises the possibility of a state being conscious, but not being conscious of anything, and of the possibility of seeing without seeing anything. The multiplicity of objects of experience is either gratuitous or incoherent, and in its attempt to rescue consciousness and intentionality from reduction, leave these phenomena as unexplained primitives. It is indeed difficult to see how this makes sense at all. At this point, the Buddhist insistence that consciousness is a relation, not a brute, intrinsic property is surely a voice necessary to bring clarity to the discussion. The confusions entailed by this version of phenomenology only multiply:

> We are never conscious of an object *simpliciter*, but always of the object as appearing in a certain way; as judged, seen, described, feared, remembered, smelled, anticipated, tasted, and so on. We cannot be conscious of an object (a tasted lemon, a smelt rose, a seen table, a touched piece of silk) unless we are aware of the experience through which this object is made to appear (the tasting, smelling, seeing, touching). This is not to say that our access to, say, the lemon is *indirect*, or that it is mediated, contaminated, or blocked by our awareness of the experience; the given experience is not an object on a par with the lemon, but instead constitutes the access to the appearing lemon. The object is given through the experience; if there is no awareness of the experience, the object does not appear at all. (Zahavi 2007, 121)

At the end of this passage we have a conclusion that, at least from a Madhyamaka perspective, is a *reductio* on the entire project. "If there is no awareness of the experience, the object does not appear at all." Once again, if the experience is the appearance of the object, this is a tautology: If there is no appearance of the object, there is no appearance of the object. The claim is only contentful, though, if the experience is more than the appearance of the object, if it is a special inner appearing. And there is simply no reason to think that when I am aware of a blue sky, I am also aware of a second thing, namely its appearance. This really does seem like a needless multiplication of entities, and even worse, entities with obscure properties, obscure identity conditions, and which turn no explanatory wheels. Once again, reflection on the Buddhist tradition of thinking of consciousness not as some intrinsic property, but as a relation between thinkers and their objects, suggests a route out of this morass.

All of this brings us back to the question of the meaning of the phrase "what it is like," that looms so large in current discussions. Uriah Kriegel (2009), as we saw above, has helpfully distinguished two aspects of the intended meaning of this phrase, what he calls *qualitative character* and what he calls *for-me-ness*. He argues that any conscious experience must have both of these two characteristics, that that is *what it is like* to be conscious. We have already found reasons to doubt the need for consciousness to have some special qualitative character. The discussion of subjectivity above can help us in dismissing the need for *for-me-ness*.

Kriegel claims that consciousness consists in a kind of penumbral halo around every experience, whether perceptual or cognitive, that reveals it as *mine*. Now, he concedes that we have no introspective evidence for this. And we might add that there is no experimental psychological evidence, either. The argument would have to be philosophical. Rather than imagine such arguments, let us look once again at the conclusion. If the argument is meant to show that when I have an experience, it is *mine*, the claim is an empty tautology. But if the claim is that beyond the experience of the blue sky, there is an experience of *me seeing* the blue sky, and that that is *not* a higher-order or an introspective experience, we are back to a regress-generating, explanatorily impotent inner state for which there is no evidence, exactly the kind of position that Candrakīrti criticizes so trenchantly.

I conclude that one consequence of this Madhyamaka take on consciousness is that the phrase "what it is like" is simply devoid of any content, if it is meant to apply to anything other than the objects of experience, and does nothing to explicate consciousness. I can say what a blue sky is like: it is blue; what a red sunset is like: it is red. But to go further and to say that there is something *more* or *different* that it is like to see a blue sky or a red sunset is simply to obfuscate, and to posit an ineffable, mysterious nothing as a mediator of my awareness of the world. We will return to this issue and explore the sense of the phrase "what it is like" in greater depth in the next chapter.

When we turn to the question of *for-me-ness*, things are even worse. For the sense of *being mine*, and the sense of a *self* that is the subject of consciousness, as we have seen earlier, are, from *any* Buddhist perspective, necessarily illusory. For this character presupposes both the awareness of a subjective *self* and the appropriation of the experience as belonging to that self. On any Buddhist view, however, there is no such self, and there is no intrinsic possession relation between a self and its experiences or faculties. There are only psychological and physical states and processes, including sensory faculties that constitute subjectivity. Together they form the basis of imputation of a conventional person, but they do not *constitute* a *self*. So, to the extent that consciousness is implicated with self-consciousness, it is not *revelatory* of its character, an idea taken for granted in virtually all of this literature, but rather *obscurational*, or, in Sanskrit, *saṃvṛti, concealing*. So, even if, despite the absence both of introspective or scientific evidence, one felt compelled to posit this explanatorily impotent property of consciousness, if the general Buddhist framework for thinking about the self is at all correct, the consequence is only that consciousness is necessarily opaque, distorting its own character as it presents it and superimposing a deceptive subject-object duality. It might be better to rethink this posit.

## 9. Zombies and Other Exotica in Consciousness Studies

> We remain simply and necessarily strangers to ourselves, we do not understand ourselves, we must be confused about ourselves. For us this law holds for all eternity: "Each man is furthest from himself"—where we ourselves are concerned, we are not "knowledgeable people."
>
> —*Nietzsche, Genealogy of Morals*

No discussion of contemporary views of consciousness would be complete without a discussion of some of the central examples—real and imagined—that animate that discussion. For part of what makes it appear obvious that consciousness is some special *thing* or *property* with a nature either intrinsic or extrinsic is that we are invited to imagine the difference between conscious and unconscious states or beings, and to imagine in them in ways that they constitute what Dennett once called "intuition pumps" (1980). It is time to dispose of those once and for all, following the lead of the Buddhist-inspired analysis offered thus far.

Zombies perhaps play the leading role in this philosophical horror show. They are deployed effectively by Chalmers (2010) among others to argue that there is a special "hard problem" about consciousness, in virtue of the fact that there could be beings functionally exactly like us, but obviously unconscious—zombies. Now, nobody claims that these zombies are *nomologically* possible; the claim is rather that they are *metaphysically* possible. Let us leave aside for now (though we introduced the topic in chapter 1 and will return to this issue in chapter 7 below) what metaphysical possibility amounts to, and how we can determine what is metaphysically possible. Let us rather ask whether, even on a generous reading of the relevant modal metaphysics and epistemology, zombies so understood *are* metaphysically possible. We shall see that in taking them to be so a question is being begged, and that the begging of that question is obvious from a Buddhist perspective.

Zombies are nonsentient duplicates of us. There are two ways to characterize the sense in which they are duplicates, however. We can think of them as *physical duplicates* without qualitative states or as *functional duplicates* without qualitative states. There are good reasons to prefer the second option dialectically. If we are asked to imagine physical duplicates of us who lack *any* cognitive states at all, we might simply balk at the imaginative exercise. That is an exercise in special effects: we are asked to imagine something that *appears to be a duplicate*, but is not. I might as well be asked to imagine a triangle whose interior angles sum to 100°. The fact that I claim to be able to do so would be no guide to metaphysics, only to my own strange imaginative powers, real or illusory. It is at least prima facie more interesting to imagine zombies who are physical and functional duplicates of us, but who lack only qualitative states. If we can make sense of this, we might motivate a dualistic theory of consciousness, and this is the goal of the zombie exercise. It is for this reason that dialectically, even if zombie discussions begin with physical duplicates, they quickly move to a discussion of functional duplicates.

In this context, a functional duplicate must be understood as a being with the same beliefs, desires and other intentional states that we have, but who lacks any states with qualitative character. The idea here is that intentional states are relational, and can be characterized in terms of their typical causes and effects—their relations to stimuli, to behavior and to other intentional states; to have qualitative character, however, is taken to be monadic, to be intrinsic to the state itself. This is what gives zombies their plausibility, and the hope that their possibility can illuminate the nature of consciousness, and hence their starring role in contemporary Western philosophy of mind. But does it yield possibility? At least in a non-question-begging way?

Let us focus on the fact that a zombie is meant to be functionally—that is, cognitively—identical to a human being, but lacking in qualitative states. If it is not really cognitively like us, there is really nothing of interest here. For then, all we are really imagining is a special effect: something that *appears* to be human in interesting senses, but is not—a product of PIXAR, perhaps. Or we are asked to fall back on the implausible—and not obviously imaginable—target of a physical duplicate that behaves exactly like us, but with nothing inside. The important point, then, is that despite behavioral equivalence—and hence, at least prima facie, cognitive equivalence—there is nothing "that it is like" to be the zombie. It has no genuine experience, no consciousness. One can feel the pull of intuition here. (Though I note, non-probatively, but as an anecdotal aside—that nobody I have ever met from a Buddhist culture has found the case even vaguely intuitively compelling.)

Now, we can see the problem for this device: for the qualiaphile zombologist, (1) our beliefs about our perceptual states are *caused by* the qualitative character of our states, as are our introspective beliefs that we have experience; (2) zombies are cognitively/functionally identical to us; (3) zombies perceive the world (unconsciously) and believe that they have qualitative perceptual states; but (4) their beliefs are *not* caused by any qualitative states, because they lack them; their perceptual beliefs and their introspective beliefs that they have experience are false. It is obvious that these four claims are inconsistent with one another. Together they constitute a *reductio* on the hypothesis of the metaphysical possibility of zombies.

I do not want to go too far down the path of zombie debates, a path that leads through many thickets. I do note that Chalmers, among others, does reply to this argument. He argues (2010) that (1) is false, because the relation between qualitative states and qualitative beliefs is one of *constitution*, not *causation*. Hence, he argues, zombies don't have beliefs about qualitative states. This reply is patently question-begging. First, it requires a unique set of intentional states that are in part constituted by their objects, but second, it denies the obvious possibility that *false* qualitative beliefs are possible, in which case there is no way to tell whether we are zombies. He denies (2) on the grounds that whereas our states are caused by (or constituted by) qualia, zombies' states are not. But this would be to deny that zombies are enough like us to be duplicates, as opposed to mockups. It is thus hard to see how one can mount a non-question-begging argument for the possibility of zombies.

So, when we claim that zombies are devoid of qualitative states, while claiming that our own are cognitively relevant to our lives, we can no longer claim that zombies are cognitively like us. This conclusion only reinforces the Madhyamaka insight that consciousness is not a thing, or a unitary property, but a complex set of relations. Moreover, it shows that the very supposition that zombies are possible is equivalent to the supposition that there is a discrete something—qualitative character, or consciousness—that we can simply subtract from ourselves to get some other possible entity, the zombie. That supposition is not only false, but is the conclusion of the argument of which the possibility of zombies is meant to be a premise. (See Garfield 1996, as well as Braddon-Mitchell 2003, Hawthorne 2002 for more detailed discussion of this problem as well as Dennett 2003, Harman 1990 and Webster 2006 for other reasons to distrust zombie intuitions.)

It might appear that in a book about the importance of Buddhist philosophy to Western philosophy I am spending far too much time on this issue. There is a reason for this attention, though. Zombies *don't* show up in Buddhist discussions of mind and consciousness, and there is a reason that they do not. To be sure, they are meant to provide arguments for the non-physical status of consciousness, and just as there are modern dualists about the conscious and the physical, there were, and are, Buddhist dualists about these matters. These Buddhist dualists should welcome this line of argument, were it sound. But Buddhist philosophers saw that one can't simply treat consciousness as a simple thing or property that one either has or does not; it is a complex of states, processes and capacities; and Mādhyamika Buddhists like Candrakīrti and Tsongkhapa saw that we can't just look inside and report on the nature of our psychological states; nor can we say *a priori* what kinds of things have or lack any of these kinds of consciousness. These lessons are both apposite here; either would have forestalled the descent into this peculiar rabbithole wonderland.

Illusions of consciousness confirm this sensible approach. The well-known phenomena of inattentional blindness (Most 2010; Most et al. 2005; Rensink 2000b; Rensink, O'Regan and Clark 1997; Noë 2007; Simons 2000a, 2000b), change blindness (Rensink 2001, 2002, 2004; Noë, Pessoa and Thompson 2000; Simons and Ambinder 2005) and blindness to the anisotropy of the visual field suggest that not only do we refer to a motley, complex set of processes and states as *conscious*, and so that there is no unitary phenomenon to be called *consciousness*, but also that we are not introspectively authoritative regarding the objects and properties to which we are responding. The well-known phenomenon of masked priming (see for instance Masson and Isaak 1999) demonstrates conclusively that our cognitive processes respond to stimuli of which we had to be conscious, but which we cannot report, and of whose effects on our thought we are completely ignorant. Our conscious life is, rather than being transparent, opaque; rather than revealing our subjectivity often occludes it and its nature.

All of this suggests that while it appears that we know ourselves and our inner life intimately from a first-person point of view, a point of view that can provide immediate data for a theory of that life, in fact, we are strangers to ourselves, and what we take to be immediate data may be nothing more than illusion. Not only is there nothing that it is like to be me, but even my judgments of what particular experiences are like are likely to be useless. If zombies are possible, we may well be zombies. If they are not, we learn nothing about consciousness from the thought experiment. Once again, the Madhyamaka insight that the mind, and even consciousness, are hidden, rather than manifest phenomena, known only by inference, and through imperfect processes, can be a useful corrective to the easy use of introspection, speculation and shallow phenomenological analysis.

Blindsight raises further problems. Blindsighters affirm sincerely that they cannot see, are introspectively unaware of any vision, and form no articulable beliefs about the visible objects in their immediate environment (Collins 2010, Danckert and Rossetti 2005, Ptito and Leh 2007). Nonetheless, they navigate successfully around obstacles using only visual cues and reliably reach in the right place and for the right objects in forced choice situations, while insisting that they are only guessing. If we take consciousness to be necessarily transparent, or introspectible, or available for verbal report, or revelatory of our subjectivity, or as "feeling like something," or to satisfy any of the characterizations prevalent in the Western literature, we would have to conclude that blindsighters are not visually conscious.

Blindsighters' actions, however, are modulated by sensorimotor processes that are shared by ordinary sighted people, and blindsight might well be exactly like the visual mechanisms that subserve the visual experience of infrahuman animals, who may well not introspect and who do not report their visual experience. And it would be odd to deny them any consciousness. From a Buddhist perspective, there is no immediate reason to believe that all visual consciousness is introspectible, or that we are capable of reporting and reflecting on all that we see. Blindsight on this model simply involves the presence of one kind of consciousness in the absence of other kinds. Visual consciousness is present—there is receptivity and responsiveness to visual information—but this is not transmitted to introspective consciousness. Once again, this perspective, like this phenomenon, suggests that the construct of consciousness as an entity or property is just too simple to do justice to that which it is called to explain.

## 10. The Epistemology of Self-Knowledge

> Though clouds' illusions I recall
> I really don't know clouds at all.
>
> —*Joni Mitchell.*

Madhyamaka and Yogācāra accounts of the mind remind us of the complexity and limitations of introspection. Even the most optimistic and, we might say, naively realistic accounts of the introspective sense faculty we find in the Buddhist literature remind us that it is very much a sense faculty. As such, even if its objects are in some sense, or in principle, known by such a sense faculty, they are known fallibly. If they are intrinsically self-revealing, on the other hand, while they are not then known through the mediation of a human sensory system, to the degree that we take up that knowledge and make use of it, it is only subject to higher-order reflection. And such reflection is imperfect on a number of dimensions, and is always deeply inflected by our conceptual framework. As a consequence, we can't think of introspection as a veridical means for simply delivering the inner world to subjectivity. Just how we can think of it is a complex matter.

Finally, and consequent upon this insight regarding the fallibility of the introspective sense, a review of Buddhist accounts of the project of self-knowledge reminds us that we may be massively confused about its structure, about its object and about the epistemic credentials of introspection or phenomenological reflection as tools for the use in the development of a theory of mind. (Schwitzgebel 2011 makes similar observations.) To inquire into the nature of self-knowledge in the first place is to grant that we don't know how it works, and so to grant that these seemingly obvious instruments may be entirely deceptive. So not only are the objects of introspection delivered in an opaque way, but the instruments we use, and even the data delivered by those instruments are, in a deep sense, opaque to us. Self-knowledge becomes very elusive indeed.[21]

To use introspective data themselves, and to treat them as constituting an unproblematic given in that investigation, is then to treat the investigation as complete before it has begun. If we truly don't know what the mind is, how it works, or how we might know about it, considerably more epistemic humility regarding what seems evident to us as we reflect on it may well be in order. If we learn nothing else from the Buddhist tradition of reflection on the mind than this, reflection on that tradition is well worth the trouble.

What does all of this suggest for current discussions of self-knowledge? While one cannot simply map Buddhist debates onto current debates, I do think that the dialectic we see developing from 5th-century India through 15th-century Tibet helps us to appreciate both the perils of immediate first-order accounts of self-knowledge, and the degree to which taking higher-order views seriously forces us closer to taking knowledge of our inner lives to be very much like knowledge of the external world. We are thus led to accept a serious falliblism about introspection, and to appreciate the complex and problematic role of inference and theory in making sense even of higher-order perceptual processes. All of this means that what we might take as unproblematic explananda for, or commonsense intuitions to be accommodated by, theories of self-knowledge, might instead be illusions or delusions to be explained away.

Long ago, Dennett (1991) made the same point, perhaps channeling Buddhist ideas unawares. He distinguishes between two approaches to phenomenology (44–45). The first takes as its task the mapping of our inner life, of inner episodes, processes and experiences as they are—of the structure of

21. We should note in this context, however, that there is a very different position also represented in classical Indian Buddhist philosophy, one which attracts a great deal of attention both in the Indian and Tibetan literature and in contemporary Buddhist Studies and cross-cultural phenomenology. (See especially Coseru 2012, Thompson 2011 and the essays in Siderits, Thompson and Zahavi 2013.) That is the position of Dignāga and his followers, according to which we have immediate verdical access to our own perceptual states, in virtue of their being self-presenting and reflexive. We will consider this position in detail in the next chapter. This is the position against which Candrakīrti and his followers react. See Coseru (2012) for a defense of this position.

consciousness, we might say—taking as authoritative introspective reports of that inner world and our sense of what it must be like. The second takes as its task mapping the claims that people make about their inner life and the popular lore about what consciousness and its contents must be like—a kind of anthropology of phenomenological reflection.

While it might appear that the former is serious philosophy and the latter is merely a superficial survey of attitudes, Dennett points out that only the second has any respectable epistemic credentials. We can know what people say about their inner lives; but only if we take people to be oracular about those lives do we have any grounds for taking the inner appearances or experiences they report seriously as entities, and that requires an improbable model of introspection, one taken for granted by almost everyone in the contemporary consciousness literature in virtue of regarding our intuitions about our own inner experience as constituting the data to which a theory of consciousness must respond.

From a Buddhist perspective, we can recast this as the distinction between exploring an illusion versus taking that illusion for granted as reality. We know that our inner sense, like our outer sense, is fallible; we know that we tend to reify ourselves and to take our introspective awareness as well as our external perceptual faculties as more reliable than they are. We know that our understanding of our lives is deeply theoretically infected and that our theories are always tentative. To take what introspection delivers as reality is therefore, from a Buddhist perspective, simply to embrace delusion. On the other hand, to take what we believe about introspection seriously as a matter for reflection is to take delusion as an object for study, and that may be the first step not to an oracular understanding of an inner reality, but at least to an understanding of our own capacity to obscure whatever that reality might be.

The Chan/Zen tradition offers one more insight we might well consider in closing. In distinguishing between (1) acting thoughtlessly; (2) acting with thought and (3) acting without-thinking, Zen theorists challenge us to reconceive the omnipresence and necessity of self-consciousness in consciousness as well as the introspectibility and explicit availability to reflection of conscious experience. Consider the mastery of a skill, such as that of playing the piano or playing football. One first might bang away at the keys or kick the ball aimlessly about the pitch with no particular thought; we might even say that one is not conscious of what one is doing. Perhaps the mind is elsewhere; perhaps there just aren't the conceptual resources to make sense of one's activity. But with a bit of coaching and prompting, one begins to play with thought, attending to where one's fingers are on the keys, to how one strikes the ball, to where one's teammates are on the field. At this point, perhaps, we might think that one is acting with maximum consciousness.

But of course when real expertise clicks in, all of that thought that was once so necessary to guide action drops off. Action becomes automatic. One is no longer able to say where one's fingers are, of what key is to be struck next, of the angle of one's foot, or even who is where on the field. One just plays, spontaneously and expertly.[22] Now, in *one sense*, that of explicit access to what is going on, that of phenomenal feel, or of self-consciousness, there is no consciousness. But this is a straightforward *reductio* on these criteria of consciousness. From the standpoint both of Chan theory and of common sense, it is in this kind of expert performance that consciousness is most manifest and most present, when our responsiveness and effectiveness are at their maximum, when we are most fully engaged, most fully present. Once we realize this, we might reflect on the fact that most of what we do—walking, interacting with one another, cooking, reading—we do with something like this expert consciousness. This is the stuff waking life is made of, and in this mode of engagement, the world is, as Heidegger would put it, ready-to-hand, not present-to-hand, in a mode of conscious engagement that is not introspected, in which the subject is not present even as periphery, and in which both higher-order and reflexive thought is absent. We will return to this topic in more detail in the next chapter.

This suggests that a Buddhist perspective can do a great deal to enrich contemporary discussions of consciousness. It brings a suite of insights that can refigure debates and ways of thinking about the topic. Instead of seeing consciousness as a singular phenomenon, a natural surd perhaps requiring non-natural explanations, the Buddhist asks us to think of consciousness as a family of relations that subjects might bear to their objects. Its different levels and manifestations may require very different kinds of explanations. But in each case they will take the form of natural explanations of the relations between psychological processes and their conditions or objects, not mysterious powers of a self or subjectivity.

22. Compare Merleau-Ponty (1962) on the embodiment of skill.

# 6 PHENOMENOLOGY

The term "phenomenology" is rather elastic in contemporary philosophical discourse. Broadly speaking, it is the study of the nature of experience, of the cognitive processes and structures that enable experience and of the nature of subjectivity. Phenomenology is concerned especially with the first-person point of view, with a deep exploration of subjectivity. None of these phrases is as clear as we would like them to be, but then neither is the topic itself.

In the West, the tradition of phenomenology is complex and replete with differences in perspective and position. It is fair to credit Husserl with the introduction of phenomenology as a particular kind of philosophical inquiry—a transcendental inquiry into the conditions of the subjectivity of experience, conducted by a bracketing of ontological questions regarding the status of the objects of experience—and as an alternative both to metaphysics and epistemology as they were practiced in the 19th century. Thompson characterizes the Husserlian program eloquently:

> Phenomenology, in is original Husserlian inspiration, grows out of the recognition that we can adopt in our own first-person case different mental attitudes or stances toward the world, life and experience. In everyday life we are usually straightforwardly immersed in various situations and projects... Besides being directed toward these more or less particular, "thematic" matters, we are also directed at the world as an unthematic horizon of all our activity. Husserl calls this attitude of being straightforwardly immersed in the world "the natural attitude," and he thinks it is characterized by a kind of unreflective "positing" of the world as something existing "out there" more or less independently of us.

> In contrast, the "phenomenological attitude," arises when we step back from the natural attitude, not to deny it, but in order to investigate the very experiences it comprises.... We are to attend to the world strictly as it appears and as it is phenomenally manifest. Put another way, we should attend to the modes or ways in which things appear to us. We thereby attend to things strictly as correlates of our experience, and the focus of our investigation becomes the correlational structure of our subjectivity and the appearance or disclosure of the world. Things remain before us, but we investigate them in a new way, namely, strictly as experienced. (2007, 17–18)

Nonetheless, it would be unduly restrictive to regard all phenomenology as Husserlian. Husserl emphasizes the "bracketing" of the external object of intentional states and the analysis of the intentional, temporal and transcendental structure of the conscious states and their immediate intentional objects themselves. Heidegger, on the other hand, emphasizes the immediate embeddedness of subjectivity in the world, and argues that such bracketing is impossible, or at least a terrible distortion of the nature of experience.

For Merleau-Ponty our embodiment and the ways in which feeling, perception and action structure our experience are the central phenomenological facts. In Sartre's work, by contrast, self-consciousness takes center stage, with an emphasis on social relations and moral experience in the wings. And de Beauvoir emphasizes the central roles that gender and gender relations play in phenomenological reflection. Phenomenology then, even as practiced by the great luminaries of the European movement, is a multifaceted phenomenon. Nonetheless, it has a recognizable core: the reflective investigation of the nature and of the transcendental conditions of the possibility of subjectivity.

Much contemporary phenomenological reflection, while drawing on the insights and methodology of these "classic" figures in the European phenomenological tradition, draws heavily as well on contemporary cognitive science. For if the goal of phenomenological reflection is to understand the structure of experience, and the motor, sensory, social, ecological and intentional processes that together constitute that experience, we do well to heed what science tells us about how we actually work. Reflection has its place, but then so do empirical data. And so we see recent work in phenomenology by such philosophers as Gallagher (2007, 2012a, 2012b), Noë (2004), Kriegel (2007), Levine (2001), Carruthers (2000), Zahavi (2004), Thompson (2014), Metzinger (2003) and others (Thompson and Zahavi 2007, Thompson, Lutz and Cosmelli 2005, Thompson and Varela 2003) relying explicitly on empirical psychology as well, giving birth to the burgeoning field of neurophenomenology.

I say all of this because while there is this vast diversity in approaches to phenomenology, and hence a tendency to fight over the term, it is fair to say that the domain is reasonably well limned; it is broad enough, however, to countenance a wide variety of approaches to detailing its geography. Broadly speaking, when we do phenomenology, we ask what it is to be a subject, and more specifically, what it is to be a *human* subject. This inquiry may well begin with introspection, but it can hardly end there, and all phenomenologists are insistent on the difference between phenomenological reflection and mere introspection (Gallagher and Zahavi 2008, 23–24). Introspective data, as we argued in the previous chapter, themselves tell us very little—at best what the most manifest contents of our experience are at a single moment. And even that may well be subject to the distortions of an imperfect introspective faculty.

The data of introspection, to the degree to which they are given to us discursively, require interpretation, and so, as Heidegger emphasized, a hermeneutic method is necessary to the enterprise of phenomenology. Moreover, introspective data are always particular. General reflection therefore requires analysis, inquiry into the transcendental conditions of experience of any kind, and reflection on the alternative modes of being and consciousness of which humans are capable. Phenomenology, that is, is theory. And hence it is always contested, even though the apparent immediacy of the data with which we begin might suggest no room for doubt or disagreement.

We can put this point in a slightly different register by distinguishing between a "naive" and a "jaded" view of introspective evidence. On the naive view, introspection is both easy and veridical: we just look inside, and our inner life is presented to us just as it is, with no possibility of illusion or error. On this view, there is all the difference in the world, to use Kantian terminology, between inner and outer sense: Outer sense is mediated and fallible; inner sense immediate and infallible. On the jaded view, when we look inside, our inner perception is as clouded, subject to error, and as theoretically infected as any external perception.

Our inner sense may be subject to cognitive illusion; our observations may be biased by theory; we may have inadequate conceptual resources to characterize what we find, and so may be unable to achieve any judgments regarding the nature of our inner life in which we have the right to place any confidence. That is, on the jaded view, our access to our inner life is mediated, just like our access to the outer world. It is mediated both by the faculty itself by means of which we introspect, which functions, as I argued in the previous chapter, as a kind of inner measuring instrument—but an instrument the operations and fidelity of which are opaque to us—and by the conceptual resources we use to formulate the judgments that encapsulate our views about our inner life, concepts of whose adequacy to the domain we use them to limn we must remain uncertain. On the jaded view, then, as I argued in the previous chapter, there is good reason to be leery about the data of introspection.[1]

One last preliminary note is in order. Since Thomas Nagel's landmark essay "What Is It Like to be a Bat?" (1974), the phrase "what it is like" has come to dominate Anglophone phenomenological discourse. Some would even characterize phenomenology as the study of "what it is like to be conscious" or to characterize consciousness as "a state that there is something that it is like to be in." Zahavi says that "most people are prepared to concede that that there is necessarily something 'it is like' for a subject to undergo an experience..." (2005, 15). Kriegel takes it as unproblematically obvious that "there is something that it is like for me to have my experience" (2009, 8). Galen Strawson writes of "the wholly concrete phenomenon of the experiential 'what-it is-likeness' of experience" (2013, 102). Coseru even glosses the Sanskrit *caitta* (or mental constituent—the fundamental phenomena that constitute mental events and processes) as "the what-it-is-likeness of experience" (2012, 69). And even Schwitzgebel, no friend of the phenomenological mainstream, defines *consciousness* as "whatever it is in virtue of which (in Nagel's 1974 terminology) there is 'something it is like' to be you, or a bat, and (presumably) nothing it's like to be a rock, or a toy robot" (2011, 93–94). We could continue this perp parade for quite a while.

Nagel's phrase has legs, to be sure. We have considered it above and will return to it below, but for now I would like to set it aside. Let us just note for now that the very nominalization it involves suggests a particular; a particular we could come to know. This may well be an instance of what Wittgenstein called "the decisive move in the conjuring trick" (*Philosophical Investigations* §308) the one we don't notice but that saddles us with an entity that we come to take for granted, and strive to understand—a set of inner mechanisms and phenomena—just like external, physical, mechanisms and phenomena, only neither external nor physical! We should begin our investigation instead with the idea, already suggested in the previous chapter, that there may well be nothing that anything is like, just because that phrase is empty, and see where we our investigation takes us. This move is suggested by Carruthers (2011) and Metzinger (2003) as well.

We will proceed by moving between Western and Buddhist approaches, drawing on the fruits of the last few chapters. I am spending so much time on

1. Note that this view that introspection is conceptually and perceptually mediated is not the view that perception—outer or inner—is *indirect*. That is, this is not the claim that perception is mediated by *representations*. It is consistent with that view, but does not entail it. Perception, on this view, might be direct in that it is not representationally mediated, despite being mediated both conceptually and through perceptual faculties.

preliminary discussions of the phenomenological enterprise because I think that phenomenological reflection is absolutely central to—but easy to miss in—Buddhist philosophy. It is easy to miss because it is not thematized as such. Buddhist phenomenological reflection is undertaken often in what appears to be a metaphysical, epistemological or even psychological or soteriological register, and it is hence easy to overlook the fact that in a particular case (and we will consider cases below) what is really at issue is phenomenology.

Phenomenology is central to Buddhist thought, because in the end, Buddhism is about the transformation of the way we experience the world. It begins with an analysis of how ordinary beings take up with the world, and how that engenders suffering. Buddhist analysis continues with an account of the cognitive and intentional structures that constitute that mode of comportment. The whole point of that analysis is to conclude with an account of how they can be transformed so as to enable us to experience the world without engendering suffering. And of course that requires an account of what the structure of such a consciousness would be. One way to think of Buddhist philosophy, then—though not the only way—is phenomenology at the beginning, the middle and the end.

## 1. Surface versus Deep Phenomenology

*There is fiction in the space between you and reality.*
*You would do and say anything*
*To make your everyday life seem less mundane.*

—*Tracy Chapman*

We need to begin with a distinction between two kinds of phenomenology, which I call "surface" and "deep" phenomenology reflecting the similar distinction that commentators such as Zahavi [2008] draw between phenomenology as introspection and phenomenology as transcendental analysis. Phenomenological reflection, even careful, illuminating reflection, and observation by sophisticated, trained observers, is directed in the first instance, almost by definition, at those cognitive states and processes that are accessible to introspection. Indeed, this is often what some philosophers and psychologists mean by "phenomenology"—the inner world of which we have, at least in psychological principle, conscious awareness, and which we can describe. (See Dennett 1978b, 182–186 and Metzinger 2003, 36.) It is not always easy to introspect in a revealing way, of course, and reasonable people disagree about what one finds when one does look within and especially what it is to look within, but we have a pre-theoretic fix on this inner world and our access to it. The sophisticated articulation of its contours is what I call "surface phenomenology."

The term "surface" here is meant not to disparage the sophistication of such reflection, or of the theories of mental life arising therefrom, but to emphasize that phenomenology in this sense—as sophisticated introspection—penetrates no further than the surface of our cognitive lives, necessarily only to that which can in principle be observed, not to the non-introspectible processes and events that underlie and generate it. This point will be clearer once we contrast surface with deep phenomenology.

Deep phenomenology is the inquiry into the fundamental cognitive, affective and perceptual processes that underlie and which are causally or constitutively—biologically or metaphysically—responsible for those we find in introspection. This is necessarily an experimental and theoretical enterprise, not an introspective one. It is the enterprise undertaken in the West not only by such philosophers as Husserl, Heidegger, Merleau-Ponty, Sartre and de Beauvoir as well as their contemporary heirs, but also by such psychologists as Simons (2000a, 2000b); Rensink (2000b); Lutz, Dunne and Davidson (2007); Lutz and Thompson (2003); Brefcynski-Lewis et al. (2007); Farb et al. (2007); Khalsa et al. (2008); McLean et al. (2010); Moore and Maliniowski (2009); Shear (2004); Shear and Jevning (1999); Raffone, Tagini and Srinivasan (2010); Varela (1996, 1999); Varela and Shear (1999); and in the Buddhist tradition first in the development of the Abhidharma, later by such philosophers as Asaṅga, Vasubandhu, Śāntarakṣita and Kamalaśila, and elaborated at length in various Chinese and Tibetan traditions.

To get a feel for the difference, consider your visual field. Right now. Is it colored or black and white? Uniform or gappy? Simultaneously or successively apprehended? Precedent or subsequent to the fixation of attention? These are questions about the phenomenology of perception. In each case, the answer is not simple: shallow and deep reflection yield very different answers, although each is accurate at its respective level, and each must be taken seriously in a complete phenomenological analysis of human perception.

Most of us experience our visual field as richly colored from left to right, top to bottom. That is true, but shallow. We also know that only the central 10% of the field is actually processed in color: the rest is black and white, with the color experience filled in by, not delivered to, central processes. Our *deep* visual phenomenology is hence largely monochrome; the *lebenswelt* of our surface phenomenology is a construction from the *ur-welt* of our deep phenomenology. (See Stiles 1959, Hurvich and Jameson 1960.) Understanding how this happens causally is a matter for the psychology of perception; understanding its significance for our self-understanding and for the interpretation of our experience is a matter for philosophical phenomenological reflection.

We experience our visual field as uniform in character. We have already noted that this is not so from a chromatic point of view at the deep level. But things at the deep level are even worse: There are holes at the center of our visual world where the optic nerve enters the retina. While these holes not introspectible, and hence not a fact of surface phenomenology, they set a task for the visual system in the construction of our introspectible experience. Moreover, our visual field is delivered to us in the form of two slightly different images that must be integrated by the visual sense faculty. At the surface level we see one world; at a deeper level, two. Philosophers and psychologists in the West since Goethe and Schopenhauer have been aware of this phenomenon.

Finally in this parade of now commonplace facts about our visual system at the *surface* level, we experience our visual field as present to us simultaneously from edge to edge. But we know that at a *deeper* level, only small parts of it are being processed from the bottom up at any moment; the arc of our vision is generated not by a photographic transfer of what is in front of us to consciousness, but through a constantly updated stitching together of moments of apprehension of different zones within that field. What is experienced as a still photograph at the surface level is a filmstrip—or a pair of damaged filmstrips—at the deeper level. (See Fisher and Weber 1993 for a good discussion.)[2]

Recent research into inattentional blindness (Most 2010; Most et al. 2005; Rensink 2000b; Rensink, O'Regan and Clark 1997; Noë 2007; Simons 2000a, 2000b) has only amplified our sense of the disjunction between the deep and surface facts of our phenomenology. Inattentional blindness really is *blindness* at the level of surface phenomenology. But we know that a refocusing of attention eliminates that blindness. We don't see (at the introspectible level)

2. Buddhist scholars have also been aware for millennia that our ordinary perceptual experience is the result of cognitive processes that operate on sensory input to yield experience of a constructed reality that is erroneously taken to be an accurate representation of an external world existing independently of our perceptual processes. For this reason it is an important voice in this discussion. But that doesn't mean that it should be the dominant voice. To be sure Buddhism does not need cognitive science to tell it that there is a *parikalpita svabhāva*—an imagined nature that we superimpose on experience. But the details regarding how this superimposition is achieved are not present in any Buddhist accounts of perception or cognition of which contemporary scholars are aware. This is not surprising. They are hard to discover. On the other hand, contemporary cognitive science is rather thin on the implications for consciousness of the complex transcendental conditions of experience that emerge when we reflect on the nature of this kind of superimposition. This is not surprising, either. These are not straightforwardly empirical matters. One more reason why Buddhism and Western philosophy need to be in dialogue with one another.

the gorilla when we are counting the basketball catches; we do see the gorilla when we look for it. But this also tells us that at a more fundamental level—the deeper, non-introspectible level—information is cognitively available and that it is actively suppressed before reaching surface consciousness. That filtering, like the invisible seams that stitch together our visual field, and like countless other such processes that we only discover through careful experimental paradigms, is essential to the construction of the surface phenomenology we enjoy (Simons 2000a, 2000b). There is far more to experience than meets the eye, or even than meets the most careful and honest introspection.

For this reason, we must countenance the possibility of significant error in introspection, just as we recognize the possibility of significant error in external perception. Some of this error derives from simple inattention to our current states; that may be remediable by psychological training, or just by the resolution to attend more carefully to our own lives. Some of that error may be caused by the adoption of inadequate or confused conceptual schemes as the categories in terms of which we understand and report to ourselves our own inner lives. After all, the unit of introspective knowledge, just like the unit of perceptual knowledge, is the observation sentence, not a mere feeling, and sentences require predicates, which require conceptual schemes.

There are multiple ways in which we might report our inner lives. Some are the stuff of Western folk psychology; some the categories or orthodox Indian philosophy of mind; some the frameworks of the Abhidharma, and some the stuff of complex tantric texts. None has a privileged claim to correctness. Then there is the possibility of simple introspective illusion. Our introspective sense may be as subject to illusion as are our external senses. And finally, summing up all of these issues, is the simple fact that our introspective faculties are opaque to us. There is no guarantee that what our introspective sense delivers bears any relation to anything really going on at deeper levels of our minds.

Why call this deeper level of our psychological life phenomenological at all? For several reasons. First, it is essential to understand this deep level in order to understand our surface phenomenology. This is not only the stuff waking life is made of; it must also be the stuff that *awakened* life is made of. Second, in the quest to understand what it is to be conscious, we need to understand not only that which we can report in introspection, but that which is waiting in the wings, sometimes introspectible in principle, but even if not, accessible to processes that appear to be making cognitive *decisions* that determine the character of our inner life: attend to this, not to this; patch this remembered bit into this hole; keep the field steady, even though the retinal image is moving, and countless other such decisions. We will see this drive to treat these subconscious, subpersonal processes phenomenologically despite their opacity to introspection mirrored in Yogācāra Buddhist discussions of distorted consciousness (*kliśṭamanas*) and the foundation consciousness below.

## 2. The Complexity of the Interior

Buddhist philosophy of mind and psychology generally promise accounts of deep phenomenology as an explanation of our surface phenomenology. Buddhist accounts of perception, memory, attention, and suffering typically refer to states and processes to which ordinary persons do not have introspective access. And many claims for meditative practice and expertise are claims to access these deep states in meditative equipoise; indeed the reports of meditators are often important—though not the only—evidence for certain Buddhist claims about deep phenomenology. These accounts of consciousness are robust theoretical accounts precisely *because* they operate at this level, and the fact that processes at these levels are regarded by most Buddhists as *conscious* processes is the final reason that it makes sense to treat this level as a phenomenological level of analysis. Indeed, one of the important features of Buddhist phenomenology is its identification of a variety of cognitive processes as kinds of consciousness, and hence an early insight into the complex, multilayered, and often cognitively impenetrable character of consciousness itself. As we have already seen, debates about the degree to which consciousness is transparent to itself are important in Buddhist philosophy, and while Buddhist philosophers offer us deep theoretical insights into conscious life some of the deepest insights are into its ineliminable opacity.

Consideration of deep phenomenology raises complex questions about the nature of consciousness. The philosophy of cognitive science has lately been much preoccupied with the nature of consciousness, and indeed there is welcome new dialogue between phenomenologists and cognitive scientists, as is evident by the success and quality of *The Journal of Consciousness Studies* and a host of recent books, articles and research programs too numerous to cite and too fecund to ignore. Buddhist philosophy has been focused on the nature of consciousness for much longer, and it might well be useful to attend to the results of that sustained reflection (as indeed many contemporary cognitive neuroscientists have under the auspices of the Mind and Life Institute dialogues over the past quarter century).

Some (see, e.g. Wallace 2008, 2009) have argued that the greatest contribution that Buddhist philosophy can make to cognitive science is an account of the nature of consciousness born of meditative introspection into the deep phenomenology that underlies our ordinary thought. Proponents of such a view argue that consciousness is immediately knowable, self-revealing and hence always in principle the object of veridical apperception. The reasons advanced for this position are far from convincing. They rely either on the assurances of experienced meditators that when they look inside they know what they see, and that their results are stable, or on an *a priori* claim that there can be no appearance–reality gulf in the domain of the psychic interior. But neither line of argument is compelling. Beyond the manifest circularity of relying on the testimony of trained introspectors that trained introspection is veridical, the fact is that meditators in different traditions find different things when they look inside. Hindu meditators find their *ātman;* Buddhist meditators find its absence, and so on. And this is not surprising given the falsity of the claim to the transparency of the inner. As we saw above, there are simply too many veils between naive introspection and our cognitive interior for there to be any security in introspective reports.

And this view is far from unanimous in the Buddhist tradition, canonical or modern. On any Buddhist view, as we have seen, consciousness is a many-leveled phenomenon. The coarsest levels of consciousness are on all accounts introspectible by ordinary agents in ordinary states; the subtler levels, however, are the ones that matter for an understanding of the nature of our experience, and these, most traditional scholars argue, are too deep for most of us to introspect. These deeper and more subtle levels of consciousness—what many in cognitive science might regard as analogues to unconscious cognitive processes—are, according to some (but not all) Buddhist traditions, accessible to the introspection of highly advanced meditators. Many Buddhist scholars, however, such as Candrakīrti and Tsongkhapa, argue that no human who has not attained full awakening (and they are *very special beings* indeed) could ever pretend to know the mind at all through introspection—that it is a hidden phenomenon from all ordinary beings.[3]

The transparency of the depths of the mind is hence a matter that is up for discussion in the Buddhist world. But very similar considerations apply to *surface* phenomenology, once we penetrate beyond mere appearances. Here we may be tempted by the image of immediate direct access to our own minds, a temptation common to Western and Buddhist epistemologists. But we must ask ourselves whether this assumption of the possibility of immediacy, of pure, uncontaminated apperception, actually makes sense at any level. Or must our

3. Carruthers mistakenly claims (2011, 30–31) that all Buddhist traditions regard consciousness as transparent to itself. This is simply an error, one that it is easy to understand if one has not read the relevant texts. Such errors demonstrate the need for more than casual conversation when we try to work across cultural boundaries and philosophical traditions.

access to the mind always be theoretically mediated? If so, what are the consequences of that mediation for our self-understanding, self-consciousness, and for the structure of subjectivity itself?

Prior to all of these questions is a meta-question about questions concerning consciousness. Some (but not all) Buddhists share with some (but certainly not all) cognitive scientists and some (but not all) phenomenologists a tendency to think of consciousness as a kind of *thing*, or at least as a discrete *property*. We can then ask, as we did in the previous chapter, how many kinds or loci of consciousness there are, whether they are physical or not, what the neural correlates of it are, whether machines can have it, etc. These questions may or may not be interesting, and may or may not have answers. But they share a common presupposition which must be interrogated in either tradition, viz., that there *is* something (or even some things that cluster meaningfully into a natural kind) denoted by *consciousness, awareness, jñāna/shes pa (shehpa), vedanā/tshor ba (tzorwa), rig pa,* and other such terms about which these questions can meaningfully be asked. We have introduced these issues in the previous chapter, but we now must engage them in more detail.

So far, we have been discussing the *vijñānas*, or cognitive functions, as kinds of consciousness, and that is natural. But part of what we regard as the landscape of consciousness in the West is subsumed in a Buddhist taxonomy not under *vijñāna*, but rather under *vedanā/tshor ba*, usually translated as *feeling, awareness* or sometimes as *hedonic tone*. The latter translation captures the fact that *vedanā* is experienced on a continuum from unpleasant to pleasant. But the former captures the fact that it is associated with the immediate sensory experience of a perceptual episode and that there is a separate kind of *vedanā* for each of the six sense faculties.

We can think of *vedanā* loosely as the sensory component of perceptual experience; it is pre-conceptual, and is immediately and primitively affective. The pleasurable scent and red sensation is *vedanā;* the awareness of it as an experience of a rose is *vijñāna*. Like *vijñāna, vedanā* is introspectible; unlike it, it is non-conceptual; it contributes the affective tone and sensory character to an episode of *vijñāna*, and gives rise to that richer form of consciousness. Buddhist and Western accounts of conscious phenomena may therefore often be accounts of different phenomena.

Now, the preliminary discussion of a Buddhist anatomy of consciousness in the previous chapter barely scratches the surface, just as we have barely scratched the surface of Western accounts of consciousness. Specific accounts of the operations and structure of different cognitive processes underlying our conscious life are rich, complex and various in that tradition. But it is enough to see that the Buddhist tradition carves things up a bit differently than does the Western tradition. Neither, when adumbrated with any sophistication, regards consciousness as a unitary phenomenon. But they see the complexity of conscious life as demanding different kinds of analyses, and different kinds of taxonomies. This would be surprising only if we thought that our conscious life is self-presenting. Instead it must be recovered by careful theoretical reflection, and theoretical reflection can yield different results if undertaken from different starting points. The Western philosopher typically starts from a horizon of a primordially given individual, unitary subjectivity; the Buddhist with the view that the experience of a self is necessarily illusory.[4]

The fact that consciousness is neither a unitary phenomenon nor is immediately available to introspection, or even to introspection supplemented by *a priori* reflection, means that deep phenomenology as an enterprise is essential to understanding ourselves. It also means that deep phenomenology is *hard*. It requires us to use techniques of examination that rely on theory and experiment, not simple observation, however sophisticated that observation may be, or however difficult it may be to cultivate it. The mind guards its secrets as jealously as any other natural phenomenon. It also means that we had better pay attention to insights that others may have, inasmuch as there may be no cultural Archimedean fulcrum for understanding the mind. Let us now explore in detail one Yogācāra exploration of the structure of subjectivity, one that takes up with the topic in a way radically distinct from any we find in the Western tradition. While we cannot hope to survey all Buddhist phenomenological approaches, or indeed all of those within the Yogācāra tradition, I hope that this will serve as an example of the utility of attention to this tradition as a way to deepen and to extend Western thought about these matters, and as encouragement to dialogue.

## 3. *Trisvabhāva* Theory and Yogācāra Phenomenology

Phenomenology is not metaphysics, but an alternative to it. Rather than ask about the ultimate nature of things, as the metaphysician does, the phenomenologist asks about our mode of subjectivity in relation to those things, and the way they manifest themselves in our *lebenswelt*. Nor is phenomenology epistemology; again, it is an alternative, asking not whether or how we know about objects in the world, but rather about how we are *aware* of the objects that figure in our experience, whether veridically or not. Now, to be sure—and

4. This does *not* mean that no Buddhist phenomenologists take for granted a primordially given horizon of subjectivity *tout court*. As Coseru argues persuasively (2012, 235–262.) Dignāga understood reflexive awareness as just such a horizon of subjectivity, albeit not the presentation of a unitary self, but rather of the fact that each distinct moment of awareness has a subjective as well as an objective aspect.

this is one of the attractions of the phenomenological project—important metaphysical or epistemological conclusions regarding human life might fall out from phenomenological analysis, but the project itself is one of interrogating experience, not its transcendental objects, if indeed there are any.

As we noted at the outset of this chapter, there is a distinction to be drawn between a phenomenological investigation of the kind Husserl conducts, in which *bracketing* the external world plays a central part, and one of the kind Heidegger conducts, in which such bracketing is regarded as literally incoherent. That methodological contrast structures much of late 20th- and early 21st-century Western phenomenology and its debates. Perhaps it need not have done so. Perhaps these are not as radical alternatives as they appear. Vasubandhu's phenomenological reflection might help us to get beyond that.

Vasubandhu introduces near the end of *Treatise on the Three Natures (Trisvabhāvanirdeśa)*, the last text he wrote,[5] a simile drawn from the *Discourse Unravelling the Thought* in order to illustrate the relationship between the three natures. The specific characters of these natures, their role in phenomenology, and the structure of conscious experience that arises from Vasubandhu's account will become clear as we proceed. The simile refers to what appears to be a classical Indian roadside magic show in which (the details are hazy, and my attempts to replicate this feat have failed spectacularly) a magician uses a piece of wood or a pile of sticks as a prop, and somehow—allegedly by the use of a mantra that affects the minds of those in the audience, though it is important to the simile that only the magician really knows how the trick works—causes the audience to see these sticks as a real elephant. In the opening verses of this section (27 and 28) Vasubandhu tells us that our perception of external objects is *in some sense* like the perception of the elephant by the naive villagers in the show. There is no elephant. But we must be careful to see what corresponds to the elephant as we adumbrate the simile.

5. See especially Lusthaus (2003) for a compelling defense of a phenomenological understanding of Vasubandhu's project, but note that Lusthaus (personal communication) also denies the ascription of the *Treatise on the Three Natures* to Vasubandhu, on the grounds first that Xuanzang does not mention or translate it, second that he finds stylistic differences between this text and other verse texts of Vasubandhu, and third that there are no Indian commentaries on the text. These are interesting arguments. But I do not think that they are compelling reasons to take the canonical attribution to be erroneous. According to the biography of Vasubandhu, he composed this text in the last year of his life. This late composition would explain some stylistic difference (after all, one ought not compare the styles of *Tractatus Logico-Philosophicus* and *Philosophical Investigations*, and conclude that they were not authored by the same person), as well as the fact that there are no commentaries (Vasubandhu himself wrote autocommentaries on his other texts, which served as the basis of later commentaries), and the dearth of commentaries could also explain Xuanzang's omission of this text in his own project. I take the matter to be unsettled, but see no positive reason to reject the authenticity of the text.

27. Like an elephant that appears
Through the power of a magician's mantra—
Only the percept appears;
The elephant is completely nonexistent.

28. The imagined nature is the elephant;
The other-dependent nature is the visual percept;
The non-existence of the elephant therein
Is explained to be the consummate.

29. Through the foundation consciousness
The nonexistent duality appears.
But since the duality is completely nonexistent,
There is only a percept.

30. The foundation consciousness is like the mantra.
Reality can be compared to the wood.
Imagination is like the perception of the elephant.
Duality can be seen as the elephant.

Let us first consider in more detail the three natures as Vasubandhu deploys them. The imagined nature is purely projected and is completely unreal, just like the elephant. The imagined nature is, on this account, the nature that we superimpose on our experience in virtue of our cognitive processes, not a nature that the objects of experience supply from their side. This is a first pass, and we will have cause to render it more precise as we proceed. But for now note that it need not be understood as *externality*, as on an idealistic reading of Yogācāra.

The dependent nature of any percept is the fact that it depends for its character as a percept on the structure of our perceptual and conceptual apparatus. Our percepts depend upon us; we only imagine them to be presented to us with all of the qualities we supply. So, to take an example we discussed above: Our visual field is *imagined* to be uniform in grain and in color. But it is not. The surface phenomenology is *imaginary*; that experience depends upon our constructive cognitive processes.

Just so, with the sticks used by the magician: they can be correctly perceived as a pile of sticks by the side of the road, as a prop for a cool trick, or mis-perceived as an elephant. The consummate nature is the absence of the imagined in the dependent, that is, the fact that since our introspectible experience depends on mind, it is empty of those qualities we superimpose, and of a dualistic relation to my subjectivity. Just so, the fact that there is no real elephant in the pile of sticks is their actual nature, what is to be understood if one sees through the trick. Let us now work deeper into Vasubandhu's perspective.

## *3.1 To Bracket or Not To Bracket: Phenomenological Reduction*

From a phenomenological perspective, we can ask the question that divides Husserl from Heidegger in the European tradition: Does it make sense, in order to understand the structure of human experience, to bracket the external world, or not? That is, do we gain insight from focusing solely on the nature of inner experience without considering its external objects or causes, or do we distort our experience in doing so? And if the latter, how do we attend to the external side of our experience while retaining a phenomenological attitude. In the discussion that follows, I will consider Indian Buddhist arguments in favor of bracketing and against it. We will see that there are compelling arguments for bracketing, against bracketing, for adopting both perspectives, and finally arguments that neither perspective is coherent in the first place. This discussion will illuminate the deep and surprising connections between Yogācāra phenomenology and Madhyamaka accounts of selflessness.

### 3.1.1 Bracketing the External World

I wish to consider a perfectly naturalistic motivation for and interpretation of phenomenological bracketing—the suspension of consideration of the external reality of the objects of consciousness in order to focus on the structure of consciousness itself. We will then extend this to a phenomenological inquiry trading on Vasubandhu's analysis in the verses under consideration. What is it to consider our experience to be all that is available as data for reflection? It is to recognize that to be subjects of experience—as central nervous systems on which our conscious states supervene—is to be dependent on input systems under the control of external forces[6] that generate my experiences. It is also for all of my efferent activity to result in actions or their effects (*karma*) whose reality is only apparent to me through those same afferent pathways. In short, it is to have no *unmediated* access to reality—that is, for all of my access to reality to be mediated by my cognitive and sensory apparatus.[7] It is also for

6. Imagined differently in the history of philosophy as Putnam's "brain in a vat" hypothesis; in Descartes's evil demon hypothesis; and in Vasubandhu's account of the workings of karma.

7. Not necessarily, however, by *representations*; mediation and a certain kind of directness of perception are consistent with one another.

all of the *mediation* to be through media *opaque* to my consciousness, and for it to be impossible to verify the veracity of these media independently. They are as opaque, one might say, as the operations of a magician at a good magic show. To take this situation seriously and to restrict ourselves in analysis to what we know immediately is to perform Husserlian *epochē*.

And we *should* take this enterprise seriously. My brain, as far as I can tell, and as far as the best scientists (real or imagined) tell me, is housed in a *human body*. It is indeed—if I can believe my experience at all—hooked up to input devices (the afferent nerves and blood supply) that are indeed controlled by external forces, including—in Quine's felicitous phrase—sensory irritations, in turn perhaps caused by such things as external objects, the chemistry of my blood, and other such causes and conditions. And indeed it is only through these afferent pathways that I can have any knowledge of the effects or reality of my own apparent activity. I have no direct *unmediated* knowledge of any reality independent of these sensory inputs, and their actual nature and relation to whatever might lie beyond them is indeed opaque to me.[8]

Note—and this is the first reason that Vasubandhu is an important partner in this conversation—that this *epochē* is not idealist.[9] It is neither to deny the materiality of the brain, nor of the body, nor to deny the reality of the world to which I have only mediated access. There is a tempting way to take this in an idealistic direction: One could argue (with Dignāga and his followers) that the *objects of my experience*—the percepts in my sensory fields, for instance—inasmuch as they are only the inner effects of distal causes about which I know nothing, are purely mental. So, one would argue, in a somewhat Berkeleyan vein—albeit a vein that leads us directly to the more nuanced view articulated by Kant—that nothing I ever know exists externally to consciousness. This includes my brain, and the body that encloses it; so whatever physicality might characterize whatever might exist in some other, unknown way, nothing I encounter is physical.

But we should resist this idealistic temptation, for at least two reasons. First, it begs the ontological question in a subtle but important way. Consider the tulip Berkeley's Hylas places before me. Even when I grant that the

8. This is also the main point of Paul Churchland's (2012), one important moral of which, defended elegantly both on neuroscientific and philosophical grounds, is that most of what we take to be the deliverances of introspection is profoundly false as an account of the actual nature of our subjectivity. Consciousness, Churchland shows, is far from transparent, and the first-person view is anything but privileged.

9. On the other hand, it is important to note that although Vasubandhu argues for idealism elsewhere, Vasubandhu's own argument for idealism is not Berkeley's, and is not a target of Kant's attack. His argument in *Twenty Stanzas* rests on the incoherence of the concept of matter.

*experience* of the tulip is an inner event, caused proximally by the input to my brain, to argue that the tulip just *is* the experience of it presupposes its conclusion—that perception is not a causal interaction with a distal object but a mere conscious episode. Berkeley may be able to achieve a standoff—maybe—but certainly not victory on this terrain.

Second, and more importantly—and we will have reason to reflect more carefully on this later—as Kant (as well as Tibetan Geluk philosophers such as Tsongkhapa, Gungthang and Dendar) was to argue, what goes for the tulip goes for the percept, too. Just as we cannot treat the external object as a thing known as it is itself, in abstraction from the sensory and cognitive faculties that deliver it to us, we cannot treat our inner experiences as things in themselves known apart from our inner sense, or, as Vasubandhu would call it, our introspective consciousness—*manas-vijñāna*. This, of course, is the central point made by Kant in the "Refutation of Idealism" in the second edition of the *Critique of Pure Reason*. There Kant argues that the idealist cannot infer that the external world is nonexistent, or at least inaccessible to knowledge, on the grounds that our knowledge of external objects is mediated by perception, whereas the inner world is obviously real, or at least better known to us, on the grounds that our knowledge of the inner is immediate. This is because, he argues—following the analysis of inner sense in the Transcendental Aesthetic—our knowledge of our inner states is subject to the form of our inner sense, and to the categories of judgment. The idealist would then be forced to agree that the inner is as problematic ontologically or epistemologically as the other. The asymmetry that idealism needs cannot be established.

The idealist, that is, needs a wedge that distinguishes the outer from the inner, giving privileged status to the latter; but all that is forthcoming is a distinction between experience and its object. This distinction is ontologically neutral. Note, for instance, that we can talk in English, as well as in Sanskrit, Chinese or Tibetan, both of *real* and of *unreal* objects of cognitive or physical acts. One can describe, wish for, or aim at the existent as well as the nonexistent. The act/object of distinction instead distinguishes only the subjective from the objective aspects of a cognitive act, enabling an anatomy of experience, but not an investigation of reality. With this distinction between idealistic and phenomenological readings of our embodiment, let us return to text in question to see what it would be to read Vasubandhu in this way:

> 27. Like an elephant that appears
> Through the power of a magician's mantra—
> Only the percept appears;
> The elephant is completely nonexistent.

28. The imagined nature is the elephant;
The other-dependent nature is the visual percept;
The non-existence of the elephant therein
Is explained to be the consummate.

29. Through the foundation consciousness
The nonexistent duality appears.
But since the duality is completely non-existent,
There is only a percept.

30. The foundation consciousness is like the mantra.
Reality can be compared to the wood.
Imagination is like the perception of the elephant.
Duality can be seen as the elephant.

Verse (27) sets out the example. In the example, the elephant is nonexistent, because the example is a conjuring trick. In (28) Vasubandhu tells us that the elephant is analogous to the imagined nature, and so we are to conclude that *that nature* is what is unreal in the same sense that the elephant is unreal in the conjuring trick, and in (30) he specifically identifies the elephant with *duality*, and hence, by transitivity, duality with the imagined nature. So, if we focus specifically on this set of verses, Vasubandhu argues that subject–object *duality* is unreal, and that, just as the mantra causes the elephant to appear, that duality in our experience is caused to appear by our foundation-consciousness, or what a Western neurophenomenologist could call our neuro-cognitive processes.

Perception in Vasubandhu's scheme has as its material condition or *de re* object *(alambanā/dmigs rkyen [mikkyen]) reality* or a pile of sticks, but delivers as the character of its *intentional object (artha/don [dön])* a subject–object duality *absent from reality itself*, or a hallucinated elephant. While the *intentional object* of perception is denied existence independent of the mind, neither perception nor the external world that occasions it is even *interrogated* ontologically here. Vasubandhu hence argues that our ordinary experience involves a confusion of the nature of *experience* with the *fundamental nature of reality*, caused by instinctive cognitive habits of which we are unaware, and leading us to ascribe the subject-object duality we superimpose in consciousness to reality itself as it is independent of that superimposition, thus confusing construction with discovery. This point is driven home in (28) and (29)—the verses that link those we have been examining. Here the point to be realized (28) is that there is no elephant at all in reality—that subject–object duality is imaginary, and that it arises (29) through our cognitive processes, in which we confuse a real percept with the unreal structure of subject standing over against object.

Vasubandhu hence shows that a phenomenological bracketing reveals part of the structure of my subjectivity. My experience (the dependent nature, characterized as percepts) is the joint product of a reality that I never directly apprehend (the sticks) and a set of psychological processes that are opaque to me (the mantra, or root consciousness). To the extent that I take my experience to be a direct deliverance of reality, to exist as it appears to me, or to be, qua experience, *external to me*, or even *transparent* to me, I am simply deceived.

I am, however, qua subject, *also* a pile of sticks by the side of the road. For, as I have been emphasizing, in foregoing the idealist's distinction of outer versus inner, in turn mapped to real versus unreal, in favor of the phenomenologist's distinction between act and content, my own existence as subject is rendered as problematic as the existence of the object I confuse with an external cause of my experience. Where I seem to come upon a world neatly divided into *me*, the *experiencer* and *it*, the *experienced*, all I find instead is *experience.*

The division into subject and object, and the subsequent reification or deprecation of one with respect to the other, depending on how I take things, is my contribution, not my discovery. So, then, on this view, what am I? I am, independent of my experience, just what the elephant is: a pile of sticks beside the road that I have never encountered directly, and, short of complete awakening, or Buddhahood, never will. The implications for the immediacy of self-knowledge and for the status of introspection are profound, as we shall see below.

### 3.1.2. On the Other Hand, Maybe We Should *Not* Bracket!

Just as Western phenomenologists are far from unanimous regarding the utility of *epochē*, so are Buddhists. Just as Western philosophy includes both idealistic and realistic voices, so does the Buddhist tradition. In order to enrich our reading of *Treatise on the Three Natures*, let us introduce Candrakīrti into this conversation. While he is often a foe of the Yogācāra analysis, and certainly a foe of any idealism, he has something to contribute here. We will begin by considering Candrakīrti's reasons for rejecting idealism, and then we will see how his insights take us one step deeper into Vasubandhu's dialectic. In *Autocommentary to an Introduction to the Middle Way* Candrakīrti argues that any attempt to discredit the reality of external objects yields arguments that, if cogent, discredit the reality of the self as well. Let us consider the relevant verses and autocommentary:

92. If there is no matter, don't hold on to the existence of mind!
If mind is existent, on the other hand, don't hold on to the nonexistence of matter!

Thus, although one might think that there is no matter, since they stand or fall together, you would have to also think that there is no mind. And if you think that there is mind, you have to also think that there is matter. Both of them are thus obviously mundane realities. And scripture supports this:

92cd. The Buddha rejects them in the same sense in the *Perfection of Wisdom*,
And treats them similarly in the Abhidharma.

According to the Abhidharma, everything from aggregates like that of matter to such things as particulars and universals are subject to the same detailed analysis. And in the *Perfection of Wisdom*, all five aggregates are rejected in the same way from "Subhuti, matter is empty of intrinsic nature" to "consciousness."

93. Thus, you would destroy the framework of the two truths—
That which is established by scripture and reason—
Since your substance has been refuted, it cannot be proven to be real.

Having asserted that even though there is no matter, there is only consciousness, how can you maintain the framework of the two truths? You would have destroyed it! Having destroyed the framework of the truths, you cannot prove your substance to be real. "Why is that?" you might ask. Because since substance has been refuted, all of your effort will be pointless.

93de. Therefore, according to a correct understanding of this framework,
Ultimately nothing arises; conventionally, arising makes perfect sense.

...

96. The Buddhas have taught that without an object of knowledge,
It is easy to eliminate the knower.
Since without an object of knowledge, the knower is refuted,
They begin by refuting the object of knowledge.

The glorious Buddhas first show through the analysis in terms of fundamental particles that everything lacks intrinsic nature. Then it is

> easy to engage with the nature of the bearer of karma.... Once the ultimate existence of the object of knowledge and its selflessness has been demonstrated, in the same way that they show them to be selfless, the Buddhas easily show that consciousness and the knower are selfless. The arguments that show the object of knowledge to be selfless show the subject to be selfless. (2009:180–187)

Here, Candrakīrti emphasizes several points relevant to the present discussion. First, mind and matter stand and fall together. Any argument that can be used to undermine the reality of the material world can be used to undermine the reality of the mental. Now, to be sure, here he takes his target to be Yogācāra idealism, and he is worried principally about the *ontological* status of mind and matter. In that sense, we can see Candrakīrti as anticipating Hume by a bit over a millennium, arguing that Berkeley's attack on the reality of material substance works just as well against mental substance.

On the other hand, Heidegger saw, the argument transposes nicely to the phenomenological domain. Any argument for bracketing the reality of the external object of knowledge is equally an argument for bracketing the reality of the subject. To the extent that we have cause to see the object as a mere construction, the subject we take to be its constructor may also be such a construction. To the extent that we are entitled to take the subject for granted as part of the horizon of consciousness, since its subjectivity consists in its engagement with objects, we are entitled to take the object for granted. (See Haugeland 2013 for an excellent discussion.)

Second, Candrakīrti emphasizes that to treat the subject and object differently is to violate the framework of the two truths. Neither is ultimately existent; neither is a substance. Both are conventionally existent; both are part of the everyday world. The only reason for so much emphasis on the status of the object in Buddhist scriptures, he argues, is that the analysis of the emptiness of the object paves the way for the homologous analysis of the emptiness of the subject. Once again, the emphasis on the non-substantiality, but conventional existence, of both subject and object anticipates Hume, and the emphasis on the need for both subject and object to constitute a world of everyday engagement anticipates Heidegger.

So, while Candrakīrti attacks the conclusion he takes the Yogācārins to defend, viz., that the mind is *more real* than external objects—that while external objects are entirely imaginary, the mind is *real*, and that it must be, if it is to be that which experiences and imputes reality to an unreal external world—he thereby neither reifies the external world nor does he deny the reality of mind. Candrakīrti argues instead that the same arguments that show external objects to be mind-dependent, impermanent and without any ultimate entity show the mind, or the self, to be mind-dependent, impermanent, and with no entity of its own.

The subject, Candrakīrti argues elsewhere in this text, is not a unitary thing, but a composite of a myriad of functions, each itself composite; it is not something that can be identified over time independent of our representation of it; he contends that it is dependent for its existence and character on innumerable causes and conditions. The self we experience and posit, the referent of the first-person pronoun, he concludes, is merely a conceptual, verbal designation on the basis of that causal stream, not even that stream itself.

> 162. In the same way, in virtue of being taken for granted in everyday life,
> And since it depends on the elements and the six sensory domains,
> One can say that the self is indeed the appropriator.

> Just as the self depends upon such things as the five aggregates, the chariot depends upon such things as the wood, the traces and wheels. Just as it is the appropriator, so is the chariot. Nonetheless, since the self is conventionally real—is accepted by mundane nominal conventions without analysis—one can, just as in the case of the chariot, call it the appropriator. It is the appropriator of such things as the five aggregates, the elements and six sensory domains; thus it is a dependent designation based upon such things as the aggregates....

> Thus, we maintain that this framework of appropriator and appropriated is merely conventionally designated, just like the framework of agent, action and object. It is all just like the chariot.

> 162d. The agent is just like the appropriator.

> Since it is a dependent designation, and is merely dependent, it doesn't actually have any characteristics such as being dependent or independent; and it cannot be conceived as permanent or impermanent.

> 163. Since it is not an existent object, it is not dependent.
> Nor is it independent. It neither arises nor ceases.
> Nor does it have properties such as permanence or impermanence.
> Nor does it have identity or difference.

> ...It makes no sense to say that something cannot be found through the sevenfold analysis is either permanent or impermanent....
>
> 164. That self to which beings constantly develop
> The attitude of self-grasping
> And with respect to which the attitude of grasping as mine arises
> Is only apparent when not analyzed, and arises out of confusion.
>
> ...Even though it doesn't exist, as a result of confusion, it is posited by convention. So, it doesn't appear to advanced practitioners... (262–268)

We know ourselves, Candrakīrti argues, not directly, but only imperfectly, using a conceptually mediated inner sense that is just as fallible as any outer sense. Candrakīrti's refutation of idealism, like Kant's, proceeds, in Kant's words, by "turning the game played by idealism against itself" (*Critique* B276), that is, by demonstrating first that idealism is essentially a contrastive doctrine, assigning the mind or the inner world a greater degree of reality than physical objects, or the external world, and second, that it fails in its attempt to distinguish those degrees of reality.

What does this all have to do with Vasubandhu's phenomenology or indeed with the nature of subjectivity? Well, once we see that the essence of idealism is the ontological contrast it draws between mind and the material world, we see that the drive to bracket the external world in order to characterize experience is already an idealistic move. I take my experience to be real; the world I imagine, I take to be, well, imaginary. Candrakīrti's analysis bites here. Husserlian bracketing takes my access to the external world to be dubious, but my knowledge of my immediate cognitive state to be secure. I know that I am experiencing a world containing trees and birds, but I leave open the ontological status of those trees or birds.

But none of this makes sense. For if the fact that my knowledge of the external world is mediated makes the epistemic status of the world dubious and renders coherent the claim that it is unreal, then the same goes for my self and my own experience. My knowledge of my own inner states and experience is mediated by my introspective processes. My representation of myself as a continuing subject of experience requires a conceptual construction of a unity from a multiplicity of cognitive processes and states occurring over time. I have no better knowledge of my inner life than I do of the external world, and no greater assurance of my own reality—if that means the kind of reality that persons have—than I do of that of the external world. So, if to be a subject means to be something assured of its own reality in intimate, veridical contact with its own experience, but with only dubious, mediated access to the external world, which may indeed by nonexistent, I am *not* a subject.

Once again, not only are there strong resonances between Candrakīrti's analysis and those of Kant, but there also are intriguing affinities to important insights of Wittgenstein both in his treatment of self-knowledge in *Philosophical Investigations* and in his discussion of idealism and certainty about the external world in *On Certainty*. In §§305– 308 of *Philosophical Investigations*, Wittgenstein notes the ways in which we use our conception of external phenomena as models for understanding the mind, leading us to posit inner mechanisms—mechanisms we neither observe nor whose nature we really understand. The critique of behaviorism and of mechanism, in the context of which these observations occurs, need not concern us here. But the insight that our self-knowledge is not *immediate*, given by an infallible inner sense, is important. We can join this with the Sellarsian insight (1963) that to the extent that we think of our inner episodes as *significant*, as *meaningful*, we understand them on the analogy of language, and language can only be a public phenomenon, inasmuch as meaning emerges from rule-governed behavior, and rules require communities to constitute them. Our inner life and subjectivity is hence constituted in part by our social context. We exist as subjects only conventionally.

This hermeneutical turn, of course, also has strong resonances with Heidegger's treatment of intentionality and of our interpretations of ourselves. On this view, to the extent that we think *anything at all*, or think that we do, we do so in virtue of being members of actual linguistic and epistemic communities. This entails that if I am a mind at all, and if I know myself at all, to bracket the external world in order to understand experience is no option.

In his consideration of Moore's refutation of idealism in *On Certainty*, Wittgenstein returns to the theme of the social dimension of knowledge. He argues persuasively that since knowledge is *justified* true belief, and since justification is a social practice that must be learned from others, and which is responsible to evidentiary practices and arguments that get their warrant from their reliability and their acceptance by others, knowledge is possible if, and only if, we participate in epistemic communities in the context of a world against which our claims are tested. Moreover, he argues, *doubt* is an epistemic activity that must be learned, and whose felicity conditions are socially and pragmatically determined.

Doubt, moreover, presupposes a background of true beliefs. To doubt a proposition requires one to know how to doubt, what justifies doubt, what it would be for the proposition to be true, and so on. Genuine doubt is impossible in the context of massive Cartesian error. These epistemic attitudes, like all others, are not individualistically characterized psychological states, but are norm-governed social epistemic practices. Therefore, even to *doubt* that there is an external world presupposes that there is one; and to *know* the truth of solipsism presupposes that I am in fact a person among persons whose beliefs are, by in large, true.

We thus see that the phenomenological dialectic drives us inexorably from Husserl to Heidegger. The very possibility of the reflection that leads us to recognize the mediation of all of our experience—in Yogācārin terms the pervasively imagined nature of our experience, and in Husserlian terms, the necessity of phenomenological reduction, in other words, the transcendental conditions of even inquiring into my subjectivity—presupposes that I am a person among persons, embedded in an external world. The transcendental *epistemic* conditions of bracketing guarantee that bracketing is incoherent. I am *not* an isolated subject. Human consciousness itself—*dasein*—presupposes the immediate presence of and engagement with a world of other conscious agents—*mitsein*—and the immediate presence of and engagement with a world of objects of experience. *Parikalpita*—the imagined nature—presupposes *paratantra*—the dependent. Or to put it another way, while the magician can do a lot, he needs those sticks and that mantra!

### 3.1.3 The Phenomenological Dialectic: We Must Both Bracket and Not Bracket

It would seem to follow from the preceding discussion that, at least from the Indian Yogācārin point of view I am asking us to take seriously, our experience is structured by a causally necessary *preconscious horizon* constituted by a linguistic and epistemic community—an embodiment and a location in a causal nexus—and on the other by cognitive reflexes that *construct* for us a surface phenomenology to which we react as though it was *given*. It would also seem to follow that the understanding of the constitution of that experience requires a bracketing of the external world as well as an interrogation of the subject–object duality that structures that experience.

I will now argue that that is so, taking us one step deeper into Vasubandhu's phenomenological project. To do so, however, I want to take a detour through yet another Indian Buddhist philosopher—Śāntarakṣita. In *Ornament of the Middle Way*, as we saw in chapter 3 above, Śāntarakṣita attempts to synthesize Vasubandhu's Yogācāra thought with the skeptical ontology of Candrakīrti's Madhyamaka, arguing that Yogācāra provides the best analysis of conventional reality, and Madhyamaka the best analysis of ultimate reality. This synthesis, given the phenomenological concerns of Yogācāra and the ontological concerns of Madhyamaka, represents an important Buddhist account of the relation between phenomenology and ontology.

As a Mādhyamika, Śāntarakṣita takes Candrakīrti's account of the conventional nature of things seriously—a thing's conventional nature is the way it appears to ordinary people. Śāntarakṣita, moreover, takes *that* to be the way things are *experienced.* But he also takes Vasubandhu's account of *experience* seriously: Things are experienced only as they appear as delivered by our senses, through input channels opaque to us, shot through with subject–object duality. Taking these three theses together allows Śāntarakṣita to conclude that *conventionally,* things are shot through with an erroneous subject–object duality and a pervasive confusion of appearance with reality.

On Śāntarakṣita's view, then, Yogācāra, by giving us an analysis of *appearance,* also gives us an *analysis* of our ordinary mode of taking up with the world, of conventional reality, even if it is not therefore an account the way in which that ordinary mode is *misconceived.* This is nonetheless an analysis of conventional truth, simply because that is what it explores; that truth remains, on this analysis, deceptive because it obtains in one manner (as construction) but appears in another (as given).

On this account, despite providing an analysis of conventional truth, Yogācāra says nothing about the *ontology* either of mind or of the external world. That is the work of Madhyamaka, and that is what gives us the ultimate truth. Śāntarakṣita's synthesis hence reconciles Yogācāra phenomenology with Madhyamaka ontology. While he urges that we get to the heart of the nature of reality only when we move *beyond* phenomenology to ontology, the move to ontology does not *undermine,* but rather *explains,* the phenomenology.

The fact that phenomenology and ontology are so independent and yet constitute two indispensible levels of analysis is one of Śāntarakṣita's deepest and most original insights. It provides the basis for his own synthesis. But it is also a promising basis for the project of joining a Madhyamaka metaphysics to a Yogācāra phenomenology as we bring Buddhism to bear on contemporary discourse. Moreover, as I will now argue, this reading of Śāntarakṣita's project animates Mipham's reading of *The Ornament of the Middle Way,* and underlies the deep insights into the philosophy of mind Mipham articulates in the context of his commentary, one we considered in chapter 3. We pick up Mipham's commentary where we left off:

> Consider a mistakenly grasped appearance such as a double moon: in this case, the *appearance* is merely consciousness itself appearing to itself. Therefore, one should not commit the error of not including it in the conventional. However, when we consider whether or not these apparent objects exist in the same way that they appear, they are just non-existent in that way. (2004, 438)

Mipham then argues that we cannot take cognitive states to have some special status, conventionally existent in virtue of depending on causes and conditions, of being neither unitary nor manifold, but nonetheless existing as they appear, apparent as the objects they are, available to non-deceptive introspection. He says that this would be to violate the dichotomy between the two truths, and to create a new, incoherent category, conventionally real in some respects, ultimately in others:

> If they were taken to exist as objects, since they would not have the characteristics of the conventional, one might think that one had discovered a third category or objects of knowledge apart from the conventional and the ultimate. If one maintained that such things exist, but are not momentary, they would be permanent appearances, and would not be false. (Ibid.)

Not only would this be ontologically incoherent, he argues, but to take inner experience to have this kind of privileged epistemic status would make discourse about inner life impossible. In a remark prescient of Wittgenstein's treatment of self-knowledge in *Philosophical Investigations*, Mipham notes that if we each could claim incontrovertible access to our inner experience, agreement about the meaning or truth of statements about mental life would be impossible, and we would abandon even the common practices of everyday life in which the possibility of both agreement and error are taken for granted:

> And if this were the case, it would follow absurdly that there could be no mutually agreed upon counterexample to a truth claim. Since one would be even more foolish than ordinary people, one would be just like a cow. (Ibid.)

Śāntarakṣita concludes his discussion of the conventional status of the mind and of the Cittamātra position by emphasizing that the analysis of the ultimate in Madhyamaka terms does not undermine the *reality* of these appearances, only their *veridicality*. While we have no guarantee that the appearance of mind to itself is verdical, this does not mean that it does not appear at all:

> 78. I do not refute entities
> That have the nature of appearance.
> Therefore the framework of proof
> And conclusion is not confused. (Ibid.)

Mipham emphasizes that this point amounts to a restatement of the Madhyamaka doctrine of the identity and mutual dependence of the two truths, but with an important twist relevant to self-knowledge. Even to say that appearances are empty of intrinsic nature is to grant their conventional reality, for if they were not real, they could not even be empty. But to say that they are empty is at the same time to say that they are only conventionally real, and to say *that* is to say that they are deceptive. Therefore, even the appearance of mind to itself is deceptive appearance.

> ...Therefore, in this context, and in that of Madhyamaka in general, one should not understand the statement that appearance is not refuted to mean that appearances have a distinct existence not characterized by emptiness of intrinsic nature. When, for instance, the moon appears in the water, it is empty, but just as there is nothing empty apart from its perceived appearance, its being empty does not imply that it is devoid of mere appearance. If there were not even mere appearance, there would not even be the emptiness of mere appearances. Therefore, mere appearance and emptiness are mutually dependent: without one, the other is impossible as well; when one is present, that entails that the other must be as well. Nor is their mode of existence like that of black and white thread—twisted around each other, but distinct, or alternating, one appearing only by excluding the appearance of the other. Appearance entails emptiness; emptiness entails appearance. (2004, 440)

We should take this last remark very seriously. The very idea of totally non-deceptive appearance is incoherent,[10] and it is as incoherent with respect to the appearance of mental states as it is with respect to external objects. Nothing of which we are aware, even in our own inner life, exists as it appears. What do we make of all of this? Well, for one thing, Śāntarakṣita's synthesis of Madhyamaka and Yogācāra shows us how Yogācāra provides an analysis of subjectivity. But Mipham takes the analysis one step further. He argues—consistent both with the perspective of Vasubandhu in *Treatise on the Three Natures* and with Candarakīrti's analysis of conventional truth in *Introduction to the Middle Way* and *Lucid Exposition*—that to take Yogācāra as delivering

10. Aside from the direct nondual appearance of emptiness ascribed by Buddhist philosophers to highly realized practitioners. But that experience is entirely different in kind from the ordinary human subjectivity being considered here.

conventional truth is to take the appearance of the mind to itself to be deceptive, and hence to take the mind to be a hidden phenomenon from itself.

If we take Śāntarakṣita's synthesis seriously, then, we see that we must bracket at one moment of analysis and must lift the brackets at another. From a phenomenological standpoint, I am nothing but a subject to which only experience is present. The self I experience and the objects I experience are nondually related, but dualistically experienced, and are mere appearances caused in ways I can never know. From an ontological standpoint, however, this view is untenable. I can only make sense of the truth even of the claim that I am only a subject if I am more than that. The very fact that I *know most intimately* that I am subject shows that I can never know my own nature, even as subject, at least to any degree greater than I can know anything else.

These facts, moreover, are not reducible to one another. Despite their apparent inconsistency, they are both true. Despite being both true, they are distinct from one another. From the mere fact of emptiness and conventional reality one cannot deduce the phenomenological character of experience. Moreover, it is not through an analysis of our experience that we gain an understanding of the fundamental nature of reality, but through ontological analysis. From the standpoint of this Buddhist phenomenological dialectic, even if, *per impossibile*, we had substantial selves, and lived in a world of things with essences, our access to them would be mediated.

To bracket the external world is to accept the cogency of a radical idealism or skepticism. And this makes no sense at all. It cannot, as we have seen, and as all Madhyamaka philosophers would argue, even be asserted coherently. But we cannot refrain from doing so. And this is so precisely because we must presuppose our embeddedness and embodiment in the world. How can this be so? Well, as we have seen, the fact that bracketing is incoherent reflects the mandatoriness of a robust realism about other persons and about the world we inhabit.

That robust realism also entails accepting a naturalistic and realistic understanding of my own sensory and cognitive apparatus, and so of the fact that my perceptual and cognitive states—including even my apperceptive and reflexively cognitive states—arise in the familiar opaque way adumbrated in contemporary cognitive science and anticipated in the Yogācāra phenomenology of Vasubandhu. Given that they do, as Śāntarakṣita and Gyeltsab point out, I must regard my own experience as possibly radically disjointed from the way the objects of my experience—even the objects of my introspective experience—in fact exist. The very phenomenological inquiry that leads me to the conclusion that experience requires embodiment and embedding leads me to the conclusion that that embodiment and embedding themselves present the world to me as though it was given.

To say *only* that that I inhabit a world would be, paradoxically, to deny my embodiment—to deny that my body is indeed an epistemically opaque organism containing my brain, and to deny the disjunction between reality as it is experienced and what reality is independent of experience. This would be to succumb to the strongest possible version of the Myth of the Given—the view that the world is given directly to consciousness as it is in itself. To say *only* that I am a subject of experience standing in relation to my objects would be to deny the role that my social and natural context plays in my cognitive life. I am therefore neither a mere part of nor ontologically apart from the world. Once again, I am a pile of sticks by the side of the road, experiencing itself as a pure subject believing that it is not one, and an embodied being knowing itself to be nothing but a pure subject. The opacity of the mind to itself and the immediacy of experience turn out to be two sides of a deeply paradoxical coin.

### 3.2 *Mu, or Radical Negation of All Four Possibilities*

In Japanese Zen literature, the term "Mu" is used to indicate a radical negation—a denial with no affirmation, a denial of the very presupposition of the question being asked. It is a fitting rubric for a final take on Vasubandhu's metaphor. We can see this entire phenomenological investigation as a grand *reductio* on a particular very compelling model of subjectivity. Let us ask, "Who or what is this thing that inquires into the transcendental character of its own subjectivity?" It is at least a metaphysical or epistemic *subject*, posited as distinct from and related somehow to, its object. Having taken its identity, reality and distinctness from its objects for granted, we can then ask about its precise status, and use the law of the excluded middle to assert that it either is or is not distinct from its objects. This is the mode of inquiry that characterizes much of Western phenomenology. But it need not be.

The set of presuppositions are analogous to those subject to critique in the negative tetralemmas in Nāgārjuna's *Fundamental Verses on the Middle Way* regarding causation, emptiness and the Buddha. In these contexts Nāgārjuna argues that none of the four possibilities—existence, nonexistence, both or neither—makes sense precisely because of such presupposition failure.[11] The same presupposition failure obtains in this case. In posing the question of our immediate subjectivity we begin with the presupposition of an unproblematic

11. See Deguchi, Garfield and Priest (2008) and Garfield (1995, 2014b) for more detail on these Nāgārjunian arguments.

subject, a subject necessarily distinct from its object, and then pose our question: Is it necessarily embedded in a world or not? But that presupposition is equivalent to the presupposition of the reality of the self, and of subject–object duality, and these are the very targets of both Yogācāra and Madhyamaka analysis, each of which is aimed at establishing selflessness and non-duality.

The very inquiry into the nature of the subject then *begs* the question against Vasubandhu, Nāgārjuna and, for that matter, the entire Buddhist tradition. It does so by presupposing an unproblematic unified subject of experience, precisely the subject that is the target of the dialectic of each of these schools. Candrakīrti's and Vasubandhu's recommendation of thesislessness with regard to the self issues from the insight that the self in question is merely a nominal posit and has no independent existence. Hence there is nothing left to say about the subject itself, as distinct from its objects. This is, however, not to be understood as a rejection of the reality of either. When understood as a Buddhist phenomenology, Yogācāra analysis does not reject the existence of the external world, only its *externality*. That is, it is not the *world* that is nonexistent, but the duality between mind and world. So, nor is the reality of our experience rejected, only its existence as a distinct *internal* world by means of which we know our external objects. Our *lebenswelt*—the only world we ever inhabit—emerges in full reality not in spite of, but in virtue of, its emptiness of independence, and in virtue of, not in spite of, its constitution through the operation of our sensory and cognitive apparatus.

### *3.3 Being in the World: What the Elephant Simile Does and Doesn't Show*

Vasubandhu's elephant simile illustrates the complex nature of our subjectivity, a subjectivity in which at the most basic level we inhabit a world in which the distinction between subject and object, internal and external, is entirely absent, but a subjectivity that also systematically mis-takes that world to be saturated with that very duality in virtue of cognitive processes that, in a kind of cognitive reflex, superimpose that structure at a higher level on an experience that does not present it at a more primordial level. That is the conjuring trick. We systematically deceive ourselves about the nature of our own experience, and hence about the world in which we live. But it is a deception through which we can learn to see.

Vasubandhu's point is that when we see elephants in the road, that experience is multi-layered. In naive introspection, we take both our own subjective state and the objectively presented pachyderm to be presented to us as they exist, related to one another as experiencing subject and experienced object.

But this is a mis-taking not only of the elephant, but also of ourselves, and of the structure of the experience at a more primordial level. At that more fundamental level, the elephant we perceive on the road is a conceptual-perceptual construction wrought by our sensory and cognitive apparatus in response to stimulation; our subjectivity is constructed by a complex network of subpersonal perceptual and apperceptual processes, and the duality we project in which we take ourselves simultaneously to be aware of self and other as distinct entities in this experience is itself constructed. That is the *conjured elephant.* We, the elephant and the moment of experience are all, finally, sticks in a pile by the side of the road.

## 4. Re-thinking Subjectivity through Buddhism

Earlier in this chapter and in the previous chapter we noted and put aside the phrase "what it is like" that structures so much of contemporary phenomenological reflection. Let us now take it up and see how it looks in light of Vasubandhu's approach. The first thing to note is that it is a nominalized phrase that purports to refer to some property or individual, suggesting that there is a relevant referent. As Candrakīrti and Vasubandhu argue, phrases like 'I' can be deceptive. They can give the appearance of reference while being empty. (Recall our discussion of the self in chapter 4.) They demand interrogation before analysis.

We might imagine that the phrase refers to *qualia*, if such things exist. But as we argued above, there really are no compelling reasons to think that they do. When we see red tomatoes, we see red tomatoes, not red qualia. If the direct object of our sensory experiences were qualia, they would lack the intersubjectivity necessary even to get reference going. They would be, in Mipham's terms, something neither conventionally nor ultimately real. To posit them as mediators between us and the world solves nothing and raises new problems of its own, leaving us, as Mipham suggests, as inarticulate as cattle.

Perhaps the phrase is meant to refer to sensations, that is, to subjective states themselves, as opposed to their ghostly inner objects. Then "what it is like" to see red is to have a red sensation; what it is like to see a sunset at Race Point is to have the sensations one has when one sees such a sunset. This is better. There are at least sensations. And if "what it is like" refers to those, the phrase is not so much pernicious as otiose. The problem is that those who deploy it might then want to ask what it is like to have a red sensation, or wonder whether, for instance, zombies might have red sensations, but yet there be nothing that it is like for them to have them. Now we are back to the act–object structure that bedevils sense-data theory, and we start thinking of our sensations not as *subjective* cognitive or perceptual states, but rather as the *objects* of further cognitive states.

The decisive move in yet another conjuring trick has been made, and it does seem so innocent. After all, we know what it is for a state to take another as an object, and we know the difference between states of which we are reflectively aware and those of which we are not. So, why not argue that what makes a perceptual state conscious is for there to be something that it is like to be in it, and then simply treat that something as other than the state? But what? If we do not retreat to the failed qualia option, we simply blow smoke.

Perhaps we mean a property, a universal. So, what it is like to experience a Race Point sunset is an abstract entity, something that all experiences of Race Point sunsets have in common. Which one? The property of being such an experience? Big deal. We were after, we thought, *what it is like to have that experience*. Nothing more is forthcoming. What more do all such experiences have in common than being such experiences? Moreover, that qualitative property would have to be experienced in order to perform any psychological or phenomenological function. And then there would be something that it is like to experience that what-it-is-likeness. We are off on a vicious regress. We should begin to suspect that "what it is like" is like the self, on Candrakīrti's analysis—a useful *façon de parler*, but nothing more, a term that simply refers to nothing at all.

There is ground to which one might be tempted to retreat at this point. We might take the phrase to refer simply to mere subjectivity, to the fact that when we have a sensation, see a sunset, bite into a tomato, the experience has a subjective as well as an objective aspect. *What it is like* is the very subjectivity of that experience. While this has all the virtues of not positing qualia as direct objects, or of taking first-order sensory states as objects of higher-order subjectivity-conferring states, and of not positing mysterious sui generis universals as essential objects of consciousness, it buys these virtues at the expense of vacuity. We were seeking an analysis of subjectivity. To say that it is for there to be something that it is like to be me, or to have an experience, and then to analyze that as mere subjectivity is simply to say that to be a subject is to be a subject. The noun phrase does nothing but obfuscate. We are looking once again, in a different guise, for the referent of 'I.'

Why does it appear so compelling to talk about "what it is like," then? I think it is this. The phrase asks us to direct our attention to our current state. Can we feel it? Of course we can. Do we know it? Sure. Is it an object of knowledge? Well, yes. Can we then ostend it? Why not? *That, the thing ostended,* is *what it is like*, or something. Note how much nonsense and unjustified reification goes on here, but how seductive each move is, if done quickly. Can we feel our current state? Not necessarily. We are in it, and it may be a feeling, but feeling a state is a higher-order state that may or may not be present. Do we *know* our current inner state? Probably not. The mind just is not that transparent. Is our current mental state an object of knowledge for us? To even ask this question is to impose a subject–object duality on subjectivity itself, making an ontological and epistemological hash of our own being. This hash can have serious methodological consequences when transferred into psychological practice. Consider this endorsement of introspective method by Thompson:

> [E]xperimental neurophenomenology employs first-person phenomenological methods in order to obtain original and refined first-person data. Individuals vary in their abilities as observers and reporters of their own experiences, and these abilities can be enhanced through various phenomenological methods.
>
> ...
>
> The relevance of these practices to neurophenomenology derives from the capacity for sustained attentiveness to experience they systematically cultivate. This capacity enables tacit and prereflective aspects of experience, which typically are either inaccessible of reconstructed after the fact according to various biases, to become subjectively accessible and describable in more accurate ways. Using first-person methods, individuals may be able to gain access to aspects of their experience that otherwise would remain unnoticed and hence unavailable for verbal report and description. (2007, 339)

The methodology here suggests that when trained introspectors look inside, they find mental reality *as it is*. This is the nature of primal confusion, of grasping to the self, and of grasping to the property of *being mine*, and of grasping that nature of that which is mine. It is precisely the confusion against which Buddhist phenomenologists warn us. Could there then be *nothing that it is like* to be me, to taste a tomato, to see red? If that question is paraphrased as "Could there be nothing more to being me than being me? To tasting a tomato than tasting a tomato? To seeing red than seeing red?" The answer is, "Damn right." It is time to get rid of the phrase, and a Madhyamaka and Yogācāra analysis can help us to do so, and to clear some fog from phenomenology.

Another way to put this point is that this kind of phenomenological reflection presupposes a unity to consciousness or subjectivity that may well be illusory. It may well be that the phenomenological project as prosecuted by Dignāga and Husserl, and as resurrected by Coseru and Zahavi, may be misguided for a simple reason: There may be nothing that it is like to be me because there is no me; there may be nothing that it is like for me to see red, because I don't. Instead of a single locus of consciousness contemplating a distinct world of objects—like a Wittgensteinian eye in the visual field or a Kantian transcendental ego—to be a person, from a Buddhist perspective, is to be a continuum of multiple, interacting sensory, motor and cognitive states and processes. Some of these are first-order intentional states and processes; some higher-order and some non-intentional. Some are introspectible; some are not. My own access to them is mediated by my ideology, my narrative and a set of fallible introspectible mechanisms. When I introspect, I impose a subject–object duality on my experience that I take for granted, although I know it is my superimposition, not an intrinsic feature of subjectivity. Whatever I take the character of my subjective experience to be is at best a reconstruction. There is nothing that it is like to be me, in part because there is no me, and in part because there is no privileged level of experience to which that phrase could attach.

Yet another way to put this point is that from the perspective of Yogācāra analysis the very idea of subjectivity as an object of transcendental analysis is an error. Subjectivity is a pole of a duality that is constructed by introspective and reflective processes that can never promise, any more than any human instruments can process, to deliver any reality to us as it is. Apprehension is always mediated, and the media through which our self-knowledge is delivered are themselves not only probably fallible, but opaque. Any understanding we gain of them is itself mediated, and so on all the way down. For the self to fail to have an ultimate nature in the Buddhist sense is for there to be nothing that it is to be a subject at all. This is why Candrakīrti says that we are neither permanent nor impermanent. Any predication of a subject suffers from presupposition failure.

Now, one might object at this point that while the veridicality of introspection may always be questioned—and so the *character* of our subjective experience may be constructed and not given—the fact of subjectivity itself cannot be constructed by cognitive processes, on pain of regress. They must themselves be either subjective, in which case we have begged the question, or not, in which case it is not clear how they could ever give rise to subjectivity.[12] But this objection misses its mark. The subjectivity we are trying to characterize is the one that presents us to ourselves as unified, continuous loci of our

12. I owe this objection to Lynne Rudder Baker (personal communication).

experience and agency, as the selves about which we care, and which we recognize. The point is that our awareness of ourselves in that guise, the only guise in which we encounter ourselves in non-reflective introspection, the guise in which I take myself to be the referent of 'I,' is constructed, and constructed by means of innumerable unconscious cognitive processes. Those processes lie below the level of introspectibility, and so never by themselves have this kind of subjective character. They are the unseen creators and scaffolding of the scenery of the theatre in which we take our lives to be enacted; subjectivity emerges in the scenery, but is wrought only in the wings. When we forget this, we can find ourselves in thickets like this one, in the context of Thompson's pondering the status of one's consciousness of a sound to which one was not at first attending:

> [H]earing the sound before noticing it should be counted as a case of phenomenal consciousness. One does consciously hear the sound before noticing it, if "noticing" means turning one's attention to it. The sound is experienced implicitly and prereflectively. One lives through the state of being affected by the sound without thematizing the sound or one's affectedness by it. This prereflective consciousness counts as phenomenal consciousness because the sound's appearance and affective influence have a phenomenal character, though an indeterminate one.... Nevertheless, there is no reason to believe that the experience is not also a case of access consciousness. After all, one is poised to make use of one's implicit and prereflective hearing of the sound. The content of the experience is at least accessible, even if it is not accessed explicitly. (2007, 264)

On this view, even if it is not introspectible, hearing the sound is part of our phenomenal subjective experience. Even if there is no determinate character to the experience of the sound, it has some character; even though we have no access to it, it is a case of access consciousness. Each of these might be taken as a *reductio* on the idea that these categories map anything we can coherently call *consciousness* as a state independent of our introspective activity to which we have any kind of access at all. Together they call this entire framework of into question. As Vasubandhu suggests, when we engage in analysis of something we take ourselves to have discovered—our own self, subjectivity or consciousness—we stumble instead on something we have constructed. To pretend to develop a science of it, to ask whether it is present even when we don't notice it, is to pretend to research the real biography of Ahab. Fictions may be useful; if a Buddhist analysis is right, they are all we have. But this does not make them more than fictions, and they outlive their utility, becoming obstacles to the truth, when we forget their status as fictions.

There is a reason that so much of Chan or Zen reflection on experience takes that experience that is most authentic, most revelatory, most conducive to awakening and to effective engagement with the world, to be that in which the self does not figure, that in which we are immersed in the world, not standing over against it. This is not because such experience feels good, or because there is something special that it is like to be in that state. It is because there is in that experience none of the fabrication that yields the false sense of self, and the polar coordinate view of reality that takes the subject to be the center of a world of objects, and, despite not being an object, being a potential object of knowledge. When reification ceases, engagement can begin. Once again, we consider Thompson's account of a pre-conceptually given state of consciousness, and we see the difficulties that emerge from the Husserlian tradition, difficulties that do not emerge in the same way in the Heideggerian or Chan tradition. These considerations take us back to the phenomenology of skilled engagement, a topic with which we concluded the previous chapter. Consider Thompson's account of this phenomenon:

> . . . [E]xperience does not have a subject-object structure in immersed skillful action. Instead, experience is the phenomenal flow of one's body-environment coupling. Furthermore, consciousness here is not detached observation of reflective self-awareness, but rather a non-reflective attunement to the interplay of action and milieu. . . . There is clearly a phenomenal flow . . . Consciousness has the structure of a non-reflective "I can" in the flow of habitual action . . . As Merleau-Ponty says, "Each maneuver undertaken by the player modifies the character of the field and establishes in it new lines of force in which the action in turn unfolds and is accomplished, again altering the phenomenal field." (2007, 314, citing Merleau-Ponty 1962, 168–169)

Note here the actual divergence between Thompson and Merleau-Ponty. Merleau-Ponty emphasizes the causal coupling between the player and others on the field, between perception and action, in terms of "lines of force"; Thompson, on the other hand, thematizes these in terms of an "I can" in a flow of consciousness. If *consciousness* here denotes nothing more than engagement with the world through perception and action, the intentional content is superfluous and the prefix *non-reflective* serves only to negate the force of the term. If, on the other hand, the term *consciousness* denotes something more—a kind of inner domain in which states unfold that we might or might not introspect, the intentional structure "I can" appears to be an illicit interpretation that undermines the claim that all of this is *non-reflective*. That this latter reading is the one intended—the one that lurks behind the myth of the givenness of consciousness—becomes clear when Thompson contrasts his own position with that of Heidegger. Responding to Hubert Dreyfus (1991), Thompson writes:

> Dreyfus (1991, p. 58), who says "absorbed action in the world does not involve an experience of acting," seems to think that the only kind of self-awareness is reflective awareness, and hence that there is no prereflective self-awareness in skillful coping. In this view, in skillful coping we experience a steady flow of activity, but we are unaware of our acting because we are absorbed in acting do not reflect on it... Although we should grant this point about reflection, it does not follow that we are completely unaware of our acting in skillful coping. The reason is that reflective self-awareness is not the only kind of self-awareness.... There is every reason to think that... prereflective self-awareness animates skillful coping. If skillful coping were not prereflectively self-aware, then it would not be different from unconscious automaticity and would have no experiential character whatsoever. And if it had no experiential character, then there could be no genuine phenomenology of skillful coping but only a logical reconstruction of it. (2007, 315)

The echo of Śāntarakṣita's claim that reflexivity is what distinguishes conscious states from unconscious states is striking. Thompson is following the tradition of Dignāga in arguing that consciousness must be reflexive, even if he wants to deny that it is always reflective. As we have seen, while that position has a great deal of traction in the Buddhist tradition, it also comes in for a great deal of trenchant criticism. To the extent that the critique of philosophers such as Candrakīrti and Tsongkhapa is successful, we might be suspicious of this approach. The Heideggerian approach to consciousness and reflexivity is anticipated by Dōgen, and offers an interesting alternative.

Dōgen wrote that "to study the self is to forget the self; to forget the self is to be affirmed by myriad things. When actualized by myriad things, your body and mind as well as the bodies and minds of others drop away" (Tanahashi 1985, 72). I hope that by this point we can take this Zen aphorism seriously, not as a mystical pronouncement, but as the result of deep phenomenological reflection in a different key. The more we pay attention honestly to our own nature, the more we realize that there is no such nature; the more we pay attention to our own subjective character, the more we realize that we are not subjects; the more we realize that, the more we realize that that to which we respond as *our* object is not apprehended as it is; and the more we can shed the myth of subject–object duality and the immediacy of our relation to subjectivity, the more honestly we can understand our participation in the reality we inhabit. This is the goal of a Buddhist phenomenology.

I close this with a poem of Dōgen:

> Being in the world.
> To what can it be compared?
> Dwelling in the dewdrop,
> Fallen from a waterfowl's beak,
> The image of the moon. (quoted in Kasulis 1981, 103)

Note that here there is no focus on subjectivity, no focus on the character of experience, only of an ephemeral, impermanent, impersonal existence pregnant with illusion, but also with beauty.

# 7 EPISTEMOLOGY

## 1. *Pramāṇa*

### *1.1 General Introduction to* Pramāṇa *Theory*

When contemporary Western philosophers address epistemological questions, the central topic is often the definition of knowledge, say as Justified True Belief ± Gettier, and most of the action is devoted to determining what counts as justification (with a bit to the Gettier problem). Buddhist epistemology is not much different in emphasis, but different enough to be interesting. The central term in Buddhist epistemology is not any that we would translate naturally as *knowledge*, but is related to *justification*. The term in Sanskrit is *pramāṇa*, or in Tibetan *tshad ma* (tsehma). Let's first talk etymology, and then semantic range, to get a feel for how Indian and Tibetan Buddhist epistemologists thought about their project.

One should also bear in mind that Buddhist epistemological reflection occurred not in a philosophical vacuum, but in the context of a broader Indian philosophical milieu in which *pramāṇa* theory was always at center stage. Philosophical schools were often identified by the range of *pramāṇas* they accepted, and epistemology was taken as foundational to all other philosophical inquiry, inasmuch as philosophical inquiry is always aimed at the acquisition of knowledge and the justification of claims. Moreover, *pramāṇa* theory played a special role in classical Indian philosophical discussion. Inasmuch as philosophical dispute often involved partisans of competing philosophical traditions—prominently including discussions between orthodox and Buddhist or Jain philosophers—the terms of debate had to be set in a non-question-begging way. There was hence considerable interest in the project of settling on a minimal set and conception of *pramāṇas* on which all sides to a debate could agree, so that at least the terms of evidence and justification could be taken for granted by all parties. The Buddhist investigation of *pramāṇa*, while central to the Buddhist project and responsive to specifically Buddhist ideas, was also always sensitive as well to broader Indian epistemological debates and dialogical concerns. (See Frauwallner 2009, Gupta 2012, Patil 2009.)

The root meaning of *pramāṇa* derives from *māṇa, to measure*. The Tibetan *tshad ma* captures this nicely, denoting measurement or degree, and was created to track the meaning of *pramāṇa*. For that reason everything we say semantically about *pramāṇa* goes over to *tshad ma*. From the standpoint of etymology, a *pramāṇa* is something that measures, or takes the measure of, things. But the semantic range of this key term is more complex. Roughly, depending on context, we can say that *pramāṇa* denotes an *instrument* of knowledge, such as perception or inference. These measure, or take the measure of, reality.

That sense is descriptive, indicating the function of a cognitive instrument, but also normative, suggesting that it is *appropriate* or *useful* to deploy that instrument epistemologically. In this sense of the term, it coordinates nicely with *prameya*, or *epistemic object*. In other contexts, *pramāṇa* denotes epistemic *warrant* more directly. So we might say that perception is *pramāṇa* because it is reliable, or we might speak of a belief as *pramāṇa* because it is warranted. The term can also sometimes be translated as *authoritative cognition*, denoting a cognitive episode that is the *result (phāla)* of warranted use of an instrument that is *pramāṇa*. The term *pramāṇa* hence conveys justification or warrant, and instrumentality as well as that which is delivered by instruments that confer warrant. Indian and Tibetan Buddhist debates about epistemology concern the nature and number of the *pramāṇas*, and the nature of their respective *prameyas*.

*Pramāṇa* theory in Indian Buddhism is generally associated with the so-called *Pramāṇavāda* school, sometimes called the *Logicians* or *Epistemologists*. The principal originary figures in this school are Dignāga and his commentator Dharmakīrti. Dharmakīrti's *Commentary on the Encyclopedia of Epistemology (Pramānavartikka)* and his other epistemological texts are in turn the subject of an enormous commentarial literature in India and Tibet and an extensive contemporary scholarly literature.[1]

To be sure, much of the most sophisticated elaboration of Buddhist epistemological theory is developed in the commentarial literature on Dignāga's and

1. See Dreyfus 1997; Dunne 2004; Patil 2009; Coseru 2012; Katsura 1969, 1984, 1991, 1992, 1999; Franco 1997, 2009; Steinkellner 1991; Hayes 1980; Kellner 2001, 2010, 2011; Hattori 1980 for a treatment of this vast literature, much of which is beyond the scope of this chapter.

Dharmakīrti's work. But it would be an error to think that the Pramāṇavādins held a monopoly on *pramāṇa* theory either in India or in Tibet, for they were in constant dialogue and debate with Mādhyamikas as well, including Nāgārjuna, Bhāviveka and Candrakīrti, who often diverged regarding the nature and number of *pramāṇas* and the proper conduct of epistemology. (See Thakchöe 2012a, 2013.) In what follows, I will suggest that we gain insight into different ways of approaching epistemological problems in part by attending to the differences between these schools.

In particular (and we will discuss this in greater detail below) while Buddhism, in virtue of the centrality of the Pramāṇavādin school to the articulation of *pramāṇa* theory, is generally associated with the view that there are only two *pramāṇas*, viz., perception (*pratyakṣa*) and inference (*anumāna*), Mādhyamikas such as Candrakīrti took on the more liberal Nyāya understanding of *pramāṇa* according to which there are four *pramāṇas*, with analogy (*upamāna*) and testimony or scriptural authority (*śabda*) added to the list. And while the Pramāṇavādins were epistemological foundationalists, the Mādhyamikas were coherentists.

## *1.2 Apoha and Buddhist Nominalism*

Let us begin by considering the two *pramāṇas* recognized by the Pramāṇavādin school and their respective *prameyas*, or epistemic objects. These represent one of the more distinctive Buddhist contributions to epistemology; the *apoha* theory of the meaning of predicates introduced in chapter 1 is another. Before entering into any discussion of this issue, we should acknowledge that there is an enormous literature on *apoha* theory itself. (See, especially, Siderits, Tillemans and Chakrabarti 2011.) We will only scratch the surface, but that surface will have plenty to interest us.

As noted above, the Pramāṇavādins defended the view that there are only two *pramāṇas*, or epistemic instruments, or means of warranting a belief, viz., perception and inference. In restricting the number to two, they are explicitly ruling out *pramāṇas* recognized by non-Buddhist Indian philosophical schools such as verbal/textual testimony or analogy. They accomplish this restriction by reducing the latter two to perception and inference. The details need not concern us here. The big issues arise when we consider the relation between inference and its epistemic object, for inference appears to be mediated by relations between universals.[2]

2. Well, not *all* of the big issues. Understanding the nature of perception—including both ordinary perception and that of highly realized practitioners (yogic perception) is also an important preoccupation in Buddhist epistemology. In particular, Dignāga, in *Investigation*

Indian logicians and epistemologists characterize this relation by the term *vyapti*. This term can be felicitously translated as *entailment* or *pervasion* or *categorization* depending on the level of discourse at which one is operating. Buddhist logic in medieval India was categorical, and so entailment between propositions was conceived as grounded in the relationships of subcategorization between classes denoted by the predicates in those propositions, much as Aristotle understood syllogistic. So, when I deduce the impermanence of sound from the fact that it is produced, it is the fact that the category of impermanent things is a subcategory of the category of produced things that validates the inference. There is *vyapti* between the property of being produced and the category of impermanence at the ontological level and *vyapti* between the propositions that sound is produced and that it is impermanent at the logical level. The important thing about this account of inference is that it appears that the *pramāṇa* of inference must put one in direct contact with universals and relations among them.[3]

This is problematic because of Buddhism's commitment to nominalism introduced in chapter 1, deriving from its metaphysical commitment to the claim that whatever is real is causally interdependent and impermanent. And this, as we have seen, in turn entails that universals are nonexistent, illusory, mere conceptual constructs with no real correlates. But that would also mean that the most obvious account of *vyapti* as a relation between universals is off the table. And that means that it is hard to make sense of how inference can be a *pramāṇa*.

*of the Percept*, devotes serious attention to understanding the relation between the causes of perceptual experience, which may well be atomic and imperceptible (atoms or *dharmas*), with the intentional object of perception, which typically is nonexistent outside of perceptual experience (enduring macroscopic objects), and to working out how perception, given this predicament, can be a source of knowledge at all. These are fascinating questions, but we will leave them aside here.

3. It is worth noting a distinctive feature of Candrakīrti's thought about logic in this context. Indeed, most Indian logicians and epistemologists after Dignāga take the logical relation *vyapti* to be first and foremost a material relation between categories, or between categories and individuals. And the most common English translation of *vyapti* is *pervasion*, signaling this fact. Candrakīrti, however, in the context of his critique of Bhāviveka's use of this logic in the latter's commentary on Nāgārjuna's *Fundamental Verses on the Middle Way*, suggests that this has to be an error. He argues that Nāgārjuna, rather than using an Indian formal argument that presupposes a shared understanding of the reference of the key terms of the argument, and hence a shared understanding of the potential material relata of *vyapti*, makes use only of *reductio (prasāṅga)* arguments that presuppose no common understanding of the meanings of terms, but only a shared commitment to inference. Inference, on this view, then, is taken as a relation between sentences (or terms, at least) and not between classes and individuals. This idea seems to die in Indian thought about logic, however, due to the pervasive influence of Dharmakīrti and his followers.

However, without inference, knowledge would be rather meager. Very meager indeed. We would be limited to knowing only what we perceive directly and currently. (This excludes memory, which, after all, involves inferences, as does reliance on testimony.) And we could have no general knowledge at all. That is bad enough. But remember that if inference is characterized as that which engages with a universal, we could not even know anything about the enduring composite dry goods that populate our ordinary world, such things as rocks, trees, cows, or other people. The reason for this is that anything composite or enduring has its identity in terms of a specific universal, a property held in common by all of its spatio-temporal parts.

When I take myself to perceive the tree outside of my window, for instance, in fact I am perceiving many momentary tree parts. To represent those momentary particulars as constituting a single tree, I must *categorize them* as *parts of the tree outside of my window*. And that seems to involve engagement with the universal *part of the tree outside of my window*. The judgment that the trunk and the branches belong to the same tree, constitutive of my perceiving the whole as a tree, involves then an *inference* from (1) The trunk has *part-of-the-tree-outside-my-window-hood*; and (2) The branches have *part-of-the-tree-outside-my-window-hood* to the conclusion, "The trunk and the branches share in the property of *part-of-the-tree-outside-my-window-hood*," and so are of the same thing.

So even what we might take to be ordinary perception, on this view, is actually inference (and this confusion, according to these Buddhist epistemologists, is part of the epistemological face of primal confusion). If inference involves engagement with universals and if there are no real universals, then even ordinary perceptual knowledge is undermined. Now, as we will see, there is a *sense* in which Buddhist epistemologists do want to undermine some of the pretensions of ordinary perceptual knowledge, but they do not want to reject the entire framework of everyday knowledge.

For these reasons, Buddhist theorists creatively developed an account of an ersatz universal—the *apoha*—as the *prameya* of inference, an idea introduced in chapter 2. The term *apoha* is a contraction of *anyapoha*, which literally means *exclusion of that which is other. Apohas*, as we have seen, are negations. Let us return to the classical example, the *apoha* analysis of what it is to be a cow, introduced in chapter 2, which always sounds bizarre at first reading, but which we can come to understand as a plausible move with the help of the commentarial tradition. At first pass, to be a cow would seem to be to possess the property of bovinity, and this is indeed how all non-Buddhist Indian traditions (quite sensibly, it might appear) see the matter. But on *apoha* theory, it is not. It is to be, on a first pass, *excluded from being a non-cow*.

Now we could immediately and uncharitably gloss this as *to possess the property of not being a non-cow*, and then by double negation elimination determine that nothing has been gained. This critical move was in fact immediately made by non-Buddhist Indian critics of *apoha* theory. But we needn't be so hasty, for a lot has to do with how we understand negation and exclusion. And the understandings of these ideas develop considerably in the course of intra-Buddhist debates about *apoha*, as well as in the context of debates between Buddhists and their orthodox critics. (See Siderits, Tillemans and Chakarabarti 2011, Dreyfus 2011b, Dunne 2004, 2011 and Patil 2003 for details.)

Let us begin with a few remarks about negation. From the standpoint of most Buddhist ontology, verbal negation denotes an absence, and this absence itself can also be referred to as a negation. So, the fact that there are no angels on my desk right now is an absence, a negation of angels. Importantly, this conveys no ontological commitment. Therefore the absence of angels, expressed by the sentence "There are no angels on my desk" does not commit me to the existence of angels, or for that matter, non-angels at all. Negations—like that represented by emptiness, discussed in earlier chapters—are thus attractive to Buddhist philosophers as ways of eschewing ontological commitment, a real desideratum in this ontologically spare philosophical framework. So, initially, we can see that the seemingly vacuous move from a positive assertion that Elsie is a cow to the negative assertion that Elsie is not a non-cow can be the starting point for an ontological evaporation scheme.

Let us put negation on hold for a moment and attend to the understanding of *anyapoha* itself. Dharmakīrti—the most important figure in the articulation of this idea—is not always clear in his discussion of the nature of *apoha* and how it is supposed to solve the problem of universals, and so contemporary scholars are at odds regarding how to interpret his views. (See Siderits, Tillemans and Chakrabarti 2011 for some of this debate.) But he does move the discussion forward. Dharmakīrti argues that the basis for taking things to be excluded (or not) by a term rests on judgments of similarity and takes these in turn to be grounded in linguistic and cognitive practice and their efficacy in fulfilling specific human purposes (*arthakrīya*) (Guerrero 2013).

Dharmakīrti argues that when we reform our naive assertion that Elsie is a cow into the slightly more nuanced claim that Elsie is not a non-cow we are noting that Elsie is different from all of the things to which the label "cow" is not applied, which, in turn, are similar to one another in not being called "cows." Dharmakīrti's critics were quick to point out that to refer to things as "similar" appears to presuppose a *dimension* of similarity, and here two problems arise. First, the most natural way to characterize such a dimension is as sharing, to some degree at least, a *property*, and we seem to have landed back in the lap of realism about universals. Second, when we seek a respect in which all non-cows are similar, things are even worse: The only thing that such things as cabbages, kings, committees, cogs and coffee share in respect of which they are non-cows is the absence of a *property*, in particular, that of *being a cow*. And now we are back in the lap not only of realism about universals in general, but of realism with respect to *bovinity*, the very universal we sought to eliminate in the first place.

There is controversy surrounding whether Dharmakīrti's own reply to these objections is cogent. Dharmakīrti argues that judgments of similarity do not presuppose commitments to properties in virtue of the possession of which things are similar. Instead, he argues that we create predicate expressions, apparently denoting properties, to encode our habitual tendencies to regard certain things as similar. The anticipations of Hume's own brand of nominalism are intriguing here. Dharmakīrti goes a bit further, though, and argues that what grounds these tendencies to agree in similarity judgments are the degrees to which things fulfill human purposes, together with innate cognitive tendencies (*vasanas*, understood by Dharmakīrti as karmic imprints formed as a result of experiences in past lives, but which can easily be naturalized as our evolutionary ancestry).[4] Non-cows don't give cow milk or produce cowdung, and humans need cow milk for nutrition and cow dung for fuel. Humans instinctively see cows as similar to one another, and as different from horses. (See Dharmottara in Arnold 2012, 190–191.)

Given these fundamental human goals and a similar perceptual neurobiology we tend to judge as similar those things that have the power to advance our goals and to judge as similar (and dissimilar from the first class) those that don't. The analytical spade on this account is turned not when we stumble upon a universal whose presence we recognize in particulars, but rather when a particular does or does not do what we want together with an innate non-conceptual tendency to see as similar things that serve similar sets of purposes reinforced by tendencies to apply common linguistic terms to those things we see as similar. This last tendency in turn gives rise to an illusion, mediated by a naive referential theory of meaning, that we are referring to universals. (See Guerrero 2013 for an extended discussion.)

4. *Vasanas* play another important naturalizing role, explaining our primitive dispositions to interact with our conspecifics in ways that facilitate the learning of language and the acquisition of norm-governed dispositions, playing the same role that our evolutionary history does in explaining the innate tendencies that make learning and socialization possible. We can thus naturalize *karma* by treating it as a placeholder for anything we inherit psychologically from the past.

I now skip a lot of history and dialectic and move to the most mature form of this doctrine that we find in the work of Dharmakīrti's 11th-century commentator, Ratnakīrti, and also to some extent in the work of his teacher Jñānaśrīmitra (10th–11th C). We might call this the "paradigm and distinction" model of *apoha*. Ratnakīrti glosses *apoha* as *determination (niścaya)*, asserting that to grasp an *apoha* is simply to be able in practice to determine which of two alternatives holds, to draw a distinction among entities. He argues that to have a concept—to be able to engage in inference or to recognize conceptually constructed composite entities—is a two-stage affair. First, he argues, we must have an *ākāra/rnam pa*—a representation[5]—of a paradigm instance of a particular that satisfies the concept in question. Second, we must have the capacity to distinguish things that are *similar to* the paradigm from things that are not.

Once again, the objection regarding the presupposition of universals in order to account for similarity can be raised, but it is not decisive. If we appeal to innate habits or dispositions to respond to some particulars in a certain way in virtue of responding to others in a particular way—a causal story—we may be able to dispense with the ontological extravagance of a universal as the explanation of that causal capacity, especially if we are Buddhists about causality, seeing it as mere dependent origination. The role of a representation of a paradigm anticipates Eleanor Rosch's (1999) account of the role of paradigms in concepts in a nice way. And the gloss of *apoha* as the ability to draw distinctions in our verbal and non-verbal behavior gives a nice nominalistic understanding that avoids the awkward double negations to which Dignāga and Dharmakīrti were committed.[6]

Geluk theorists in Tibet, particularly Gyeltsap, took things a step further, asking whether the *representation* of a paradigm is necessary at all to this story. Adopting something like a direct realist theory both of perception and of cognition, they argued that conceptual thought merely consists in the ability to draw distinctions and to use words and concepts to codify those distinctions we draw in perception and action. Some capacities to distinguish may be innate; some depend on our language; but all are matters of convention, in the sense that each of these constitutes a way in which we construct a shared reality, as opposed to being ways in which we discover an independently existing

5. Once again, bear in mind the complex semantic range of this term, which can also connote an image, or an aspect, or even, as Kellner and McClintock (2014, 1–6) suggest, phenomenal content. But here *representation* seems clearly to be what is at issue.

6. For a nuanced treatment of *apoha* and a persuasive pragmatist interpretation of Dharmakīrti's theory of truth and meaning see Guerrero 2013.

reality awaiting our transparent epistemic faculties. In this story—one might call it *articulation without representation*—neither universals nor representations play any central role at all.

*Apoha*, on this view, is merely the ability to draw distinctions. All we have are particulars, our responses to them, and the language with which we describe those responses. To have a concept is to behave in a particular way; to believe that to have one is to grasp a universal is merely to reify. To draw an inference is to respond at a discursive level (in thought or in language) to the distinctions we draw in behavior. The story is nominalistic, particularistic, and non-conceptual all the way down, and yet is an account of how we engage conceptually with a world of particulars.

It is important to note before we leave *apoha* theory that this is also a story according to which any conceptual knowledge—including what we in the West would regard as perceptual knowledge of composite, enduring objects—is at best conventional, not ultimate truth. We can return to Candrakīrti's analysis of convention to unpack this claim. It means for one thing that it depends upon our biology, our conceptual apparatus and our language. For another, it does not deliver reality in a way that withstands analysis, reality as it is independent of how we engage with it. Analysis reveals the properties we take ourselves to register to be mere imputations. And finally, in virtue of this, conception is always *deceptive*. While it is a *pramāṇa*, an instrument of knowledge,[7] it is a second-rate instrument, standing behind perception as a guide to reality, simply in virtue of always presenting itself as engaging with that which is not real.

Inference and perception are then both *pramāṇas*, but Buddhist nominalism and the *apoha* theory it inspires establish a hierarchy in the Pramāṇavāda tradition we have been exploring. Perception engages directly and causally with particulars, and can in principle, though not for most of us in practice, deliver these momentary tropes as they exist. Inference, on the other hand, always presents itself as an engagement with the universal, and while we can analyze that away, it never escapes the taint of language, conception and deception. But the fact that we need at least these two *pramāṇas* to get anywhere in the world, to accomplish any of our *puruṣārthas*, together with the fact that our categorization depends upon our contingent *vasanas*, guarantees that the world with which we engage is always merely conventionally real according to this tradition.

7. A status they have in virtue of their *reliability* in delivering knowledge. Dharmakīriti and many of his followers—and like most non-Buddhist Indian epistemologists—are classical reliablists, unlike, for instance, Nāgārjuna and his followers who, as we will see, are coherentists.

## 1.3 *How Many* Pramāṇas? *Pramāṇavāda versus Madhyamaka*

While Buddhism is often identified on the epistemological side as the school that recognizes only two *pramāṇas*, this is true only of the Pramāṇavāda school we have just been examining. Candrakīrti, in *Lucid Exposition*, rejects this position, arguing that there is no good reason for Buddhists to reject the Nyāya *pramāṇas* of testimony and analogy,[8] and so that four *pramāṇas* should be taken seriously. His argument is simple and compelling, and is developed in the context of his commentary on Nāgārjuna's *Fundamental Verses on the Middle Way*.

When we ask about *pramāṇa*, Candrakīrti points out, we must be talking about knowledge from either the conventional or the ultimate perspective. But, he also urges, it makes no sense at all to say that anything is ultimately real, including *pramāṇas*. The activity of gaining knowledge is something we do in the conventional context, using conventional means. If we are asking how our ordinary mundane conventions pertain to acquiring knowledge of the external world, and how we actually engage in epistemic discourse with others, epistemology must be a *descriptive* enterprise, a kind of anthropology of human investigative practices, albeit a descriptive enterprise with normative implications. When we actually describe how we come to know, we see that a great deal of our knowledge in fact does come from testimony, from the spoken or written words of others. Moreover, a good deal of our understanding also relies on drawing analogies (a point made forcefully by Wittgenstein in *On Certainty*).

To be sure, inference is involved in these activities, but it is also involved in perception. We must infer from our knowledge of the reliability of our sense faculties that the information they deliver is accurate. And our confidence in inference is grounded on the words of others, who teach us how to reason. The assignment of a special primacy to two of the four *pramāṇas*, Candrakīrti argues, amounts to a covert assertion that they have some special *ultimate* status. Once we give that up, we should, he argues, let all plausible *pramāṇas* into the epistemological playing field. And given that the Buddhists' most prominent interlocutors were the Nyāyikas, the full set of Nyāya *pramāṇas* recommended itself. (See Thakchöe 2012a, Cowherds 2011.)

8. Candrakīrti does devote some space to arguing that testimony is, at least conventionally, a distinct *pramāṇa*, in virtue of the fact that speech is intentional and constitutive of the domain of convention (we might say that it puts the *sam* [together] and the *vṛt* [speech] in *saṃvṛti* [convention]). But it is ironic, given that he, like so many Buddhist philosophers, makes such heavy use of analogy in his own writing, that he says nothing much about how analogy works. We will have occasion to consider this issue in the next chapter when we talk about Buddhist theories of metaphor and of the nature of meaning.

At one level, Candrakīrti's response to Pramāṇavāda methodology is a debate about how to count epistemic instruments and is simply a familiar analytic debate about whether certain epistemic activities are reducible to others. At another, it is an interesting move in a discussion of epistemological foundationalism. [9] Candrakīrti is challenging the project of reducing the set of *pramāṇas* to a privileged pair from which all others can be derived, arguing that our full range of epistemic practices instead form an interdependent set. And at yet another level, Candrakīrti is anticipating a naturalization of epistemology, urging that in asking about how we know, we are asking an empirical question about human practices, and the answer to that is to be given by asking what we in fact *do* as knowers, not by adopting a prescriptive account of what *knowledge* is, once again challenging, as does Wittgenstein, the very cogency of a solipsistic hypothesis in the context of a discourse about knowledge.[10] Candrakīrti's analysis suggests that we see these three levels of analysis as tightly related.

Candrakīrti's more expansive approach to the enumeration of *pramāṇas* is shared by several early Chinese Buddhist epistemologists. The 6th-century Chinese epistemologist Huiyuan, in his *Essay on the Three Means of Valid Cognition* (translated in Lin 2014) agrees precisely with Candrakīrti in accepting all four of the Nyāya *pramāṇas*.[11] Moreover, Huiyuan, like Candrakīrti, despite using frequent analogies in his text, confines his epistemological analysis to the other three *pramāṇas*. He argues in particular that we require the separate *pramāṇa* of testimony or scriptural authority in order to come to know things that are outside of the scope of our own perceptual or inferential capacity, but are known by others in whom we have independent reason to trust (Lin 2014, 14–15, translation at 22).

Huiyuan's analysis, however, is very different from the Indian view of these *pramāṇas* and their relations to their respective *prameyas*. Huiyan does

9. A note about my use of the word "foundationalism" is in order here. The term often is used only to denote an epistemological position according to which certain sentences or cognitive episodes are taken to be self-warranting and to stand as the foundation for all other knowledge. That is a foundationalism of *content*. But there is also a foundationalism of *method*, according to which certain faculties or methods of knowing are taken to be self-warranting and foundational. Descartes's use of clear and distinct perception in the *Meditations* is a good example of this kind of foundationalism. It is this latter kind of foundationalism that Nāgārjuna is here concerned to refute.

10. See Thurman (1980) for an insightful treatment of the homologies between the thought of Candrakīrti and that of Wittgenstein, emphasizing their shared commitment to the centrality of a domain of shared practices in the constitution of knowledge and meaning.

11. Lin notes that in translating Indian *pramāṇa* literature, Kumārajīva uses the Chinese term *xin*, meaning *trust, warrant* or *assurance*, bringing this normative dimension of *pramāṇa* into Chinese (2014, 3).

not distinguish among the *pramāṇas* on the basis of their respective objects of knowledge, but rather in terms of the kinds of cognition they generate. In fact, he argues that each of the *pramāṇas* of perception, inference and scriptural authority can take particulars or universals as their objects. This divergence from Indian Buddhist epistemology is interesting, and is explained in part by the fact that for Huiyuan, what is known, in the end, is the truth of *sentences* (even though he takes all language to be merely metaphorical—see the next chapter for more on this), and sentences contain nouns and predicate expressions that must be understood as referring to individuals and predicating universals of them. Huiyuan seems to infer from the unity of the object of knowledge, and from its comprising both particulars and universals, that whatever is known, no matter by what means it is known, involves both.

Huizao (7th–8th C) was more directly influenced by Dignāga (Lin 2013). He follows Dignāga in taking particulars as the *prameya* of perception and universals as the *prameya* for inference. Nonetheless, it is important to Huizao that if universals are objects of knowledge—if inference is to be a genuine *pramāṇa*—those universals are real in some sense. His solution is conceptualist: universals, he argues, are mental representations and are the noematic contents of inference. He hence argues that inference does have a real object—these intentional contents of mind are real things—but that there is nothing non-conceptual to which they correspond. He then follows Dignāga in offering an *apoha* understanding of the relation of predicate expressions and the representations they express to reality: While predicates positively refer to conceptual representations, the only function of those representations is to enable us to draw distinctions. Scholars are only beginning to investigate seriously the Chinese Buddhist epistemological tradition, and there may be a great deal more of value forthcoming in the near future.

## 2. *Pramāṇa* and Convention

### *2.1 The Problem*

Candrakīrti's firm insistence that epistemology is an inquiry into our conventions for justification and inquiry raises the problem of epistemic relativism. If epistemic practices are merely conventional, then how are we to decide between competing conventions? The attack on the Pramāṇavāda tradition can be seen as an attack on the possibility of any such Archimedean standpoint. In the Buddhist context, this problem is even more poignant, given the association of *convention* with *ignorance*, or *primal confusion*, inviting the suspicion that a consequence of Buddhist epistemological commitments to the conventional status of the *pramāṇas* and the deceptiveness of the conventional, that there is no genuine knowledge at all. Let us explore the dimensions of the problem before examining the Madhyamaka solution.

Tsongkhapa, following Candrakīrti closely, writes that "*Convention*[12] refers to a lack of understanding or ignorance; that is, that which obscures or conceals the way things really are" (2006, 480–481). Candrakīrti himself puts the point this way:

> Obscurational truth[13] is posited due to the force of afflictive ignorance, which constitutes the limbs of cyclic existence. The śrāvakas, pratyekabuddhas and bodhisattvas, who have abandoned afflictive ignorance, see compounded phenomena to be like reflections, to have the nature of being created; but these are not truths for them because they are not fixated on things as true. Fools are deceived, but for those others—just like an illusion—in virtue of being dependently originated, they are merely obscurational. (Ibid., 481–482)

So it might seem that for Candrakīrti and Tsongkhapa conventional truth (understood here as *obscurational truth*) is merely illusion, wholly false, accepted only by the fools it deceives. In this case, even to talk about *pramāṇa* or knowledge conventionally would make no sense.

But of course that can't be the whole story, for several reasons. First of all, both Candrakīrti and Tsongkhapa refer to conventional truth as a *truth*. Indeed in *Introduction to the Middle Way* VI: 24 and its commentary, Candrakīrti explicitly argues that there is a big difference between conventional truth and conventional falsehood. Second, he points out in *Lucid Exposition* that the term "convention," though it can mean *concealing* (2009, 439), can also refer to *mutual dependence* and to *signifiers* (2006, 480), *Introduction to the Middle Way*, 252b, 2009, 439–440). In *Lucid Exposition*, Candrakīrti emphasizes the

12. There is a translational problem posed throughout this discussion by the terms *vyāvahāra* and *saṃvṛti* in Sanskrit and *tha snyad (thanyet)* and *kun rdzob (kundzop)* in Tibetan. I will use *convention* to translate the first members of these pairs and *obscuration* to translate the second. The only time that this difference is important is where they are glossed. Both Candrakīrti and Tsongkhapa regard them as absolutely coextensive.

13. Here I am using the term *obscurational truth* instead of the normal *conventional truth* to reflect the gloss Candrakīrti is developing for the Sanskrit *saṃvṛti*. In general, in this chapter, as we will be occasionally referring to his and Tsongkhapa's gloss of this term, we will require this alternative translation to make sense of what they are doing.

presence of these more positive meanings, asserting that "positing the person as a dependent designation based upon the aggregates" is an example of mundane convention (2009, 439), and that *mutual dependence* is a meaning of "conventional"; and therefore he claims that "term and referent; consciousness and object of knowledge, and all such things, *so long as they are non-deceptive, should be known as conventional truth*" (2009, 440).

Third, Candrakīrti also asserts that "it has been shown that each phenomenon has its own two natures—a conventional and an ultimate nature" (*Introduction to the Middle Way*, 253a, Tsongkhapa 2006, 483). The fact that these are natures of phenomena means that they are in some sense both *existent*. In fact, the very fact that Candrakīrti refers to these as *natures* of objects indicates that he does *not* reduce the sense of "conventional" (*saṃvṛti, vyavahāra*) to *illusory*. Fourth, Nāgārjuna asserts quite plainly, in the verse to which all of the passages to which I have just adverted are commentaries, that "the Buddha's teaching is based on two truths: a truth of worldly convention and an ultimate truth" (*Fundamental Verses on the Middle Way* XXIV: 8, Tsongkhapa 2006, 479). Finally, given the doctrine of the identity of the two truths (*Fundamental Verses on the Middle Way* XXIV: 18–19), a doctrine of which both Tsongkhapa and Candrakīrti approve, if the ultimate truth is a truth, a conventional truth that is identical with it just has to be true in some sense. And knowledge of it has to be possible in some sense.

It is important therefore to see how Candrakīrti and Tsongkhapa understand the idea of conventional truth, most specifically, in the sense in which, and the reasons for which, they regard conventional truth as *true*. We must therefore reconcile the claims that conventional truth is *concealing, deceptive, truth only for fools* with its *identity* with ultimate truth, and its being one of the two *natures* of any object. We thus also must explain the sense in which conventional truth is distinct from, and the sense in which it is identical to, ultimate truth, and why these two claims are mutually consistent.

## *2.2 Two Reasons that Conventional Truth Is a Truth (Preliminaries)*

There are two prima facie reasons for treating conventional truth as a truth both in the work of Candrakīrti and in that of Tsongkhapa. First, there is a very important sense in which the conventional truth is the only truth that there is. There are two ways of making this point. First, as we noted above, the two truths are, in an ontological sense, identical. If that is true, then even ultimate truth is only conventional. Second, the ultimate truth is emptiness, the absence of true, or inherent, existence in things. The ultimate truth is thus the fact that they are merely conventionally existent.

Now, neither Tsongkhapa nor Candrakīrti would put the point this way. They present two different arguments for the status of the conventional as truth. First, Tsongkhapa argues, following Candrakīrti very closely, that the ultimate truth—emptiness—is an external negation, a mere elimination of any intrinsic existence in things, and of any conceptualization (2006, 52–23). But this in the end amounts to the same thing, since to be merely existent is to lack any intrinsic identity. The ultimate truth is hence, even for Tsongkhapa, that the conventional truth is all that there is. We will return to this consideration at the end of this chapter.

The second reason will be more important in what follows. Tsongkhapa and Candrakīrti each emphasize that conventional truth is the domain of conventional *pramāṇa*, and hence that conventional truth is a domain about which there is a difference between getting it wrong and getting it right, and that one can be *correct* about conventional truth in two different but equally important senses. First, ordinary people can be right about the fact there is a rope on the ground, or they could be wrong about the fact that there is a snake there. The fact that there is a rope, not a snake, is hence in some sense *true*. Moreover, it is important to Buddhist soteriological theory that accomplished beings can know the conventional nature of conventional reality in a way that ordinary fools cannot. What is deceptive to fools is not, according to philosophers in this tradition, deceptive to *āryas*—highly accomplished practitioners—although it is merely conventional. In that sense, too, convention can be seen *truly*. Buddhist epistemology is hence in an important sense *progressive*, or *optimistic*, holding out the possibility that careful use of our *pramāṇas* can lead to entirely new and improved means of access to reality.

But there is a deeper point here concerning the very relation between truth and knowledge. It is easy to take for granted the idea that reality, or truth (and remember that in Sanskrit and Tibetan these are denoted by the same term, *satya/bden pa*) is foundational to knowledge, in that knowledge is defined in terms of access to truth, or to reality. But it is also important to remember that for both Candrakīrti and Tsongkhapa, it is the fact of epistemic authority that guarantees truth in convention and the reality of the conventional. When we ask why conventional truth is a *truth*, the answer will turn on the fact that epistemic practice allows us to draw a distinction *within* the conventional between truth and falsehood, as well as to talk about truth *about* the conventional. The fact that in epistemic practice there is something that counts as getting it right about conventional reality is what anchors our concepts of truth and reality, not the other way around. This is one of the distinctive contributions of Indo-Tibetan Madhyamaka to epistemology. We will explore this contribution first by considering Candrakīrti's and Tsongkhapa's account of conventional truth.

## *2.3 Mirages for Mādhyamikas*

Among the many similes for conventional truth that litter Madhyamaka texts, the most fruitful is that of the mirage. Conventional truth is false, Candrakīrti tells us, because it is deceptive (*Commentary on Sixty Stanzas of Reasoning Yuktiṣaṣṭikāvṛtti*, 7b in Loizzo, 2007). Candrakīrti spells this out in terms of a mirage. (Once again, given his liberality concerning *pramāṇas*, allowing *upamāna* or analogy into the set, his regular use of analogies is instructive.) A mirage appears to be water, but is in fact empty of water—it is deceptive, and in that sense, a false appearance. On the other hand, a mirage is not *nothing*: it is an *actual* mirage, just not actual water.

The analogy must be spelled out with care. A mirage appears to be water, but is only a mirage; the inexperienced highway traveler mistakes it for water, and for him it is deceptive, a false appearance of water; the experienced traveler sees it for what it is—a real mirage, empty of water. Just so, conventional phenomena appear to ordinary beings to be inherently existent, whereas in fact they are merely conventionally real, empty of that inherent existence; to those who see reality as it is, on the other hand, they appear to be merely conventionally true, hence to be empty. For us, they are deceptive, false appearances; for them, they are simply actual conventional existents with the capacity to deceive.

We can update the analogy to make the point more plainly. Imagine three travelers along a hot desert highway. Alice is an experienced desert traveler; Bill is a neophyte; Charlie is wearing polarizing sunglasses. Bill points to a mirage up ahead and warns against a puddle on the road; Alice sees the mirage as a mirage and assures him that there is no danger. Charlie sees nothing at all and wonders what they are talking about. If the mirage were entirely false—if there were no truth about it at all—Charlie would be the most authoritative of the three (and, importantly from a Buddhist framework that takes seriously the possibility of full awakening, Buddhas would know nothing of the real world). But that is wrong. Just as Bill is deceived in believing that there is water on the road, Charlie is incapable of seeing the mirage at all, and so fails to know what Alice knows—that there is an actual mirage on the road, which appears to some to be water, but which is not. There is a truth about the mirage, despite the fact that it is deceptive, and Alice is authoritative with respect to it precisely because she sees it as it is, not as it appears to the uninitiated.

## *2.4 Constraints on Conventional Truth in Madhyamaka Epistemology*

Tsongkhapa, in his discussion of the status of arising and ceasing, and the other pairs of opposites in the context of the negations presented in the Homage verses for *Fundamental Verses on the Middle Way*, remarks:

> [I]f there were no place for conventional phenomena, the existence of which is established by the epistemic instruments, these phenomena would be like the snake—that is, the rope grasped as a snake—of which no cause or effect is possible...
>
> [I]f one were forced to maintain that there is no place for bondage, liberation, etc. in the meaning of "conventional existence," and that these must be placed only in the erroneous perspective, that would be a great philosophical error.
>
> Even worse, as long as convention is conceived [as entirely nonexistent], since there would be no role for the epistemic instruments, neither the proposition maintained nor the person who maintains it nor the proof—including scriptural sources and reasoning—could be established by epistemic instruments. So it would be ridiculous to maintain that there are no genuine phenomena delivered by the epistemic instruments. (2006, 30–31)[14]

Tsongkhapa makes it plain here that conventional phenomena, unlike the snake thought to be perceived when one sees a rope (but like the thought that it is a snake), have causes and effects, and are actual. Moreover, he argues that the repudiation of the reality of the conventional would undermine the possibility of epistemic authority, undermining even the ability to argue cogently that the conventional does not exist. Such a position would be self-refuting.

Tsongkhapa comments that although ignorance is not a necessary condition of positing conventional truth, it is the source of the superimposition of inherent existence on that which is conventionally existent.

14. I have made slight changes in the translation that appears in (2006) for greater clarity in this context.

> This does not demonstrate that those who posit the existence of conventional truth posit through ignorance, nor that from the perspective of the śrāvakas, pratyekabuddhas and bodhisattvas... it is not posited as conventional truth.... Since it is through afflictive ignorance that one grasps things as truly existent, the object that is thereby grasped cannot exist even conventionally, and whatever is an obscurational truth must exist conventionally.
>
> ...When it is said that compounded phenomena are "merely conventional" from their perspective, the word "mere" excludes truth, but in no way excludes conventional truth....Thus, the sense in which the conventional truth is true is that it is true merely from the perspective of ignorance—that is, obscuration.
>
> [When] Candrakīrti...says, "since it is conventionally true, it is obscurational truth" [*Commentary to Introduction to the Middle Way*, 98] [he] means that conventional truth is that which is true from the perspective of ignorance—obscuration—but not that it is truly existent from the standpoint of nominal convention. (2006, 482)

Tsongkhapa notes that the fact that something is "only" conventionally true does not make it *false*. Things that are conventionally true are indeed *true*, but only conventionally so. And so he glosses Candrakīrti's apparent claim to the contrary as merely drawing a distinction between conventional and ultimate truth. Tsongkhapa next turns to the question of whether the distinction between conventional and ultimate truth is drawn on the basis of two distinct perspectives on the same reality or on the basis of two distinct natures of that reality. Following Candrakīrti, he adopts the latter position, arguing that when we distinguish conventional from ultimate truth we are distinguishing between two aspects of the object, not between two ways of apprehending the object, despite the fact that we indeed apprehend these aspects by using different faculties:

> Each of the internal and external phenomena has two natures: an ultimate and a conventional nature. The sprout, for instance, has a nature that is found by a rational cognitive process, which sees the real nature of the phenomenon as it is, and a nature that is found by a conventional cognitive process, which perceives deceptive or unreal objects. The former nature is the ultimate truth of the sprout; the latter nature is the conventional truth of the sprout.

> [Candrakīrti's assertion that] "it has been shown that each phenomenon has two natures—a conventional and an ultimate nature" [*Commentary to Introduction to the Middle Way*, 98–99] does not show that a single nature is in fact two truths in virtue of the two perspectives of the former and latter cognitive process. (2006, 483)

The distinction between the two natures, or two truths about a phenomenon, is drawn, according to both Tsongkhapa and Candrakīrti, on the basis of the kind of *pramāṇa* appropriate to each, and it is important that there is a kind of *pramāṇa* that is authoritative with respect to each. To be empty and to be deceptive are different. It is one thing for a mirage to be *empty of water*; it is another thing for it to be a *deceptive appearance*. These are two natures of the mirage, and the distinction between them is not the difference between two perspectives on the mirage, but between two objects of knowledge, which in turn are apprehended through different cognitive processes.

When one perceives the emptiness of a phenomenon, one perceives a nature that that phenomenon has, regardless of one's perspective on it, and the kind of cognitive process that perceives that emptiness is one that is authoritative with respect to ultimate truth; when one perceives the conventional character of a phenomenon, one perceives its deceptive nature, both the way it appears and the fact that it does not exist in that way. Moreover, the kind of cognitive process that perceives that is one that is authoritative with respect to the conventional. On the other hand, to perceive a conventional phenomenon as inherently existent is not even to be authoritative with respect to the conventional.

> ...In order to ascertain a pot for instance, as a deceptive or unreal object, it is necessary to develop the view that refutes...the object of fixation that is the object grasped as truly existent. This is because without having rationally refuted its true existence, its unreality is not established by *pramāṇas*. So, for the mind to establish anything as an object of conventional truth, it must depend on the refutation of its ultimate existence. (2006, 483)
>
> ...
>
> Ordinary beings grasp such things as pots as truly existent, and grasp them as ultimately existent as well. Therefore, from the perspective of their minds, such things as pots are ultimately existent, but they are not conventional objects. The things, such as pots, which are ultimately existent from their perspective, are conventional objects from

> the perspective of the *āryas*, to whom they appear as illusionlike. Since they cannot be posited as truly existent as they are apprehended by an *āryan* consciousness, they are referred to as merely conventional.
>
> . . .
>
> That which is perceived by ordinary people
> By being grasped through unimpaired sense faculties
> Is regarded by ordinary people as real.
> All the rest is said to be unreal. (*Introduction to the Middle Way* VI: 25 in Tsongkhapa 2006, 484)

Finally, there is a standard of correctness for conventional truth. Truth, for Candrakīrti and for Tsongkhapa, must contrast with falsehood. And the standard for the truth of a judgment regarding conventional truth is that it is vouchsafed by the authority of conventional *pramāṇas* and cannot be undermined by them, just as the standard of truth of a judgment regarding the ultimate is that it is vouchsafed by the authority of ultimate *pramāṇas* and not undermined by cognition of that kind. This in turn requires a distinction between sound and impaired conventional faculties:

> The internal impairments of the sense faculties are such things as cataracts, jaundice, and such things as hallucinogenic drugs one has consumed. The external impairments of the sense faculties are such things as mirrors, the echoing of sounds in a cave, and the rays of the autumn sun falling on such things as white sand. Even without the internal impairments, these can become the causes of grasping of such things as mirages, reflections and echoes as water, etc.
>
> The impairments of the mental faculty are . . . such things as erroneous philosophical views, fallacious arguments and sleep. . . . .
>
> Taking conventional objects grasped by such unimpaired and impaired cognitive faculties to be real or unreal, respectively, merely conforms to ordinary cognitive practice. This is because they actually exist as they appear or do not, according to whether or not they are undermined by ordinary cognition. This distinction is not drawn from the perspective of the *āryas*. This is because just as such things as reflections do not exist as they appear, such things as blue, that appear to exist through their own characteristics to those who are afflicted by ignorance do not actually exist as they appear. Therefore there is no distinction between

> those two kinds of cognitive faculties in terms of whether or not they are erroneous. (2006, 485)

Note the emphasis on ordinary cognitive practice. Conventional truth, according to Tsongkhapa, is that which is delivered by unimpaired cognitive faculties when they are used properly. This is not an accidental generalization; instead it is *constitutive* of conventional truth. It entails that any judgment about truth is in principle revisable, but that to be true is to endure through revision. The distinction between the conventionally true and the conventionally false has nothing to do with ultimate truth. Conventional existents and conventional nonexistents are all false from the perspective of ultimate truth.[15] Those who are taken in by the conventional fail to understand its deceptive character, and so fail to understand the two truths. That failure, however, is consistent with a lot of conventional knowledge about a lot of conventional truth.

## 3. Coherentism, Fallibilism and Pragmatism

### *3.1 Epistemic Authority for Mādhyamikas*

Inasmuch as the role of the authority of *pramāṇas* in Madhyamaka metaphysics plays a significant role in Buddhist epistemology, a few remarks on Nāgārjuna's and Candrakīrti's account of the source of the authority of the *pramāṇas* are necessary. It is often urged that Nāgārjuna, in *Reply to Objections (Vigrahavyāvārtanī)*, rejects the intelligibility of any *pramāṇas* (Siderits 2011). I believe that this is incorrect. Nāgārjuna, in that text, criticizes a Nyāya account of *pramāṇas* and their authority according to which the *pramāṇas* are taken to be *foundational* to all knowledge. He does so because this kind of foundationalism would require their intrinsic identity and authority as instruments, and so would undermine his more general account of emptiness.

The Nyāya interlocutor in *Reply to Objections* argues that Nāgārjuna himself cannot argue cogently for his own position, as that would presuppose that it is delivered and so justified by a *pramāṇa*; that, in turn, the interlocutor argues, requires that the *pramāṇas* be self-verifying, and hence non-empty. Hence, he argues, Nāgarjuna must presuppose non-empty epistemic categories in order to argue for the emptiness of everything, and so is self-refuting.

15. Nāgārjuna's glosses *falsehood* in this context in *Introduction to the Middle Way* XIII: 1 as *deceptiveness*. So to say that the conventional is false is to say that it is deceptive, as when we call someone a false friend or refer to a fake gun. It is not to say that the conventional is nonexistent, but to say that exists in one way, but appears to exist in another. See Cowherds (2011), especially chapter 4, for more on this.

5. Suppose one were to deny the things
One apprehended through perception.
That by which one apprehended things—
Perception itself—would be nonexistent!

That is, as the autocommentary makes clear, the opponent is reasoning that any argument for the emptiness of the objects of knowledge is an equally good argument for the emptiness of the *pramāṇas*. But if the *pramāṇas* are empty, they cannot serve as foundations for knowledge, and so in the absence of such foundations, there would be no reason to believe even the Mādhyamika's claims. (See Westerhoff 2010a for details.)

Nāgārjuna replies not by denying the utility of the *pramāṇas*, but rather by arguing, in what must be the first explicit defense of epistemological coherentism in the history of world philosophy, that the *pramāṇas* are themselves useful precisely because they are dependent. Once again, a terminological clarification is needed. The kind of coherentism Nāgārjuna is defending is not one in which all *beliefs* are mutually supportive, but rather one according to which the warrant of mechanisms of attaining knowledge and the warrant of the beliefs they deliver are mutually supportive. The *pramāṇas*, Nāgārjuna argues, are dependent upon their *prameyas*, the objects of knowledge.

40. If *pramāṇas* were self-established,
They would be independent of *prameyas*.
These *pramāṇas* you would establish,
Being self-established, would depend on nothing else.

41. If, as you would have it, the *pramāṇas*
Are independent of their objects, the *prameyas*
Then these *pramāṇas*
Would pertain to nothing at all.

. . .

46. So, as far as you are concerned, by establishing the *pramāṇas*
The *prameyas* are thereby established.
So, as far as you are concerned,
Neither *pramāṇas* nor *prameyas* can be established.

Foundationalism, even of this methodological kind, according to Nāgārjuna, makes no sense. Neither instrument nor object of knowledge can serve as foundations. We are entitled to rely on epistemic instruments, that is, just because they deliver epistemic objects; we are entitled in turn to have confidence in our judgments about our epistemic objects just because they are delivered by these epistemic instruments. For instance, you are entitled to believe that your vision is good just because it delivers visible objects to you; in the same way, you are entitled to believe that those objects are present just because your vision is good. (See Thakchöe 2012a.)

Candrakīrti, as we have seen, is even more explicit in his endorsement of the full set of Nyāya *pramāṇas* (perception, inference, analogy and scriptural authority). He enumerates them specifically, but argues that they have only a dependent, conventional validity, concluding, "therefore, in this context [that of mundane knowledge] the four *pramāṇas* make the mundane object known" (2003, 55). Moreover, Tsongkhapa makes explicit use of this theory of *pramāṇas* and their objects, using this theory as an account of authority or warrant throughout his corpus. It is therefore a serious mistake to think that Madhyamaka, at least as articulated by Nāgārjuna, Candrakīrti and Tsongkhapa, eschews reliance on, or an account of, epistemic authority. But it is equally incorrect to ignore their radical pluralism and coherentism about such authority.

### *3.2 Pragmatism and Fallibilism*

Not only is there an important strain of coherentism in Buddhist epistemology, but there is also an important strain of pragmatism.[16] We have encountered one source of this pragmatism in Dharmakīrti's attempt to ground *apoha* theory through the appeal to *puruṣārtha* or human ends and *arthakrīya*, the ability to accomplish those ends. Here we have an explicit appeal to non-discursive as well as discursive human practices at the basis of concept formation and judgment. But as we follow the trajectory of Buddhist epistemology into Candrakīrti's Madhyamaka, the pragmatism goes deeper yet. For Candrakīrti explicitly treats justification and the process of coming to know as conventional practices alongside any others, whose justification as practices consists simply in the fact that they fit into a network of everyday conventions and practices that work for us. When asked for any ultimate ground, such as direct contact with reality or transcendental justification, the Mādhyamika shakes her head, suggesting that the very idea of such a ground is incoherent; convention, human practice, is all we have, and all we need. This justification

16. Many, including Kalupahana (1976) and Guerrero (2013), have noted the broad philosophical affinities between many ideas developed in many Buddhist traditions and American pragmatist thought, particularly that of John Dewey and William James. There is a lot to be said for this insight, and I thank Andrew Connor for calling this connection to my attention, but I will not pursue those analogies here.

and understanding of pragmatism in epistemology is another signal contribution of Buddhist theory to our understanding of knowledge.

Moreover, this epistemology is fallibilist in at least two senses. First, and most obviously, while we may know some things to be conventionally true, everything we say conventionally, whether true or false, fails to be ultimately true. What we know is hence always false in one very important sense. But this is old hat within a Madhyamaka framework, as we have seen in our discussion of the two truths. More interestingly, and more relevant to contemporary Western discussions of knowledge, since knowledge is understood in terms of the deliverances of the *pramāṇas*, and since the *pramāṇas* are only validated in terms of evolving social epistemic practices and the *prameyas* they deliver, we can never take knowledge, on this model, to be a finished enterprise.

Conventional knowledge is thus not only *ultimately false*, but much of it is very likely to turn out to be *conventionally false* as the ongoing equilibrium between *pramāṇa* and *prameya*, as well as the ongoing calibration of *pramāṇas*, advances. This is simply another version of the "pessimistic induction" on knowledge: when we focus epistemological reflection on the *pramāṇas*, when we couple that with a careful account of just in what the warrant of the *pramāṇas* consists, and when we focus on the relationship between knowledge, truth and the role of convention in constituting each, this conclusion is unavoidable. This is another contribution of Buddhist epistemology to contemporary discourse.

## 4. The Centrality of Epistemic Authority to Ontology

The authority of the *pramāṇas* is hence central to Madhyamaka accounts of truth and reality in two respects. First, conventional truth is conventionally *true* precisely because it is that which is delivered by conventional *pramāṇas* and not undermined by it. My knowledge that snow is white is delivered by vision, corroborated by the vision of others, and is not undermined by any other conventional *pramāṇa*. Without an antecedent account of the *pramāṇas* and their authority, there is no way to distinguish conventional truth from conventional falsity. On the one hand, without such an account, we might take only the ultimate *pramāṇas* to be authoritative. But then, since all phenomena are ultimately unreal, reliance on these instruments only would deliver the verdict that everything is false, and we would have no domain of truth whatsoever. On the other hand, in the absence of such an account, we might take the object of *any* cognition to be conventionally existent. But that would make a hash of all inquiry, as there is always somebody crazy or deluded enough to believe, or to believe *in*, anything. It is therefore the fact of conventional authority—of the robustness of ordinary epistemic standards—that allows us to distinguish truth from falsity and to engage in inquiry in the first place.

Second, the genuine actuality of conventional truth is a consequence of the fact that according to Candrakīrti and Tsongkhapa the *pramāṇas* of *āryas*—of those who have transcended the primal ignorance that fabricates inherent existence—deliver conventional phenomena as *actual*, although deceptive, phenomena. Once again, the authority of their *pramāṇas* doesn't so much *reflect* the fact that it is true that conventional phenomena are existent but *constitutes* their existence, as it constitutes a standard by means of which we can distinguish the true from the false.[17]

Truth for Candrakīrti and Tsongkhapa is always that which is delivered by *pramāṇas*. But what makes these *pramāṇas* authoritative? Here is where the epistemic rubber hits the soteriological road and where the term "conventional" (*vyāvahara/tha snyad*) gets its punch. An ultimate *pramāṇa* is simply defined as one that is authoritative with respect to ultimate truth. It is hence the kind of cognition finally necessary to attain awakening and the kind engaged in awakened consciousness. A conventional epistemic instrument, much more straightforwardly, is just one that is authoritative with regard to what we conventionally accept. As we have seen, Nāgārjuna argues in *Reply to Objections* that this is not a static set—*pramāṇas* depend on their *prameyas* for their authority, and these objects, in turn, depend on the *pramāṇas* for their actuality in a coherentist spiral that defies grounding, but characterizes epistemic practice in the only way we could ever hope to do so. Candrakīrti follows Nāgārjuna in accepting the authority of conventional *pramāṇas* in the conventional domain.

## *4.1 Seeing Mirages Correctly*

We can now see why it is so important to Buddhist epistemology that we actually see mirages, and that we can come to see *that* mirages *are* mirages. Mirages are genuine parts of our world, and they cause real problems. If one were to spend one's life in polarizing sunglasses, one would never know this, and one would be less useful to everyone else. To see a mirage as water is not to see conventional truth, but conventional falsehood, for conventional *pramāṇas* undermine the assertion that there is water on the road. But conventional

17. See Westerhoff (2011) and Finnigan and Tanaka (2011) for interesting explorations of how this constitution might be modeled.

*pramāṇas* vindicate the claim that there is a mirage that appears to be water. That is *why* it is conventionally existent.

There are two levels of apprehension of mirages, though. There is a difference between the *novice* desert driver who *sees* the mirage *as water*, but then *infers* its mirage-status and the *experienced* driver who sees it *as a mirage*. They each apprehend conventional existence, but the first does so as do most of us ordinarily, but as sophisticated Mādhyamikas do, inferentially. The latter sees the mirage as an *arhat* sees conventional existence—immediately, perceptually, non-inferentially. *We* see it as deceptive because we are, at least in the first moment of perceptual consciousness, deceived. *She* sees it as deceptive because she knows what we see. The transcendence of primal ignorance is hence not the transcendence of the *apprehension* of the conventional, but the transcendence of *deception* by it. Buddhist epistemology is deployed to make sense of the possibility and the process of this kind of transcendence.

Buddhism, as we noted in chapter 1, is about solving a problem—the problem of the omnipresence of suffering—and the central intuition of Buddhism is that the solution to that problem is the extirpation of ignorance. Epistemology is located at the foundation of morality and gets its point just from that location, but it also has profound ontological consequences. The mechanism of the extirpation of ignorance is the competent use of our *pramāṇas*. What truly competent use delivers is hence, at least indirectly, always of soteriological significance—always instrumental to liberation. Inasmuch as that is the central moral virtue and inasmuch as epistemology is so tightly bound to the soteriological project, it is also the central epistemic virtue, and what we call the goal of epistemic activity is *truth*. Conventional truth is hence not to truth as blunderbusses are to buses, nor as fake guns are to real guns, but rather is, instead, simply one kind of *truth*. And knowledge must be defined in reference to it. The primary Buddhist insight is that the most obvious direction of explanation is in fact to be reversed.

## *4.2 Epistemology and the Two Truths*

One of the Buddha's deepest insights was that there are two truths, and that they are very different from one another. They are the objects of different kinds of cognition, and they reflect different aspects of reality. They are apprehended at different stages of practice. Despite the importance of the apprehension of ultimate truth, one can't skip the conventional. Despite the soteriological efficacy of ultimate truth, even after Buddhahood, omniscience and care for others require the apprehension of the conventional.

Nāgārjuna's deepest insight was that despite the vast difference between the two truths in one sense, they are, in an equally important sense, identical. We can now make better sense of that identity that we discussed at length in chapter 2, and of why the fact of their identity is the same fact as that of their difference. The ultimate truth is, from a Buddhist perspective, emptiness. Emptiness in Madhyamaka thought is the emptiness of *inherent existence*, not of *existence simpliciter*. To be empty of inherent existence is to exist only conventionally, only as the object of conventional truth. The ultimate truth about any phenomenon, on the analysis of this doctrine I have been defending, is hence that it is merely a conventional truth. Ontologically, therefore, the two truths are absolutely identical. This is the content of the idea that from a Madhyamaka standpoint the two truths have a single basis: that basis is empty phenomena. Their emptiness is their conventional reality; their conventional reality is their emptiness.

But to *know* phenomena conventionally is not to *know* them ultimately. As objects of knowledge—that is, as intentional contents of thought, as opposed to as mere phenomena; that is, as external objects considered independently of their mode of apprehension—they are objects of different kinds of knowledge, despite the identity at a deeper level of those objects. Hence we see the difference between the two truths. But the respect in which they are different and that in which they are identical are, despite their difference, also identical. A mirage is deceptive because it is a refraction pattern and it is the nature of a refraction pattern to be visually deceptive. The conventional truth is merely deceptive and conventional because, upon ultimate analysis, it fails to exist as it appears—that is, because it is ultimately empty. It is the nature of the conventional to deceive. Ultimately, since all phenomena, even ultimate truth, exist only conventionally, conventional truth is all the truth there is, and that is an ultimate, and therefore, a conventional, truth. To fail to take conventional truth seriously as truth is therefore not only to deprecate the conventional in *favor* of the ultimate, but to deprecate *truth*, per se. That way, according to any Buddhist school, lies suffering.

Buddhist epistemology is aimed at the extirpation of suffering, but, as I hope to have shown, it is of more than soteriological interest. It represents a distinctive way of picking up the problem of knowledge. It develops a distinctive account of the nature of justification and a distinctive account of the relationship between knowledge and its objects, as well as a distinctive approach to thinking about the structure of concepts and judgments. To be sure, all of this is entwined with a Buddhist account of ontology, both with its nominalism and with its focus on the two truths. One not predisposed to Buddhist metaphysics might therefore find the epistemology of little interest. On the other hand, to the extent that the epistemology makes sense—and in my view that is a considerable extent—this might provide reason to be sympathetic to Buddhist metaphysics as well. In any case, it is clear that this is a distinctive voice in epistemology, and one that belongs in discussions of knowledge as they are prosecuted in the contemporary West.

# 8 LOGIC AND THE PHILOSOPHY OF LANGUAGE

Formal logic as we know it since Frege was not a feature of the classical Indian landscape. A categorical logic reminiscent of Aristotelian syllogistic logic was introduced to Buddhist thought by the Nyāya school in about the 4th century, and developed in some detail by Indian and Tibetan Buddhist epistemologists, particularly Dignāga and Dharmakīrti. While this "Buddhist Logic" has received considerable attention in Buddhist Studies per se, it never reaches a level of sophistication that would lead us in the modern world to take it seriously as a sophisticated account of reasoning or of consequence relations in general. And Buddhist logical thought makes almost no inroads into East Asia at all. So, while the history of Buddhist accounts of formal reasoning and debate are to be sure interesting to the *historian* of logic, it would be useless to look to medieval Indian Buddhist logic as a source of formal insights today.

This does not mean, however, that there are no resources in Buddhist logical theory for contemporary philosophical logic. To find those resources we travel back in time, prior to the Nyāya intervention in Buddhist philosophical thought, to the deployment by the Buddha himself and later by Mādhyamikas, of the *catuṣkoṭi*, or *four-cornered* logic. This structure represents the first serious program in four-valuational logic in world history, recognized by Routley (1975) as an important anticipation of the Meyer-Dunn semantics for first-order entailment (Meyer and Dunn 1972). It is also a clear anticipation of Belnap's four-valued logic for computer reasoning (Belnap 1977a, 1977b). In this framework, while some sentences are simply *true*, and others simply *false*, some are *both true and false*, and some are *neither true nor false*.[1]

1. I use the term "four-valuational" logic to emphasize that while Mādhyamikas were happy to recognize both truth value gaps and gluts, the only truth *values* they recognized (whether singly, together, or altogether absent) are *true* and *false*. This emphasizes a deep kinship between their paraconsistency and paracompleteness, on the one hand, and the logics more familiar to those whose

And while formal logic may not have preoccupied Buddhist philosophers, the philosophy of language certainly did. Language, as we have already seen, occupies a complex position in Buddhist philosophical reflection. On the one hand, *Buddhavacana* (the speech of the Buddha), although clearly linguistic, is valorized if not as a *pramāṇa*, then at least as something awfully close, capable of clinching a doctrinal argument, and even when its meaning is disputed, requiring interpretation as true in the context of intramural Buddhist dialectics. And no Buddhist philosopher, in any tradition, has been shy about using language, despite some apparently extralinguistic "utterances" by Zen masters and certain valorized silences to which we will return below.

On the other hand, language is always associated with conceptuality, with reification, and with predication that implicates universals. Ultimate truth, access to which is the epistemic goal of Buddhist reflection and practice—and which is indeed the subject of much Buddhist speculation carried out in Pāli, Sanskrit, Tibetan, Chinese and other *languages*—is regarded as ineffable, as beyond discursive thought or description. So language is always regarded as *deceptive*, as in need of transcendence. This tension, not surprisingly, gives rise to paradoxes, the resolution of which may require the device of the *catuṣkoṭi*.

The conjunction of the obvious utility of language—acknowledged both implicitly in its use, and explicitly in reflection on its use—and its necessary ultimate inadequacy and deceptive nature raises important broad questions that Buddhist philosophers took very seriously: What does language actually do? What is the nature of meaning? How can something so deceptive and inadequate nonetheless be useful in the pursuit of truth? Addressing these questions, especially in the context of tantric Buddhism, leads to interesting speculations about the genus of which language is a species. In this chapter we will take up each of these linked topics in turn.

## 1. Logic—the *Catuṣkoṭi*

Let us begin with the *catuṣkoṭi*. This Buddhist approach to logic is often characterized as a *four-valued* logic, but I think that is misleading. It is a two-valued logic that allows four *valuations*. We can bring this point home with the

logical reference points are Boole and Frege, on the other hand. Of course those logics can also be specified with only a single truth value, *true*, and two valuations—*true* and *not true*—although they are rarely conceived by their proponents in that parsimonious way. There is also a kind of awkwardness in using this anachronistic language to discuss Buddhist logic. For as we have seen, Buddhist philosophers are resolutely nominalist, and in helping ourselves to the apparatus of evaluation functions, we may be using a rather Platonist metalanguage. Thoughts about how to nominalize that metalanguage are for another day.

following simple analogy. Suppose that you invite my wife and me to dinner. There are four possibilities: (only) she comes; (only) I come; we both come; or neither of us comes. The fact that there are four possibilities for our attendance does not mean that there are four of us, only that there are four subsets of the set comprising the two of us.

The insight behind the *catuṣkoṭi* is simply that truth values, like spouses, dispose themselves independently. While the only truth values are *true* and *false*—and all Buddhist philosophers of language are insistent on this fact—these truth values are independent of each other. A sentence may be (only) true; (only) false; *both* true and false; *neither* true nor false. The *catuṣkoṭi* hence partitions logical space into four possibilities, which we can represent by thinking of a valuation function that maps sentences not onto *members* of the basic set of truth values, but rather onto *subsets* of the set of truth values. Hence four *valuations*, not four *values*.

While the *catuṣkoṭi* is deployed in certain Pāli *suttas* and in the *Perfection of Wisdom sūtras* that constitute the foundation of Madhyamaka (Westerhoff 2009, Garfield and Priest 2009, Tillemans 2011a), its locus classicus is in Nāgārjuna's *Fundamental Verses on the Middle Way* and in the commentarial literature that follows it. Shortly after the period of Nāgārjuna, this logical approach is eclipsed by the much less interesting categorical logic of the Nyāyikas, brought in to Buddhist discourse by such philosophers as Bhāviveka and Dignāga, and developed most extensively by Dharmakīrti and his commentators.[2]

In Nāgārjuna's hands, the *catuṣkoṭi* comes in two forms: a positive and a negative form. In the positive form, generally asserted from a conventional perspective, all four limbs are asserted. That is, Nāgārjuna argues that some sentences can be understood as true, false, both and neither, from that perspective. For instance, in the eighteenth chapter of *Fundamental Verses on the Middle Way*, he says:

> 8. Everything is real; and is not real;
> Both real and not real;
> Neither real nor not real.
> This is the Lord Buddha's teaching.

In such cases, the four corners are parameterized. So, there are two principal readings of this verse. On one reading, these represent sequential stages in understanding. One begins by urging people to take phenomena seriously.

2. The interested reader can consult Chi (1984), Tillemans (1989), Matilal and Evans (1986), Perdue (2008) and Matilal (1998) on Buddhist formal argument as needed.

They are real. But then it is important to teach that phenomena are in fact empty, that they do not exist in the way they appear to exist, and so are unreal as they appear. Since this can lead to nihilism, it is important then to teach that their ultimate nonexistence is perfectly compatible with their conventional reality. And finally, it is necessary to urge that neither of these assertions conveys the ultimate reality of things, because that is beyond characterization by words. But this must be contrasted with the *negative catuṣkoṭi* in which all four limbs are denied. Tsongkhapa draws this contrast as follows::

> We do not assert both of these; nor do we assert neither that he [the Tathāgata] exists nor does not exist because *ultimately* none of these four alternatives can be maintained. On the other hand, if we did *not* assert these *conventionally*, those to whom we speak would not understand us. So, from the standpoint of the conventional truth and for conventional purposes, we say "empty" and "nonempty," "both empty and nonempty," and "neither empty nor nonempty." We say these having mentally imputed them from the perspective of those people to whom we are speaking. Therefore, we simply say that "they are asserted only for the purpose of designation." (2006, 448)

The last statement, on this interpretation, leads directly to a paradox of expressibility, of course. That is, in asserting that ultimate reality is inexpressible, it expresses something about ultimate reality, namely its inexpressibility. (See Garfield and Priest 2003, 2009; Deguchi, Garfield and Priest 2013a, 2013b, 2013d.) A second way to read this is as the assertion that everything exists (conventionally), does not exist (ultimately), both exists (conventionally) and does not exist (ultimately) and neither exists (ultimately) nor does not exist (conventionally). Interestingly, more canonical commentaries take the first reading than the second.

When Nāgārjuna is discussing the *ultimate* perspective in chapter XXII, on the other hand, he resorts to *negative catuṣkoṭis* in which all four possibilities are *denied*.

> 11. We do not assert "empty."  
> We do not assert "non-empty."  
> We assert neither both nor neither.  
> These are used only nominally.

This suggests a more radical possibility for a valuation function—that it is *partial*, and not only partial but radically so. Some sentences get no evaluation at all, *not even the empty set of truth values.* (See Garfield and Priest 2009.) In this case, Nāgārjuna's point is that all language—no matter how useful—fails to characterize reality, simply because it deals in unreal universals, superimposing concepts on a non-conceptualized world. To the extent that language is necessary at all, it is a necessary evil; while it can never succeed, it gives us the illusion that we have somehow encompassed the world as it is.

This lands us once again in an expressibility paradox. Some Buddhist philosophers, noting this looming paradox, attempt and fail to defuse it. Candrakīrti glosses the possibility of this kind of refusal to assert or deny anything at all in terms of a distinction between *non-implicative,* or *external,* negation, in which a sentence is simply denied without anything being implicated, not even its falsity or lack of any truth value. This distinction is an old one in Sanskrit grammatical traditions. It corresponds roughly to the Western distinction between *internal* or predicate negation and *external* or sentential negation, but with a pragmatic dimension as well. So, the non-implicative negation rejects a sentence without suggesting anything at all about its subject term, while an implicative negation rejects a sentence implicating that its subject term satisfies a property contrary to the one asserted by the sentence.

So, when I say that my horse is not brown, I implicate that I have a horse of a different color, while if I say that I do not have a brown horse, I do not implicate that I have a horse at all. This draws the distinction in terms of logical form. Sanskrit grammarians, however, also draw it pragmatically: An implicative negation is any negation that carries a clear implicature regarding the subject term; a non-implicative negation is one that does not. So, to take a stock example, "that fat man does not eat during the day" implicates that he eats at night, while "that fat man has no son" does not implicate that he has a daughter. The two negations are then regarded as distinct in type despite the identity of logical form. This alerts us to the fact that negation as an operator is conceived somewhat differently in this tradition, not simply as a kind of denial, but as a family of speech acts.

In the case of the negative tetralemma, Candrakīrti urges that emptiness is an external, or non-implicative negation. So when we say that things are empty, we deny that they have any nature; we do not implicate that they have some other nature, in particular, that they have the nature of being empty. For this reason, he suggests, the negative tetralemma is not contradictory. For in denying that things are empty, we are denying that they have the nature of emptiness; in denying that they are non-empty, we are denying that they have any nature at all, etc. Unfortunately, given that emptiness is also asserted to be the ultimate nature of phenomena, and that that nature is to have no nature, paradox is nonetheless inevitable. (See Garfield and Priest 2009, Deguchi, Garfield and Priest 2013a, 2013b.)

In the Chan and Zen traditions in China and Japan, this negative tetralemma is glossed as an *absolute negation*, or *MU*, the refusal to say anything, even that. In Tibet, this radical negation is taken to indicate the complete ineffability of ultimate truth—that to say anything about it, or anything that purports to characterize reality as it is, is to say something that is not even truth-valueless, something not even suitable for evaluation. Gorampa argues for this position, stating that the ultimate truth is "beyond all conceptual fabrication" (Kassor 2013), and so that no statements about it have any content whatsoever.

Sometimes, on the other hand, the *catuṣkoṭi* is neither simply asserted nor simply denied, but rather is used as a partition of the logical space for the purposes of *reductio*. In *Fundamental Verses on the Middle Way* XXII we find the following:

13. One who holds firmly
    That the Tathāgata exists
    Will have to fabricate his nonexistence
    After having achieved nirvana.

14. Since he is essentially empty,
    Neither the thought that the Buddha exists
    Nor that he does not exist
    After having achieved *nirvāṇa* is tenable.

15. Those who develop fabrications with regard to the Buddha—
    The unextinguished one who has gone beyond all fabrication—
    And are impaired by those cognitive fabrications,
    Fail to see the Tathāgata.

16. Whatever is the essence of the Tathāgata,
    That is the essence of the transmigrator.
    The Tathāgata has no essence.
    The transmigrator has no essence.

This argument is often taken to be a *reductio* on an imagined opponent's presupposition that the Buddha exists ultimately, as some kind of soul, or substantially real continuum. The argument is then that one of the four alternatives would have to obtain after the Buddha has entered *nirvāṇa*, but that each is absurd. If he continued to exist, then since the post-*nirvāṇa* Buddha would be identical to the pre-*nirvāṇa* Buddha, he would have the same properties, and would not be awakened; if he did not exist, then *nirvāṇa* would simply be extinction, and would be useless. To both exist and not exist in the same sense is impossible—particularly if neither conjunct is true—and anything substantially real must either exist or not exist at any moment.

While this use of the *catuṣkoṭi* might seem less radical than its simple assertion or more radical denial, it still implicates the partition of logical space into four possibilities rather than two. So, even in cases such as this, the use of the *catuṣkoṭi* framework presupposes the cogency in general of the assertion of contradictions and the cogency of truth value gaps, even if they are not cogent in a particular case. In any of these three uses of the *catuṣkoṭi* the Madhyamaka perspective on logic is clear: Logic must be both paraconsistent and paracomplete.

This Madhyamaka logical commitment is not, I emphasize, a recommendation of irrationalism, or some kind of antinomian rejection of canons of reasoning. Instead it is a specific account of what rationality demands, and a specific proposal for a particular canon of reasoning. We can make perfectly good sense of the contradictions that arise at the limits of thought, expressibility and ontology that arise naturally from these Buddhist analyses. The tools of modern paraconsistent logic demonstrate the cogency of such reasoning and the rationality of the endorsement of certain contradictions (Priest 2006, 2010; Garfield and Priest 2009; and Garfield 2014b). Moreover, the standard semantics for entailment and the most powerful database logics validate this approach. In each of these cases, we have compelling arguments for each conjunct of the relevant contradiction, a commitment to accepting the rational consequences of rationally justified beliefs, and no reason to believe that contradictions are to be rejected per se, as there is no commitment in this tradition to the principle of *ex contradictione quodlibet*, or *explosion*. Without a commitment to this principle—one hard to defend without begging the question—the Mādhyamika recommends a tolerance of contradiction.

But we can also make sense of presupposition failure issuing in the assignment of the empty set as a valuation for a sentence. This is a perfectly natural approach to be taken in the case of fictional discourse, and Madhyamaka can be cogently interpreted as a kind of pan-fictionalism. (See Garfield 2006a.) That is, conventional truth is entirely a fiction, a collectively constituted fiction, a fiction sufficient to ground conventional truth just as ordinary fictions ground truths about the fiction. But just as fiction has its gaps, and it is neither true nor false, for instance, that Ahab's mother was blonde, conventional truth has its gaps. It is neither true nor false that I remain the same person today that I was tomorrow, since the basis of identity—the self—that would either verify or falsify that claim does not exist.

Logic follows metaphysics quite naturally in Madhyamaka. We may or may not adopt a Madhyamaka metaphysical framework, and the purpose of this study is not to recommend, but to articulate that framework. Nonetheless, if logic is a canon of inference that enables us to think cogently in any domain, the four-valuational approach suggested by early Buddhist thought recommends itself to us. It does not require that we augment our set of truth values; nor should it. Truth and falsity constitute the most natural way to evaluate sentences. But it does permit us to reason in domains where contradictions may be true, or when truth may be underdetermined.

Of course there are those—including many in the Buddhist philosophical world—who believe deeply that our own world is consistent. If it is consistent, though, that is a metaphysical fact, not a logical fact. Others—once again, including many in the Buddhist world—believe that our world is complete, and determines the truth or falsity of every sentence. Once again, that is metaphysics, not logic, and our logic should not commit us to that view. Still others might believe the world to be complete and paraconsistent; still others that it is paraconsistent but not paracomplete. Once again, these are metaphysical theses. Logic transcends metaphysics: It is a canon of reason, not a theory of reality, and a canon of reason ought to be equally valid no matter how the world is. That is the early Buddhist insight, one we might well take seriously now, whatever we think of the metaphysics that underlies it.

## 2. Language, Conception and Deception

It is a central thesis of virtually every Buddhist school that language is deceptive and that it distorts reality (and this thesis is often expressed eloquently and elaborated upon at great length). Ultimate truth is almost universally asserted to be indescribable, inconceivable, beyond all discursive categories. Of course, as we have already noted, this ends up in paradox, and we will consider the paradox of expressibility in more detail in the next section. Let us first remind ourselves of why so many Buddhist theorists are so critical of language as a vehicle for truth.

There are really two problems: one on the subject side, and one on the predicate side. On the subject side we find ostensibly referring terms, terms, which, if they fail to refer, would render a sentence false, or truth-valueless. The assertion of any sentence then implicates the existence of its subject, and in much of our ordinary discourse, its endurance over time. But composite enduring things, on a Buddhist account, do not really exist. They are conceptual fictions. Language hence misleads us into taking to be ultimately real that which is only conventionally real. And when we try to use language to talk explicitly about ultimate reality, things are even worse. For nothing exists ultimately, and so there are no referents for words at all in such a discourse.

On the predicate side, things are just as bad. For predication implicates property possession, and properties are most naturally conceived as universals. As we have seen, Buddhists are resolutely nominalist with regard to universals. The implicature of participation of (illusory) particulars in nonexistent universals—and the sense that the truth conditions of sentences consist in this participation means that language is misleading with regard to predicates just as it is with regard to subjects.

There is a perfectly natural way to think about this. I tell you that the weather is beautiful here today. It seems natural to us that that sentence, *the weather is beautiful today*, if true (and it is) tells you something about the day—that it somehow *corresponds* to the weather. But nothing in that sentence conveys the blue of the sky, the fluffiness of the clouds, the remnants of cherry blossoms fluttering in the cool breeze. Even these words leave so much out. And when we try to specify what a *correspondence* relation would look like, we run into notorious difficulties. There simply does not seem to be any natural relation that connects sounds, inscriptions or types thereof to the particulars, universals, relations and logical functions to which they are meant to "correspond," nor any account of how satisfying any such relation would explain the phenomenon of meaning.

Here is a natural way to think of this point. As Wittgenstein emphasizes in his metaphor of a toolbox (*Philosophical Invesigations*, §11), there are many kinds of tools. Hammers pound; screwdrivers turn; pliers grab. There is no single common function that all tools perform. Similarly, some meaningful words refer; some characterize; some function purely grammatically. There is no single common function that all words perform. Nothing *corresponds* to *thank you*, or to *perhaps*. We might be able to make some metaphorical sense of the correspondence relation for some words (maybe); but there is no reason to think that meaning in general is captured by any correspondence relation. To the extent that the meaning of *any* class of terms is to be understood in terms of correspondence, then, that is a special case of a more general phenomenon. Buddhist philosophers of language are convinced that that phenomenon is to be understood in terms of our conventions for using signs.

There is a further, more metaphysical problem with correspondence as a fundamental semantic notion in the context of Buddhist linguistic nominalism. A relation requires two relata, and the most natural relatum on the language side for correspondence to the world when we try to explain truth and falsity is the *proposition*, or in Sanskrit, *pratijñā*. The *pratijñā* is—in orthodox Indian semantic traditions just as the thought or proposition is in Fregean semantic traditions—the content of a sentence, the bearer of truth value, what intertranslatable sentences have in common (and hence—as we will see—what orthodox Indian semanticists saw as the *svabhāva*, or essence of a sentence), the argument of negation and what the mind grasps. For a sentence to be meaningful is for it to express a *pratijñā*. But the *pratijñā*, unlike the token of the sentence whose meaning it is taken to be, is timeless and abstract. In short, it is a universal, and is independent. And for a Buddhist *nothing* has these qualities, and so there can be no *pratijñā*. But without a *pratijñā*, there is no determinate meaning for any sentence, no content. So, correspondence can never be a general account of the semantic value of a sentence, or the primitive notion of semantic theory. And so language always fails to correspond to reality, or to anything for that matter.

Nonetheless, we take ourselves in sharing this sentence as speaker and hearer to have grasped something of the quiddity of the day. You may even imagine a day that would ground these sentences. But it wouldn't be this day. That is the deceptive character of language and thought. Where we are after particulars—real moments of real things—all we can characterize are vague generalities. After all, how many days are there that could justify such a sentence, and in how many respects do they differ from one another? And where we take our words to bear some determinate, graspable relation to the world, such a relation is not to be found, still less to be grasped.

In *Reply to Objections*, Nāgārjuna, considering a set of Nyāya objections to arguments he offers in *Fundamental Verses on the Middle Way*, considers the objection that if he, Nāgārjuna, is correct that everything is empty, than his language must be empty as well, in precisely this sense. But if his language is empty—that is, if there is no core to his assertions that could be captured by synonymous assertions—then he expresses no proposition. And if he expresses no proposition, then he fails even to say that things are empty. And if he is not saying anything at all, he cannot even *deny* that he is saying anything at all, since negation presupposes an argument, and there is no propositional argument for the negation function to take. We see in this discussion an articulation of the classical Nyāya version of a correspondence theory of meaning in a framework we would recognize as that of intensional semantics. Here is how the opponent's argument is articulated. (I quote only the verses, not the autocommentary):[3]

1. If no essence can be found anywhere in anything, your assertion, being essenceless, is incapable of refuting essence.
2. On the other hand, if your assertion exists essentially, it refutes your own thesis. Otherwise, it is an exception, and you owe us an explanation.

3. Translations are mine. For a good translation of the entire text, with autocommentary, see Westerhoff 2010a.

3. You can't reply that this is just like saying, "Don't make a sound." For this is just to prevent a future sound by making a present sound.
4. So, this is not the correct account of the negation of a negation. Thus your thesis, not mine, is undermined by this characterization.

How does this argument go? In the first two verses, the opponent sets out a destructive dilemma: When Nāgārjuna asserts that everything is empty, *everything* either includes that very statement or it does not. If it does, then that statement is empty, which means that it does not express any proposition, since a proposition, as we noted above, is the essence of a statement. If it does not express any proposition, however, it cannot assert that all things are empty. If, on the other hand, it does express a proposition, then it constitutes a counterexample to its own claim, or a special case that cannot be explained. Moreover, the opponent continues, Nāgārjuna cannot simply trade on the claim that the term *empty*, glossed here as *essenceless*, is a negation, and so that he is not *asserting* anything, but merely *denying*. This is because the negation must attach to something—there must be a proposition negated for the negation to make any sense (unlike the case of "be quiet," which can cancel a future sound).

On many plausible (Indian or Western) views of what it is to be meaningful or to connect to reality, then, language as understood by a Mādhyamika—or indeed by any Buddhist—fails to be meaningful, and fails to mediate between us and reality. Nonetheless, it is obvious that even in stating this, as Nāgārjuna's imaginary Nayāyika interlocutor points out, we presuppose that language is meaningful; otherwise we could not even indicate its meaninglessness. Even in denying that sentences convey propositions, we are negating *what those sentences say*, and the negation operator would seem to require an argument, and what could that argument be save a proposition?

Nāgārjuna's reply is elegant.

21. My assertion is neither among the combination of causes and conditions nor distinct from them. So, why can't an essenceless thing demonstrate that things are empty?
22. Dependent origination is explained to be emptiness, for anything dependently originated is essenceless.
23. This negation is just like the case of an illusory man who stops another illusory man from doing something, or like that of one illusory man conjuring up another illusory man.

24. Since my assertion does not exist essentially, it does not undermine my position. Since it is not an exception, I don't owe any special explanation.
25. The example "Do not make a sound" is not apposite. Although it is the prevention of a sound by a sound, it is not analogous to the present case.
26. If the essencelessness of things were refuted by something essenceless, then by giving up on essencelessness, essence would indeed be established.

. . .

29. If I asserted any proposition, I would commit this error. But since I do not assert any proposition, I do not commit this error.

This is a subtle rejoinder. Nāgārjuna opens by affirming that his statement, like everything else, is indeed essenceless, in virtue of its dependent origination. He points out that essencelessness does not, however, preclude causal or dialectical efficacy. He explicitly embraces the position that emptiness is a negation, but adopts a different account of negation from that presupposed by his opponent, pointing out that to adopt the opponent's theory that negation must take a proposition as an argument—something that exists essentially, in virtue of being abstract and uncaused—is to beg the question. Instead, Nāgārjuna points out that there are plenty of cases of negation operating on that which is in fact nonexistent.

We can recast Nāgārjuna's examples of magic in terms of cinema to make the point clear. We don't think that the images on the screen in the cinema are real people. Nonetheless, when the image of Omar Sharif in *Doctor Zhivago* crosses the screen, we have no trouble saying that he, Dr. Zhivago, fell in love with Lara. Just as characters empty of reality can bear relations to one another, negations empty of intrinsic reality can deny the truth of sentences that do not express propositions. Just as characters in a film can exist in a different way—as cinematic characters—sentences can be meaningful in a different way—as devices we use to cause cognitive states in one another, such as the realization that phenomena are empty and that sentences are only meaningful insofar as they have uses, not in virtue of relations to abstract objects such as propositions.

Nāgārjuna points out in conclusion that if a Buddhist theory of meaning posited propositions as the meanings of sentences, the *reductio* advanced by his opponent would indeed be successful. But, Nāgārjuna continues, he asserts no proposition. This is not to say that he says nothing—after all, he is not only producing words, but arguing. But it is to say that he sees the functions of his words not as mirrors that reflect reality, but as *instruments*, as discursive tools by means of which he can cause his interlocutor to see things in a certain way. The words are not taken to express abstract entities, but simply to be effective means of intellectual and behavioral coordination, including this use to coordinate our thought so as to enable us to see that words do no more than coordinate our behavior! The deceptive character of language is its tendency to get us to think that it is more than this. The parallels to ideas to be advanced two millennia later by Wittgenstein in *Philosophical Investigations* are striking.

Language is hence deceptive but indispensable, another aspect of that complex fiction called *saṃsāra*, the cycle of confusion, attraction and aversion that generates the mass of difficulties that is our life. But language is more than just a necessary evil; it is also the ladder that enables one to climb out of this sea of conceptual and affective difficulties. But it is a paradoxical ladder, one that we will see cannot, perhaps, bear the weight it needs to bear. We have been circling around the edge of those paradoxes, noting that even to say that linguistic expressions are, in a deep sense, meaningless is to express that meaning. We will now go the heart of linguistic paradox as it emerges in Buddhist philosophy of language.

## 3. Paradoxes of Expressibility and the Context of Silence

We have already noted that the ultimate truth is inexpressible. Since nothing exists ultimately, and nothing has any properties ultimately; since the ultimate is the way things are independent of our conceptualization, and since language is necessarily encodes our conceptual categories, language is inadequate to express the ultimate. But everything we have just said about the ultimate is true, and is expressed in language. This limit contradiction, which has been called Nāgārjuna's expressibility paradox (Garfield and Priest 2003; Deguchi, Garfield and Priest 2013a, 2013b, 2013c, 2013d; Garfield 2002c), is inescapable once we take seriously the Buddhist insights that the way things are ultimately is independent of and transcends the way any particular kind of consciousness takes them to be, and that language reflects our form of consciousness.

One frequent Buddhist admonition in the face of this paradox is to forego speech. There are many admonitions of this kind in Mahāyāna *sūtras*, and extensive development of this idea in meditative practice and in the Chan/Zen tradition, with its many references (all discursive, of course!) to non-discursive techniques for bringing about realizations, precisely because of the supposition that any discursive techniques are inadequate to this purpose.

The locus classicus, however, and the episode that directly inspires much of the Chan/Zen tradition, is surely the so-called *Lion's Roar of Silence* in the ninth chapter of the *Discourse of Vimalakīrti* (Thurman 1976). In that chapter, Vimalakīrti, the hero of this *sūtra*, asks an assembly of bodhisattvas how to understand nonduality, a way of indicating ultimate truth. A few dozen answers are given, each indicating that a distinction commonly drawn is in fact artificial, and that understanding that artificiality and the illusory nature of the putative distinction is the way to understand nonduality. For instance:

> The bodhisattva Dharmavikurvana declared, "Noble sir, production and destruction are two, but what is not produced and does not occur cannot be destroyed. Thus the attainment of the tolerance of the birthlessness of things is the entrance into nonduality."
>
> The bodhisattva Śrīgandha declared, "'I' and 'mine' are two. If there is no presumption of a self, there will be no possessiveness. Thus, the absence of presumption is the entrance into nonduality."
>
> The bodhisattva Śrīkuta declared, "'Defilement' and 'purification' are two. When there is thorough knowledge of defilement, there will be no conceit about purification. The path leading to the complete conquest of all conceit is the entrance into nonduality." (Thurman 1976, 88)

After a number of such proposals, Vimalakīrti asks Mañjuśrī, the celestial bodhisattva of the perfection of wisdom, and so the representation of the very highest understanding of such matters, for his account. Mañjuśrī replies that all of the previous explanations were good attempts, but all failed, since all were expressed in language, and language is inherently dualistic. Only by transcending language and the distinctions it encodes, he says, can we enter into an understanding of nonduality.

> Mañjuśrī replied, "Good sirs, you have all spoken well. Nevertheless, all your explanations are themselves dualistic. To know no one teaching, to express nothing, to say nothing, to explain nothing, to announce nothing, to indicate nothing, and to designate nothing—that is the entrance into nonduality." (90)

Mañjuśrī then turns to Vimalakīrti and asks for his explanation. Vimalakīrti remains silent.

This moment is dramatic enough. But it is even more poignant given the larger context of the *sūtra* as a whole. Two chapters earlier, Śāriputra, the paragon of the *śrāvaka* or early Buddhist practitioners so often pilloried in polemical Mahāyāna *sūtras* such as this one, attempts just such a move when asked a set of rather sharp philosophical questions by a mysterious goddess who has just emerged from a closet. When he remains silent—stymied by the goddess's dialectic—she asks him why he says nothing. He replies that ultimate truth is inexpressible, only to be upbraided, with the goddess pointing out that the Buddha himself talked extensively during his lifetime.

> ŚĀRIPUTRA: Since liberation is inexpressible, goddess, I do not know what to say.
> GODDESS: All the syllables pronounced by the elder have the nature of liberation. Why? Liberation is neither internal nor external, nor can it be apprehended apart from them. Likewise, syllables are neither internal nor external, nor can they be apprehended anywhere else. Therefore, reverend Sariputra, do not point to liberation by abandoning speech! Why? The holy liberation is the equality of all things! (67)

Vimalakīrti's silence is articulate precisely because of its place in a larger discourse, like a rest in a piece of music or John Cage's *4′33″* in the context of the tradition of Western musical performance.[4] Discourse may be limited, and silence may be necessary, but only when that silence is *articulate*—that is, when it is also discursive. And we are back to paradox. For if it is discursive, it is more than just silence; it is one more symbol. Śāriputra's silence fails precisely because, absent the discursive context that gives it sense, it is senseless; but a silence that has the requisite sense—a sense that no speech can convey—has that sense only when it becomes a kind of speech.

This paradoxical approach to meaning is of course familiar to many Western philosophers. It involves the relegation of the most meaningful not to the sound in the foreground, but to the silence in the background, to the context that enables speech rather than to speech itself, hence rendering that very silence, or background, a kind of speech, and hence a new foreground.

4. There is critical debate regarding whether 4′33″ is in fact silent, and a broad critical consensus (though not a unanimous one) that it is not—that it in fact essentially comprises the ambient noise in the concert hall (Kania 2010). I dissent from that consensus, but this is hardly the place to fight that battle. Nonetheless, even if 4′33″ is not silent, the analogy to the silence of Vimalakīrti goes through—this is the kind of *absence* that only make sense in the context of a tradition of *presence*. Moreover, as Kania points out, there are clear examples of silent music (in fact predating Cage), such as Erwin Schulhoff's "In Futurum" from his *Fünf Pittoresken*. I thank Ben Blumson for drawing my attention to this issue.

It is prescient of Wittgenstein's worries about the limits of expression in the *Tractatus*, of his emphasis on the role of inarticulate brute convention in the constitution of meaning—or the bedrock that turns the semantic spade—in the *Philosophical Investigations* (§217), of Heidegger's ruminations on poetic language, and of Derrida's drive to write *sous erasure* in *Grammatology*, despite the fact that even the *erasure* must, per impossibile, stand *sous erasure.*

When these issues move into China, silence is valorized even further, first by such philosophers as Jizang (6th C CE) in the San Lun or Three Treatise tradition, and later, under his influence, by the even more antinomian Chan tradition. Jizang, in his text *The Profound Meaning of Mahāyāna (Dasheng xuanlun)*,[5] writes:

> Other schools take only 'Being' as conventional truth, and 'Emptiness' as ultimate truth, and claim nothing else. Now let me make clear that either of them, whether it is Being or Emptiness, is conventional truth, and Non-emptiness and Non-being can be first named as ultimate truth. Thirdly—let us call Emptiness and Being as 'Two' and Non-Emptiness and Non- Being as 'Non-two'—all of Two and Non-two are conventional truth, whereas Non-two and Non-non-two can be first named as ultimate truth.

At this point, Jizang takes us through the ground level of the tetralemma, asserting that although one might take the third and fourth limbs (both and neither) to constitute an ascent to ultimate truth, all are simply conventional. All, as he says in the next phrase, are assertions. Nothing that can be expressed expresses reality.

> Fourthly, all of these three sorts of two truths are mere doctrines. Those three are preached only for making people understand Non-three. Having no foundation is alone named as way of things.
>
> Question: Do you take all the former three as conventional truth and Non-three as ultimate truth?
>
> Answer: Yes I do.

5. This text, however, is almost certainly not written by the historical Jizang. Most scholarship dates it at least several centuries after his death, and there is reason to believe that it is composed in Korea or in Japan. We can think of it as the work of some pseudo-Jizang (Ito 1971, 1972; Mitsugiri 1970a, b; Plassen 2007; Choi 2007). Thanks to Yasuo Deguchi for invaluable help on this.

So here, Jizang asserts that the fourth limb, the denial of the first three, constitutes a reference to ultimate truth. He then refers obliquely to the *Discourse of Vimalakīrti*, indicating that although the conventional is expressible and the ultimate inexpressible, they are no different from one another.

> Question: Then why do doctrine and the way of things differ with each other?
>
> Answer: I take Two Truths as doctrines and Non-Two (truths) as way of things. But the distinction between them is merely superficial and occasional, and there is no barrier between them.
>
> Question: Why do you claim this Fourfold Two Truth?
>
> Answer: Against the Abhidharma's two truths of phenomena and truth, the first two truths; i.e., Emptiness and Being, is claimed. Against people who are based on Vasubandhu's *Thirty Verses* and uphold two truths of Emptiness and Being, I claim that since your two truths of Emptiness and Being are merely our conventional truth, Non-Emptiness and Non-Being is really ultimate truth. That's why I made the second two truths.

Jizang argues that a linguistic *via negativa*, a writing *sous erasure*, can even indicate the nature of reality, that the articulation of the two truths in the Indian tradition, in virtue of their positive mood, are necessarily deceptive, and that ultimately, even these negative formulae have to be rejected as deceptive:

> Thirdly, against people who are based on Asaṅga's *Anthology of the Mahāyāna (Mahāyāna-saṃgraha)* and take 'Two'; i.e., interdependent nature and discriminative nature as conventional truth, and non-interdependent nature and non-discriminative nature; that is to say, true nature as 'Non-two' as ultimate truth, I claim that either of the 'Two' or 'Non-two' is merely our conventional truth and 'Non-two and Non-non-two' is really ultimate truth. Hence we have the third two truths.
>
> Fourthly, other Mahāyāna people say that Yogācāra's three are conventional and the three naturelessnesses or non-firmly-established truth is ultimate truth. That is why I claim that either of your two truths, i.e., interdependent nature and discriminative nature; or two truth that is not two, or firmly-established truth on the one hand, and 'Non-two and Non-non-two'; i.e., three non nature or non-firmly-established

truth on the other hand, is merely my conventional truth, whereas 'Forgetfulness of words and annihilation of thoughts' is really ultimate truth. (Taisho, vol.45, 15, trans. Deguchi, 2014)

Jizang hence uses the rubric of the tetralemma as a radical way to explore linguistic meaning, presenting a dialectical treatment prescient of a Hegelian analysis. We can see it this way: Jizang begins with assertion, or what he calls *being (wu)*. At this level, we can say things about the empirical world, ordinary things, like *Snow is white* or *The cat is on the mat*. At this level, the theory of meaning is roughly Fregean, and the theory of truth roughly Tarskian. Sentences aim to represent reality, in virtue of their referring expressions denoting entities, their predicate expressions denoting properties, and the sentences are true if, and only if, the sequence of referents in fact satisfies the relevant properties. Jizang is not explicit about the details, but the story is at least close.

The second level of the dialectic is the level of *mu*, of *non-being* or *negation*. The negation here is a kind of strong pragmatic cancellation. The assertions made at the first level, together with the semantic theory they implicate, are to be cancelled. There is no ultimately real snow; there are no ultimately real cats; the properties of being white and being on the mat are unreal; the pretense language that has to somehow mirror the world or deliver truth is just that, a pretense, a deception to be seen through, not one in which we should participate.

But there is a third level of this dialectic, corresponding to the third position in the *catuṣkoṭi*; Jizang advises that at this third level, we assert both *wu* and *mu*, that we both affirm conventional truth and use language as it is, for what it can do, *and* cancel the ontological and semantic implicatures it carries. An irenic solution indeed. Note that at this point, and from here on through the dialectic, though, the naive reference-and-truth semantics for language have been discarded, and we are treating language as merely instrumental in a strong sense. Note also that on this reading, the negations that take us through the dialectic are cancellations of speech acts, not truth-functional operators.

But there is one more *koṭi*, and a lot more dialectical ascent to go! After all, however irenic the third *koṭi* appears to be, it is unstable. For it involves a *statement* that we should both use language conventionally, that is, instrumentally, *and* that we should refuse to endorse its representational or truth-conveying character. And that statement itself purports to be true. It, too, requires cancellation. At the fourth level of the dialectic, then, Jizang urges that we assert *neither wu* nor *mu*, that we simply refuse *both* to use language conventionally *and* to assert that we reject its pretensions.

And this, if we remained with Nāgārjuna's *catuṣkoṭi* framework, would be the end of the matter. It would seem that at this point, we have reached a place of complete silence, and a total rejection of all language. But Jizang takes us further. His dialectic raises the Madhyamaka dialectic one *catuṣkoṭi* and then some. At the next level, we realize that the *Neither* phase itself contains the seeds of its own destruction. For if we maintain (in any sense) that we must refuse both to assert and to cancel, it is because we *assert* that we should do so *and* that we cancel that assertion. But this means that we are now committed *both* to the *both* and *neither* phases of the first four-fold phase of the dialectic, and this is in fact its fifth moment, or the first moment of the second, higher-order *catuṣkoṭi* phase.

On the other hand, of course, the cancellation means that in fact we are committed linguistically to *neither* the *both* nor to the *neither* phase of the first dialectic, since we are committed to nothing, and cancel all apparent ontological or semantic commitment. And this higher *neither* phase is the sixth moment. The sixth generates the seventh in a now predictable fashion: Since each of *both and neither* and *neither both nor neither* are indispensable, mutually implicative moments of this debate, so is their conjunction, in a higher-order image of the first *catuṣkoṭi*. And this takes us immediately to what would appear to be the final limb of an infinite hierarchy of dialectical positions, neither *both and neither* nor *neither both nor neither*, a refusal to maintain any of the positions in the hierarchy, since no way of using language can escape its deceptive nature, but no refusal to use language can, either.

The second, higher-order *catuṣkoṭi* yields an important insight, though, and that is the insight that this dialectic is endless. That insight, of course, is Mañjuśrī's insight in the *Discourse of Vimalakīrti*. And that is the insight that takes us directly to Vimalakīrti's own solution to that problem: silence. And that, we might say, is the position at which Jizang says that this series converges. But let us note that like the *Vimalakīrti*, Jizang quite deliberately locates that final silence in the context of informative discourse, demonstrating that even silence, if it is to be articulate, itself becomes discourse, bringing us inevitably back to paradox. Inevitably, but with an understanding of our predicament, just as awakening brings us back to the world, back, but with insight replacing confusion.[6]

6. Yasuo Deguchi (2014) presents this dialectic as an intricate alternation between conventional and ultimate truth. We begin at stage 1 with the conventional assertion of being (*p*). But at this stage, ultimately we assert emptiness (–*p*). At the second stage, we can sum these by conventionally asserting conventional being and ultimate emptiness (*p*&–*p*). But ultimately we deny that. (–(*p*&-*p*)). At the third stage we conventionally assert the conjunction of the conventional and the ultimate at the second stage, and so on. Note that at each

This situation is mirrored in the storied Zen Oxherder pictures on pages 262 and 263. The series begins with the ox of the mind running wild, the understanding of reality elusive, and the oxherder merely aspiring to tame the mind and to grasp reality. In the second image he obtains a rope, a method for subduing the mind, and for fixing an understanding of the world. In the third the ox is pursued and in the fourth, the mind is disciplined, reality is grasped, but only discursively, and the ox remains tied tightly by the rope. In the fifth image the ox follows the boy easily and freely, but remains bound by discursive thought—the mind is better understood, but still is taken to be an object, not fully inhabited; in the sixth, the ox can be trusted to go its own way, representing a mind in complete harmony, understood implicitly. Reality is understood effortlessly, and analysis is no longer required. In the seventh the ox disappears; the need to penetrate reality as it is has been cast off and the mind is no longer an object of inquiry. And in the eighth we find emptiness. Subject and object vanish; nothing is depicted at all. In the ninth, illuminated by emptiness, the world is completely manifest, though with no mind, and hence with no subject-object duality, and in the tenth, the boy returns to social life, back to the ordinary world, engaged in ordinary transactions, just as before, but now spontaneously engaging with it *as ordinary*. Emptiness is not the annihilation of convention, but the ability to return to convention, seeing it merely as conventional. Discursive thought returns; language is again used, but now understood merely as a tool, not as a mirror of reality itself.

It is important to remember that the pictures end not with the empty circle, but with the return. The return to the world and to discourse is the inevitable goal—neither an accidental consequence nor a *reductio*—of the quest for a non-discursive space or a trans-lingusitic insight into language. But as we have seen, even in the Zen tradition, there is plenty of room for language and plenty of appreciation of its value and significance, albeit carefully qualified. Dōgen, in an echo of the *Vimalakīrti-nirdeśa*, says in his essay *Entangled Vines (Kattō)*:

> My late master Rujing once said: "The vine of a gourd coils around the vine of another gourd like a wisteria vine." . . . [T]his refers to studying

stage what is asserted conventionally is denied ultimately; at each stage we assert conventionally (and deny ultimately) the conjunction of what we asserted at the previous stage. This sequence has a nice feature. If we sum up at omega, we get all of the assertions at the conventional level, and all of the denials at the ultimate. In one sense, these are quite distinct: all assertions on one side; all denials on the other. But at the same time, every formula that occurs on the conventional side occurs on the ultimate side as well. The two truths are hence also identical. The identity and difference between the two truths emerge quite naturally from this interpretation.

FIG. 1

FIG. 2

FIG. 3

FIG. 4

FIG. 5

FIG. 6

FIG. 7

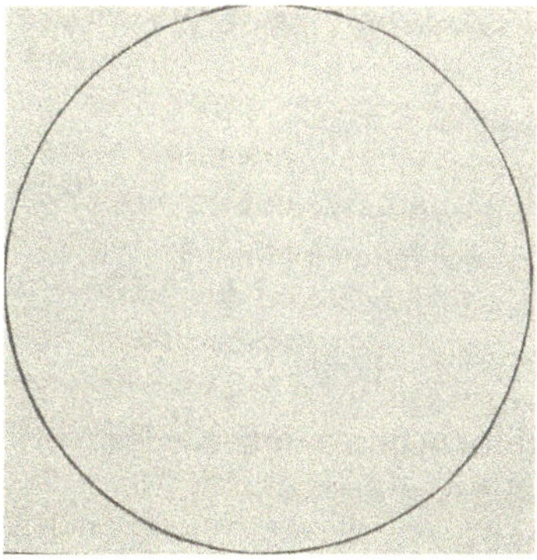

FIG. 8

FIG. 9

FIG. 10

the Buddhas and patriarchs directly from the Buddhas and patriarchs, and to the transmission of the Buddhas and patriarchs directly to the Buddhas and patriarchs....

> The twenty-eighth patriarch said to his disciples, "As the time is drawing near for me to transmit the Dharma to my successor, please tell me how you express it."
>
> Daofu responded first. "According to my current understanding, we should neither cling to words and letters, nor abandon them altogether, but use them as an instrument of the Dao."
> The master responded, "You express my skin."
>
> Then the nun Zongshi said, "As I now see it, the Dharma is like Ānanda's viewing the Buddha-land of Akshobhya, seeing it once and never seeing it again."
> The master responded, "You express my flesh."
>
> Daoyou said, "The four elements are emptiness, and the five *skandhas* are non-being. But in my view, there is not a single dharma to be expressed."
> The master responded, "You express my bones."
>
> Finally, Huike prostrated himself three times, and stood silently in his place.
> The master said, "You express my marrow."

Huike became the second patriarch as a result of this, and he received the transmission of the Dharma as a result of this, and he received the transmission of the sacred robe.

You must study the first patriarch's saying, "You express my skin, flesh, bones and marrow" as the way of the patriarchs. All four disciples heard and realized this saying all at once. Hearing and learning from it, they realized the skin, flesh, bones and marrow of the casting off of body-mind. You should not interpret the teachings of the patriarchs and masters from a single specific viewpoint. It is a complete manifestation without partiality. However, those who do not fully understand the true transmission think that "because the four disciples had different levels of insight, the first patriarch's saying concerning the 'skin, flesh, bones and marrow' represents different degrees in recognizing the superficiality of depth of understanding. The skin and flesh are further from the truth than the bones and marrow." Thus they say that Bodhidharma told Huike

> that he "expressed the marrow because the second patriarch's understanding was superior." But interpreting the anecdote in this manner is not the result of studying the Buddhas and patriarchs or of realizing the true patriarchal transmission. (Heine and Wright 2000, 151–152)

This is a wonderfully complex discussion. Dōgen begins with the metaphor of two vines entangled with one another. One is a gourd, the other a wisteria; so one is useful in the mundane world, and one a thing of pure beauty. But they are completely intertwined, supporting one another, and inseparable. One is the study of the transmission of the Dharma, a discursive practice; the other is the transmitted Dharma, completely inexpressible. These two are completely intertwined, completely inseparable.

The metaphor opens the story of the transmission of the Dharma from Bodhidharma to the second patriarch in China. The standard Chan reading of the story is clear: the first disciple, Daofu, does OK, but is too reliant on language when reality is inexpressible and language always deceptive; Zhongshi is much better: she sees that reality is momentary, and that it can only be glimpsed, but not expressed; but like Mañjuśrī, she falls down when she tries to express that; Daoyou comes closer still, stating that everything, including what he says, is inexpressible, at least explicitly undermining his own speech. But only Huike rises to the heights of Vimalakīrti in maintaining silence. So he gets the robe and the transmission.

While this is an orthodox Chan reading, Dōgen undermines it, taking the four perspectives, which we might see as the four moments in Jizang's tetralemmic dialectic, as mutually interdependent. As organisms, marrow only makes sense if it is encased in bones, bones only function if they are covered with flesh, and we only live in our skins. Dōgen then reinterprets a metaphor of depth into a metaphor of organic unity, taking silence itself to be but one more discursive practice.

We might end there, taking Dōgen to anticipate Tsongkhapa in the re-centering of language as a mode of access to reality. But that might be hasty. In a related text, *A King Requests Saindhava (Ōsakusendaba)*, Dōgen opens with the following verse, echoing the title of *Entangled Vines*:

> Words and wordlessness:
> Like tangled vines to a tree,
> Feeding a mule to feeding a horse,
> Or water to the clouds. (Ibid., 156)

Here things are very different, and we are again climbing Jizang's hierarchy. For now words and silence are related as tangled vines to a tree—a disorderly mess to a beautiful, strong organism; like a mule to a horse—a mere expedient to an honorable ride worthy of a king; or to something that actually quenches one's thirst, as opposed to a distant promise. The tangled vines of discursivity and silence are themselves taken to be but a precursor to a higher silence, and the poetic images as the vehicles to its realization.

The Buddhist approach is more than a historical curiosity anticipating in India and China later developments in the West. I hope that it has become clear from this discussion that Nāgārjuna, the shadowy authors of the Mahāyāna *sūtras*, and those who followed them in this tradition of semantic reflection thought at least as systematically about the origins of these paradoxes, their connections to ontology and to the relation between thought, language and reality as their 20th-century Western successors, and in a very different, perhaps complementary, register. This account does not leave the paradoxical impotence of discursive practice as a curious *aporia*, but locates it firmly in a logical and ontological framework, connected to a set of related paradoxes that make sense in a grand metaphysical system.[7]

## 4. What Does Language *Do*?

But language is necessary, and Buddhist philosophers use quite a lot of it, however much they disparage it. So, we might ask, what does language actually do, and why are Buddhist philosophers entitled to it? One thing that language does, and does well, is to engage conventional truth.[8] As we have seen, despite the doctrine of the two truths, and the merely conventional and illusory character of the world as we engage it, conventional truth is all of the truth we actually have, and engagement with it is necessary for life and for any accomplishment. Language is hence not to be disparaged, as the goddess reminded Śāriputra; even though the limitations Mañjuśrī tried and failed to make clear must be recognized.

Language facilitates our engagement with the world, on a Buddhist view, because it functions at the broadest level not as a vehicle for reference and

7. See Sharf (2007) for an excellent discussion of the treatment of language and silence and of the roots of this treatment in the *Discourse of Vimalakīrti*.

8. Of course given the identity of conventional and ultimate truth, and the impossibility of expressing ultimate truth, there is another paradox here, Nāgārjuna's Paradox, explored in detail in Garfield and Priest 2003, 2009, and in Deguchi, Garfield and Priest 2013a, 2013b, 2013c, 2013d, but we leave that aside for present purposes.

predication, but as a complex cognitive tool for social coordination, for cognition and the expression of cognition. As we saw above, Nāgārjuna emphasizes this when he replies to his Nyāya critic in *Reply to Objections*, saying that he doesn't pretend to express any *pratijñā*, only to *use words*. Candrakīrti makes the same point when he says that "words are not prowling policemen, they are our tools" (2003, 78). On a Buddhist account of meaning, anticipating, as Thurman (1980) noted, Wittgenstein's account in the *Philosophical Investigations*, language can be used non-deceptively to the extent that we are not taken in by the "picture that holds us captive." Tsongkhapa, in his *Essence of Eloquence (Legs bshad snying po)*, writes:

> We might suppose here, as the mundane person engages in a great deal of analysis—"Is it happening or not?" or "Is it produced or not?"—that it must be improper to reply to such inquiries, "It happens" or "It is produced." However, this type of inquiry (conventional analysis) and the above analytic method (analysis into the ultimate nature of things) are utterly different. The mundane person is not inquiring into coming and going through analysis into the meaning of the use of the conventional expressions *comer, goer, coming, going* out of dissatisfaction with their merely conventional usage. He is rather making spontaneous inquiry into the spontaneous usage of the expressions *coming* and *going*. (Thurman 1980, 329–330)

Tsongkhapa's point is straightforward: While the philosopher might think that analysis requires a precise specification of the meanings of terms, and even a theory of meaning to guide that specification, ordinary inquiry remains satisfied with terms as rough and ready tools that permit social and intellectual intercourse, no more. Vasubandhu, Sthiramati and the great Tibetan philosophers Sakya Paṇḍita in the 14th century and Mipham in the 19th and 20th centuries make a similar point when they argue that the putative distinction between literal and metaphorical language must be jettisoned, as *all* linguistic usage is figurative. Jonathan Gold puts it this way:

> Whereas we ordinarily think of language as literal, it cannot be, [Vasubandhu] says, since (given that all things are appearance only) there is no literal reality to which such words might refer. Instead, as we see in Vasubandhu's opening verse, as interpreted by his great commentator Sthiramati (470–550), all language refers figuratively to the transformation of consciousness—to the illusory play of mind itself:

> A varied figurative use of "self " and "things" is what sets things going—that is to say, in the world and in treatises. It is with regard to the transformation of consciousness. (from *Ornament to the Māhāyana sutras [Mahāyānasūtrālaṃkāra]*)
>
> What this means is that whenever we use terms that refer to either "self " or "things" (and in this system all terms do one or the other), we are in fact using figures—metaphors—wherein the illustrative terms are these self and things and the topic illustrated by the metaphor is the transformation of consciousness. What makes them say that words can only be only figurative?
>
> Sthiramati's commentary is very clear: "This is so because selves and things do not exist outside of the transformation of consciousness." (*Commentary to the Ornament of Mahāyāna Sūtras*) Since there are no real things (only illusions), all reference to things must be merely figurative—and to prove this Sthiramati need only restate the traditional Sanskrit grammarians' definition of metaphorical reference: "[A word] is used figuratively with regard to something which is not there, as when [one calls] a Bahikan [person] an ox." (2007, 12)

As Gold (2013) and Tzohar (2013) emphasize independently, this view of the role of language in our cognitive lives and of the structure of meaning maps nicely onto the Yogācāra rubric of the three turnings of the wheel of Dharma and, more importantly, onto the rubric of the three natures and the three naturelessnesses. The *Discourse Unravelling the Thought* emphasizes that the third turning of the wheel of doctrine is definitive in *meaning*, but that it does not represent a shift in *doctrine* and merely explicates the intention of the first two turnings.[9]

9. The rubric of the three turnings of the wheel of Dharma is a common hermeneutical device in Mahāyāna Buddhist commentarial literature, distinguishing three cycles of texts attributed to the Buddha and the attendant treatises and commentaries. The first turning comprises the Pāli *suttas* and the treatises and commentaries that depend upon them. The second comprises the *Perfection of Wisdom sūtras* and the Madhyamaka texts that take them as their scriptural basis. The third comprises the *Sūtra Unravelling the Thought, The Entry into Lanka Sūtra* and the *Flower Garland Sūtra*, among others, and the Yogācāra literature inspired by those texts. Śrāvakayāna schools recognize only the first as authentic; Mahāyāna schools recognize all three as authoritative. But within the Mahāyāna tradition there is a split: Mādhyamikas take the second turning to be the definitive expression of Buddhist doctrine and the third to constitute a way station for those incapable of understanding that position; Yogācārins take the third turning to be definitive, and the second turning to be the halfway house.

On this (admittedly polemical, but nonetheless philosophically useful) view, the approach to language suggested in the first turning is literalist and referential. The words spoken by the Buddha in the suttas and their adumbration in the Pāli Abdhidharma are to be taken as true, and true in virtue of their correspondence to reality. In the second turning—represented in the *Perfection of Wisdom sūtras*, this view is undermined. These texts, according to this *sutra*, take all language directed at the conventional world to be merely a useful instrument, as nothing in the conventional world literally exists as it is described in language: language implicates true existence, but everything exists merely conventionally. On the other hand, on this reading, the language directed at the ultimate indicates a reality, but does so merely figuratively, for the ultimate, by its lights, is inexpressible. The meaning of this language is to be taken seriously, on this view, but not the language itself.

The third turning, on this view, detaches language entirely from the mechanism of reference, and from any pretense of representation or connection to truth. From the standpoint of the *Discourse Unravelling the Thought*, the only possible meaning is figurative meaning; the only possible understanding of the utility of language is causal and instrumental. To think that for language to be meaningful or to be useful requires that any of its terms denote, that any of the predicates it employs correspond to properties, or that any sentences bear some special relation to truth is simply to misunderstand how we use sounds to coordinate our behavior and to interact with reality. Our sound-making behavior on this view is no different from our locomotion, perception, or tactile behavior. It can be more or less efficacious in achieving our ends. But that is all.

To put this into the framework of the three natures, we might say that the *imagined* nature of language is its ability to represent reality; this is how we naively take it to be, and this is that in which we take meaning to consist. On the other hand, the *dependent* nature of language is the fact that its performing any function at all depends not on primitively semantic properties, but on *causal* properties; that our linguistic behavior is dependent upon determinate sets of causes and conditions, and in turn conditions the behavior of ourselves and others. The *consummate* nature of language is the absence of the imagined in the dependent, that is, the fact that performing these functions does not require semantic properties at all, or literal meaning, or representation, or the possibility of expressing truth. Language is ultimately empty of all of that.

Finally, to put this in terms of the three naturelessnesses, we might say simply that the emptiness of language with respect to characteristic is the fact that it is empty of the semantic properties it appears to have; that its emptiness with respect to production is the fact that it lacks any independent abstract status as a system of meanings—it is merely the product and the producer of human interactions and thought; that its ultimate emptiness is the fact that there is no literal meaning to be found anywhere, even here. All meaning, on this view, is figurative. It goes without saying, of course, that all of this lands us back in paradox, but that is familiar terrain by now. More importantly—and this may need saying—what goes for language goes for any form of expression, including thought. Our own thinking is, on this view, just as figurative, just as instrumental, and is just as disconnected from the activity of representation or truth-grasping as public language. This is perhaps the deepest and most disturbing level of Buddhist analysis of meaning.

We might think in a post-Fregean world that metaphorical meaning is parasitic on literal meaning, and that literal meaning can be understood in term of reference and satisfaction of predicates. These Buddhist philosophers of language challenge the idea that there is such a basic use of language. If to be figurative means to be meaningful despite reference and satisfaction failure, all language is figurative. All is grounded in a loose set of conventions for use. Reference and predication can then be recontextualized not as the foundation of meaning, but rather as activities undertaken within the context of convention, with the understanding that the nominal objects of reference, just as the nominal properties ascribed by predicates, are merely nominal, fictional entities.

Taking figuration to be nothing but one more way to use language, hence lightening the ontological baggage to be carried by semantic theory, may make more sense of language as one more human activity. Taken in this way it is nothing more than a system of social behavior and an epistemic instrument like any other, and not so special as it pretends to be. Language so understood is neither a mirror of reality nor a shrine for truth. Sakya Paṇḍita elsewhere refers to linguistic usage as nothing more than a way of coordinating action and realizing intention. To the degree to which we take words or phrases as indicating any non-linguistic referents, that is merely a special case of this more general function, to be understood only practically, and not in any sense the central function of language, and explicitly locates word meaning in relation only to other words and to linguistic and other non-linguistic activity. (See Gold 2007, 45–53)

Tsongkhapa, in *The Essence of Eloquence,* addresses these issues when he uses the philosophy of language as an important doxographic tool. In another move prescient of Wittgenstein (see Thurman 1980, 1978) Tsongkhapa characterizes *Mādhyamikas who advance their own positions* as being committed to a semantic theory according to which the meanings or words are specified by necessary and sufficient conditions for reference, conditions that underpin linguistic usage, and which specify the conventional natures of things. So, for instance, a proponent of this position (such as, according to Tsongkhapa, the Indian Mādhyamikas Bhāviveka and Jayānanda) would argue that if a word like *cow* is to have any meaning at all, there must be commonly agreed-upon conditions for its usage, a conventional essence of bovinity.

Now, since this is a Madhyamaka position, Tsongkhapa notes, it is not a position according to which these conditions reflect intrinsic natures in the things themselves; rather, they reflect conventional intrinsic natures—what Tsongkhapa calls, *conventional existence as having a distinguishing characteristic* (*rang gi msthan nyid gyis yod pa [rang gi tsenyid ki yöpa]*).[10] Nonetheless, according to this view, even if it is *we* who decide what it is to be a cow, in this decision about the necessary and sufficient conditions for the application of the predicate, we thereby fix its meaning, and any usage of the term can be assessed against that criterion.

Though the exegetical argument that results in ascribing this position to this group of commentators is complex, the central issue is this: Because they are committed to the view that Mādhyamikas such as Nāgārjuna (on whose texts they comment) must be able to offer positive arguments for their own positions, they are committed to the view that the terms in which those arguments are couched must be understood in the same way by all parties to the argument, including non-Mādhyamikas and even non-Buddhists. But the presupposition that these terms have shared meanings independent of one's philosophical position, Tsongkhapa argues, is the presupposition that the meanings are fixed not by the way that the terms are used, but rather by a set of independent criteria for their use.

Tsongkhapa contrasts this position with that he ascribes to Mādhyamikas who wield *reductio* arguments such as Candrakīrti. These Mādhyamikas, whose position Tsongkhapa regards as more sophisticated, eschew positing necessary and sufficient conditions for the applications of terms, arguing that all there is to semantic character is use, with no independent criteria for that use. They are freed from the commitment to independent criteria for the correct application of words, Tsongkhapa argues, because they are committed not to presenting independent arguments for their positions in terms acceptable both to themselves and to their interlocutors, but only to demonstrating the incoherence of their interlocutors' positions *on their own terms*. Therefore, they can adopt a way of using language acceptable to their opponents without

10. This Tibetan neologism is a somewhat tendentious gloss of the Tibetan term *rang mtshan (rangtzen)* that translates the Sanskrit *svalakṣaṇa*, a term that generally simply denotes a particular.

any commitment to the entities or properties to which their opponents are committed, only agreeing about how the language works in the discourse in question. This, Tsongkhapa argues, is what it really is to take meaning to be conventional—it is the conventions themselves that ground meanings; they are not grounded *in* meanings.

When we understand conventional truth *as conventional*, when we see *through* the deception, as we saw in the discussion of mirages in the previous chapter, its deceptive character is rendered harmless and merely potential. In the same way, when we see through its deceptive character, language can cease to deceive us into taking it as accurately representing an independent reality. Language is not so much a ruler that measures reality as a screwdriver that operates on it. It can then, to continue to torture this metaphor, dismantle the barriers that prevent understanding. This is the promise of a non-conceptual, immediate confrontation with reality central to Buddhist soteriology. Even if one doubts the possibility of utility of that kind of understanding, the analysis of linguistic meaning is compelling.

The term used for this kind of analysis in Buddhist literature is *upāya/thab mkhas (thapkheh)/fāngbiàn*. The history of its semantic tone in Sanskrit, Tibetan and Chinese is instructive here, partly for understanding the trajectory of Buddhist philosophy in those traditions, but also for understanding the Janus-faced character of this idea and of Buddhist attitudes toward language. The term connotes *technique* or *means to an end*. In Sanskrit it is a term of neutral valence. It can either connote a useful savoir faire or a kind of devious manipulation or expedient.

Indian Buddhist literature often valorizes *upāya* as a necessary characteristic of anyone who wants to benefit others, or to accomplish goals. Vimalakīrti, for instance, is praised as a master of *upāya*. The Buddha is praised for his *upāya*. But *upāya* is often also regarded as something desirable *only* because of the ends it can achieve, and itself distasteful. In the familiar story from the *Lotus Sūtra* the father lures his children from a burning house they are reluctant to vacate by making false promises of gifts. The lie, itself undesirable, is a necessary expedient to achieving an important goal, and so is regarded as *upāya*.

This ambiguity forks when Sanskrit is translated into Tibetan and Chinese. In Tibetan it is translated as *thab mkhas*, a term with valorizing connotations (indeed often conferred on monks as an ordination name), associated with a kind of wisdom (*mkhas pa [khepa]*), or pedagogical understanding. In Chinese, on the other hand, it is translated as the pejorative 方便 (*fāngbiàn*), connoting a mere expedience—something necessary but distasteful.[11]

11. Douglas Duckworth points out that instant noodles are referred to as 方便 (*fāngbiàn*) noodles in contemporary Chinese, confirming the point!

When we think about attitudes toward language in the Tibetan and Chinese tradition, we see a divide that tracks this distinction. In Tibetan Buddhist literature, commentarial practice, eloquence in exposition and precision in reasoning are valorized as *thab mkhas*; while discursive practices are always regarded as merely conventional, and potentially deceptive, they are regarded as indispensible pedagogical means of transmitting wisdom and of asserting truths. A precise analytic literature is the consequence, as well as extensive reflection on the nature of meaning, and on logic.

In the Chinese Buddhist traditions, on the other hand, discursive practices—also widely undertaken—are disparaged as mere方便/*fāngbiàn*, and the consequence is a corpus of highly metaphorical, cryptic and poetic writing, writing that deliberately aims at transcending in practice the limits the tradition sees in discursive practice itself. Here we see both Mañjuśrī's and Vimalakīrti's responses to the illusions of discourse. Attention to this character of language, so explicitly thematized in the Buddhist tradition, is still at the margins of Western philosophical thought about language. It may be time to move it to center stage. This approach to language has natural affinities, for instance, to the intentionalism advanced by theorists such as Grice (1989) and Shiffer (1972, 1987), tying meaning to what we *do* with words and how we interact with each other using words.[12]

## 5. Vajra Hermeneutics

In his essay "Vajra Hermeneutics," (1978) Robert Thurman introduces another important insight regarding language to be derived from the Buddhist tradition, one deriving from much older Indian thought regarding language and sound. (It is no accident that the Tibetan word *sgra [da]* denotes either a *word* or *sound*.) Once again, just as in the case of our discussion of *pramāṇa* theory above, while I will be emphasizing specifically Buddhist deployment of these ideas, it is important to note the broader Indian context of this line of thought. From the Vedic and Upaniṣadic literature on up, the role of speech as sound has been conceived causally in Indian thought, most evidently in the theory of mantra and in Indian poetics.[13] Thurman points out that attention to the

12. See Hansen (1992) for extended discussion of Chinese theories of language. He argues persuasively for a semantic account focused upon the uses of language as opposed to a representational model of meaning. Hansen's treatment of Chinese philosophy of language and of Chinese philosophy more broadly is an excellent example of how the study of a non-Western tradition can force a dramatic re-thinking of assumptions we take for granted in the practice of Western philosophy.

13. One might see Aurobindo's poetics as an intriguing modern continuation of this approach. See Aurobindo 2000.

way that sound in general, and language in particular, are treated in Buddhist tantric traditions, which follow this older view of sound and language, sheds light not only on tantra per se—a topic well outside the scope of the present investigation in any case—but on Buddhist thought about language more generally. I conclude this chapter with an exploration of ideas arising from reflection on that essay.

Thurman notes, as we have, that it may be a mistake to regard the primary purpose of language to be to convey meaning, or to take the goal of utterance to be understanding of the content of the utterance, as much Western thought about language would have it. Instead, he argues, much language may be intended to be cryptic, and much language is used in order to *cause things to happen*, as opposed to *conveying meaning*. There are cases where this is obvious: commands to dogs, or to computers; lullabies sung to small children; poetry in some aspects; spells, and in the Indian and later Chinese Buddhist contexts, the mantras central to tantric practice that are meant to transform the mind as a direct effect of sound.

These cases are all in a broad sense *mantras*, or utterances produced and taken to be efficacious in virtue of their physical or sonic properties, as opposed to any *semantic* properties. Attention to the phenomenon of *mantra* may lead to a further recontextualization of semantically pregnant language, and suggest new directions in the philosophy of language.[14] The point is to focus not on *meaning* as a sui generis category, but rather on *causation*, and on meaning only as a special case of that larger phenomenon.

While this discussion focuses on sound, regarded in the Indian and Tibetan context as the primary vehicle of language, nothing hinges on that modality being taken as paradigmatic. The same points could be made regarding manual signs, semaphore or written language. For the sake of cultural fidelity, though, I will focus on sound. Sound is, obviously, part of the network of dependent origination. It is caused, and has effects. And as a physical phenomenon in the range of our sense of hearing, it has physical effects on us—on our sensory apparatus, and on our nervous system. Those phonological effects must underwrite even any semantic analysis of language.

All of this seems painfully obvious, but like so much that is obvious, it is also painfully easy to ignore these facts in philosophical reflection. Ignoring it, from a Buddhist perspective, leads to a kind of mystification of language and eventually of thought. That mystification—treating language and thought, in

14. Śri Aurobindo in *The Future Poetry* intriguingly characterizes *mantra* as the primordial form of language, and as fundamental to poetic structure.

virtue of being meaningful, as putting us in direct touch with a third world of abstracta that stand between us and the rest of reality—takes us straight to the duality of subject and object, representation and represented. That dualism in turn leads to worries about correspondence or other reference- or meaning-inducing relations, the relation of the self to the world, of mind to body, and the whole raft of confusions that result from forgetting that the self or subject, to the extent that it is real at all, must be part of the world, not something standing over against it.

How does this go? We begin by distinguishing the semantic from the causal aspects of sound. We then focus on the semantic aspects we have isolated, understanding the effectiveness of language and its relation to thought as a matter of relationship to *content*, and thinking of that content as constituted by abstract entities, such as *propositions*, themselves understood perhaps as *functions from indices to truth values*. And of course mathematical functions are the wrong kinds of things to be causally produced or to have effects. The efficacy of language has thus effectively been mystified precisely in the attempt to understand how it can actually function to enable our epistemic and cultural activity.

Given the fact that we, as physical organisms, are part of a causal nexus, we know that the real story has to be a causal one. Of course we also know that when we are talking about language and thought, semantic categories will emerge as part of that causal story. There has to be an explanation of the fact that sounds that are as different as those produced when an English woman says *Snow is white* and when a Tibetan man says *khang dkar po red (khang karpo reh)* have similar causes and effects. But that story itself has to be causal, on pain of further mystification. Semantic evaluability, that is, has to emerge from, not provide an alternative to, or an explanation of, causal efficacy.

This in turn means that, as Wittgenstein points out in the very beginning of *Philosophical Investigations*, the focus in understanding the nature of language on the truth conditions of the declarative sentence are misleading.

> 11. Think of the tools in a tool-box: there is a hammer, pliers, a saw, a screw-driver, a rule, a glue-pot, glue, nails and screws.—The functions of words are as diverse as the functions of these objects. (And in both cases there are similarities.) Of course, what confuses us is the uniform appearance of words when we hear them spoken or meet them in script and print. For their application is not presented to us so clearly. Especially when we are doing philosophy.

> 12. It is like looking into the cabin of a locomotive. We see handles all looking more or less alike. (Naturally, since they are all supposed to be handled.) But one is the handle of a crank which can be moved continuously (it regulates the opening of a valve); another is the handle of a switch, which has only two effective positions, it is either off or on; a third is the handle of a brake-lever, the harder one pulls on it, the harder it brakes; a fourth, the handle of a pump: it has an effect only so long as it is moved to and fro.

The fundamental insight of Vajra hermeneutics, of seeing language from the standpoint of *mantra*, as opposed to *pratijñā*—sound as opposed to proposition—is that meaning, however special it is, is nothing more than a *special case* of natural causal efficacy. Just as Sellars was to argue a few millennia later, Buddhist philosophers of language saw meaning as a kind of functional classification. But in even a more naturalistic spirit than that of Sellars, they saw this not *au fond* as a kind of *functional* classification, but as a kind of *causal* classification (of which the functional, once again, might be one intermediate special case).

Just as the recitation of a *mantra* was held to *cause* one to become more compassionate (a claim whose truth or falsity is irrelevant to the point in question), singing a German lullaby to an English baby might cause her to drift off to sleep. Just as the lullaby might induce sleep, an utterance of *attention!* might *cause* a soldier to straighten up. And just as the command causes the soldier to behave in a certain way, the assertion that Buddhist philosophy is indeed worthy of attention might cause a Western philosopher to take it more seriously.

To be sure, on this view the explanations of the causation in question drive us to generalizations that are progressively more aptly framed in terms of content. And Tibetan semantic theory introduces a raft of concepts proper to language to explain this, including *term universals* that aggregate functionally isomorphic words or phrases and *meaning universals* that aggregate the cognitive states they bring about. But again, like all universals, these are in the end fictions to be nominalized away. If this perspective is right, what we see is a continuum and not a dichotomy. Moreover, if this perspective is right, at no point on this continuum do we leave causality behind, and at no point on this continuum do we need an appeal to a fundamental duality between vehicle and content, or representation and represented. Communication is tantric all the way down.

This tantric approach to thinking about meaning is worth taking seriously, particularly in the context of the drive to naturalize epistemology and the philosophy of mind. Part of that worthy enterprise—an enterprise of which, as I hope that this investigation has shown, any Buddhist would approve—has to be the naturalization of semantics. For if we cannot provide a naturalistic account of the meaningfulness of linguistic tokens, we cannot hope for a naturalistic account of the content of thought. And without that, epistemology is a non-starter.

To the extent that the representational model of meaning is committed to the idea of a fundamental duality of representation and represented, and to content as abstract, this naturalization is impossible. And it is hard to see what is left of representationalism if that commitment is abandoned, for if there are no universals, there is no *relatum* on the language side, and without such a relatum it is hard to see how a relational model such as representationalism can get off the ground. In the end, then, we might see this tantric strain of the philosophy of language implicated by Buddhist theory and practice as one of history's most radical and profound attack on the representational model of thought and language, and one of the most serious blows in the battle for naturalism. That is worth taking seriously.

# 9 ETHICS

## 1. Introduction: The Subject Matter of Ethics

Contemporary normative ethics is dominated by debates between deontologists, consequentialists of various stripes and areteic ethicists with varying degrees of allegiance to Aristotle, with a few anti-realists thrown in. That is, moral theorists are debating the subject matter of ethics. Does it concern our obligations and rights? Or is it concerned with the preconditions of happiness or human flourishing? With the maximization of good and the minimization of harm? Or perhaps with our feelings and dispositions? Or is there perhaps no subject matter at all? Of course despite all of this theoretical debate, there is a great deal of common ground between divergent ethical theories regarding the moral valence of most states of affairs, maxims of action and traits of character. We can fruitfully see these debates, and, as we shall see, the Buddhist intervention into these debates, as a kind of generalization of the *Euthyphro* problem: Are deontological maxims good because they maximize utility, or the other way around? Are virtues good because they conduce to the discharge of duty, or the other way around? In short, what, if anything, grounds moral value? I will argue that Buddhist moral theory enters this debate not through disagreements about the value of happiness, virtue or duty, but rather by arguing that these values depend on a more fundamental value: our phenomenological orientation toward the world.

It is important when approaching Buddhist moral theory to resist the temptation to assimilate Buddhist ethics to some system of Western ethics. Succumbing to this temptation usually results in portraying it either as some form of utilitarianism (Goodman 2008) or virtue ethics (Keown 2005). In Buddhist philosophical and religious literature we find many texts that address moral topics, and a great deal of attention devoted to accounts of virtuous and vicious actions, states of character and lives. However, we find very little direct attention to the articulation of sets of principles that determine which actions, states of character or motives are virtuous or vicious, and no articulation of sets of obligations or rights. So, while in many chapters of this volume I have argued for significant homologies or overlap between Buddhist and Western ideas, here I will be suggesting a dramatically different way of addressing important philosophical problems.

Buddhist moral theory provides an alternative voice to those in contemporary debates, and a different view of the subject matter of ethics. Buddhist moral theorists see ethics as concerned not *primarily* with actions, their consequences, obligations, sentiments or human happiness, but rather with the nature of our *experience*. That is, as we will see, Buddhist ethics is a *moral phenomenology* concerned with the transformation of our experience of the world, and hence our overall comportment to it.

This is not because Buddhist moral theorists were and are not sufficiently sophisticated to think about moral principles or about the structure of ethical life, and certainly not because Buddhist theorists think that ethics is not important enough to do systematically. It is instead because from a Buddhist perspective there are simply too many dimensions of moral life and moral assessment to admit a clean moral theory.[1] Buddhist ethical thought has instead been concerned with understanding how the actions of sentient beings are located and locate those beings within the web of dependent origination, or *pratītya-samutpāda*. This web is complex, and there is a lot to be said. And so Buddhists have had a lot to say. But the web is also untidy, and so what Buddhists have had to say resists easy systematization.

There is one last temptation to resist, and that is to see the various Buddhist philosophical and religious traditions as constituting a homogenous whole. An enormous variety of positions have been defended within the Buddhist world on just about every philosophical position, and ethics is no exception. Here I will confine my remarks to one strand of Buddhist moral thought, that beginning with the articulation of the four noble truths at Sarnath and running through the work of Nāgārjuna in his *Jewel Rosary of Advice to the King*, Candrakīrti in *Introduction to the Middle Way*, and Śāntideva in *How to Lead an Awakened Life*. In particular, I will be ignoring a rich lode of moral literature comprised by the *Jātaka* tales and the vast corpus of Buddhist morality tales that populate Buddhist literature, offering a range of moral examples, ideals and cases for consideration (Rotman 2008).

1. There is hence reason to think of Buddhist ethical thought as *particularist* in certain respects.

I hope that the observations I offer regarding this narrow path through Indian Buddhist moral thought will serve to show that Buddhist moral thought represents a reasonable alternative way of thinking about our moral life, one that can engage Western moral theory in profitable dialogue. Each tradition of ethical thought has a great deal to learn from the other, and that learning begins with attention to what each has to say on its own terms. The discussion that follows will be grounded in Buddhist ethical texts and discussions, and sometimes on oral commentary to which I have been privy. But it will also involve a certain amount of rational reconstruction extrapolating from those texts and commentaries. Often the Buddhist tradition is not as explicit as one would expect on topics in ethics (Hayes 2011) and reflection and reconstruction is often necessary; indeed it is often a central task of oral teaching in this tradition.

## 2. Ethics and Interdependence

Thinking about the good from a Buddhist perspective begins from the first principle of Buddhist metaphysics—the fact of thoroughgoing interdependence. As we have seen, from a Buddhist perspective, every event and every phenomenon is causally and constitutively dependent upon countless other events and phenomena; and it, in turn, is part of the causal ancestries and constitutive bases of countless other phenomena. Moral reflection on action must take all of these dimensions of dependence into account. To focus merely on motivation, or on character, or on the action itself, or on its consequences for others, would be to ignore much that is important.

Interdependence is relevant when thinking about identity and interest as well. Many Western moral theorists begin by taking a kind of ontological and axiological individualism for granted in several respects. First, agency is taken to reside in individual actors, with an attendant focus on responsibility as a central area of moral concern. Second, interest is taken to be *au fond* an individual matter, and even when the self is consciously deconstructed, as it is by Parfit, interest is taken to attach to individual stages of selves. Third, and consequent on these, a conflict between egoistic and altruistic interests and motivations is taken to structure ethical deliberation and acting on egoistic motives regarded as at least prima facie rational, if not morally defensible or ultimately rational.

Buddhist accounts of identity reflect the commitment to interdependence. The boundaries between self and other are regarded as at best conventional and relatively insignificant, and at worst deeply illusory. Agency is not taken as a primary moral category, at least if taken to indicate a unique point of origin of action in an individual self, and so moral responsibility, duty and desert are not foregrounded in moral reflection. Interest is hence also seen as a shared phenomenon, and egoism as fundamentally and obviously irrational. We will work out the ramifications of these views as we proceed. (See Garfield 2010/11, 2012.)

Nāgārjuna argues that to understand dependent origination is to understand the four noble truths. The truth of suffering sets the problem that Buddhism sets out to solve. The universe is pervaded by *dukkha* and the causes of *dukkha*. As we saw in chapter 1, the Buddha did not set out to prove this at Sarnath. He took it as a datum, one that is obvious to anyone on serious reflection, though one that escapes most of us most of the time, precisely because of our evasion of serious reflection in order not to face this fact. The Buddha also assumed that suffering is a bad thing. If one disagrees with this assessment, from a Buddhist perspective, moral discourse has no basis: There is no problem to be solved. If you just love headaches, don't bother taking aspirin. If you don't, you might consider how to obtain relief. Once again, the Buddha took it as a datum that people don't like *dukkha*, and Buddhist ethics is aimed at its relief.

The Buddha then argued that *dukkha* does not just happen. It arises as a consequence of actions conditioned by attachment and aversion, each of which in turn is engendered by confusion regarding the nature of reality. This triune root of *dukkha* is represented in the familiar Buddhist representation of the Wheel of Life with the pig, snake and rooster at the hub representing primal confusion, aversion and attraction, respectively; the six realms of transmigration (or aspects of the phenomenology of suffering as we might understand them less cosmologically) turning around them, structured by the twelve links of dependent origination (a detailed psychology of perception and action), all of which is depicted as resting in the jaws of death, the great fear of which propels so much of our maladaptive psychology and moral failure.

Attention to the second noble truth allows us to begin to see how very different Buddhist moral thought is from most Western moral thought: the three roots of *dukkha* are each regarded as moral defilements, and are not seen as especially heterogeneous in character. None of them is seen as especially problematic in most Western moral theory, and indeed each of the first two—attachment and aversion—is valorized in at least some contexts in some systems, particularly that of Aristotle, who characterizes virtues in part in terms of that to which we are attracted and averse.

The third, confusion, is rarely seen in the West as a moral matter, unless it is because one has a duty to be clear about things. But this is far from the issue in Buddhist moral theory. Buddhism is about solving the problem of *dukkha*;

the three root vices are vices because they engender the problem. The moral theory here is not meant to articulate a set of imperatives, nor to establish a calculus of utility through which to assess actions, nor to assign responsibility, praise or blame, but rather to solve a problem. The problem is that the world is pervaded by unwanted *dukkha*. The diagnosis of the cause of the problem sets the agenda for its solution.

The third truth articulated at Sarnath is that, because *dukkha* depends upon confusion, attraction and aversion, it can be eliminated by eliminating these causes. And the fourth, which starts getting the ethics spelled out in a more determinate form, presents the path to that solution. The eightfold path is central to an articulation of the moral domain as it is seen in Buddhist theory, and careful attention to it reveals additional respects in which Buddhists develop ethics in a different way than do Western moral theorists. The eightfold path comprises correct view, correct intention, correct speech, correct action, correct livelihood, correct effort, correct mindfulness and correct meditation.

While many, following the traditional Tibetan classification of three trainings, focus specifically on correct speech, action and livelihood as the specifically ethical content of the path, this is in fact too narrow, and misses the role of the path in Buddhist practice and in the overall moral framework through which Buddhism recommends engagement with the world. The eightfold path identifies not a set of rights or duties, nor a set of virtues, but a set of areas of concern or of dimensions of conduct.

The path indicates the complexity of human moral life and the complexity of the sources of suffering. To lead a life conducive to the solution of the problem of suffering is to pay close heed to these many dimensions of conduct. Our views matter morally. It is not simply an epistemic fault to think that material goods guarantee happiness, that narrow self-interest is the most rational motivation, that torture is a reasonable instrument of national policy or that women are incapable of rational thought. Such views are morally problematic.[2] To hold such views is not to commit a morally neutral cognitive error, like thinking that Florida is south of Hawai'i. It is to be involved in a way of taking up with the world that is at the very root of the *dukkha* we all wish to alleviate.

It is not only what we do that matters, but what we intend. Intention grounds action, and even when it misfires, what we intend to do determines who or what we become. The great 5th-century Theravāda philosopher Buddhaghosa in *The Path of Purification (Visuddhimagga)* explores the role of intention (*cetanā*) in great detail, as do his slightly older, but roughly contemporary Mahāyāna

2. This is not, of course, to say that none of these views were held by important Buddhist scholars or that they were not prevalent in Buddhist cultures.

colleagues Asaṅga and Vasubandhu, in *Encyclopedia of the Abhidharma* and *Investigation of the Five Aggregates (Pañcaskandhaprakaraṇa)*, respectively. It is worth spending some time on this term and its role in Buddhist psychology and moral psychology at this point, as *cetanā* constitutes an important focus of Buddhist thinking about agency and morality in all major Buddhist traditions.

The term, as we noted above, is perhaps best translated as *intention* (or, as Meyers 2010 prefers, *intending*). Its semantic range is roughly consistent with that of *intention* in English, connoting *directedness* in its various forms. So it can indicate the purposive intentionality of action, the directedness of perception on an object or of thought on its content. So right in the eightfold path, we have an emphasis not only on what we intend to *do*, but on what we think *about*, and under what descriptions we think about and act on the world around us. And Buddhaghosa and Asanga explicitly draw our attention to the relationship between *cetanā* and our orientation to objects and persons around us as pleasant or unpleasant, allies or enemies, or in terms of other such categories, all orientations with moral as well as cognitive dimensions.

It is also worth considering, as we note the centrality of intention in this complex sense to Buddhist moral psychology, the ways in which the ascription of intentionality is always a matter of interpretation, even when that is self-ascription, or self-interpretation. And given the embeddedness of the practice of interpretation in narratives, as the backgrounds against which we make sense of action, we would expect an important narrative dimension to Buddhist moral thought, a dimension we will in fact discover. We will return to the role of *cetanā* and other prima facie simply cognitive attitudes, but, in a Buddhist framework, deeply ethical dimensions of experience below.

The eightfold path, which represents the earliest foundation of Buddhist ethical thought, must always be thought of as a path, and not as a set of prescriptions. That is, it comprises a set of areas of concern, domains of life on which to reflect, respects in which one can improve one's own life (as well as those of others), and, in sum, a way of moving cognitively, behaviorally and affectively from a state in which one is bound by and causative of suffering to one in which one is immune from suffering and in which one's thought, speech and action tend to alleviate it.

The eightfold path may be represented as broadly consequentialist, but it is certainly not utilitarian, and it is consequentialist only in a thin sense—that is, what makes it a path worth following is that things work out better to the extent that we follow it. By following this path, by attending to these areas of concern in which our actions and thought determine the quality of life for ourselves and others, we achieve greater individual perfection, facilitate that achievement for those around us and reduce suffering. There is no boundary drawn here that circumscribes the ethical dimensions of life; there is no distinction between the obligatory, the permissible and the forbidden; there is no distinction drawn between the moral and the prudential; the public and the private; the self-regarding and the other-regarding.[3] Instead, there is a broad indication of the complexity of the solution to the problem of suffering.

## 3. Action Theory and Karma

The term *karma* plays a central role in any Buddhist moral discussion. It is a term of great semantic complexity and must be handled with care, particularly given its intrusion into English with a new range of central meanings. Most centrally *karma* means *action*. Derivatively, as Tsongkhapa makes clear (2006, 355) it means *the consequences of action*. Given the Buddhist commitment to the universality of dependent origination, all action arises from the karmic consequences of past actions, and all action has karmic consequences. Karma is not a cosmic bank account on this view, but rather the natural causal sequelae of actions. Karma accrues to any action, simply in virtue of interdependence, and karmic consequences include those for oneself and for others, as well as both individual and collective karma.

Buddhist action-theory approaches human action, and hence ethics, in a way slightly divergent from that found in any Western action-theory, and it is impossible to understand moral assessment without attention to action theory. Buddhist philosophers distinguish in any action the *intention*, the *act* itself (whether mental, purely verbal, or non-verbally physical as well) and the *completion* (or, as we would say in more contemporary language, the *immediate consequence*) or the final state of affairs resulting directly from the action itself. If I intend to give ten dollars to Oxfam and hand over the ten dollars to an Oxfam worker, who then uses it to bribe a policeman, beneficial karma accrues from the intention, beneficial karma from the act, but non-beneficial karma from the completion. If I intend to steal your medicine, but instead pocket the poison that had been placed on your bedstand by your malicious nurse, thereby saving your life, negative karma accrues from the intention, but positive karma from the act and from the completion, and so forth.

It is important to see that karma isn't additive or subtractive. There is no calculus of utility or of merit points here. The fact that something I do is beneficial

3. The trope of "self and other" as in "for the benefit of self and others" is common in Buddhist literature. But this expression does not inscribe but undermines the distinction in question. The point is *not* that self and other are to be treated differently, but that they are to be treated in the same way.

does not cancel the fact that something else I do is harmful. It just means that I have done something good and something harmful. I have generated both kinds of consequences, not achieved some neutral state. No amount of restitution I pay for destroying the garden you worked so hard to cultivate takes away the damage I have done. It only provides you with some benefit as well. Truth and reconciliation commissions do indeed reveal the truth and promote reconciliation, and that is good. But to pretend that they thereby erase the horrific consequences of the deeds they reveal for those who are reconciled is naive.[4]

Note as well that the relevant kinds of karma include the impact on my character and that of others, such as the tendency to reinforce or to undermine generosity or malice, and the degree to which the action promotes general well-being. Behaving in wholesome ways can be habit forming; so can behaving viciously. There is hence attention both to virtue and to consequence here, and attention to the character of and consequences for anyone affected by the action. The fundamental facts relevant to moral assessment are causal interdependence and the moral equivalence of all moral agents and patients.

Buddhist moral assessment and reasoning hence explicitly takes into account a number of dimensions of action. We cannot characterize a particular action as good or evil *simpliciter* in this framework, nor can we enumerate our obligations or permissions. Instead we examine the states of character reflected by and consequent to our intentions, our words, our motor acts, and their consequences. We ask about the pleasure and pain produced, and about how actions reflect and enhance or ignore and undermine our universal responsibility. In sum, we ask how these actions are relevant to solving our collective problem—the omnipresence of suffering. The fact that a terrible outcome ensues from a good intention does not make the outcome morally acceptable; nor does a good outcome somehow cancel malicious intent. Each component of action has its consequences and reflects morally relevant features of its genesis.

Attention to this approach to moral assessment and reasoning reveals that in this framework there is no morally significant distinction between self-regarding and other-regarding actions. Nor is there any distinction between moral and prudential motivations. Motivations that appear to be immoral but prudential are, on deeper analysis, simply confused. Nor is there any limit to the domain of the ethical. Karma is ubiquitous; interdependence is endless. Responsibility, on this model, as the Dalai Lama XIV constantly reminds his audiences, can only be universal.

4. Once again, this is not to say that nobody in any Buddhist culture has thought this way, and indeed a good deal of folk morality in Buddhist societies proceeds in just such a manner.

## 4. Beyond Virtue, Consequence Obligation: Toward Moral Perception

We can now see that Buddhist moral theory is neither purely consequentialist nor purely areteic nor purely deontological. Elements of each kind of evaluation are present, but there is no overarching concern for a unified form of moral assessment. And none of these is thematized as the focus of moral assessment. Rather, as I emphasized at the outset, the concern of Buddhist reflection on ethics is the solution of a fundamental, pervasive problem, the problem of *dukkha*. The problem is complex, its roots are complex, and so its solution can be expected to be complex.

Suffering is both caused and constituted by fundamental states of character, including preeminently egocentric attraction, egocentric aversion and confusion regarding the nature of reality. Hence the cultivation of virtues that undermine these vices is morally desirable. Suffering is perpetuated by our intentions, our acts and their consequences. Hence attention to all of these is necessary for its eradication. Because our own happiness and suffering are intimately bound up with that of others, we are responsible for others and obligated to take their interests into account.

Buddhism hence represents a distinct moral framework addressed to problem-solving that takes action not to issue from a free will bound by laws, but from a dependently originated, conditioned continuum of causally interdependent psychophysical processes. It takes the relevant consequences of action not to be pleasure and pain conceived of as introspectible experiences of persons, but to be states of sentient continua of genuine suffering, that which conduces to suffering, genuine liberation, or that which conduces to genuine liberation, whether or not those are desired or detested, or experienced as desirable or detestable by the sentient beings imputed on the basis of those continua.

The relevant categories of assessment, and the relevant considerations in deliberation, are unified by an overarching vision of the complexity of ethical life, by an overarching vision of the purpose of moral reflection and of moral cultivation, and by an overarching vision of the nature of agency and of the nature of life. If we fail to attend to this framework, we see a patchwork of ad hoc admonitions and assessments. When we attend to the framework, we see a unitary, alternative way of taking up with ethics.

Buddhist ethical thought is articulated with considerable care both in Pāli literature—preeminently by Buddhaghosa and his commentators—and in the Mahāyāna tradition, as developed in texts such as *How to Lead an Awakened Life* and *Introduction to the Middle Way*. There are important differences in emphasis in these two bodies of literature, but they are more complementary than competitive, and together offer a rich view of moral psychology that can contribute a great deal to Western approaches to moral theory.[5]

Central to each is an account of perception grounded in Abhidharma psychology, a framework devoted to the detailed anatomy of the psychology of experience expressed in a set of lists of kinds of mental episodes, processes and factors together with an account of the ways in which fundamental subpersonal mental phenomena combine to yield the relatively macroscopic cognitive and affective states of which we are aware. There is not space in this volume to scout that terrain in full. For present purposes, it is important to note that there are several fundamental processes taken to be involved in all perceptual awareness, referred to as the *sarvaga/kun 'dro (kundro) (constantly operative)* mental factors.

We have already encountered one of these—*cetanā*, or intention, and have considered its role in perception and in moral consciousness in a preliminary way. To this we add *sparsa/reg pa (rekpa) (contact), vedanā/tshor ba (tsorwa) (feeling* or *hedonic tone), samjñā/'du shes (dusheh) (ascertainment)* and *chanda/'dun pa (dönpa) (action selection)*. On this model of the perceptual process, perception involves not only bare sensory contact, but also intentionality, an initial sense of the sensory and affective valence of the object (pleasant or unpleasant; to be approached or avoided; friend or foe...), a cognitive ascertainment or determination of what the object is (perception is always perception-as, but on this model, not only as a thing of a kind, but as a thing with an affective valence) and all of this readies action with respect to the object.

What does all of this have to do with ethics? Everything. Each of our perceptual encounters, whether with other people or with the animate and inanimate objects around us, involves hedonic or affective tone. We may find ourselves averse to people who don't look like us or attracted to objects that lend us status, for instance. And every morally charged interaction begins with perceptual encounter. These affective sets are neither morally neutral nor fixed. Changing the affective dimensions of our perceptual experience is both possible, and can lead us to be better (or worse) people, can lead us to experience and to create more or less suffering. This is part of the work of ethical development.

5. The idea that moral evaluation is so multidimensional is not, of course, unique to Buddhism. See Feltz and Cokely (2013) for evidence that it is in fact part and parcel of our intuitive moral framework.

We have already encountered the moral dimensions of *cetanā*, of intentionality. The way we direct our attention, the categories in terms of which we perceive, that which grabs our attention are all matters of moral concern, but are all matters not of what we do *after* perception, but condition and direct our perception of the world. Nonetheless, while intention drives much perceptual processing, it is not an autonomous foreign force in our experiential lives, but rather a force we can come to control, and which can either take us in morally salutary or deleterious directions. Once again, moral development is seen to consist in the cultivation of essentially perceptual skills.

When we engage perceptually, we categorize. We see others as colleagues, adversaries, friends, family members, or strangers, superiors or subordinates, white, black, male, female, and so forth. And of course often these categories are far from morally neutral, and their moral valence may vary considerably with context. But perception is impossible without ascertainment of this kind. And once again, this ascertainment process is one that while present in any moment as a kind of perceptual reflex, is also malleable. We develop skills of ascertainment constantly in daily life, as when we learn to recognize kinds of flowers, genres of art, or the work of particular composers. But we can also hone our skills in moral ascertainment. Indeed, we used to have a term for this—*consciousness raising*.

Finally, part of perception is the readying of action. Our motor systems are fully integrated with perception, and this can be the basis of thoughtless reflex action, as when we strike out in anger upon perceiving a threat or an insult, flinch when we hear something uncomfortable, or reach out spontaneously in embrace. Once again, this aspect of our perceptual engagement with the world, while automatic in the moment, is malleable, and while deeply cognitive is also deeply moral. As we cultivate ourselves ethically, we develop the motor sets that are part of our spontaneous perceptual engagement with the world around us. (See Heim 2013 for a detailed discussion of Buddhaghosa's account of the structure of perception and of its moral dimensions.)

Ethical engagement, on this Buddhist view, has its foundation in perceptual engagement, and perceptual engagement on this view is far from passive, far from fixed. The project of leading a life that is a solution to, rather than a reinforcement of, the problem of universal suffering is at least in large part the project of reordering our perceptual engagement with the world. This is a very different orientation from one focused on action, duty or even the cultivation of a broad set of action-based virtues. Let us now see how this orientation to moral engagement through perception and our mode of experiencing the world articulates in the two great living Buddhist ethical traditions—that of the Theravāda and that of the Mahāyāna.

## 5. Theravāda Ethics: The Four Immeasurables and the Narrative Context

The Theravāda tradition emphasizes the cultivation of the four *brahmavihāras* or divine states: *karuṇā (care), muditā (sympathetic joy), mettā (love)* and *upekkhā/Skt: upekṣā (equanimity)*. The account of these states of character provides a moral psychology that articulates with a more general Buddhist phenomenology and metaphysics.

*Karuṇā* is a central concept not only in the Pāli tradition, but also, as we shall see, in the Mahāyāna, where it is thematized as the heart of morality. The translation of *karuṇā* as *compassion* has become standard in Buddhist Hybrid English. But I can no longer stick with it. While the root of *compassion* is *passio*, meaning to experience, or to suffer, and connoting being a patient, rather than an agent, the root of *karuṇā* is *kṛ*, meaning *to act.*[6] And *karuṇā* connotes not just an emotive response to another, but a commitment to act on behalf of others to relieve their suffering. The standard translation is hence etymologically paradoxical, and can be misleading. The term *care* nicely captures this commitment to act, as in the case of *caregiving, caring for*, and other such expressions.

To cultivate care in this sense is to recognize both the omnipresence of suffering and our interconnectedness through the web of dependent origination; it is to recognize that one cannot solve even the problem of one's own suffering without caring about that of others, as well, given our essentially social nature and the claims that nature ensures that we make upon one another. It is to recognize that not to care about others is to suffer from profound alienation, and to adopt an attitude with which one can never be comfortable. But to adopt a caring attitude is more than an act of recognition; it is also to adopt a mode of comportment to the world, a mode in which the welfare and suffering of others is that which is ascertained in perception, in which sentient beings are perceived intentionally *as suffering*, and in which the actions that are readied in the perceptual cycle are actions designed to alleviate suffering. In short, *karuṇā* is tied directly to the phenomenology of perception as well as to the ideology of the four noble truths and of dependent origination.

*Mettā* is an attitude of spontaneous positive emotion and well-wishing toward others, an attitude of beneficence. It joins with *karuṇā* in signaling a recognition of interdependence and a lack or self-grasping, but focuses

6. Jenkins (personal communication) notes that this etymology may be spurious. But it is widely cited in Buddhist literature, and even if it is spurious, canonical Buddhist glosses of *karuṇā* emphasize this active dimension of its meaning.

intentionally and cognitively not specifically on the suffering of others, but on positively promoting their welfare. Again, it is not a reflective attitude, but a perceptual set.

*Muditā* or *sympathetic joy* is a distinctively Buddhist moral psychological state, the mirror image of *schadenfreude*. To cultivate *muditā* is to cultivate an attitude in which the good fortune, the positive traits of character, the happiness and the accomplishments of others are a source of immediate joy to oneself. It counteracts envy, and also reflects the sensibility of selflessness, of an absence of self-grasping—that recognition that happiness and accomplishment are good per se, not because they are good for *me*.

Once again, the disposition to such sympathetic joy represents not simply a post-perceptual cognitive judgment and appraisal, but part of a perceptual set, a way of being embedded in the world. For it is once again to be intentionally oriented to, and to ascertain, others' achievements in perception; for the hedonic tone of that awareness to be positive, and neither negative as in envy nor neutral as in the mutual disinterest celebrated by modern economists; and for celebration and support to be the actions readied in this perceptual engagement.

Finally among these four aspects of morally awakened perception we encounter *upekkhā* (Pāli) or *upekṣā* (Sanskrit). This is an attitude of equanimity. In the context of these other affectively charged states, this one might seem odd. But it is not. Equanimity in this sense is at the heart of selflessness and at the foundation of moral effectiveness. In equanimity we dislodge the sense that the world revolves around us or even the sense that the events in our immediate environment revolve around us. Equanimity in this sense is not a refusal to care about what happens to us. On the contrary, because it allows us to detach from egocentric involvement with the world, it allows us to care about what happens per se, not about its impact on *us*.

The sense that the world does revolve around us—that we as subjects stand at the center of our universe—is, as we have seen, a central aspect of the Buddhist conception of self-grasping. It is the foundation of the subject–object duality that not only makes a hash of our metaphysical and phenomenological orientation to the world, but which grants us a prima facie reason to isolate ourselves as deserving of special regard, and so is also a foundation of egoism. More than that, however, it is the foundation of a set of what Peter Strawson (1962) called "reactive attitudes," such as resentment and gratitude, attitudes that are affective reactions to the morally charged actions of others.

From a Buddhist point of view, these reactive attitudes, along with their cousins such as anger and egocentric affection, are in fact *kleśas*, or dysfunctional cognitive states. They impair our judgment, orient us to our own reactions and not to the circumstances around us, and make us less, rather than more, morally effective. In resentment we feel *ourselves* wronged; we take others to be *personal agents* of harm; we isolate perpetrators and victims from a complex web of interdependence; we end up *reacting*, rather than *responding* to circumstances, and in the end, make things worse for ourselves and others, not better.

Once again, both the self-grasping orientation that underpins this kind of pathological reactivity and the attitude of selflessness that permits the equanimity that can underlie non-self-interested moral intervention are perceptual sets, ways of experiencing and taking up with the world. It is one thing to see the world with oneself at the center, and hence immediately to develop hedonic and action-readying responses grounded in that sense of self and ownership, and another to see a de-centered world in which one's own perspective is but one among many, and one's own experiences but some among many. Doing so, Theravāda ethicists such as Buddhaghosa argue, allows us not only to see the world more *accurately*, but more *ethically* as well.

This is but the briefest introduction to the *brahmavihāras* and hence to this profound Theravāda analysis of moral phenomenology.[7] I hope, however, that it is sufficient to see that this is a perspective on the subject-matter of ethics, and on the nature of moral cultivation, that deserves to be taken seriously, one grounded in moral perception, and one grounded in a compelling analysis of the nature of perception and experience itself.

Another feature of Theravāda (and indeed of all Buddhist) moral discourse deserves mention here, and that is the explicitly *narrative* character of Buddhist moral discussion. Whether we attend to early Buddhist *Avadāna* (stories of virtuous activity) literature (Rotman 2008), *vinaya* (monastic discipline literature), the moral admonitions in the vast *sutta* literature, or even such systematic commentarial literature as Candrakīrti's commentary on Ārydadeva's *Four Hundred Stanzas (Catuḥśataka)* (Lang 2003), Buddhist moral thought is often presented in the context of narratives. A story is told about an event, perhaps in one of the Buddha's previous lives, perhaps an event in the history of the monastic community, or perhaps the life of one of the Buddha's interlocutors, or even a folk tale. The moral lesson derived is not a "moral of the story" abstracted from the tale. Instead, the narrative is essential for making sense of the actor's actions, and of the moral assessment of and response to those actions.[8]

7. For more detailed discussion of the *brahmavihāras* and the relation of moral and perceptual cultivation see Buddhaghosa 2003, Heim 2013 and Saddhatissa 1999.

8. It is useful to contrast the role of narrative in, for instance, Platonic dialogues with that in Buddhist moral literature. Platonic dialogues indeed have narrative structure, but that

In the canonical story of Kisagotami, for instance, a young grieving mother asks the Buddha to restore her child to life. The Buddha tells her that he can do so if, and only if, she brings him a mustard seed from the house of a family that has never known death. Kisagotami, overjoyed at the prospect of the miracle, travels from house to house, only to find that death has visited each one. Gradually it dawns on her that her loss is not unique and that death is a normal part of life, and her grief eases. In this case, simply to state that everyone dies and that everyone loses loved ones is to thin the narrative beyond the bounds of its sense. The repetition of Kisagotami's actions, the blindness of grief, the determination to find a miracle and the gradual realization are all essential parts of the story of how a person comes to grips with suffering.

The fact that the narrative makes sense to us is an essential part of its power. Our coming to make sense of the narrative is what teaches us as we read the narrative, and absorption in the narrative brings us as readers to see the world differently; that transformation in vision, which appears not only in the protagonist, but in the reader as well, is the goal of moral practice in this tradition. (See Bhushan 2009 for an excellent discussion of the Kisagotami story; see Rotman 2008 and Heim 2013 for a textured discussion of the role of narrative in Buddhist ethics.) One might indeed read a great deal of Buddhist ethical literature looking for moral theory and fail to see it simply because of its embedding in so much narrative.

Only by understanding this essential role of narrative and the centrality of a transformation of vision can we make sense of ethical discourse in Indian Buddhist literature. Ethical thought is a way of making sense of our lives, individually and collectively. To see our actions and our situations ethically is to see them in relation to their social context, and to the context of our own lives, options, perceptual skills and acculturation, to see our actions and our lives as having meaning in the context of a larger story that gives them meaning, a story that we must understand in order to grasp their meaning. Ethical assessment is ineliminably hermeneutical, and ethical response is an attempt to complete a story in a way that makes sense to the central ethical actor, to those affected by his or her actions, and to ourselves as a culture. This is why so much courtroom time is spent telling stories about the lives of perpetrators and of victims. This is why when we raise children ethically we do so through narrative.

is more dramatic or dialectical framing than part of the philosophical story. Any of the dialogues could be written in essay form without any loss of content. In much Buddhist ethical literature, by contrast, the narrative plays a crucial hermeneutical role, as the story is essential to making sense of the behavior, comportment and transformation of the protagonist. (See Haugeland 1979 and Hutto 2007 for more on narrative and understanding.)

But from a Buddhist perspective, things run deeper, since from this perspective, our very being as ethical agents comes into existence through narrative. This is because from any Buddhist perspective, as we have emphasized at length above, persons are *constructed*. They are constructed through the appropriation of aggregates, through recognizing a body as mine, thoughts as mine, values, dispositions, and intentions as mine. In turn, those physical and cognitive processes are also constructed in relation to that person, and the person is appropriated by them as a locus. That appropriation and construction is itself accomplished through the narration of a life in which a person emerges as a character (Garfield 2014a). The very English term *person*, deriving from *persona* or *mask*, with its theatrical resonances suggests this idea.

That appropriation and narration of a life is, moreover, not a solo affair. We narrate and construct each other constantly in the hermeneutical ensemble act that is social life. (See Hutto 2008 and Bogdan 2011 for more recent Western developments of this idea, but of course as Nehamas 1985 points out, this idea in the West goes at least back to Nietzsche.) None of us is innocent in our own creation; but at the same time none of us is *autonomous* in that creative activity. Our identities are negotiated, fluid and complex in virtue of being marked by the three universal characteristics of impermanence, interdependence and the absence of any self. It is this frame of context-governed interpretive appropriation, instead of the frame of autonomous, substantial selfhood that sets metaphysical questions regarding agency, and moral questions regarding responsibility in a Buddhist framework.

What is it to act, in a way relevant to moral assessment or reaction? It is for our behavior to be determined by reasons, by motives we and/or others regard as our own. It is therefore for the causes of our behavior to be part of the narrative that makes sense of our lives, as opposed to being simply part of the vast uninterpreted milieu in which our lives are led, or bits of the narratives that more properly constitute the lives of others. This distinction is not a *metaphysical* but a *literary* distinction, and since this kind of narrative construction is so hermeneutical, how we do so—individually and collectively—is a matter of choice, and sensitive to explanatory purposes. That sensitivity, on the other hand, means that the choice is not *arbitrary*.[9]

So, from a Buddhist point of view, when we make choices or when we perform acts that merit moral assessment or assign responsibility to agents for

9. It is important to remember that not all narratives are equally good. Some makes good sense of our lives, or those of others; some are incoherent; some are facile and self-serving; some are profound and revealing. It is possible for people to disagree about whether a particular event is an action or not, or about the attribution of responsibility. It is possible for us to wonder about whether we should feel remorse for a particular situation or not. These

their actions, when we absolve others and when we assess acts morally, we do not settle questions about the ultimate structure of reality or about sui generis moral facts. Instead, we locate ourselves and others in collectively constituted moral narratives within which we make sense of our actions and theirs, and which, when read, help us to better see how we could participate in further narratives in which we would like to figure, narratives of greater happiness, of less suffering, of more human flourishing. Once again, this suggests a different way of thinking about ethical discourse from those that dominate Western ethical theory. Let us now continue this exploration of the Buddhist framework through attention to the developments that emerge in the context of the Mahāyāna tradition.

## 6. The Bodhisattva Path and Buddhist Moral Psychology

As I have been emphasizing, Buddhist ethics is directed at solving the problem of suffering in the context of the nexus of dependent origination. Careful attention to the nature of suffering and its causes in this context reveals that the causes and effects of any one sentient being's suffering include the states of indefinitely many other sentient beings, and that there is nothing special about the suffering of any particular sentient being that gives it pride of place in moral consideration. Together these drive one to a universal concern for the enlightened welfare of all sentient beings and to the cultivation of states of character that reflect this awareness and commitment, and this insight is the foundation of Mahāyāna moral theory. Let us take these points in turn, and then consider the relevant range of virtues as adumbrated in Buddhist moral psychology.

First, it is an important fact about human beings in particular, but more generally about any beings with sufficient sentience, to have moral standing, that their cognitive, affective and motivational states are linked inextricably with those of indefinitely many others in a vast causal nexus. For present purposes, let us focus on the case of those social animals we know as *Homo sapiens*. Our happiness, suffering and moral progress depends at all times on the actions and attitudes of others, as well as on their welfare.

questions are in the end, on this account, questions about which narratives make the most sense. While these questions may not always be easy (or even possible) to settle, the fact that they arise saves this view from the facile relativism that would issue from the observation that we can always tell *some* story on which this is an action of mine, and *some* story on which it is not, and so that there is simply no fact of the matter, and perhaps no importance to the question.

If others cooperate and support our projects and our development, success is far more likely; if their attitudes are hostile, happiness and progress are difficult to obtain.

If we know of others' weal or woe, we are either motivated to celebrate or to regret. Celebration of others' welfare benefits both ourselves and others; schadenfreude is not only detrimental to those around us, but ultimately, through undermining the relations that sustain us, to ourselves as well. *Muditā* is not only good for others, but good for ourselves as well. Similarly, our own actions, mental, verbal and physical, have endless ramifications both for our own affective and moral well-being and for that of those around us. These are natural facts, and to ignore them is to ignore the nature of action and its relevance to our moral, psychological and social lives.

Confusion regarding the nature of reality in the moral realm, from a Buddhist perspective, as we have seen, manifests itself most directly in the grasping of oneself and of that which most immediately pertains to oneself as having special importance and justifiable motivational force. The twofold self-grasping issues directly in the moral duality of self and other. Such a duality leads to the distinction between prudential and moral concern, self-regarding and other-regarding acts and between those to whom one owes special regard and those to whom one does not. All of these are taken by Buddhist philosophers to be spurious, and in general to reflect a view of the world as comprising *me, et al.*, a view not rationally sustainable once one sees that it is equally available, and so equally unjustifiable, for any moral subject. It is for this reason, at bottom, that confusion is a root moral delusion, and not simply an epistemological problem.

In the Mahāyāna tradition, moral attention is focused on the cultivation of a set of perfections, or virtues, including those of generosity, patience, propriety, attention, meditation and wisdom. Once again, this list might seem odd to the Western ethicist, in virtue of the inclusion of such prima facie non-moral virtues as those of attention, meditation and wisdom on the same list as generosity, patience and propriety. Once again, though, attention to the focus of Buddhist ethics on solving the problem of suffering, and attention to the role of inattention, failure to develop the insights and traits of character cultivated in meditation, and ignorance as causes of and maintainers of suffering, should dispel this sense of oddness, and we should be well on the way to normalizing these concerns.

Although a signal conceptual innovation in the Mahāyāna movement is the overlay of this prima facie areteic conception of moral development on the framework of the eightfold path with its delineation of areas of concern, and on the account of the nature of action and karma familiar from earlier Buddhism, this innovation is not an abandonment of the more basic framework, but an enrichment and a refocusing. The eightfold path remains a central guide to the domains in which the perfections figure, and the perfections are manifested in the propensity to perform cognitive, verbal and physical actions of the kind assessable in the familiar framework of Buddhist action theory. The framework of the perfections hence represents only an approach to morality more focused on states of character than on their manifestations as the fundamental goals of moral practice.

The most important innovation in Mahāyāna moral theory, however, is not the framework of the perfections but the installation of *karuṇā*, or care as the central moral value and the model of the bodhisattva's caring and careful engagement with the world as the moral ideal. *Karuṇā*, as we have seen, is not a passive emotional response, and not a mere desire. That is sloppy sympathy, and benefits nobody. Instead it is a genuine commitment manifested in thought, speech and physical action, to act for the welfare of all sentient beings.[10] It is in the Mahāyāna tradition of Buddhist ethics, and its development of the Theravāda anticipations of such moral theorists as Hume and Schopenhauer, that Buddhist moral theory makes its closest contact with Western ethics.

Care in the Mahāyāna tradition is founded upon the insight that suffering is bad, per se, regardless of whose it is. To fail to take another's suffering seriously as a motivation for action is itself a form of suffering and is irrational. This is a deep insight, and one over which we should not pass too quickly: The bodhisattva path is motivated in part by the realization that not to experience the suffering of others as one's own, and not to take the welfare of others as one's own, is to suffer even more deeply from a profound existential alienation born of a failure to appreciate one's own situation as a member of an interdependent community. Our joys are social joys; our sorrows are social sorrows; our identity is a social identity; the bounds of our society are indefinite. We either suffer and rejoice together in the recognition of our bonds to one another, or we languish in self-imposed solitary confinement, afflicted both by the cell we construct, and by the ignorance that motivates its construction.

Care, grounded in the awareness of our joint participation in global life, hence, from the Mahāyāna perspective, is the wellspring of the motivation for the development of all perfections, and the most reliable motivation for morally decent actions. Care is also, on this view, the direct result of a

10. It is important to note that the scope of ethical concern in all Buddhist moral discussions is universal—comprising not only human beings, but all sentient beings. While I do not focus on this fact in the present discussion, it must be taken as understood throughout.

genuine appreciation of the emptiness and interdependence of all sentient beings. Once one sees oneself as nonsubstantial and existing only in interdependence, and once one sees that the happiness and suffering of all sentient beings is entirely causally conditioned, the only rational attitude one can adopt to others is a caring and careful one.

Care, Mahāyāna moral theorists argue, requires one to develop *upāya*, or moral skill, in order to realize one's objectives. Caring intention is only genuine if it involves a commitment to action and to the successful completion of action, enabled by the skills requisite for that action. A desire to eradicate world hunger is not genuinely caring in this sense if it leads nowhere. But moving to eradicate world hunger requires that one know how to act, if only to know to which organizations to donate, let alone to help others to grow or distribute food. It is in the domain of *upāya* that Buddhist and Western ethics converge in practice and it is in this domain that each can learn from the other.

Often the best way to ensure that minimal human needs are met, for instance, is to establish rights to basic goods, and to enshrine those rights in collective moral and political practice. Often the best way to ensure that human dignity is respected is to enshrine values that treat persons as individual bearers of value. Often the best way to ensure plenty is to develop social welfare policies. And often the best way to develop flourishing citizens is to articulate a theory of virtue. Western moral theorists have been good at this. Liberal democratic theory and a framework of human rights has been a very effective device for the reduction of suffering, though hardly perfect or unproblematic. So has utilitarian social welfare theory. And virtue theories have been useful in moral education. These Western articulations of the right, the good and the decent provide a great deal of specific help in the pursuit of the bodhisattva path.

On the other hand, Buddhist moral theory provides a larger context in which to set these moral programs, and one perhaps more consonant with a plausible metaphysics of personhood and action, and with the genuine complexity of our moral lives. To the extent that that world is characterized by omnipresent suffering, and to the extent that that is a real problem, perhaps the fundamental problem for a morally concerned being, Buddhist moral theory may provide the best way to conceptualize that problem *in toto*. But Buddhist moral theory and Western moral theory can meet profitably when we ask *how* to solve that problem in concrete human circumstances, and it is in these concrete human circumstances that we must solve it.

It is useful to attend to the work of the 20th- and 21st-century Vietnamese Buddhist philosopher the Ven. Thich Nhat Hahn, who eloquently characterizes the essentials of Buddhist moral development in his essay "Fourteen Mindfulness Trainings" (1998, reprinted in Edelglass and Garfield 2009, 421–427). There, Thich Nhat Hahn emphasizes that moral cultivation comprises the development of traits such as *openness*, which he glosses as "awareness of the suffering created by fanaticism and intolerance" (Edelglass and Garfield 2009, 421); non-attachment and freedom of thought, also glossed in terms of kinds of awareness (Ibid., 422). In these cases and that of others on his list, Thich Nhat Hahn argues that the primary object of moral cultivation—the state at which ethical practice aims—is not a disposition to act, not to become an agent who regularly maximizes utilities, and not respect for duty. Instead, ethical perfection consists primarily in a way of seeing things, in a kind of awareness of others and of one's place in the world. The goods most Western moral theorists are likely to emphasize flow from this mode of ethical comportment and from this quality of experience. But it is validated not because it leads to these goods, but because of its congruence with an understanding of the nature of existence and of human life. It is for this reason that I prefer to see Buddhist ethics as a kind of moral phenomenology.

Among the qualities of ethical awareness, Thich Nhat Hahn also notes "dwelling happily in the present moment." (Ibid., 424) Once again, he is characterizing a mode of awareness, one that reflects an understanding of the possibilities of life, and of interdependence and its fruits. The important point here is that this is not a recommendation for personal satisfaction, but a component of moral comportment, and a component that reflects an understanding of reality. Even dispositions that might appear to be traditional Western virtues, such as generosity and propriety are treated as kinds of *awareness*. Thich Nhat Hahn concludes his presentation:

> Studying and practicing the mindfulness trainings can help us to understand the true nature of interbeing—we cannot just be by ourselves alone; we can only inter-be with everyone and everything else. To practice these trainings is to become aware of what is going on in our bodies, our minds, and the world. With awareness, we can live our lives happily, fully present in each moment we are alive, intelligently seeking solutions to the problems we face, and working for peace in large and small ways . . . (Ibid., 427)

This approach to ethics as moral phenomenology is hardly new in the Buddhist tradition with Thich Nhat Hahn. It has old roots, beginning with the Pāli *suttas* themselves and the work of Buddhaghosa, and articulated with great force by Śāntideva, to whose work we now turn.

## 7. Moral Phenomenology in *Bodhicaryāvatāra*

### *7.1 Introduction to the Text*

Let us now turn directly to *How to Lead an Awakened Life*. Śāntideva's understanding of how to lead an awakened life, or a life aimed at awakening, is distinctive for its sophistication and for the detail with which it is articulated and defended.

The central moral phenomenon taken up in the text is that of *bodhicitta*, a term I prefer to leave untranslated. This term is usually translated either as *the awakened mind* or as *the mind of awakening*. But that's not very helpful, in part because of the different connotations of *citta/sems (sem)* and *mind* in Buddhist and Western philosophy, respectively, and in part because of the unclarity of the bare genitive construction in English. Avoiding the temptation to follow attractive philological and metaphysical byways, let me offer this preliminary reading of the term: *Bodhicitta* is a complex psychological phenomenon. It is a standing motivational state with conative and affective dimensions. It centrally involves an altruistic aspiration, grounded in care, to cultivate oneself as a moral agent for the benefit of all beings.[11]

That cultivation, as we shall see, demands the development of the skills in moral perception, moral responsiveness and traits of character we have already encountered, as well as an insight into the nature of reality so deep that it transforms our way of seeing ourselves and others, and what we would call practical wisdom. In short, *bodhicitta* entails a commitment to attain and to manifest full awakening for the benefit of others. A bodhisattva is one who has cultivated *bodhicitta* in at least one of two senses adumbrated by Śāntideva, and distinguished below.

Śāntideva's account of morality has been read in the West as a distinctively Buddhist theory of moral *virtue*, that is, as structurally Aristotelian, even if very different in content from Aristotle's account of virtue and the good life (Keown 2005, 2007). It has also been read as consequentialist (Goodman 2008, Siderits 2007). Each of these readings, I fear, is a symptom of the dangerous hermeneutic temptation to force Buddhist ethics into a Western mold against which I warn at the opening of this chapter, and while each reading reflects something of the content of Śāntideva's approach, each misses the heart of the matter. *How to Lead an Awakened Life* addresses the nature of *bodhicitta* and the means of cultivating

11. We must tread with care, here however. As Susanne Mrozik has pointed out to me, Stephen Jenkins argues (1998) that "altruism" may be a bit strong, since, as we shall see below, *bodhicitta* and the motivations and skills connected to it are beneficial to the bodhisattva as well as to others. It is, as Śāntideva will emphasize, always in the end in one's own interest to cultivate *bodhicitta*.

it. We can therefore better read it as a treatise on the distinction between the phenomenologies of benighted and of awakened moral consciousness.

It is true, as proponents of the areteic reading note, that Śāntideva focuses in *How to Lead an Awakened Life* on the cultivation of traits of character, and it is true that he contrasts moral virtues such as patience and care with moral vices such as a irascibility and selfishness, and recommends virtue over vice, focusing on states of the agent as opposed to actions or obligations. On the other hand, for Śāntideva the point of all of this is not to lead a happy life, or even to be a good person: *Bodhicitta* does not take the moral agent as its object. The point is to benefit others, as well as oneself. Perfection itself, in other words is, for Śāntideva, neither an end in itself, nor final, nor self-sufficient. This is no virtue theory, and awakening, while analytically related to the perfections, is not a kind of *eudaimonia* analytically related to virtues.

It is also true that Śāntideva urges us to care for the happiness of others, and to reduce their suffering. And it is even true that we can find verses in the text that enjoin us to compare how little our own happiness or suffering is in comparison to that of all sentient beings in order to motivate us to sacrifice our own interests for that of others. Here is an example many (e.g., both Goodman 2008 and Siderits 2006) cite in support of a consequentialist reading:

> III: 10 Without any hesitation, I relinquish
> My body, my pleasures,
> And all virtues achieved throughout all time
> In order to benefit all sentient beings.[12]

But to take such verses to be the expression of a kind of consequentialism would be to take them seriously out of context, and to miss the heart of Śāntideva's account. This verse in particular, as we will see below, occurs in the context of a resolution to abandon selfishness, and to broaden one's moral gaze to universal scope, to cultivate a way of seeing oneself in the context of a much broader whole in which one's own interests are a rather small affair. Śāntideva does not argue that *bodhicitta* or the perfections cultivated by the bodhisattva are valuable *because of the consequences* they entail; and there is

12. All translations are my own, from the sDe dge edition of the Tibetan text, as reprinted in rGyal tshab (1999). As Wallace and Wallace note in Śāntideva (1997), the Tibetan version of the text differs in many—usually minor—ways from the available Sanskrit edition of the text. It appears that even early on there were at least two versions of the text, and there is no way of determining whether the Sanskrit edition from which the Tibetan and Indian translators worked was in some respect preferable to that which survives today or not. But it is worth noting that because of the importance this text attained in Tibet, most of the significant commentarial literature refers to the Tibetan version. The notable exception is Prajñākaramati's *Bodhicaryāvatāra-pañjikā*, which follows the available Sanskrit.

never a suggestion that the suffering of one can be balanced against the happiness of another. Whereas for a consequentialist, balances of benefits and harms are the ground of the value of actions or attitudes, but not necessarily their objects, for Śāntideva, the good of others is an *object* of *bodhicitta*, but not the *ground* of its value. Its value is grounded instead in the fact that it is the only rational way of taking up with the world.

It is the burden of the text to defend this thesis. For Śāntideva, it is egoism, not care, that requires defense, because egoism presupposes the uniqueness of a particular practical standpoint, viz., my own. And for Śāntideva, everything I think I can best achieve by egoism is not only thereby unattainable, but is better sought through an attitude of mutuality and care. And comparison, or tradeoff of suffering and benefit, is never on the table.[13] Buddhist ethics, we have seen, is not a method for resolving moral dilemmas or for choosing action, but rather an approach to our comportment toward the world. Śāntideva takes this project one step further.

## *7.2 Fear and Refuge: Suffering, Aspiration and Awakening as Moral Development*

The role that fear plays in Śāntideva's account of the phenomenology of moral life is striking, and the diagnosis of this fear is subtle. It is one of the most original contributions he makes to Buddhist moral psychology. The centrality of fear in our lives to which he directs our attention connects deeply with the centrality of the practice of taking refuge in Buddhist life, and one can read this text profitably as an extended meditation on refuge.[14] The very need for refuge itself suggests an overarching experience of fear—perhaps a fear whose dimensions and objects are to a large extent opaque to the sufferer.

13. Moreover, as Jenkins points out (1998), in the end there never is a tradeoff—most accounts of virtuous action end up with the claim that *everyone* benefits, even those who apparently suffer temporary adversity, although perhaps one must take the long view to see those benefits.

14. Taking refuge is an essential—perhaps *the essential*—Buddhist religious practice. In fact, the definition of a Buddhist, in the religious sense, is one who has taken refuge in what are known as the "three jewels," the Buddha, Dharma and Sangha (and often, in Tibetan traditions, a fourth jewel—the lama). The idea is that the beginning of Buddhist practice is in the recognition of the first two of the four noble truths—that human existence is fundamentally unsastisfactory, permeated by *dukkha*, and that the causes of that situation lie in deep psychological dysfunction, coupled with the confidence that the only solution to this predicament is that offered in the third and fourth truths and the acceptance of the fact that that requires a Buddhist practice.

The Buddha as refuge object is twofold: first, the historical Buddha, Siddhartha Gautama is taken as a refuge object, in the following sense: the fact that *he* realized full awakening

The ultimate source and object of this fear is depicted graphically in the Indian and Tibetan representation of the wheel of life (*bhāvacakra/srid 'khor [sikhor]*), in which all of existence takes place in the jaws of death. The iconography suggests that our cognitive and emotional lives, the constant cycling between states of mind and the experience of being buffeted about by events—whether external or internal—that are beyond our control, gives rise to so much suffering and is driven in large part by the unconscious awareness and fear of the inevitability of death.

That fear engages us psychologically at the hub. Although the awareness of our own impermanence and that of all about which we care constitutes the horizon of our experience, we suppress that fear in confusion, living our lives as though these impermanent phenomena are permanent. This is why Tsongkhapa (2006, 34–35) remarks that confusion, in this sense (*avidya/ma rig pa [marikpa]*) is not simply the absence of knowledge, but the direct opposite of knowledge—a psychologically efficacious and destructive *denial* of the truth.[15] In this case, as Śāntideva is aware, it is a denial of what we at a deeper level know to be true, of a troubling knowledge.

This confusion (born, as we have seen, of fear) generates attraction and aversion. Our attachment to ourselves, to our own well-being, to our possessions, to our conventions and practices, and in general to all that in the end is a source of suffering, Śāntideva urges, is at bottom a reflexive defensive reaction to the fear of loss. Our aversion to that which we find distasteful is at bottom a reaction to the fact that it reminds us of our own impermanence and vulnerability. Our conviction that we are independent agents interacting with other independent agents—a feature of our moral experience that runs both so very deep and so contrary to all that we know upon reflection—he urges, is a way of warding off the fear of interdependence, of being out of control, of being subject to the natural laws that issue in our aging, infirmity, reliance on others and eventual demise. And around the hub cycle our emotions, desires, actions and experiences.

constitutes a proof that it can be done, just as a mountaineer attempting to scale Chomolungma (Everest) might take refuge in the fact that Tenzing, Hillary and a few hundred others have done it in the past. This gives rise to the second sense of the Buddha as refuge, viz., that one takes one's own confidence in one's own future awakening as a refuge. The second refuge—Dharma—is Buddhist doctrine, taken as the only way to dispel the confusion, attraction and aversion that together constitute the root of *dukkha*. And the third is the *sangha*, or spiritual community, taken in some traditions to be the community of monks and nuns, in others to be the community of practitioners more broadly, and in some to be the community of already awakened beings. The idea is that the achievement of awakening is very difficult, and requires support.

15. This is nicely captured in the Sanskrit term *ahaṃkāra—the construction of I*, a term used frequently to indicate the *manufacture—as* opposed to the mere *experience—*of the illusion of a self.

II: 38 Thus, since I have not realized
That I am ephemeral,
Through confusion, attachment and aversion,
I have committed many kinds of vicious deeds.

II: 42 O Protectors, through being inattentive
And heedless of this danger,
For the sake of this impermanent life
I have achieved much that is vicious.

But *fear* and *awareness of fear* are two very different things. Though we all *live* in fear, we are not, Śāntideva thinks, all *aware* of that background of fear, or of its impact on our lives. Moral sensibility properly so-called, according to the account of *How to Lead an Awakened Life*, arises when one becomes truly aware of the terror that frames one's life and that lies at the root of self-deception and vice. That awareness generates the impulse to take refuge and to strive for awakening, and as a consequence, the cultivation of aspirational *bodhicitta*.

II: 47 From this very moment I go for refuge to
The victors, protectors of all beings,
Who strive for the purpose of protecting all,
And who have great power to completely eliminate all fear.

II: 48 Likewise, I honestly go for refuge to
The Dharma in which they are completely engaged,
Which completely eliminates the fear of cyclic existence,
As well as to the assembly of bodhisattvas.

II: 49 Overwhelmed by fear,
I offer myself to Samantabhadra,
And of my own accord,
I offer this, my body to Mañjugoṣa.

II: 50 In despair, I cry out for help to
The protector, Avalokiteśvara,[16]
Who acts compassionately and inerrantly,
Begging him to protect my vicious self.

16. Samantabhadra, Mañjugoṣa and Avalokiteśvara are each celestial Bodhisattvas, or highly awakened beings, if taken literally, in the Buddhist pantheon. Samantabhadra is associated with meditation, Mañjughoṣa is a form of Māñjuśrī, and is the bodhisattva of wisdom, and Avalokiteśvara (familiar in China as Guanyin and in Japan as Kanon) is the bodhisattva of

> II: 53 Now, because of what you said before,
> Having experienced great terror,
> I approach you with refuge so that you
> Might quickly dispel my fear.

Moral development is hence, once again, revealed to be a transformation of moral *experience*; this time a transition from a life conditioned by terror and unreason—albeit perhaps unconscious terror and unrecognized unreason—to a life conditioned by confidence and clarity; from a life constituted by phenomenological self-deception to a life constituted by introspective awareness; from a life in which vice is inevitable and taken to be unproblematic just because it is not recognized, or recognized *as* vice, to a life in which the cultivation of virtue is at the centre of one's consciousness.

## *7.3 The Importance of Mindfulness*

Chapter V, on maintaining awareness, connects these insights to the importance of mindfulness we discussed earlier. Mindfulness, which I take to be the union of *smṛti/dran pa (denpa)* and *samprajñana/shes bzhin (sheshin)*, is taken up as the very foundation of all of moral practice and development. The first of these terms is often translated as *memory* or *attention*. It has the sense of *calling to mind*. The second is often translated as *maintaining attention* or *restraining the mind*. Each is often translated, depending on context, as *mindfulness*. I use the English term "mindfulness" to translate their union as it is characterized in *How to Lead an Awakened Life* and its commentaries, intending the calling to mind and retaining in mind.

Mindfulness in this sense is regarded by scholars and practitioners of many Buddhist traditions (in particular in the Pāli and Mahāyāna traditions of India and in Tibet) as essential not only for the development of insight, but also for the cultivation and maintenance of ethical discipline.[17] In the

care. So, together this trio represents meditative insight, intellectual discernment and moral concern. While celestial bodhisattvas such as these are often understood quite literally as beings, in much Buddhist meditative practice, and in particular in the tantric meditations in which they figure most prominently, they are taken as iconic representations of aspects of one's own mind. So, to invoke Samantabhadra is to resolve to develop one's meditative insight; to invoke Māñjuśrī is to resolve to develop one's understanding, and to invoke Avalokiteśvara is to resolve to cultivate an attitude of universal care.

17. Indeed—and this is no news to Buddhist scholars or practitioners, though it is sometimes surprising to non-Buddhist ethicists—the cultivation of ethical discipline is generally regarded in the Buddhist philosophical tradition as a necessary condition of the cultivation of insight and wisdom.

Pāli canon, particularly in the *Great Discourse on Mindfulness* (*Mahāsatipaṭṭāna-sutta*), but elsewhere as well, we encounter admonitions to train in mindfulness as the foundation of all Buddhist practice. Why is mindfulness so important? Śāntideva puts the point in the following memorable way at the beginning of chapter V of *How to Lead an Awakened Life*:

V:1 One who wishes to protect his practice
Should be careful to protect his mind.
If one does not protect one's mind
It is impossible to protect one's practice.

V: 2 The elephant of the mind
Causes much harm and degradation.
Wild, mad elephants
Do not cause so much harm.

V: 3 Nonetheless, if the elephant of the mind
Is restrained by the rope of mindfulness,
Then all fear is banished,
And every virtue falls into our hands.

Śāntideva here argues that the cultivation of a moment-to-moment awareness of one's own cognitive and emotional states is central to leading an awakened life. It is possible to remain utterly inattentive to one's own moral life, failing to notice situations that call for moral response, failing even to recognize one's own moral attitudes, dispositions and motivations, even if one is obsessed with the *idea* of morality. From this perspective, we can think of the three fundamental dysfunctional psychological states of confusion, attraction and aversion in the first instance as distracters, leading us away from the attention that is necessary if we are to live effectively, insightfully and compassionately; awakening consists in part in replacing that inattention with mindfulness.

These opening verses emphasize the fact that mindfulness is necessary in order to combat the natural tendency to *mindless* action driven not by care and insight, but rather by blind passion and confusion. Without attention to our motivation as well as to the situations in the context of which we act, moral conduct is impossible. Later in the same chapter, Śāntideva emphasizes, using the metaphors of Buddhist hell imagery, a second *moral* dimension of mindfulness, that is, that mindfulness is necessary not only in order for us directly to alleviate the suffering of *others*, but also in order to extirpate the deep existential suffering in ourselves that leads us to moral failing in virtue of our inability to see beyond our own misery. He emphasizes here that this suffering is entirely endogenous, and that moral development is entirely mental cultivation:

V: 7 Who so purposefully forged
The implements of sentient beings' hell?
Who constructed the floor of burning iron?
And whence have those women come?[18]

V: 8 The Sage has explained that
The vicious mind gives rise to all of these.
So, there is nothing whatever in the triple world[19]
More terrifying than the mind.

Because our own mental activity is the root of primal confusion, it is the root of vicious attraction and aversion, of all vice and so of all suffering. Because our own mental activity is the only possible root of insight and understanding, it is the only possible root of care, of virtue and so of liberation. Left to its own devices, it is the mad elephant and the architect of hell. But mindfulness can tame it, and it can become the supple, disciplined instrument of our own and others' happiness. Mindfulness, from this perspective, is therefore important because without it no other virtue can be manifest; and because with it, all other virtue emerges.

Maintaining the focus on the relationship between the dissipation of fear and moral development, Śāntideva argues that the cultivation of a moment-to-moment awareness of one's own cognitive and emotional states is central to leading an awakened life. The morally benighted are characterized by an inattention to their own mental lives; awakening consists in part in replacing that inattention with mindfulness. It is in this context that Śāntideva emphasizes the centrality of self-cultivation to moral development in these verses.

Perhaps the most widely studied and most beautiful chapter in *How to Lead an Awakened Life* is that on patience. In this chapter Śāntideva emphasizes the

18. To a reader coming to this text for the first time, this must be one of the stranger lines. The reference is to a description of a Buddhist hell in which hideous, terrifying women lurk in trees threatening the poor denizens. Śāntideva's point is that these women, like the floors or burning iron in other such hell realms, are not literally existent entities that torment people in some other realm, but are metaphors for the cognitive states that we generate consequent upon vicious action. That is, we create our own hells.

19. Another standard Buddhist trope, referring to three kinds of universe: the desire realm (where we find ourselves); the realm of material form (physical, but without desire); and the immaterial realm. This religious cosmology is irrelevant to our present concerns.

pervasiveness of anger and aversion in the morally immature state, and the enormous—though often unconscious—suffering they bring in train, feeding on a cycle linking anger to fear and aggression.[20] The predominance of these emotions prior to the cultivation of *bodhicitta* contrasts with the patience that characterizes awakened moral experience.

The final two chapters of *How to Lead an Awakened Life* address the more directly cognitive aspects of the awakened moral life, those concerned with establishing how to *see* reality properly. Meditation is central to Śāntideva's account, for it is through meditation that one embeds discursive knowledge into one's character. In the following three verses he focuses on various aspects of attachment, its consequences and how to relinquish it. The first of these considers the impact of the understanding of impermanence on the release from attachment to others, and the development of equanimity.

The second addresses attachment to self, and once again, its connection to fear; the third emphasizes more graphically the role of meditation in reconstructing not our behavior or sense of duty, but our way of seeing the world. In each case, Śāntideva presents the topics as objects of meditation, emphasizing that the task of this philosophical project is not simply to develop cognitive insight, but to embed that insight so deeply into our psychology that it transforms our way of taking up with the world.

VIII: 5 What impermanent being
Attaches himself to what impermanent being?
For sadly, he will not see her
For thousands of lifetimes.

VIII: 17 If one thinks such thoughts as
"I am very rich and respected,
And many people like me,"
When death approaches, fear will arise.

VIII: 52 If you do not lust for the impure,
Why do you repeatedly embrace another
Who is only flesh-smeared bones
Bound together with sinew?

20. The unwary Western reader might think that there is a confusion here between *emotional* immaturity and *ethical* immaturity. This thought should be resisted, as it rests on a presumption that our emotional life is independent of our moral life. It is central to Śāntideva's—and indeed, any Buddhist—conception of the domain of the moral that our emotions are morally significant and morally evaluable. Emotional immaturity is one dimension of moral immaturity; emotional maturity one dimension of moral maturity. (See Dreyfus 2003.)

Finally, in the chapter on wisdom, Śāntideva emphasizes both the importance of a deep understanding of metaphysics for moral life, and, more specifically, the fact that the relevant metaphysical view is the Madhyamaka view according to which all phenomena are empty of essence, interdependent, and have only conventional identities. It is important to note here not just that Śāntideva recommends this metaphysical position as the foundation of awakened life and morality, but also, especially in the context of the preceding chapter, that it is a foundation for such a life precisely because once internalized, this view (and for Śāntideva *only* this view) transforms one's very experience both of the external world and of oneself, generating a metaphysical *vision* that enables a moral *engagement*, thus enabling engaged *bodhicitta*.[21]

> IX: 1 The Sage taught all of these matters
> For the sake of wisdom.
> Therefore, if one wishes to avoid suffering,
> And to attain peace, one should cultivate wisdom.
>
> IX: 48 Without an understanding of emptiness
> A mental state that has ceased will arise once again,
> Just as when one engages in non-conceptual meditation.
> Therefore, one should meditate on emptiness.
>
> IX: 77 Pride, which is the cause of suffering,
> Increases due to delusion regarding the self.
> Since from one, the other necessarily follows,
> Meditation on selflessness is supreme.

The excursion into abstract metaphysics and epistemology is so important to Śāntideva, and its location at the conclusion of the treatise, and not, as one might think, given the foundational role of insight in Buddhist theory, at the beginning, is significant. It is a central theme of *How to Lead an Awakened Life*, as it is a central theme of the Buddhist diagnosis of the existential problem of suffering generally, that suffering and the egocentric tendencies it generates and which in turn perpetuate it, are grounded in a fundamental confusion about the nature of reality—taking what is in fact interdependent,

21. Of course this means that it is not as easy as it sounds to attain moral perfection. Perfect care requires perfect wisdom. Nonetheless, this does not mean that it is impossible to cultivate *any* virtue: the cultivation even of mundane care increases wisdom; the cultivation of even a basic understanding of emptiness increases care.

impermanent and essenceless, on both the subjective and objective side to be independent, enduring and substantial.

This attitude, Śāntideva urges, is not the result of careful metaphysical reflection, but an innate cognitive instinct. A truly awakened life requires its extirpation. This extirpation requires philosophical reflection, but such reflection is not sufficient, given the depth of the cognitive set.[22] Even receptivity to that argument requires the cultivation of a moral sensibility that loosens the attachment and aversion implicated with the metaphysical error. But meditative practice is also necessary, in order that reflective thought can become a spontaneous cognitive set, a way of *being in the world*, rather than a way of *thinking about the world*, in which we experience ourselves and all around us as we are, interdependent, impermanent, insubstantial.[23]

This transformation of vision, and consequent transformation of mode of being, even though it is cast in *How to Lead an Awakened Life* as a direct understanding of ultimate reality, and an understanding of the relation between this ultimate reality and conventional reality, amounts not to seeing *behind* a world of illusion, but rather to coming to see a world, about which we are naturally deceived, just as it is, not being taken in by the cognitive habits that issue in that deception. For this reason, just as the historical Buddha emphasized that one's view of the nature of reality is a moral matter in the presentation of the eightfold path at Sarnath, Śāntideva, in his analysis of an awakened life, urges that our metaphysics and epistemology are central to our moral lives. It is because it is this vision that finally transforms aspirational to engaged *bodhicitta* that this chapter comes at the end, not at the beginning of the text.

This whirlwind tour through *How to Lead an Awakened Life* of course cannot do justice to the richness of Śāntideva's insight and moral thought. On the other hand, I hope that it gives the reader a glimpse of the development of the fundamental Buddhist orientation to ethics through moral phenomenology, and of the rich possibilities of this orientation. When Śāntideva asks about moral life, he asks not what our duties are, nor what actions are recommended, nor what the relation is between the good and our actions, nor even what would make us individually happy. Instead, he starts with a problem that is to be solved—that of the ubiquity of suffering—and the standard Buddhist diagnosis of that problem in terms of attachment and aversion rooted in fundamental ontological confusion. He then asks how to solve that problem.

22. A mere addition of insight to injury, as a psychoanalyst friend of mine used to say about some cognitive therapies.

23. Once again, the fact that meditative practice may be necessary to achieve virtuoso ethical status does not mean that meditation is the sine qua non of *any* moral progress.

Like his predecessors in the Theravāda tradition, Śāntideva develops a deeper diagnosis of the problem through an analysis of our own experience of ourselves and of our place in the world. And so, like them, he seeks the solution to this problem not—at least not directly—in a transformation of the world, or even of our conduct, but rather in a transformation of that experience. The task of leading an awakened life—a morally desirable life—is the task of transforming our phenomenology. Śāntideva extends this tradition of reflection by pushing deeper into the phenomenology of fear as a driving force in ordinary life, and by articulating a further set of morally relevant character traits. He also locates care, and the distinctive attitude of *bodhicitta*, at the center of this moral discourse.

I hope that it is clear by now that we cannot force this account into a familiar Western form, or even just to graft it on to one, as the phenomenological adjunct to consequentialism or Aristotelian aretaism. The value of this engagement with Buddhist ethics is that it allows us to open ourselves to the possibility of a very different way of understanding ethical aspiration and engagement—in this case, the path of the bodhisattva.

## 8. Care and Rationality

I alluded above to the Buddhist rejection of the presumption so common in Western ethical theory that egoism is a rational starting point for ethical reflection, and that the burden of proof is on the moralist to demonstrate the rationality of moral demands as motivations for action. Now that we have a general sketch of the Buddhist understanding of the ethical landscape, and of the Mahāyāna understanding in particular, we can return to this issue and we will see that Śāntideva offers an argument that shifts that burden of proof. We will begin with an important passage in chapter VIII of *How to Lead an Awakened Life*.

> VIII: 90 "Self and others are the same,"
> One should earnestly meditate:
> "Since they experience the same happiness and suffering,
> I should protect everyone as I do myself."

Here Śāntideva introduces the conclusion: there is no moral or motivational difference between moral subjects. He then offers several arguments or analogies to make this point: First, the ontology that takes individual organisms as the relevant unit of analysis for the purpose of moral assessment of motivation is arbitrary:

VIII: 91 Divided into many parts, such as the hands,
The body is nonetheless to be protected as a single whole.
Just so, different beings, with all their happiness and suffering,
Are like a single person with a desire for happiness.

Second, it is not the *locus* but the *fact* of suffering that makes it bad. So worrying about whether it is mine or someone else's is simply beside the point:

VIII: 92 Even if my own suffering
Does no harm to anyone else's body,
It is still my own suffering.
Since I am so attached to myself it is unbearable.

VIII: 93 Just so, even though I do not experience
The sufferings of others,
It is still their own suffering.
Since they are so attached to themselves, it is hard for them to bear.

VIII: 94 I must eliminate the suffering of others
Just because it is suffering, like my own.
I should work to benefit others
Just because they are sentient beings, as am I.

Third, to single myself out as uniquely deserving of moral concern, or as a unique source of motivation for action is arbitrary:[24]

VIII: 95 Since I am just like others
In desiring happiness,
What is so special about me
That I strive for my happiness alone?

VIII: 96 Since I am just like others
In not desiring suffering,
What is so special about me
That I protect myself, but not others?

24. There is a nice anticipation of Sidgwick and his attack on the rationality of egoism on the grounds that it presupposes a strong metaphysics of personal identity and on the grounds that it privileges one's own pleasure and pain as moral considerations over those of others, overlooking the naturalness of care and affection.

VIII: 97 If, because their suffering does not harm me,
I do not protect them,
When future suffering does not harm me,
Why do I protect against it?

Fourth, the facts of personal identity militate against egoism. There is no strict identity relation between successive stages of the continuum I regard as denoted by 'I.' So, the fact that I take my future self seriously in practical reasoning already suggests that I take the welfare or suffering of those not numerically identical to myself seriously in these ways. It is therefore irrational to distinguish motivationally between temporally distinct states of my own personal continuum and states of others' continua.

VIII: 98 The idea that this very self
Will experience that suffering is false:
Just as when one has died, another
Who is then born is really another.

VIII: 99 If another should protect himself
Against his own suffering,
When a pain in the foot is not in the hand,
Why should one protect the other?

VIII: 100 One might say that even though it makes no sense,
One acts this way because of self-grasping.
That which makes no sense with regard to self or to others
Is precisely the object you should strive to abandon!

Finally, and perhaps most germane to the present topic, neither the self nor others, nor the relations of identity or difference among persons, nor even the suffering to be eliminated, exist ultimately. All are conventional. But that conventional status is not a reason *not* to take suffering seriously. It is, on the other hand, a reason to take *all* suffering seriously. Conventional reality, as we saw in chapter 4 above, is not, from a Madhyamaka point of view, *unreality*. It is, instead, the only way that things can be real. But once we see that, we see that all suffering has precisely this kind of reality, and hence precisely the same claim on us. *Care* is therefore the only appropriate reaction to the actual mode of existence both of sentient beings and their mode of being in the world. It is the only rational mode of *mitsein* and hence of *dasein*.

To fail to take another's suffering seriously as a motivation for action is hence, Śāntideva argues, itself a form of suffering—a kind of mental illness that manifests in irrationality. This irrationality, I think, goes beyond mere "enlightened self interest." The point is not that I myself would be happier or have more pleasure if other sentient beings were happy, and that this responsive pleasure or happiness should be the motive for action. The irrationality at issue is not the irrationality of acting against my own hedonic self-interest. Instead, Śāntideva thinks, (again, anticipating Sidgwick) it is the irrationality of failing to be able to give a reason for any distinction between the treatment of similar cases. Once I grasp the fact that suffering is bad, that is by itself a reason for its alleviation. It is therefore simply irrelevant whose suffering it is.[25]

Care, grounded in the awareness of our individually ephemeral joint participation in global life, Śāntideva argues, is hence the wellspring of the motivation for the development of all perfections, and the most reliable motivation for morally decent actions. This is why of all of the *brahmavihāras*, or divine states, it is located so centrally in the Mahāyāna framework. Care is also, on the Mahāyāna view, the direct result of a genuine appreciation of the essencelessness and interdependence of all sentient beings.[26] And this is so simply because *egoism*—its contrary—is rational if, and only if, there is something very special, very independent about the self, something that could justify the distinction between my suffering or well-being and that of others as a motive for action.

Care hence emerges not as a positive phenomenon, but as the absence of the irrational egoism born of taking the self to exist ultimately, and to be

25. It might appear that this is a direct challenge to a Humean theory of motivation, according to which desire and belief are jointly necessary to motivate action, as egocentric desire is explicitly rejected here as a defensible motive. But that might be a bit too swift. For in Buddhist moral psychology we can distinguish between *desire*, which is always egocentric, and *aspiration*, which is disinterested. The latter is just as conative as desire, but represents a positive orientation to action simply because of the good that it does, emerging from a morally appropriate engagement with the world. Now, a typical Humean might deny that this is possible; that is a matter for debate in moral psychology. But if it is possible, then, if we take the core of the Humean doctrine of motivation not to be that belief must join with desire per se to motivate action, but simply with a non-doxastic conative state, the account might still be Humean.

26. Hence Candrakīrti's homage to *care* in the opening verses of *Introduction to the Middle Way*:

> Kindness itself is the seed of the abundant harvest of the conquerors,
> The rain that nourishes it over time,
> And the ripening agent that yields the bounty.
> For this reason, I begin by praising care! (I:2)

Here Candrakīrti emphasizes the role of care as the motivation and the cause for the development of wisdom and other moral qualities, as that which sustains moral development, and, in its perfected state, as the consequence of the development of those qualities.

an object of special concern, just as emptiness is not a positive phenomenon, but the absence of intrinsic nature. The parallel of this account to that of Schopenhauer in *On the Basis of Morality*—perhaps the most unjustly neglected moral treatise in the Western tradition—is intriguing.

As I noted above, this transformation of vision, and consequent transformation of mode of being, even though it both conduces to and issues from a direct understanding of ultimate reality, and an understanding of the relation between this ultimate reality and conventional reality, amounts not to seeing a distinct truly existent reality *behind* a world of illusion, but rather to coming to see a world about which we are naturally deceived just as it is, not being taken in by the cognitive habits that issue in that deception. For this reason, just as the historical Buddha emphasized that one's view of the nature of reality is a moral matter, Śāntideva, in his analysis of an awakened life, urges that our metaphysics and epistemology is central to our moral lives. And it is partly for this reason that ethics is so deeply implicated in conventional reality. There is no other reality in which it can be grounded, and all that good metaphysics can ever deliver in the end is a precise understanding of the nature of conventional reality.

I have been emphasizing throughout this chapter the roots of Buddhist ethics in Buddhist metaphysics and phenomenology. This view of the conventional but nonetheless fundamentally important status of ethics is no exception. It has its roots in the earliest Mahāyāna literature. Nāgārjuna makes the same point in a metaphysical register in *Fundamental Verses on the Middle Way* XXIV:

8. The Buddha's teaching of the Dharma
Is based on two truths:
A truth of mundane convention
And an ultimate truth.

9. Those who do not understand
The distinction between these two truths
Do not understand
The Buddha's profound teaching.

10. Without depending on the conventional truth
The meaning of the ultimate cannot be taught
Without understanding the meaning of the ultimate,
Nirvana is not achieved.

Nāgārjuna here warns against the disparagement of the conventional in favor of the ultimate in the metaphysical domain and reminds us that the understanding of ultimate truth does not replace, but rather depends upon our grasp of conventional truth. He is, of course, on the way to an account a few verses later of the nonduality of the two truths. But at this point, he is emphasizing not their *unity*, but their *difference*. The conventional is the domain of conceptual thought, of objectification, of language and of intention. The ultimate transcends all of that. But one cannot achieve transcendence (especially that transcendence that amounts to a return to immanence) without a firm grasp of the immanent world to be transcended (and re-affirmed).

Śāntideva makes the same point in the ethical register. We might be tempted to disparage ordinary ethical life, or the ordinary motivations for ethical life—a better life for ourselves and those around us, less suffering, a clearer understanding of reality, the possibility of advancement of our most fundamental projects and values—because all of that is ultimately empty, and because the only *real* values are unconditional ultimate values. But that impulse to disparagement must be resisted for two reasons. First, we are on our way to a nondual understanding of the relation between the ultimate and the mundane, and so to disparage the latter is to disparage the former. But more importantly, the state of transcendence that one might think can validate all values can only be achieved through conventional engagement in conventional actions, directed by conceptually involved, hence conventional intention. This is the domain of the path, and this is the domain of ethics. If we disparage this, we have no ethical world left. In the end, a conventional account of ethics, and a conventional ground of ethical motivation, must be accepted, simply because that is the only ethical domain that makes any sense.

This does not, however, amount to an abandonment of a commitment to serious ethical principles, of a distinction between right and wrong, or a descent into trivial relativism. Just as conventional truth requires and enables a distinction between truth and falsity, it enables a distinction between paths that lead to liberation and those that do not, and a distinction between actions, attitudes and states of character that are consistent with a correct understanding of the world and those that are not. The eightfold noble path is ennobling because of the kinds of beings we are and because of the way the world is, not optionally, not ultimately, but conventionally.

The bodhisattva path is the means to cultivate a liberative way of being in the world because of the kinds of beings we are, and because of the nature of reality. Ethical engagement then requires us to take our ultimate nature and the ultimate nature of reality seriously. But to take our emptiness and the emptiness of all around us seriously is to take our conventional reality and the conventional reality of the world seriously. To take the conventional world seriously is to take seriously the distinction between conventional truth and conventional falsehood and to do so in all domains, including the ethical. To take the conventional world seriously is therefore to take ethical considerations to be conventional, and hence to be as serious as any concerns could ever be.

Let us return now to the question of the relation between Buddhist moral theory and the great Western systems with which we began. We started this chapter by considering a generalization of the *Euthyphro* problem. That is a question in the end about the priority in explanation of moral phenomena that may well be biconditionally connected. That is, it might be, for instance, that an action is recommended by consequentialism if, and only if, it is one that a virtuous person would perform, or that an action is deontologically obligatory if, and only if, it maximizes utility. We might still wonder, though: Is it the consequences that explain why the action is virtuous, or the fact that it is virtuous that explains why it has such wonderful consequences? Is an action obligatory because it maximizes utility? Or does it manage to maximize utility because it is obligatory? We have now added a new dimension to this problem, and the Buddhist analysis suggests a bold answer to this generalized *Euthyphro* problem. For another way of understanding the good is that it is the mode of engagement that emerges from an awakened experience of the world, and a mode of engagement that reflects that awakened awareness.

The Buddhist answer to the problem of explanatory priority is this: the states of character, the actions and the principles we find morally praiseworthy are those of the person whose experience of the world is awakened. That experience, or comportment toward the world, is valuable, on this view, for a straightforwardly epistemological reason: It gets things right, reflecting an awareness of selflessness, impermanence and interdependence, and an attunement to suffering, its causes and the ways of alleviating it. In turn, the virtues we value are the states of character manifested by one who engages with reality in this way; the actions we value are those motivated by those virtues. Those virtues are praiseworthy, but not because of the life they reflect, but because of the experience in which they are grounded; those actions indeed conduce to the reduction of suffering and the increase of happiness, but their value derives from the experience they evidence. Morality, on this view, is a matter of how we see the world, each other and ourselves; moral cultivation is the cultivation of an appropriate engagement with reality.

I have been emphasizing thus far the ways in which a Buddhist voice in contemporary ethics discourse would be *distinctive*, in particular in offering a different way of approaching ethics, through a moral phenomenology. Our current discourse can be enriched by expanding the kinds of questions we ask about morality, and by envisioning different goals for moral practice and *paedaia*. In particular, we can focus more on moral *perception* and the development of the relevant skills and sensitivities that enable moral engagement that enframe moral discourse and decision-making. This can lead both to greater effectiveness where immediate spontaneous response is demanded, as well as to more sensitive engagement in complex moral discourse regarding dilemmas and policy. But it is also important to be cognizant of the *affinities* between Buddhist moral theory and Western moral theory, for these allow us to see where there is common ground, basis for an easier entrée into this different approach. In this vein, I would point to the work of David Hume and other British sentimentalists.

Hume emphasizes in Books II and III of the *Treatise* the degree to which our passions determine how we see ourselves and others, and the degree to which moral education—that of our children by their parents, and of all of us by our collective social and discursive practices—consists in training our passions so that we come to see ourselves and others *differently*, in ways that facilitate such virtues as justice and benevolence, to which Buddhist theorists might refer as *śīla* (proper conduct) and *karuṇā* (care). For Hume to enter into a moral community is to extend the kind of concern nature determines we extend to ourselves and those near us to others more distant, and he emphasizes that to undertake this discipline, to develop this second nature, is a rational thing to do. It makes our lives individual lives better by making our collective lives better.

In arguing that reason is a "slave of the passions" (415), Hume emphasizes that the attempt to reduce morality to a set of principles to which one can be compelled to assent, or even to encapsulate its contents in such a form, is futile, in part because the domain is so irregular, but also because the transformative power we desire from morality requires a deeper form of transformation than reason can deliver. But in arguing that it is rational to engage in that deeper transformation, Hume locates morality as a good we can defend, and that we can understand. The Buddhist perspective I have been offering is not so far from this, although the moral psychology that underlies it is one Hume might not recognize.

This is not to say that Buddhist ethics is Humean ethics. It is rather to say that, to the extent that we find Hume a useful partner in contemporary ethical discussions, as, for instance Annette Baier (1985, 1995, 2008, 2009, 2010a, 2010b, 2011) has urged he is, we can find Buddhist moral theorists to be partners as well. Their approach is not so different from his to be utterly alien, but different enough to provide something new.

# 10 METHODOLOGICAL POSTSCRIPT

A late colleague of mine—a very prominent Anglophone philosopher, I might add—once accosted me at a conference, arguing that my attention to Asian philosophy is entirely a waste of time. He argued as follows: Either Asian philosophy is just the same as Western philosophy or it is different. If it is the same, we can learn all we need to learn philosophically from the West and not trouble ourselves learning to read difficult languages and texts written in unfamiliar styles and idioms. Why bother, if all of that effort leads us to what we already have? On the other hand, if it really is all that different (as he suspected) it isn't really *philosophy* at all, but rather some form of religious discourse or an oracular "wisdom tradition." If that is the case, then while it makes all the sense in the world for anthropologists or philologists or religious studies scholars to read that material, there is no reason for a *philosopher* to do so. Philosophy is what we do in *our* departments, in the Western tradition. That other stuff is, in virtue of being *different*, not *philosophy*. In either case, no Western philosopher should waste his (*sic.*) time reading Asian philosophy.

This book is an extended reply to that screed. I have been arguing that contemporary philosophy cannot continue to be practiced in the West in ignorance of the Buddhist tradition. It is too rich, too sophisticated to be disparaged. Its concerns overlap with those of Western philosophy too broadly to dismiss it as irrelevant. Its perspectives are sufficiently distinct that we cannot see it as simply redundant. Close enough for conversation; distant enough for that conversation to be one from which we might learn. In short, if you have followed me this far, I hope that you agree that to continue to ignore Buddhist philosophy (and by extension, Chinese philosophy, non-Buddhist Indian philosophy, African philosophy, Native American philosophy...) is indefensible. This is an argument for engagement. But it isn't, except by a few examples, a discussion of *how* to engage. It is with that topic that I now conclude.

## 1. The Hermeneutical Predicament

In the Mahāyāna version of the *Sūtra on the Occasion of the Entry of the Buddha into Final Nirvāṇa (Mahāyāna Mahāparinirvāṇa-sūtra)*, the Buddha famously enunciates the four reliances: "Rely on the teaching, not the teacher; rely on the meaning, not the words; rely on the definitive, not that which requires further interpretation; rely on direct insight, not conceptuality." That would seem to make Buddhist philosophy and interpretation easy: all we need to do in order to engage successfully with the Buddhist philosophical tradition is to use our non-conceptual insight to read definitive texts, attending precisely to what they mean. But of course, that's not so easy. And why it's not so easy to implement the four reliances indicates some of why it's not so easy to say what we are in fact doing when we engage philosophically with the Buddhist tradition.

When we pick up a text—any text, no matter where or when it is composed, or what it is about—all we have are words. Meanings do not lie on the pages but are at best indicated by what does lie thereon. Perhaps meaning lies ready for archeological excavation in the mind of a long-dead author; perhaps it emerges in the sustained engagement with the text by a scholastic commentarial tradition; perhaps it emerges in our own contemporary interrogation of the text, informed not only by that tradition, but by our own horizon of philosophical prejudices and interpretative practices. The terrible thing, though, is this: whatever our hermeneutic methodological prejudices, we must rely on the words to find the meaning, even if that meaning eventually releases us from the thrall of the words themselves.

And how do we choose the definitive from that which requires interpretation? Traditional Buddhist commentators often provide us with doxographies that purport to do the job; but of course there are rival doxographies, and choice between them can only be based on interpretation. So even to know what is definitive requires that we interpret. The admonition to choose the definitive is thus the empty advice to buy low, sell high. And as for insight over conceptual thought, so often valorized in canonical Buddhist hermeneutical thought: that might work at the end of the path, but nowhere along the way. All *we* can do is read, interpret and argue. So, the four reliances, rather than giving us guidance, only indicate the depth of our predicament as readers and as philosophers.

Despite these formidable obstacles, the last few decades have seen an explosion in interest in *doing* Buddhist philosophy. Dozens of articles in journals such as *Philosophy East and West, Journal of Indian Philosophy, Journal of the International Association of Buddhist Studies, Asian Philosophy* and *Sophia* might be cited. But I also note monographs and anthologies such as Arnold (2008, 2012), Cowherds (2011), D'Amato, Garfield and Tillemans (2009), Goodman (2009), Patil (2009), Tillemans (1999), Siderits (2007), Westerhoff (2009), Coseru (2012), Ganeri (2007, 2011, 2012), Ganeri and Carlisle (2010), Carpenter (2014) to name but a few salient examples. By "doing Buddhist philosophy," I do not mean developing an account of the history of Buddhist philosophy—the exegetical project of figuring out what Buddhist philosophers said. Nor do I mean the mere assessment of the cogency of Buddhist philosophical arguments. Instead, I mean the attempt to address serious philosophical problems, of interest in their own right, some arising from the Buddhist tradition itself, some from the West, in conversation with the Buddhist tradition, taking it seriously as a source of puzzles and of insights, and taking its horizon of concerns seriously as a backdrop for philosophical reflection. That is what I hope to have demonstrated to be possible and valuable in the preceding chapters.

To take those different horizons seriously is perhaps most important, for what marks philosophical traditions one from another most clearly is not what texts they comprise, or what theses they advance, but rather what concerns are salient; what questions are important; what counts as a problem or a solution. It is only in the last half century, with a minor explosion only in the last quarter century, that Western philosophy has taken seriously a Buddhist horizon, in which the problem of suffering frames philosophical reflection; in which interdependence is a default metaphysical position; in which questions concerning the nature of emptiness, the two truths and their relation to one another are central; and in which questions concerning *pramāṇa* structure epistemology. This nascent literature takes the problems arising within that horizon as genuine and compelling philosophical problems, and takes the insights and critiques offered by others who have worked within that tradition as a source for solutions or refutations. This is what marks contemporary Buddhist philosophy. I reflect in what follows on how that is possible and how it is to be done.

I began this chapter by indicating the familiar predicament of understanding, a hermeneutical predicament that arises in any philosophical reflection and in any historical engagement with any intellectual tradition. But there is a second hermeneutical problem facing those of us who would think philosophically with classical Buddhist texts, and who would do so by self-consciously reaching across traditions. What exactly are we doing? If we are just doing *philosophy*, relying, as it were, on the teaching, not the teacher, why are we worried about what a bunch of old books say? We could simply address philosophical questions on their own, taking the most recent issues of professional journals as determining the state of play from which we depart. On the other hand, if we are just doing the *history of philosophy*, then why do we care about truth, cogency or contemporary issues? All that would seem to matter is what the texts themselves *say*.

Note that this methodological puzzle has nothing specific to do with *Buddhist* philosophy, per se. Instead, it is a general problem for that sub-discipline of philosophy we call "the history of philosophy." The question, "Why, and how, do we read Plato or Aristotle?" is no different in principle from "Why, and how, do we read Nāgārjuna?" Nonetheless, the answer to the more specific question, "What are we doing when we engage philosophically with the Buddhist tradition?" forces us to face the often-unacknowledged scholasticism of Western philosophy, even as it is practiced today. While we often take ourselves to be asking abstract questions that arise from pure, context-free reflection, this is serious false consciousness.

Our philosophical questions emerge from our engagement with our tradition, and are answered often by judicious revisiting of the insights proffered by our predecessors. While this fact may escape us pre-reflectively, and while many who identify themselves as "analytic philosophers" might deny it, it is painfully obvious to some of us that the questions we pose and the range of answers we take seriously emerge from a specific intellectual tradition. Sometimes in order to see that the ideas and intuitions we take as bedrock are not transcendental facts, it is necessary to follow Nietzsche in a genealogy of our thought, to discover the historical roots of our thought, and thereby to see the singularity or even arbitrariness of that we take to be necessary, or to see how our current arguments recapitulate those of our intellectual forbears. This is why the discipline of philosophy must contain its own history. Without it, we don't even know what we are doing, or why. Our engagement with Buddhist philosophy is hence not novel in its attention to a *tradition* in the development of a philosophical problematic, but only in its extension of our purview beyond Europe and its diaspora.[1]

1. Now, to be sure, there are philosophers who would reject this historicist reading of our discipline, and who see philosophy as an ahistorical search for the truth in which contemporary philosophy has no more connection to its history than does physics. I find this self-understanding very foreign, although I know many who adopt it. Even on that view, however, to the extent that one takes the history of Western philosophy to be a legitimate or an important domain of study for philosophers (and I don't know anybody who disputes

The extension of the history of philosophy across cultural boundaries, however, does introduce problems of its own. Some are philological in character. To take a textual tradition such as the Buddhist tradition seriously is to undertake the serious task of figuring out what the texts are, how best to understand and to translate key terms, and how to adjudicate difficult questions of authorship, influence, and other such matters. These are non-trivial problems, and while they certainly emerge even in classical Western scholarship, they emerge with particular poignancy when we cross so many centuries and deal with so many languages. Context becomes harder to establish; intertextual relations are harder to discern; translation is simply more difficult. When we resolve to cross traditions in this way, we undertake to treat these obstacles seriously, and as opportunities for further philosophical insight.

As philosophers engaged in this enterprise, we owe our philologist colleagues debts of gratitude and considerable deference. But beyond the thorny hermeneutical problems to which we will shortly return, and the philological problems we will set aside for present purposes, there are significant problems in the choice of modes of textual engagement. For instance, we sometimes encounter in the Buddhist traditions texts that urge us to transcend reason and conceptual thought. Should we set reason and conceptuality aside as we read them? If so, how? When we address texts whose *authors* grasp only a classical Indian categorical logic, is it appropriate to avail *ourselves* of the tools of modern mathematical logic? And when we address texts that take certain possibilities or certainties for granted, such as the possibility of full awakening, or the probative value of non-conceptual insight, can *we* take them for granted when we read those texts, or can we make sense of those texts if we set these ideas aside? We will return to these questions below, but let us begin with another question of engagement: Buddhist hermeneutics is avowedly a hermeneutic of authorial intent, even if authorship and intentionality are often very differently understood in that tradition. Can we follow that interpretative path in good faith?

## 2. Hermeneutics and Intent

If we turn to the Buddhist tradition for guidance, we find ourselves admonished to interpret texts in order to determine authorial intent. If the text is *Buddhavacana* (taken to be the speech of the historical Buddha), we are after the intention of the Buddha. When Candrakīrti comments on Nāgārjuna or on Āryadeva, he is clear that he takes himself to be illuminating the author's

*that)* it is, I hope, clear that to restrict that study to the history of *Western* philosophy is irresponsible.

intent. And indeed there are many contemporary commentators who take themselves to be doing much the same thing. Gombrich (2009) is a good example of a scholar who takes himself to be revealing precisely *what the Buddha thought.* But many of us have become suspicious of this undertaking, and however much we might take ourselves to be the inheritors and propagators of a Buddhist commentarial tradition (and for many of us, that is a very great extent), we part with that tradition in its self-understanding.

This departure from a hermeneutic of authorial intent is motivated by several considerations. First, with the texts we are considering, it is sometimes hard to identify authors beyond names that have no more referential force than the definite description "the author of this text." (Though to be sure, there are also many cases where we in fact know quite a bit about authors.) Foucault's (1982) insight that often the author is a mere function created to unify a corpus is apposite here. That is, when we are trying to interpret a text, our only access to what an author, or a group of authors, might have meant by the words we are trying to understand is often those words themselves, or perhaps the words of other texts. Indeed, to the extent that we might think that we have independent access to the intention of an author, that access is almost always through other words. Escaping from the evidence of signs to non-semiotic evidence regarding the meaning of those signs is often simply impossible.

We often, for instance, hear Nāgārjuna identified as "the author of the six treatises of reasoning," or something like that, prior to a speculation regarding whether he is really the author of some other text. And there are serious debates about whether there were two, three or even more Nāgārjunas. If all we know of an author is his authorship, and if we are often not even sure of which texts a single shadowy individual is the author, how are we to pretend that in ascribing an intention we are doing more than figuring out what the texts mean to the best of our ability? We do not, as would many of our more canonical colleagues, sort matters out by assigning texts to authors merely on the authority of classical categories, and then employ a canonical view of the author's intentions in order to interpret them; nor do we sort them into canonical doxographic categories, imposing a view on the author in virtue of his supposed affiliation. To do so only raises the same methodological problem one level up in a hermeneutical hierarchy.[2]

All *suttas/sūtras*, even the Mahāyāna *sūtras*, are traditionally taken to be composed by the Buddha himself (or at least recited in his presence and

2. One is reminded here of Huxley's alleged quip that the author of the *Iliad* is either Homer, or if not, someone else of the same name!

approved by him). But of course he wrote nothing at all. The Pāli *suttas* purport to be the written record of oral teachings presented centuries before their literary ossification. There is so much opportunity for deliberate or accidental editorial intervention or pure creation that divination of the intent of an author of the discourses that lie behind these texts, especially at the remove at which we now stand, would be an impossible task. This situation is bad enough to discredit such a hermeneutical method. But things get worse. When we turn to *sūtra* and tantra literature, the authorship attributions are so murky as to be useless. We know that the Mahāyāna *sūtras* were written centuries after the death of their ascribed author and know nothing about their actual authors. (Even if you believe that they were composed by the Buddha and entrusted to the *nāgas*, we need to worry about the fidelity of ancient undersea preservation techniques!) Intention-attribution here is even more quixotic a practice.[3]

The impossibility of determining authorial intent for most of the Buddhist philosophical texts with which we engage is hence principled. In the case of *sūtra* material, we have no idea who the authors were; and even in the case of many scholastic treatises, we know little more than a name. Many texts, despite ascription to a single author, in fact coalesce over centuries through the contributions and editing of many unknown scholars who may have disagreed among themselves regarding the content of the texts. Some of these texts exist in multiple versions, rendering even the identity conditions for a text problematic. In these cases, to figure out what intention lies behind a text is no more or no less than to work out an interpretation of the text. There is often no extratextual evidence that could be brought to bear, and so whoever put quill to palm leaf falls out of the interpretative equation entirely. And once again, even when we do have an author, we often know no more about him than that he authored the text in question, and hence an identified author is no better than no author at all.[4]

This is not to deny that these texts had authors, but to point out that first that we often don't know who, or how many people, wrote the texts we had in

3. To be sure, there are well-known cases of Indian texts, particularly the Vedas, being preserved orally with astonishing fidelity, but we have no independent evidence that a similar textual practice preserved the oral teachings of Śakyamuni Buddha.

4. Note that although it may appear to be, this refusal of a hermeneutic of authorial intent is not inconsistent with a neo-Gricean theory of meaning, according to which understanding a speaker's intent is essential to understanding an utterance. For when we read these texts, no speakers are present. Instead, we *construct*, or *posit* a speaker to whom we *assign* a Gricean intention. It is the fact that this speaker or author is our construction, and that the only evidence we have on the basis of which to construct that authorial voice is what is on the page, that constitutes the truth of the Gadamerian approach, *even if* one is a Gricean about utterance meaning.

front of us. Nor is it to deny that those authors meant something by the words they wrote. It is only to say that whether one adopts an interpretative theory according to which the meaning of a text is constituted (at least in part) by authorial intent (and there are many ways to parse this out)[5] In the end, our only access to authorial intent is textual, and so as interpreters of a tradition, we should focus not on the psychology of unknown authors, but on the meanings of the words in front of us.

This inability to locate authors to whom intentions might be ascribed is not necessarily a bad thing. To regard this as hermeneutical tragedy would make sense if we also believed that we would get *more* insight into textual meaning by knowing the intentions of the authors of these texts. But it is not clear that this would help us at all. The reason for this is straightforward. Most of these texts are significant in the first place not because of their *origins*, but because of their *sequelae*. In Buddhist terms, they exist, and are objects of knowledge, precisely because they are *functioning things*, that is, objects with *effects*. The relevant effects are the commentarial traditions they generate, the insight they generate in their readers, the debates they initiate or settle. Therefore, when we ask what these texts mean, it is their effects, rather than their causes, that are most important. And fortunately, given the richness of the Buddhist scholastic traditions, we can often say quite a lot about these effects, and so say quite a lot about textual meaning.

How do we read without attributing intent to shadowy authors? The answer is simple: we read. We interpret the texts we have on the basis of the words they contain and on the basis of the intertextual relations we can determine, relying on the acumen of our philological brothers and sisters for lexical and historical assistance. Our reading and interpretation is constrained not by imagined psychobiography of the authors, but rather by our understanding of the language in which the text is written and the complex web of intertextual relations in which the text in question figures. This is the great hermeneutical advantage we are afforded when we work in a scholastic tradition (or family of scholastic traditions) such as the Buddhist tradition. We are assisted in reading texts, and forced to interpret them in restricted ways, by the commentaries that reflect on them, by the texts they take as their foundations, and by those with which they are in critical dialogue.

Just as in interpreting a text one hermeneutical circle calls upon us to read each passage in the context of the meaning we assign to the whole, even as

5. For an excellent discussion see Avramides (1989). For instance, one does not need to commit to the view that authorial intent is irrelevant (Gadamer 1976, 2004). One might argue that the divination of intent is essential, but that one can only do so by interpreting the text itself (Sellars 1997, Brandom 1998).

we assign meaning to that whole as a function of the meanings of those parts, a second, larger circle, forces us to read each text in a tradition in light of our understanding of the tradition as a whole, even as we assign meaning to that tradition as a function of those we assign to the texts it comprises. There is nothing new here, and no reason to incorporate theories about authorial intent into this procedure.

Moreover, not only does focus on these hermeneutical circles set authors and their intentions aside as interpretative reference points, but it undermines another hermeneutical myth that often haunts Buddhist Studies, that of the *uniqueness* of textual meaning. Debate about how to read texts is an old and healthy practice in every Buddhist tradition, and a practice very much alive today, both in Asia and in the West. The fact that the meaning of any eminent text emerges and develops in the context of commentarial traditions guarantees that meanings will be unstable and multiple.

This means that interpretation does not *settle* meaning—however much that may the aim of each interpreter—but *creates* an ineliminable polyvalence in texts, a polyvalence that must be honestly acknowledged by even the most passionate partisan of any particular reading. To acknowledge this polyvalence, however, as opposed to mere diversity of opinion about a text that nonetheless has a single, determinate meaning, is once again to diverge in hermeneutical practice from most canonical commentators.

Practicing Buddhist philosophy, then, if it is to be done by contemporary philosophers in good faith, is necessarily to diverge in important ways from textual practices on which philosophers in the Buddhist tradition would have insisted. This is but one respect in which Buddhist philosophy must, true to its own commitments, evolve as a constantly changing continuum of texts and textual practices. For once again, whether we are intentionalist or not about meaning, as scholars, we still have only texts before us. This is not to betray the tradition, although some traditionalists might see it that way. Instead, to insist on fossilization even of methodological commitments in the interests of a fetishized authenticity would be the real betrayal. For this reason, we might add, not only do we as Western philosophers benefit from taking Buddhist philosophy seriously, but the Buddhist tradition benefits from engagement with us. Dialogue is a two-way affair.

## 3. Textual Dialogue

There is still an obvious question. Why should we 21st-century philosophers bother reading classical Buddhist texts? Here is one answer, the one I have been trying to make plausible in this book: They make excellent partners in philosophical dialogue. That is to say, they engage with questions and problems in which we are interested, sharing enough common ground for us to understand what they have to say, and contributing enough that is new that we have some reason to listen to it. They invite us to inhabit a new philosophical horizon, different enough from our own to set new questions, and new phenomena in relief, but familiar enough that many of them will be recognizable as philosophical puzzles and insights. That is the nature of real dialogue—not casual conversation, but serious interchange between participants who voluntarily undertake a common task. And so to take someone, whether a person or a text, on as a dialogical partner, is to make a set of dialogical commitments. Without an acknowledgment and respect for these commitments, dialogue in the full sense is impossible. At best, we get a shouting match.

First among those is a commitment to openness, that is, a commitment to treat our partner with *respect*. Openness, or respect, in this case, entails a commitment to the possibility that our interlocutor is *correct* about at least a good deal of what is at issue in the conversation. This is not, of course, the demand to take our interlocutor—whether a live human or an old text—as oracular, or even the demand that we end up agreeing about *anything* at the *end* of the conversation. It is merely the demand that when we read a text (for that is what we care about here) we read with "charity" (Davidson) or an "anticipation of perfection" (Gadamer). We interpret, insofar as we can, consistent with the constraints of philology and canonical holism noted above, the claims in the text so as to make them as true as possible, the arguments so as to make them as compelling as possible, and the broad pictures sketched so as to make them as interesting as possible.

Doing so necessarily requires us often to engage in a delicate tightrope walk between the careful attention to scholastic and textual context that is necessary in order to fix lexical meaning in the first place and the decontextualization that is needed in order to yield truth and contemporary engagement. So, for instance, when we read Candrakīrti's sevenfold analysis of the self in the sixth chapter of *Introduction to the Middle Way*, and we consider his response to the idea that the self is the *shape* of the aggregates, we need both to recognize his response to a particular interlocutor to understand *why* this is an important position to refute, and how Candrakīrti's argument refutes it.

To be sure, it is important to see that Candrakīrti is making this move in the context of an archaic scholastic debate, refuting the position that the self is an abstract entity over and above the aggregates, namely, the way that they are arranged. But it is equally important to see that Candrakīrti is advancing an argument that has a place in present discussions of constitution and identity. He is pointing out that while at any time the aggregates so arranged may *constitute* the basis of designation of an individual's conventional identity, neither they, not their arrangement, nor they so arranged are *identical* to that individual. To note that present debates about constitution and identity would have been unknown to Candrakīrti and his contemporaries is important to the philology, to how we *translate* the argument, but not to philosophical methodology, to how we *interpret* it. Otherwise, we have little to learn.

To take another example, when we read *Reply to Objections* and see Nāgārjuna criticizing Nyāya semantics and epistemology as we did in chapter 7, there is nothing wrong with extrapolating his arguments as general attacks on what we would regard as a Fregean program in natural language semantics or a foundationalism in epistemology, even though these broader categories would have been unavailable to Nāgārjuna. By doing so, we recognize both the historical context and the contemporary relevance of Nāgārjuna's work. If it did not have this contemporary relevance, there would be no *philosophical* reason to engage with his corpus. Moreover, when we appreciate this philosophical relevance, it allows us a new perspective on the history of Indian philosophy, allowing us to see nascent concerns that otherwise might escape notice.

When we ask about the logic that Nāgārjuna employed, or might have endorsed (Garfield and Priest 2003, Priest 2009, Huntington 2007, Garfield 2008), we do not pretend that Nāgārjuna was thinking explicitly about modal logic. But we do think that he implicitly endorsed certain inference patterns and not others. For instance, Nāgārjuna was committed to the use of the *catuṣkoṭi* or tetralemma as a schema for portioning logical space, and so implicitly to a logic involving four valuations (in addition, perhaps, as we saw earlier, to no valuation at all). We also think that he is committed to endorsing some contradictions, and so to a paraconsistent logic. Of course we do not assert that he explicitly said as much, or even that logical theory was part of his problematic. Nonetheless, in conversation with his text, we can make those endorsements explicit so as to make the best overall sense of his text. While some might see this as violence to his work, it is in principle no more violent than Candrakīrti's ascription to him of a commitment to using only *reductio* inference, or a conventional endorsement of the Nyāya *prāmaṇas*, even though none of this is explicit in *Fundamental Verses on the Middle Way*.

Finally, and perhaps most dramatically, in contemporary Yogācāra studies many scholars have turned to reading Vasubandhu, Sthiramati and their followers, and even the *Discourse Unraveling the Thought* not as idealist, but as phenomenological texts (Lusthaus 2003; Mackenzie 2007, 2008). There is overwhelming textual evidence that in India and Tibet these were always regarded as idealistic, and overwhelming textual evidence (viz., the *Twenty Stanzas*) that Vasubandhu took himself to be arguing against the possibility of matter (Schmithausen

2014). But idealism has little traction nowadays, and phenomenology is interesting; moreover, many of the arguments developed in the Yogācāra tradition convert quite naturally into phenomenological analysis, in which context they sustain interpretations that yield rich insight (and indeed connect them in productive ways to much later phenomenological developments in the Chan/Zen tradition).

Some might say that this is so tendentious a reading, so philologically unjustified that it amounts to a distortion of the texts. But this is only textual distortion if one insists that Vasubandhu's texts, or the *Discourse Unravelling the Thought* have unique, fixed meanings. If we take textual polyvalence seriously, however, such a reading is instead the kind of creative textual engagement that marks the best history of Western philosophy as well as the best commentarial work in the Buddhist tradition.

The second dialogical commitment central to serious, respectful conversational engagement is what Ricoeur felicitously called "hermeneutical suspicion." When we engage with an interlocutor, to treat her seriously is not only to credit her, *ab initio*, with cogency and a fair grasp of the truth, but also to credit her with the same attitude toward us. Otherwise the conditions of genuine interchange are not satisfied. That in turn means that we have to treat her as crediting our own cogency and views, even though our views may diverge from her own, and our arguments might lead down paths she would prefer not to tread. And *that* means supposing that we, too, might have some grasp of the truth, and hence that our partner may well be *wrong* about a great deal. That is, in short, while we cannot begin conversation with the assumption that our conversational partner is crazy, or wrong about everything—that we have nothing to learn and everything to teach—nor can we begin by assuming that she is an oracle. That would not be conversation but obeisance.

Transposed to the textual domain, this means that while we strive to get the best, the strongest reading possible from a text consistent with philological and historical fidelity, we cannot treat Buddhist texts as oracular. After all, they disagree with one another, and they were written by fallible human beings in an epistemological context in which a lot less was known about the world than is known now. A hermeneutic of suspicion demands a critical reading in which we locate error and fallacy and diagnose it, just as we locate truth and cogency, and learn from it. This is textual respect. As Aristotle said of Plato and Platonism, "our friends are dear, but the truth is dearer" (*Nicomachean Ethics* 1096a15).

None of this is to provide a recipe for reading, for translating, or for using the texts we encounter in the classical Buddhist scholastic traditions. It is instead to identify the challenges implicit in the project of reading this tradition philosophically, which entails a fusion of our postmodern global horizon and those of the classical Asian Buddhist traditions, a task necessary even for philology, even for translation. Understanding requires such a fusion. We can no more transpose ourselves into the historical context of the texts we read than we can expect their authors to address directly the literature to which we now contribute. But the meaning that emerges in our encounter with and deployment of these texts in our own philosophical activities must be responsive to a new horizon constituted by elements from each. That new horizon is the contemporary stage of a continuous scholastic tradition in which—even if we pretend only to study and to draw from it—we are the most recent, but certainly not the last, participants.

## 4. Learning from Old Books and Dead Robed Men

What do we learn when we inhabit this new horizon? For one thing, we encounter new philosophical problems and new ways of posing those problems. Thinking about metaphysics through the idea of *svabhāva*, for instance, forces us to ask questions distinct from those often asked in the West, and forces us to ask about the interrelations among our own cluster of concepts such as those of *essence, substance, intrinsic properties,* and the like. Are they really independent of one another? How do they connect to causation and to impermanence? Doing epistemology in terms of *pramāṇa* is different from thinking about knowledge as justified true belief.[6] Epistemology may be more easily naturalized in a framework in which epistemic instruments are treated causally, and in which there is no principled distinction drawn between the cognitive and perceptual aspects of knowledge-acquisition. Ethics, I have argued, is constructed differently in Buddhist philosophy. By addressing classical Buddhist texts, we may therefore gain a new window on our own concerns.

Buddhist philosophy introduces us to the fecund—although perhaps, to a Western audience, at first a bit strange—doctrine(s) of the two truths or two realities. The very fact that, as we have seen, the Sanskrit *satya* and Tibetan *bden pa* are equally well translated as *truth* or *reality* raises both philological and philosophical issues worthy of close attention. The precise nature of the truths, the characterization of each, and the account of their relationship to one another are matters of extensive debate and subtle philosophical analysis in the history of Buddhist philosophy. This extensive literature involves

6. Stoltz (2007), for instance, argues that Gettier problems may not arise in this context (although it is arguable that Śrīharṣa does indeed develop a version of the Gettier problem [Ganeri 2007]).

Buddhist theorists in sophisticated investigation into the nature of truth itself and of reality, and into equally sophisticated investigation of the relation between language, truth, thought and reality. I do not want to claim here that this tradition of inquiry is necessarily philosophically *more* sophisticated than that developed in the West (or, for that matter, that it is *less* sophisticated), only that the framework of the debate is sufficiently different that Western philosophers can learn from it, while the problematic is sufficiently similar to that of Western philosophy that Western philosophers would benefit from that learning.

Addressing the Buddhist canons also forces us to think explicitly about, and even to revise, our normal textual practices. Our attention is drawn in this tradition to the role of commentary to a greater degree than it is in much contemporary philosophy. The difficulty of mapping important philosophical terms in Asian languages to terms of art in European languages forces us to confront not only questions about translation itself, but also the arbitrariness of certain distinctions or absences thereof. For example, when we worry about translating *pramāṇa*, and realize that it could as well be translated as *warrant, epistemic instrument, warranted cognition*, we must pause regarding the relationship between these terms. We must take seriously an epistemology that combines a kind of process reliabilism with a naturalistic psychology of knowledge, and allow the epistemic categories and questions that frame that tradition call into question those that frame our own. When we consider *essence, substance, intrinsic nature*, or some neologism as translations of *svabhāva*, similar questions arise. Is there a single concept or a cluster of concepts here, as the Buddhist might take there to be, or a confusion of ideas that need to be kept distinct, as some Western philosophers would argue?

*Karma (action, object of action, consequence of action), dharma (truth, entity, fundamental constituent, virtue, duty, doctrine...)* and other essential Buddhist terms of art each raise a host of similar issues. Each draws together what appears from a Western point of view to be a vast semantic range into what appears from a Buddhist perspective to be a semantic point. Translation, and the cross-cultural encounter in which it plays such a central role, thus forces us to reconsider, and to appreciate the somewhat arbitrary character of, our own fundamental philosophical vocabulary and the topology of our conceptual apparatus.

We also encounter philosophical texts composed in forms that challenge our sense of what an argument looks like, texts composed in highly allusive verse, for instance, or arguments framed from the standpoint of doxography. All of this is a good thing—stretching our conceptual boundaries and methodological perspective. Reading texts that are often antinomian, or at least highly suspicious of the role of reason and language in human cognitive life, also raises significant and difficult methodological questions about the role of reason and of reasoning in philosophical practice. Is it permissible, or appropriate, to take reason as a transcendental condition of the possibility of philosophical inquiry? After all, if a text argues that reason and conceptual thought inevitably distort reality, and that the truth is inexpressible, eschewing reason as probative, is it appropriate for us to demand arguments, or even to seek for them in the text, to assess them, or to mobilize arguments of our own in understanding those texts?

This is an intriguing challenge. Huntington (2007), for instance, answers in the negative, arguing that to employ reason, and in particular, the techniques of logic, to interpret or to criticize texts that reject the probative force of logic and rational arguments is to do violence to those texts, begging the question against them in the very act of interpreting them. I have argued in (2008) that this is wrong. Even arguments against the probative force of logic must use logic; even claims to the non-discursivity of certain knowledge must themselves be discursive, and even if we read texts to offer these arguments, even if we accept their conclusions, our arguments for those readings, and even for the correctness of those conclusions must themselves be discursive, rational, and probative. Reason is thus a transcendental condition of interpretation both in the sense that we can only vindicate an interpretation to the extent that we read the text as rational, and we can only justify a reading rationally. Paradoxically, this is true even if, on the most antinomian reading of these texts, they are correct in their radical critique of reason itself. (See Dreyfus and Garfield as well as Dreyfus in Cowherds 2011.)

## 5. Reflexivity: Reading Our Own Texts

A pernicious version of the subject–object duality that Buddhism targets so assiduously arises quite naturally in Buddhist Studies itself, and demands vigilance. That is the conceit that we as contemporary Western scholars are writing *about* the scholastic Buddhist tradition, and that our own texts are to be read in a fundamentally different way from the canonical texts we interpret. We thus set ourselves up as privileged subjects writing hermeneutically closed texts that illuminate the Buddhist philosophical tradition with the cool light of scholarly objectivity. This is doubly dangerous. On the one hand, it hides the intertextuality and scholastic context of our own texts, their liability to interpretation by others and their own polyvalence. On the other hand, it fossilizes the Buddhist tradition as a complete, mummified object of primarily curatorial interest. Each of these errors cuts off dialogue. We expect to be heard, but not to be interrogated; our presumed interlocutor is the object only of an epitaph.

In fact nothing could be further from the truth. The Buddhist philosophical tradition is so fascinating in large part because it is alive, because the discussions that proceed in our own time and the texts we and others publish are not *about*, but are moments *within* that tradition, extending the practice of critical reflection, reinterpretation and dialogue that has characterized the tradition from the very beginning. We sometimes do what Candrakīrti and Śāntarakṣita did, sometimes what Śaṅkara or Gaṅgeśa did. We just have more hair, wear different clothes and speak in strange tongues. And of course there are many living, practicing Buddhist philosophers—Asian and Western—who see the Buddhist tradition as constituting the primary horizon of their own philosophical practice. Contemporary Buddhist philosophical thought thus reflects the fact that the continuum of Buddhist thought, like the personal continuum, is neither permanent nor terminated; it is a constantly changing, dependently originated sequence of dialectical events, beginning in the indefinite past, and stretching into an indefinite future.

The contemporary dialogue of Buddhist thought with Western textual traditions, Western hermeneutical methods and presuppositions, Western science and Western academic practice is thus, while new in one sense, old in another. It is new in that the conversational partner and the cultural context are new, only about 150 years old. For this reason, we are still feeling each other out, adjusting vocabulary, assimilating conceptual categories and scholarly presuppositions. Hence the present project.

But it is also old. While it is true that Buddhism officially denies its own progressive character, depicting itself as a tradition with roots in an omniscient founder that has been steadily declining from a golden age, as insights are lost in transmission and translation, this self-image is hard to sustain. In fact, Buddhism has been self-reflective, internally complex, and philosophically progressive from the start. Buddhist philosophy has evolved in response to debate with and influence from other traditions from the beginning, including classical Indian traditions, traditions from East Asia, and more recently from the West. While the teachings of the Buddha obviously form the foundation for this vast and diverse scholastic edifice, it is equally obvious that many of the later developments in Buddhism that we now regard as so central to Buddhist philosophy were not present in the Pāli canon (including much of the Mahāyāna), even if they were somehow, or to some degree, implicit. Buddhist philosophy, like all philosophy, has developed and become more sophisticated over time. This is as it should be—it is a sign of life, not of weakness.

A corollary of this fact is that the impact of Buddhist philosophy on the West is both old and new. It is old in that, first, Buddhism has transformed many civilizations and intellectual traditions in the past, and there is no reason to expect that that should cease now, and in that, second, the Western tradition has never been closed, Eurocentric commentators to the contrary notwithstanding. But it is new in that, perhaps with the exception of some early interaction mediated by Bactria, until the nineteenth century, the Buddhist tradition has not been one of its principal sources of ideas. (See McEvilley 2002 for an excellent history of the interaction of early Buddhist and Mediterranean thought.) That, however, is a rather insignificant matter in the grand scheme of intellectual history.

While all of this history of ideas may seem to be nothing but truisms, it is nonetheless worth bearing in mind as we find our way in contemporary Buddhist philosophy. It is important to distinguish between the role of a curator of philosophical mummies and that of the role of a participant in an ongoing dialogue, and it is all too easy, for instance to treat Śāntarakṣita as a distant, isolated curio, while treating Aristotle as one of us. When we do that, we distinguish living philosophy from dead ideas on the basis of an arbitrary criterion of cultural proximity, and in doing so, license an intellectual attitude toward that which we designate as distant that we would never permit toward that which we regard as proximate. Another way of putting this point is that in commenting on Buddhist texts, or in using them for our own philosophical purposes, we must be careful of pretending to transcendence, of adopting a view, if not from *nowhere,* at least from some Archimedean point outside of the tradition we take ourselves to study, permitting an objectivity that we would never ascribe to one within the tradition, and in the end distinguishing ourselves as scholarly subjects from our interlocutors as philosophical native informants.

This reflexivity in practice therefore also demands that we treat our own work and that of our contemporaries in the same way that we treat the older canon. We are participants, not curators. We must thus extend the same principle of charity in reading to contemporary texts, making the best of them, as opposed to constructing the straw men that fuel the bushfires of academic debate. In that way, we can learn from each other's insights, and move Buddhist philosophy along. But we must also approach our own texts and those of our colleagues with the same hermeneutic of healthy suspicion, alert for heresy, apology and all the ills that hermeneutical flesh is heir to.

The Buddhist and Western traditions (and indeed we could say the same of the great Chinese traditions of Confucianism and Daoism) are made for each other, as each is articulated through an open canon, each is internally diverse, each constantly in dialogue both internally and with external critics and interlocutors. Our task as Western Buddhist philosophers (however we understand that deliberately ambiguous phrase) is to do our part to advance both traditions along the increasingly broad and pleasant path they tread together. That won't be so hard, as long as we remember that that is what we are doing.

> Here is the place; here the way unfolds. The boundary of realization is not distinct, for the realization comes forth simultaneously with the mastery of Buddha-dharma.
>
> Do not suppose that what you realize becomes your knowledge and is grasped by your consciousness. Although actualized immediately, the inconceivable may not be apparent. Its appearance is beyond your knowledge.
>
> —*Dōgen, Genjōkōan* (trans. R. Aitken and K. Tanahashi)

# REFERENCES


Anacker, S. (1984). *Seven Works of Vasubandhu*. Delhi: Motilal Banarsidass Publications.

Anscombe, G.E.M. (1975). "The First Person" in S. Guttenplan (ed.), *Mind and Language*, pp. 45–65.Oxford: Clarendon Press.

Aristotle. (1962). *Nicomachean Ethics*. M. Ostwald (trans.). Indianapolis: Bobbs-Merrill Educational Publishing.

Armstrong, D.M. (1968). *A Materialist Theory of the Mind*. New York: Humanities Press.

Armstrong, D.M. (1978). *Universals and Scientific Realism*. Cambridge: Cambridge University Press.

Armstrong, D.M. (1989). *Universals: An Opinionated Introduction*. Boulder: Westview Press.

Armstrong, D.M. (2005). "Four Disputes about Properties," *Synthese* 144:3, pp. 309–320.

Arnold, D. (2008). *Buddhists, Brahmins and Belief*. New York: Columbia University Press.

Arnold, D. (2009). "Dharmakīrti and Dharmottara on the Intentionality of Perception: Selections from the Nyāyabindu (An Epitome of Philosophy)," in Edelglass and Garfield (eds.) (2009), pp. 186–196.

Arnold, D. (2012). *Buddhas, Brains and Believing*. New York: Columbia University Press.

Āryadeva. (2001). *bZhi rgya pa (Catuḥśataka)*. Sarnath: Kargyud Relief and Protection Committee, Central Institute of Higher Tibetan Studies.

Aurobindo, Śri. (2000). *The Future Poetry*. Pondicherry: Sri Aurobindo Ashram Press.

Avramides, A. (1989). *Meaning and Mind: An Examination of a Gricean Account of Language*. Cambridge, MA: MIT Press.

Baier, A. (1985). *Postures of the Mind: Essays on Mind and Morals*. Minneapolis: University of Minnesota Press.

Baier, A. (1991). *A Progress of Sentiments: Reflections on Hume's Treatise*. Cambridge, MA: Harvard University Press.

Baier, A. (1995). *Moral Prejudices: Essays on Ethics*. Cambridge, MA: Harvard University Press.

Baier, A. (2008). *Death and Character: Further Reflections on Hume*. Cambridge, MA: Harvard University Press.

Baier, A. (2010a). *Reflections on How We Live*. New York: Oxford University Press.

Baier, A. (2010b). *The Cautious Jealous Virtue: Hume on Justice*. Cambridge, MA: Harvard University Press.

Baier, A. (2011). *The Pursuits of Philosophy*. Cambridge, MA: Harvard University Press.

Baker, L.R. (1995). *Explaining Attitudes: A Practical Approach to the Mind*. Cambridge: Cambridge University Press.

Baker, L.R. (2000). *Persons and Bodies: A Constitution View*. Cambridge: Cambridge University Press.

Baker, L.R. (2007). *Metaphysics of Everyday Life: An Essay in Practical Realism*. Cambridge: Cambridge University Press.

Bar-On, D. (1993). "Indeterminacy of Translation—Theory and Practice," *Philosophy and Phenomenological Research* 53:4, pp. 781–810.

Bar-On, D. (2004). *Speaking My Mind: Expression and Self-Knowledge*. Oxford: Clarendon Press.

Bartley, C. (2011). *An Introduction to Indian Philosophy*. London, New York: Continuum International Publishing Group.

Belnap, N.D. (1977a). "How a Computer Should Think," *Episteme* 2, pp. 2–37.

Belnap, N.D. (1977b). "A Useful Four-Valued Logic," in J.M. Dunn and G. Epstein (eds.), *Modern Uses of Multiple-Valued Logics*, pp. 8–37. Dordrecht: Reidel.

Berkeley, G. (1947). *Three Dialogues Between Hylas and Philonous*. R.M. Adams (ed.). Indianapolis: Hackett Publishing Company, Inc.

Bermúdez, J.L. (1998). *The Paradox of Self-Consciousness*. Cambridge, MA: MIT Press.

Bhattacharyya, K.C. (1930). *The Subject as Freedom*. Amalner: Indian Philosophical Congress.

Bhushan, N. (2009). "Towards an Anatomy of Mourning," in Bhushan, Garfield and Zablocki (2009), pp. 167–181.

Bhushan, N., J. Garfield and A. Zablocki (eds). (2009). *TransBuddhism: Transmission, Translation, Transformation*. Amherst: University of Massachusetts Press.

Blackmore, S. (2004). *Consciousness: An Introduction*. New York: Oxford University Press.

Bliss, R. (2015). "On the Incompatibility of the Humean Regularity Account of Causation and the Madhyamaka Doctrine of Emptiness." In Deguchi, Garfield, Priest and Tanaka (eds.) (2015).

Block, N. (1995). "On a Confusion about a Function of Consciousness," *Brain and Behavioral Sciences* 18, pp. 227–247.

Block, N., O.J. Flanagan and G. Güzeldere (eds.). (1997). *The Nature of Consciousness: Philosophical Debates*. Cambridge, MA: MIT Press.

Blumenthal, J. (2004). *The Ornament of the Middle Way: A Study of Madhyamaka Thought of Śāntarakṣita*. Ithaca: Snow Lion Publications.

Bogdan, R. (2011). *Our Own Minds: Sociocultural Grounds for Self-Consicousness*. Cambridge, MA: MIT Press.

Braddon-Mitchell, D. (2003). "Qualia and Analytical Conditionals," *The Journal of Philosophy* 100, pp. 111–135.

Braddon-Mitchell, D. and K. Miller. (2006). "Talking about a Universalist World," *Philosophical Studies* 130:3, pp. 499–534.

Bradley, F.H. (1930). *Appearance and Reality*. Oxford: Clarendon Press.

Brandom, R. (1998). *Making It Explicit*. Cambridge, MA: Harvard University Press.

Brefcynski-Lewis, J.A., A. Lutz, H.S. Schaefer, D.B. Levinson and R.J. Davidson. (2007). "Neural Correlates of Attentional Expertise in Long-Term Meditation Practitioners," *Proceedings of the National Academy of Sciences* 104:27, pp. 11483–11488.

Buddhaghosa. (2003). *Visudhimagga: The Path of Purification*. Bhikkhu Nāṇamoli (trans.), Columbo: Pariyatti Publishing.

Cabezón, J.I. (1994). *Buddhism and Language: A Study of Indo-Tibetan Scholasticism*. Albany: State University of New York Press.

Campbell, J. (2004). "The First Person, Embodiment, and the Certainty that One Exists," *The Monist* 87:4, pp. 475–488.

Candrakīrti. (1998). *Rigs pa drug cu pa'i bgrel pa. (Yuktiṣaṣtikavṛtti)*. sDe dge edition of the Tibetan Canon, vol. ya, 1b–30b. Dharamasala: Paljor Press.

Candrakīrti. (2003). *dBu ma rtsa ba'i 'gral pa tshig gsal ba (Prasannapadā)*. Sarnath: dGe lugs pa Student Welfare Committee.

Candrakīrti. (2009). *dBu ma la 'jug pa'i shad pa (Madhyamakāvatāra-bhāṣya)*. Sarnath: Kagyu Relief and Protection Committee.

Candrakīrti. (2012). *Autocommentary on the "Introduction to the Centre."* T. Tsering and J.S. Tillmann (trans.). Varanasi: Sattanam.

Carpenter, A.D. (2014). *Indian Buddhist Philosophy*. London: Routledge.

Carruthers, P. (1996). *Language, Thought, and Consciousness*. New York: Cambridge University Press.

Carruthers, P. (2000). *Phenomenal Consciousness: A Naturalistic Theory*. Cambridge: Cambridge University Press.

Carruthers, P. (2011). *The Opacity of Mind*. New York: Oxford University Press.

Cartwright, T. (1983). *How the Laws of Physics Lie*. Oxford: Clarendon Press.

Cassam, Q. (1997). *Self and World*. New York: Oxford University Press.

Chalmers, D.J. (2010). *The Character of Consciousness*. Oxford, New York: Oxford University Press.

Chan, W.-T. (trans., ed.). (1963). *Sourcebook in Chinese Philosophy*. Princeton: Princeton University Press.

Chatterjee, A. (2011). "Funes and Categorization in an Abstraction-Free World," in Siderits, Tillemans, and Chakrabarti (eds.) (2011), pp. 247–257.

Chi, R.S.Y. (1984). *Buddhist Formal Logic: A Study of Dignāga's Hetucakra and K'uei-chi's Great Commentary on the Nyāyapraveśa*. Delhi: Motilal Banarsidass.

Choi, Y. (2007). "On the Identification of the Daesung Saron Hyeonu Gi," *Journal of Korean History* 136, pp. 1–27.

Churchland, P. (1979). *Scientific Realism and the Plasticity of Mind*. Cambridge: Cambridge University Press.

Churchland, P. (2012). *Plato's Camera: How the Physical Brain Captures a Landscape of Abstract Universals*. Cambridge, MA: MIT Press.

Clifton, C. and M. Hogarth. (1995). "The Definability of Objective Becoming in Minkowski Space-Time," *Synthese* 103, pp. 355–387.

Collins, G. (2010). "Blindsight: Seeing without Knowing It," *Scientific American*, April 22, 2010. http://blogs.scientificamerican.com/observations/2010/04/22/blindsight-seeing-without-knowing-it/.

Conze, E. (trans.) (1973). *The Perfection of Wisdom in Eight Thousand Lines and Its Verse Summary*. San Francisco: Four Seasons Foundation.

Coseru, C. (2012). *Perceiving Reality: Consciousness, Intentionality, and Cognition in Buddhist Philosophy*. New York: Oxford University Press.

Coventry, A. (2007). *Hume: A Guide for the Perplexed*. London: Continuum.

Coventry, A. (2008). *Hume's Theory of Causation*. London: Continuum.

Cowherds. (2011). *Moonshadows: Conventional Truth in Buddhist Philosophy*. New York: Oxford University Press.

Cowherds. (2015). *Moonpaths: Ethics in the Context of Conventional Truth*. New York: Oxford University Press.

Dalai Lama XIV (Tenzin Gyatso). (2001). *Ethics for the New Millenium*. New York: Riverhead.

Dalai Lama XIV (Tenzin Gyatso). (2005). *The Universe in a Single Atom: The Convergence of Science and Spirituality*. New York: Random House.

Damasio, A. (1999). *The Feeling of What Happens*. San Diego: Harcourt.

D'Amato, M., J. Garfield and T. Tillemans. (2009). *Pointing at the Moon: Buddhism, Logic and Analytic Philosophy*. New York: Oxford University Press.

Danckert, J. and Y. Rossetti. (2005). "Blindsight in Action: What Can the Different Sub-Types of Blindsight Tell Us About the Control of Visually Guided Actions?" *Neuroscience and Biobehavioral Reviews* 28:7, pp. 1035–1046.

Davidson, D. (1984a). "Truth and Meaning (1967)," in D. Davidson, *Inquiries into Truth and Interpretation*, pp. 17–36. Oxford: Clarendon Press.

Davidson, D. (1984b). "Radical Interpretation (1973)," in D. Davidson, *Inquiries into Truth and Interpretation*, pp. 125–140. Oxford: Clarendon Press.

Davidson, D. (1984c). "On the Very Idea of a Conceptual Scheme (1974)," in D. Davidson, *Inquiries into Truth and Interpretation*, pp. 183–198. Oxford: Clarendon Press.

Davidson, D. (1984d). "The Method of Truth and Metaphysics (1977)," in D. Davidson, *Inquiries into Truth and Interpretation*, pp. 199–215. Oxford: Clarendon Press.

Deguchi, Y. (2014). "The Logic of Provision: Sānlūn Meets Non-Classical Logic," National Chengchi University-Kyoto University-Yale-NUS College-National University of Singapore Workshop in Asian Philosophy, unpublished manuscript at Kyoto University.

Deguchi, Y., J.L. Garfield and G. Priest. (2008). "The Way of the Dialetheist: Contradictions in Buddhism," *Philosophy East and West* 58:3, pp. 395–402.

Deguchi, Y., J.L. Garfield and G. Priest. (2013a). "Does a Table Have Buddha-Nature? A Moment of Yes and No. Answer! But Not in Words or Signs: A Response to Mark Siderits," *Philosophy East and West* 63:3, pp. 387–398.

Deguchi, Y., J.L. Garfield, and G. Priest. (2013b). "How We Think Mādyamikas Think: A Response to Tom Tillemans," *Philosophy East and West* 63:3, pp. 426–435.

Deguchi, Y., J.L. Garfield, and G. Priest. (2013c). "A Mountain by Any Other Name: A Response to Koji Tanaka," *Philosophy East and West* 63:3, pp. 335–343.

Deguchi, Y., J.L. Garfield, and G. Priest. (2013d). "Those Concepts Proliferate Everywhere: A Response to Constance Kassor," *Philosophy East and West* 63:3, pp. 411–416.

Deguchi, Y., J. Garfield, G. Priest, and K. Tanaka. (2015). *The Moon Points Back: Buddhism, Logic and Analytic Philosophy*. New York: Oxford University Press.

Dennett, D.C. (1978b). "Two Approaches to Mental Images," in D. Dennett, Brainstorms, pp. 174–189. Montgomery, VT: Bradford Books.

Dennett, D.C. (1980). "The Milk of Human Intentionality," *Behavioral and Brain Sciences* 3:3, pp. 428–430.

Dennett, D.C. (1991). *Consciousness Explained.* New York: Little, Brown and Co.

Dennett, D. (2003). "Who's on First? Heterophenomenology Explained," *Journal of Consciousness Studies* 10:9, pp. 19–30.

Derrida, J. (1998). *Of Grammatology*. Baltimore: Johns Hopkins University Press.

Descartes. (2003). *Meditations on First Philosophy*, trans. Cottingham. Cambridge: Cambridge University Press.

Dignāga. *dMigs pa brtag pa'i 'grel pa*. sDe dge. 174: 175–177.

Dignāga. *Tshad ma mdo kun las btus pa (Pramānasammucāya)*. Toh 4204.

Dōgen. (1985). "*Genjōkōan* (Actualizing the Fundamental Point)," in Tanahashi (1985), pp. 69–73.

Dōgen. (2009a). "*Kattō* (Entangled Vines)," S. Heine (trans.) in Edelglass and Garfield (eds.) (2009), pp. 151–156.

Dōgen. (2009b). "*Ōsakusendaba* (A King Requests Saindhava)," S. Heine (trans.) in Edelglass and Garfield (eds.) (2009), pp. 156–158.

Donnelly, M. (2011). "Endurantist and Perdurantist Accounts of Persistence," *Philosophical Studies* 154:1, pp. 27–51.

Dreyfus, G.B.J. (1995). "Meditation as Ethical Activity," *Journal of Buddhist Ethics* 2, pp. 28–54.

Dreyfus, G.B.J. (1997). *Recognizing Reality: Dharmakīrti's Philosophy and Its Tibetan Interpretations*. Albany: State University of New York Press.

Dreyfus, G.B.J. (2003). *The Sound of Two Hands Clapping: The Education of a Tibetan Buddhist Monk*. Berkeley, Los Angeles, London: University of California Press.

Dreyfus, G.B.J. (2011a). "Can a Mādhyamika Be a Skeptic? The Case of Patsab Nyimadrak," in Cowherds (2011), pp. 89–114.

Dreyfus, G.B.J. (2011b). "Apoha as a Naturalized Account of Concept Formation," in Siderits, Tillemans, & Chakrabarti (eds.) (2011), pp. 207–227.

Dreyfus, G.B.J. and S.L. McClintock (eds.). (2003). *The Svātrantika-Prāsaṅgika Distinction*. Boston: Wisdom Publications.

Dreyfus, H. (1991). *Being in the World: A Commentary on Heidegger's Being and Time Division I*. Cambridge, MA: MIT Press.

Dunne, J.D. (2004). *Foundations of Dharmakīrti's Philosophy*. Boston: Wisdom Publications.

Dunne, J.D. (2006). "Realizing the Unreal: Dharmakīrti's Theory of Yogic Perception," *Journal of Indian Philosophy* 34:6, pp. 497–516.

Dunne, J.D. (2011). "Key Features of Dharmakīrti's Apoha Theory," in Siderits, Tillemans, & Chakrabarti (eds.) (2011), pp. 84–108.

Edelglass, W. and J.L. Garfield (eds.). (2009). *Buddhist Philosophy: Essential Readings*. New York: Oxford University Press.

Emmanuel, S.M. (ed.). (2013). *A Companion to Buddhist Philosophy*. West Sussex: John Wiley & Sons.

Evans, G. (1982). *The Varieties of Reference*. Oxford: Oxford University Press.

Farb, N.A.S., Z.V. Segal, H. Mayberg, J. Bean, D. McKeon, Z. Fatima and A.K. Anderson. (2007). "Attending to the Present: Mindfulness Meditation Reveals Distinct Neural Modes of Self-Reference," *Social Cognitive and Affective Neuroscience* 2:4, pp. 313–322.

Fazang. (1963). "A Treatise on the Golden Lion (*Chin-shih-tzu chang*)," in W.-T. Chan (trans., ed.) (1963), pp. 409–414.

Feltz, A. and E. Cokeley. (2013). "Virtue and Consequences: The Folk Against Pure Evaluative Internalism," *Philosophical Psychology* 26:5, pp. 702–717.

Fendrich, R., S. Demirel and S. Danziger. (1999). "The Oculomotor Gap Effect with a Foveal Fixation Point," *Vision Research* 39:4, pp. 833–841.

Ferlinghetti, L. (1958). "The World is a Beautiful Place," in L. Ferlinghetti, *A Coney Island of the Mind*, pp. 108–110. New York: New Directions Books.

Fine, K. (2008). "In Defence of Three-Dimensionalism," *Royal Institute of Philosophy Supplements* 83:62, pp. 1–16.

Finnigan, B. and K. Tanaka. (2010). "Don't Think! Just Act!" in G. Priest and D. Young (eds.), *Philosophy and the Martial Arts: Beating and Nothingness*. Chicago, La Salle: Open Court.

Finnigan, B. and K. Tanaka. (2011). "Carnap's Pragmatism and the Two Truths," in The Cowherds (2011), pp. 181–188.

Fisher, B. and H. Weber. (1993). "Express Saccades and Visual Attention," *Behavioral and Brain Sciences* 16, pp. 553–567.

Fogelin, R.J. (1985). *Hume's Skepticism in the Treatise of Human Nature*. London: Routledge and Kegan Paul.

Foucault, M. (1982). *The Archaeology of Knowledge*. New York: Random House

Franco, E. (1993). "Did Dignāga Accept Four Types of Perception?," *Journal of Indian Philosophy* 30:2, pp. 191–211.

Franco, E. (1997). *Dharmakīrti on Compassion and Rebirth*. Vienna: Weiner Studien zur Tibetologie und Buddhismuskunde.

Franco, E. (ed.) (2009). *Yogic Perception, Meditation and Altered States of Consciousness*. Vienna: Verlag der Österreichischen Akademie der Wissenschaften.

Frauwallner E. (2009). *A History of Indian Philosophy*. New Delhi: Motilal Banarsidass.

Gadamer, H-G. (1976). *Philosophical Hermeneutics*. Berkeley: University of California Press.

Gadamer, H-G. (2004). *Truth and Method*. New York: Continuum Press.

Gallagher, S. (2000). "Philosophical Conceptions of the Self: Implications for Cognitive Science," *Trends in Cognitive Science* 4, pp. 14–21.

Gallagher, S. (2003). "Self-Narrative, Embodied Action, and Social Context," in A. Wiercinski (ed.), *Between Suspicion and Sympathy: Paul Ricoeur's Unstable Equilibrium (Festschrift for Paul Ricoeur)*, pp. 409–423. Toronto: The Hermeneutic Press.

Gallagher, S. (2007). "Neurophilosophy and Neurophenomenology," in L. Embree and T. Nenon (eds.), *Phenomenology 2005*: 5, pp. 293–316. Bucharest: Zeta Press.

Gallagher, S. (2012a). "In Defense of Phenomenological Approaches to Social Cognition: Interacting with the Critics," *Review of Philosophy and Psychology* 3:2, pp. 187–212.

Gallagher, S. (2012b). *The Phenomenological Mind*. New York: Routledge.

Gallagher, S. and D. Zahavi. (2008). *The Phenomenological Mind: An Introduction to the Philosophy of Mind and Cognitive Science*. New York: Routledge.

Ganeri, J. (2007). *The Concealed Art of the Soul: Theories of Self and Practices of Truth in Indian Ethics and Epistemology*. Oxford: Oxford University Press.

Ganeri, J. (2011). *Artha: Meaning*. New Delhi: Oxford University Press.

Ganeri, J. (2012). *The Self: Naturalism, Consciousness, and the First-Person Stance*. New York: Oxford University Press.

Ganeri, J. and C. Carlisle. (2010). *Philosophy as Therapeia: Royal Institute of Philosophy Supplement* 66, pp. 187–218. Cambridge: Cambridge University Press.

Garfield, J.L. (unpublished). "What I Learned from Al MacKay: Meaning, Synonymy and Translation."

Garfield, J.L. (1988). *Belief in Psychology*. Cambridge: MIT Press.

Garfield, J.L. (1990). "Epoché and Sunyatā: Scepticism East and West," *Philosophy East and West* 40:3, pp. 285–307. Reprinted in Garfield (2002a), pp. 3–23.

Garfield, J.L. (1994). "Dependent Co-origination and the Emptiness of Emptiness: Why did Nāgārjuna Begin with Causation?" *Philosophy East and West* 44, pp. 219–250.

Garfield, J.L. (1995). *Fundamental Wisdom and the Middle Way: Nāgārjuna's Mūlamadhyamakakārikā*. New York: Oxford University Press.

Garfield, J.L. (1996). "Casting Out Demons and Exorcising Zombies: Exposing Neocartesian Myths in Frank Jackson's Philosophy of Mind," in P. Dowe, M. Nicholls and L. Shotton (eds.), *Australian Philosophers*, Hobart: Pyrrhro Press, pp. 55–95.

Garfield, J.L. (1998). *Western Idealism and Its Critics*. Hobart: Pyrrho Press.

Garfield, J.L. (2001). "Nāgārjuna's Theory of Causality: Implications Sacred and Profane," *Philosophy East and West* 51:4, pp. 507–524. Reprinted in Garfield (2002a), pp. 69–85.

Garfield, J.L. (2002a). *Empty Words: Buddhist Philosophy and Cross-Cultural Interpretation*. New York: Oxford University Press.

Garfield, J.L. (2002b). "Emptiness and Positionlessness: Do the Mādhyamika Relinquish All Views?," in Garfield (2002a), pp. 42–68.

Garfield, J.L. (2002c). "Sounds of Silence: Ineffability and the Limits of Language in Madhyamaka and Yogācāra," in Garfield (2002a), pp. 170–186.

Garfield, J.L. (2002d). "Temporality and Alterity: Dimensions of Hermeneutic Distance," in Garfield (2002a), pp. 229–250.

Garfield, J.L. (2006a). "Reductionism and Fictionalism: Comments on Siderits," *APA Newsletter on Asian and Comparative Philosophy* 6:*1*, pp. 1–8.

Garfield, J.L. (2006b). "The Conventional Status of Reflexive Awareness: What's At Stake in a Tibetan Debate?" *Philosophy East and West* 56:*2*, pp. 201–228.

Garfield, J.L. (2008). "Turning a Madhyamaka Trick: Reply to Huntington," *Journal of Indian Philosophy* 36:4, pp. 507–527.

Garfield, J.L. (2010/2011). "What Is It Like To Be a Bodhisattva? Moral Phenomenology in Śāntideva's *Bodhicāryāvatāra*," *Journal of the International Association of Buddhist Studies* 33:(*1–2*), pp. 327–351.

Garfield, J.L. (2012). "Mindfulness and Morality," in German as Achtsamkeit als Grundlage für ethisches Verhalten in M. Zimmermann, C. Spitz and S Schmidtt (eds.), Achtsamkeit 227–250. Stuttgart: Hans Huber and Thai Journal of Buddhist Studies.

Garfield, J.L. (2014a). "Just Another Word for Nothing Left to Lose: Freedom of the Will in Madhyamaka," in M. Dasti and E. Bryant (eds.), *Freedom of the Will in a Cross-Cultural Perspective*, pp. 164–185. New York: Oxford University Press.

Garfield, J.L. (2014b). "Madhyamaka Is Not Nihilism," in J. Liu (ed.), *Nothingness in Asian Philosophy*. London: Routledge, pp. 44–54.

Garfield, J.L., et al. (eds., trans.). (forthcoming). *Alaṃbanāparikṣā*.

Garfield, J.L. and G. Dreyfus. (2011). "Madhyamaka and Classical Greek Skepticism," in The Cowherds (2011), pp. 115–130.

Garfield, J.L. and W. Edelglass (eds.). (2011). *The Oxford Handbook of World Philosophy*. New York: Oxford University Press.

Garfield, J.L. and G. Priest. (2003). "Nāgārjuna and the Limits of Thought," *Philosophy East and West* 53:*1*, pp. 1–21.

Garfield, J.L. and G. Priest. (2009). "Mountains Are Just Mountains," in Garfield, Tillemans and D'Amato (eds.) (2009), pp. 71–82.

Garrett, D. (2002). *Cognition and Commitment in Hume's Philosophy*. New York: Oxford University Press.

Gennaro, R. (2011). *The Consciousness Paradox: Consciousness, Concepts, and Higher-Order Thoughts*. Cambridge, MA: MIT Press.

Gethin, R. (1998). *Foundations of Buddhism*. Oxford: Oxford University Press.

Gold, J.C. (2007). *The Dharma's Gatekeeper: Sakya Paṇḍita on Buddhist Scholarship in Tibet*. Albany: State University of New York Press.

Gold, J.C. (2013). "Reading the Madhyāntavibhāga as a Method for Interpreting Scripture," Yogācāra Group Panel on *Madhyāntavibhāga-bhāsya*, American Academy of Religion Meeting, Baltimore.

Gombrich, R. (2009). *What the Buddha Thought*. London: Equinox.

Gómez, L.O. (1999). "The Way of the Translators: Three Recent Translations of Śāntideva's Bodhicaryāvatāra," in *Buddhist Literature, Vol. 1*, pp. 262–354

Goodman, C. (2008). "Consequentialism, Agent-Neutrality, and Mahāyāna Ethics," *Philosophy East and West* 58:*1*, pp. 17–35.

Goodman, C. (2009). *Consequences of Compassion*. New York: Oxford University Press.

Gopnik, A. (2009). "Could David Hume have Known about Buddhism? Charles François Dolu, the Royal College of La Flèche and the Global Jesuit Intellectual Network," *Hume Studies* 35: 1,2, pp. 5–28.

Gorampa Sonam Sengye. (2011). *lTa ba'i shan 'byed (Freedom from the Extremes)*. Sarnath: Sakya Student Union.

Gorampa Sonam Sengye. (2012a). *lTa ba ngan sel (Elucidation of the View)*. Sarnath: Sakya Student Union.

Gorampa Sonam Sengye. (2012b). *Ngas don rab gsal (Perfectly Clear Ascertainment of the Meaning)*. Sarnath: Sakya Student Union.

Gregory, P.N. (1991). *Tsung-mi and the Sinification of Buddhism*. Princeton: Princeton University Press.

Grice, H.P. (1989). *Studies in the Way of Words*. Cambridge, MA: Harvard University Press.

Guenther, H.V. (1976). *Buddhist Philosophy in Theory and Practice*. Boston: Shambala Publications.

Guerrero, L. (2013). "Knowledge for the Rest of Us: Dharmakīrti's Philosophy of Language." PhD dissertation, University of New Mexico.

Guirao, A. and P. Artal. (1999). "Off-Axis Monochromatic Aberrations Estimated from Double Pass Measurements in the Human Eye," *Vision Research* 39, pp. 207–217.

Gupta, B. (2012). *A History of Indian Philosophy*. London: Routledge.

rGyal tshab dar ma rin chen. (1999). *Byang chub sems pa'I spyod pa la 'jug pa'I mam bshad rgyal sras 'jug ngogs* (Commentary on Bodhicāryāvatāra). Sarnath: Gelugpa Student Welfare Committee.

Hansen, C. (1992). *A Daoist Theory of Chinese Thought: A Philosophical Interpretation.* New York: Oxford University Press.

Harman, G. (1990). "'The Intrinsic Quality of Experience', Philosophy of Mind and Action Theory," *Philosophical Perspectives* 4, pp. 31–52.

Harman, G. (1996). "Qualia and Color Concepts," *Philosophical Issues* 7, pp. 75–79.

Hattori, M. (1980). "Apoha and Pratibha," in M. Nagatomi, B.K. Matilal, J.M. Masson, and E. Dimock, *Sanskrit and Indian Studies, Festschrift in Honor of Daniel H.H. Ingalls*, pp. 61–73. Dordrecht: Reidel.

Haugeland, J. (1979). "Understanding Natural Language," *Journal of Philosophy* 76, pp. 619–632.

Haugeland, J. (2013). *Dasein Disclosed: John Haugeland's Heidegger.* (J. Rouse, ed.). Cambridge: Harvard University Press.

Hawthorne, J. (2002). "Advice for Physicalists," *Philosophical Studies* 109, pp. 17–52.

Hayes, R. (1980). "Dignāga's Views on Reasoning (*Svārtānumāna*)," *Journal of Indian Philosophy* 8, pp. 219–277.

Hayes, R. (2009). "Sensation, Inference and Language: Dignāga's *Pramāṇasammuccāya*," in Edelglass and Garfield (eds.) (2009), pp. 107–115.

Hayes, R. (2011). "Consequences of Compassion: An Interpretation and Defense of Buddhist Ethics: A Review," *Journal of Buddhist Ethics* 18. http://blogs.dickinson.edu/buddhistethics.

Heidegger, M. (1962). *Being in Time.* J. Macquarrie and E. Robinson (eds.). New York, Evanston: Harper & Row, Publishers.

Heim, M. (2013). *The Forerunner of All Things: Buddhaghosa on Cetanā.* New York: Oxford University Press.

Heine, S., and D. Wright. (2010). *The Koan: Texts and Contexts in Zen Buddhism.* New York: Oxford University Press.

Hirakawa, A. (1963). "The Rise of Mahāyāna Buddhism and its Relationship to the Worship of Stūpas," *Memoirs of the Research Department of the Toyo Bunko* 22, pp. 57–106.

Hopkins, J. (1996). *Meditation on Emptiness.* Somerville, MA: Wisdom Publications.

Hume, D. (1896). *A Treatise of Human Nature.* L.A. Selby-Brigge (ed.). Oxford: Clarendon Press.

Huntington, C.W. (2007). "The Nature of the Mādhyamika Trick," *Journal of Indian Philosophy* 35:2, pp. 103–131.

Huntington, C.W. Jr., with N. Wangchen. (1987). *The Emptiness of Emptiness: An Introduction to Early Indian Mādhyamika* Honolulu: University of Hawai'i Press.

Hurvich, L. and D. Jameson. (1960). "Color Vision," *Annual Review of Psychology* 11, pp. 99–130.

Hutto, D. (ed.) (2007). *Narrative and Understanding Persons.* Cambridge: Cambridge University Press.

Hutto, D. (2008). *Folk Psychological Narratives: The Sociocultural Basis of Understanding Reasons*. Cambridge, MA: MIT Press.

Imbo, S.O. (1998). *An Introduction to African Philosophy*. Lanham, MD: Rowman & Littlefield.

Ito, T. (1971). "Authenticity of Pa-pu-i," *Journal of Indian Buddhist Studies* 19:2, pp. 148–149.

Ito, T. (1972). "Authenticity of of Pa-pu-i in the Ta-cheng-hsuan-lun," *Journal of Buddhist Studies, Faculty of Buddhism, Komozawa University* 3, pp. 98–118.

Ito, T. (2009). "The Problem of the Dasheng Solum Xuanyi Ji," *Journal of Buddhist Studies, Faculty of Buddhism, Komozawa University* 40, pp. 83–91.

Jenkins, S. (1998). "The Circle of Compassion: An Interpretive Study of Karuṇā in Indian Buddhist Literature." PhD dissertation, Humboldt State University.

Jinpa, T. (2002). *Self, Reality and Reason in Tibetan Philosophy*. London: Routledge Curzon.

Jizang. (unpublished). *The Profound Mystery of the Middle Way*. Y. Deguchi (trans.).

Kalupahana, D.J. (1976). *Buddhist Philosophy: A Historical Analysis*. Honolulu: University of Hawai'i Press.

Kania, A. (2010). "Silent Music," *Journal of Aesthetics and Art Criticism* 68:4, pp. 343–353.

Kant, I. (1965). *Critique of Pure Reason*. N.K. Smith (trans.). New York: St. Martin's.

Kant, I. (1969). *Foundations of the Metaphysics of Morals with Critical Essays Edited by Robert Paul Wolff*. L.W. Black (trans.). Indianapolis: Bobbs-Merrill Educational Publishing.

Kapstein, M. (2002). *The Tibetan Assimilation of Buddhism: Conversion, Contestation, and Memory*. New York: Oxford University Press.

Kassor, C. (2013). "Is Gorampa's 'Freedom from Conceptual Proliferations' Dialetheist? A Response to Garfield, Priest, and Tillemans," *Philosophy East & West*, 63:3, pp. 399–410.

Kasulis, T.P. (1981). *Zen Action Zen Person*. Honolulu: University of Hawai'i.

Katsura, S. (1969). "Jñānaśñmitra on *Apoha*," in B.K. Matilal and R. Evans (eds.), *Buddhist Logic and Epistemology*. Dordrecht: Reidel, pp. 171–183.

Katsura, S. (1984). "Dharmakīrti's Concept of Truth," *Journal of Indian Philosophy* 12:3, pp. 213–235.

Katsura, S. (1991). "Dignāga and Dharmakīrti on *Apoha*," in Steinkellner (ed.) (1991), pp. 129–146.

Katsura, S. (1992). "*Pramāṇavārttika IV.202–206—Towards the Correct Understanding of Svabhāvapratibandha*," *Journal of Indian and Buddhist Studies* 40:2, pp. 1047–1052.

Katsura, S. (ed). (1999). *Dharmakīrti's Thought and Its Impact on Indian and Tibetan Philosophy: Proceedings of the Third International Dharmakīrti Conference, Hiroshima, November 4–6, 1997*. Vienna: Verlag der Österreichisschen Akademie der Wissenschaften.

Kellner, B. (2001). "Negation a Failure or Success? Remarks on an Allegedly Characteristic Trait of Dharmakīrti's Anupalabdhi Theory," *Journal of Indian Philosophy* 29:(*5–6*), pp. 495–517.

Kellner, B. (2003). "Integrating Negative Knowledge into Pramāṇa Theory: The Development of the dṛśyānupalabdhi in Dharmakīrti's Earlier Works," *Journal of Indian Philosophy* 31:(*1-2*), pp. 121–159.

Kellner, B. (2010). "Self-Awareness (*Svasaṃvedanā*) in Dignāga's Pramāṇasamuccaya and Vṛtti: A Close Reading," *Journal of Indian Philosophy* 38:*3*, pp. 203–231.

Kellner, B. (2011). "Self-Awareness (*Svasaṃvedanā*) and Infinite Regresses: A Comparison of Arguments by Dignāga and Dharmakīrti," *Journal of Indian Philosophy* 39:(*4–5*), pp. 411–426.

Kellner, B. and S. McClintock (eds.). (2014). Special Issue on *ākāra*. *Journal of Indian Philosophy* 42.

Keown, D. (2005). *Buddhist Ethics: A Very Short Introduction*. New York: Oxford University Press.

Keown, D. (2007). "Buddhism and Ecology: A Virtue Ethics Approach," *Contemporary Buddhism* 8:*2*, pp. 97–112.

Khalsa, S., D. Rudrauf, A. Damasio, R. Davidson, A. Lutz and D. Tranel. (2008). "Interoceptive Awareness in Experienced Meditators," *Psychophysiology* 45, pp. 671–677.

Koller, John. (2012). *Asian Philosophies*. 6th ed. Macmillan College Division. Upper Saddle River, NJ: Prentice Hall/Pearson.

Kriegel, U. (2007). "The Phenomenologically Manifest," *Phenomenology and the Cognitive Sciences* 6, pp. 115–136.

Kriegel, U. (2009). *Subjective Consciousness: A Self-Representational Theory*. New York: Oxford University Press.

Kripke, S.A. (1980). *Naming and Necessity*. Cambridge, MA: Harvard University Press.

Kripke, S.A. (1982). *Wittgenstein on Rules and Private Language*. Cambridge, MA: Harvard University Press.

Lai, K.L. (2008). *An Introduction to Chinese Philosophy*. Cambridge: Cambridge University Press.

Lang, K. (2003). *Four Illusions: Candrakīrti's Advice for Those on the Bodhisattva Path*. New York: Oxford University Press.

Laumakis, S.J. (2008). *An Introduction to Buddhist Philosophy*. Cambridge: Cambridge University Press.

Levine, J. (2001). *Purple Haze: The Puzzle of Consciousness*. New York: Oxford University Press.

Lewis, D. (1995). "Should a Materialist Believe in Qualia?," *Australasian Journal of Philosophy* 73:*1*, pp. 140–144.

Lin, C-K. (2013). "How to Attain Enlightenment Through Cognition of Particulars and Universals? Huizhao on *Svaalakṣana and Sāmānyalakṣana*," International

Workshop on Ontology of Asian Philosophy: Perspectives from Buddhist Studies and Analytic Philosophy," Kyoto University. (Manuscript at Chengching National University.)

Lin, C-K. (2014). "Epistemology and Cultivation in Jingying Huiyuan's *Essay on the Three Means of Valid Cognition*." Unpublished manuscript. National Chengchi University.

Loftus, E.F. (1998). "Illusions of Memory," *Proceedings of the American Philosophical Society* 142, pp. 60–73.

Loftus, E.F. and J.C. Palmer. (1974). "Reconstruction of Automobile Destruction: An Example of the Interaction between Language and Memory," *Journal of Verbal Learning and Verbal Behavior* 13, pp. 585–589.

Loizzo, J. (2007). *Nāgārjuna's Reason Sixty (Yuktiṣaṣṭikā) with Candrakīrti's Commentary (Yuktiṣaṣṭikāvṛtti)*. New York: Columbia University Press.

Lopez, D.S. (ed.). (2002). *Religions of Asia in Practice: An Anthology*. Princeton: Princeton University Press.

Lusthaus, D. (2003). *Buddhist Phenomenology: A Philosophical Investigation of Yogācāra Buddhism and the Ch'eng Wei-Shi Lun*. New York: RoutledgeCurzon.

Lutz, A., J.D. Dunne and R. Davidson. (2007). "Meditation and the Neuroscience of Consciousness: An Introduction," in Zelazo, Moscovitch and Thompson (2007), pp. 499–554.

Lutz, A. and E. Thompson. (2003). "Neurophenomenology: Integrating Subjective Experience and Brain Dynamics in the Neuroscience of Consciousness," *Journal of Consciousness Studies* 10:(*9–10*), pp. 31–52.

Lycan, W. (1997). "Consciousness as Internal Monitoring," in N. Block, O. Flanagan and G. Güzeldere (eds.), *The Nature of Consciousness*, pp. 755–772. Cambridge: Cambridge University Press.

Mack, A. (2003). "Inattentional Blindness: Looking Without Seeing," *Current Directions in Psychological Science* 12:*5*, pp. 180–184.

Mackenzie, M. (2007). "The Illumination of Self-Consciousness: Approaches to Self-Awareness in the Indian and Western Traditions," *Philosophy East and West* 57:*1*, pp. 40–62.

Mackenzie, M. (2008). "Self-Awareness Without a Self: Buddhism and the Reflexivity of Awareness," *Journal of Indian Philosophy* 18:*3*, pp. 245–266.

Masson, M. and M. Isaak. (1999). "Masked Priming of Words and Nonwords in a Naming Task: Further Evidence for a Nonlexical Basis for Priming," *Memory and Cognition* 27:*3*, pp. 399–412.

Matilal, B.K. (1998). *The Character of Logic in India*. Albany: State University of New York Press.

Matilal, B.K. and R.D. Evans. (eds.). (1986). *Buddhist Logic and Epistemology: Studies in the Buddhist Analysis of Inference and Language*. Dordrecht: Reidel.

McEvilley, T. (2002). *The Shape of Ancient Thought*. New York: Allworth Press.

McGinn, C. (2004). *Consciousness and Its Objects.* Oxford: Oxford University Press.

McLean, K.A., E. Ferrer, S.R. Aichele, D.A. Bridwel, A.P. Zanesco, T.L. Jacobs, B.G. King, E.L. Rosenberg, B.K. Sahdra, P.R. Shaver, B.A. Wallace, G.R. Mangun and C.D. Saron. (2010). "Intensive Meditation Training Improves Perceptual Discrimination and Sustained Attention," *Psychological Science* 21:6, pp. 829–839.

Merleau-Ponty, M. (1962). *The Phenomenology of Perception.* C. Smith (trans.). London: Routledge and Kegan Paul.

Metzinger, T. (2003). *Being No One: The Self-Model Theory of Subjectivity.* Cambridge, MA: MIT Press.

Meyer, R. and J.M. Dunn. (1972). "A Semantics for Relevant Logic," *Journal of Philosophical Logic* I, pp. 53–73.

Meyers, K. (2010). "Freedom and Self-Control: Freedom in South Asian Buddhism." PhD dissertation, University of Chicago, the Divinity School.

Miller, K. (2005a). "Blocking the Part from Vagueness to Four Dimensionalism," *Ratio* 18:3, pp. 317–331.

Miller, K. (2005b). "A New Definition of Endurance," *Theoria* 71:4, pp. 309–332.

Miller, K. (2008). "Endurantism, Diachronic Vagueness and the Problem of the Many," *Pacific Philosophical Quarterly* 89:2, pp. 242–253.

Miller, K. (2009). "Ought a Fourth-Dimensionalist to Believe in Temporal Parts?" *Canadian Journal of Philosophy* 39:4, pp. 619–646.

Mipham. (2004). *Speech of Delight: Mipham's Commentary on Śāntarakṣita's Ornament of the Middle Way.* T.H. Doctor (trans.). Ithaca: Snow Lions Publications.

Mipham. (2005). *Introduction to the Middle Way by Candrakīrti with Commentary by Ju Mipham.* Padmakara Translation Group (trans.). Boston: Wisdom Publications.

Mitsugiri, J. (1970a). "Eightfold Negation in the Ssu-lun hsüan-i by Hui-chün in Comparison with the Eightfold Negation in the Ta-ch'eng hsüan-lun," *Buddhist Seminar* 12, pp. 31–45.

Mistugiri, J. (1970b). "The Eightfold Negation in the Ta-ch'eng hsüan-lunin: Comparison with the Eightfold Negation in the Ssu-lun hsüan-i by Hui-chün," *Buddhist Seminar* 17, pp. 30–37.

Moore, A., and P. Maliniowski. (2009). "Meditation, Mindfulness and Cognitive Flexibility," *Consciousness and Cognition* 18:1, pp. 176–186.

Most, S.B. (2010). "What's 'Inattentional' about Inattentional Blindness?" *Consciousness and Cognition* 19:4, pp. 1102–1104.

Most, S.B., B.J. Scholl, E. Clifford and D.J. Simons. (2005). "What You See Is What You Set: Sustained Inattentional Blindness and the Capture of Awareness," *Psychological Review* 112, pp. 217–242.

Müller, F.M. (ed.) (2005). *The Questions of King Milinda.* T.W.R. Davids (trans.). London: Routledge-Curzon.

Myers, K. (2010). "Freedom and Self-Control: Free Will in South Asian Buddhism." PhD dissertation, University of Chicago.

Nagao, G.M. (1991). *Mādhyamika and Yogācāra*. L.S. Kawamura (trans.). Albany: State University of New York Press.

Nagel, T. (1974). "What Is It Like To Be a Bat?" *Philosophical Review* 83, pp. 435–450.

Naht Hahn, Thich. (1998). *Interbeing: Fourteen Guidelines for Engaged Buddhism*. Berkeley: Parallax Press.

Nattier, J. (1992/1993). "The Heart Sūtra: A Chinese Apocryphal Text?," *Journal of the International Association of Buddhist Studies* 15:2, pp. 153–223.

Nehamas, A. (1985). *Nietzsche: Life as Literature*. Cambridge, MA: Harvard University Press.

Nida-Rümelin, M. (2007). "*Grasping Phenomenal Properties*," in Alter and Walter (2007), pp. 307–338,

Nishida, Kitaro. (2009). *The Problem of Japanese Culture*. In Edelglass and Garfield (2009), pp. 358–369.

Noë, A. (2002). "Is the Visual World a Grand Illusion?" *Journal of Consciousness Studies* 9:(5–6), pp. 1–12.

Noë, A. (2004). *Action in Perception*. Cambridge, MA: MIT Press.

Noë, A. (2007). "Inattentional Blindness, Change Blindness, and Consciousness," in M. Velmans and S. Schneider (eds.), *The Blackwell Companion to Consciousness*, pp. 504–511. Malden: Blackwell.

Noë, A., L. Pessoa and E. Thompson. (2000). "Beyond the Grand Illusion: What Change Blindness Really Teaches Us About Vision," *Visual Cognition* 7:(1–3), pp. 93–106.

Parfit, D. (1986). *Reasons and Persons*. Oxford, New York: Oxford University Press.

Patil, P. (2003). "On What It Is That Buddhists Think About—Apoha in the Ratnakīrti-Nibandhāvali—," *Journal of Indian Philosophy* 31:(1–3), pp. 229–256.

Patil, P. (2009). *Against a Hindu God: Buddhist Philosophy of Religion in India*. New York: Columbia University Press.

Perdue, D. (2008). "The Tibetan Buddhist Syllogistic Form," *Chun-Hwa Buddhist Journal* 21, pp. 193–211.

Perry, J. (1993). *The Problem of the Essential Indexical*. New York: Oxford University Press.

Plassen, J. (2007). "On the Significance of the Taesüng Saron Hyönyu ki for Research on Early Korean Buddhist Thought: Some Initial Observations Focusing on Hwajaeng," *Journal of Korean History* 136, pp. 29–52.

Powers, J. (trans.) (1995). *Wisdom of Buddha: The Saṃdhinirmocana Mahāyāna Sūtra*. Berkeley: Dharma Publishing.

Powers, J. (1998). *Jñānagarbha's Commentary on Just the Maitreya Chapter from the Saṃdhinirmocana-sūtra: Study, Translation and Tibetan Text*. New Delhi: Indian Council of Philosophical Research.

Powers, J. (2007). *Introduction to Tibetan Buddhism*. Ithaca, Boulder: Snow Lions Publications.

Priest, G. (2002). *Beyond the Limits of Thought*. New York: Oxford University Press.

Priest, G. (2006). *In Contradiction: A Study of the Transconsistent*. New York: Oxford University Press.

Priest, G. (2009). "The Structure of Emptiness," *Philosophy East and West* 59:4, pp. 466–478.

Priest, G. (2014a). *One*. New York: Oxford University Press.

Priest, G. (2014b). "The Structure of Emptiness," in Deguchi, Garfield, Priest and Tanaka (2015).

Prosser, S. and R. Recanati. (2012). *Immunity to Error through Misidentification: New Essays*. New York: Cambridge University Press.

Pryor, J. (1999). "Immunity to Error through Misidentification," *Philosophical Topics* 26:(*1–2*), pp. 271–304.

Ptito, A. and S.E. Leh. (2007). "Brain Mechanisms of Blindsight," *Neuroscientist* 13:5, pp. 506–518.

Quine, W.V. (1969). *Ontological Relativity and Other Essays*. New York: Columbia University Press.

Raffone, A., A. Tagini and N. Srinivasan. (2010). "Mindfulness and the Cognitive Neuroscience of Attention and Awareness," *Zygon* 45:3, pp. 627–646.

Rensink, R. (2000b). "Visual Search for Change: A Probe Into the Nature of Attentional Processing," *Visual Cognition* 7:(*1–3*), pp. 345–376.

Rensink, R.A. (2001). "Change Blindness: Implications for the Nature of Visual Attention," in M. Jenkin and L. Harris (eds.), *Vision and Attention*. New York: Springer, pp. 169–188.

Rensink, R.A. (2002). "Change Detection," *Annual Review of Psychology* 53, pp. 245–277.

Rensink, R.A. (2004). "Visual Sensing Without Seeing," *Psychological Science* 15, pp. 27–32.

Rensink, R.A., J.K. O'Regan and J.J. Clark. (1997). "To See or Not To See: The Need for Attention to Perceive Changes in Scenes," *Psychological Science* 8, pp. 368–373.

Ricoeur, P. (1976). *Interpretation Theory: Discourse and the Surplus of Meaning*. Abilene: Texas Christian University Press.

Rorty, R. (1979). *Philosophy and the Mirror of Nature*. Princeton: Princeton University Press.

Rosch, E. (1999). "Reclaiming Concepts," *Journal of Consciousness Studies* 8:(*11–12*), pp. 61–77.

Rosenthal, D. (2005a). *Consciousness and Mind*. Oxford: Clarendon Press.

Rosenthal, D. (2005b). "The Higher-Order Model of Consciousness," in R. Carter (ed.), *Consciousness*. Berkeley, Los Angeles: University of California Press.

Rotman, A. (2008). *Divine Stories: Divyāvandāna Stories, Part I*. Boston: Wisdom Publications.

Routley, R. (1975). "The Role of Inconsistent and Incomplete Theories in the Logic of Belief," *Communication and Cognition* 8, pp. 185–235.

Saddhatissa, H. (1999). *Buddhist Ethics.* Boston: Wisdom Publications.

Śāntideva. (1997). *A Guide to the Bodhisattva's Way of Life (Bodhicāryāvatāra).* V.A. Wallace and B.A. Wallace (trans.). Ithaca: Snow Lions Publications.

Scharfstein, B. (1998). *A Comparative History of the World Philosophy: From the Upanishads to Kant.* Albany: State University of New York Press.

Schechtman, M. (1996). *The Constitution of Selves.* Ithaca: Cornell University Press.

Scheer, R. (ed.) (1969). *Eldridge Cleaver: Post Prison Writings and Speeches.* New York: Random House.

Schmithausen, L. (2014). *The Genesis of Yogācāra-Vijñānavāda: Responses and Reflections.* Tokyo: International Institute of Buddhist Studies.

Schopen, G. (1999). "The Bones of a Buddha and the Business of a Monk: Conservative Monastic Values in an Early Mahāyāna Polemical Tract," *Journal of Indian Philosophy* 27:4, pp. 279–324.

Schopenhauer, A. (1965). *On the Basis of Morality.* E.F.J. Payne (trans.). Indianapolis: Bobbs-Merrill Educational Publishing.

Schwitzgebel, E. (2011). *Perplexities of Consciousness.* Cambridge, MA: MIT Press.

Searle, J.R. (1997). *The Mystery of Consciousness.* New York: New York Review of Books, Inc.

Sellars, W. (1963). *Science, Perception and Reality.* London: Routledge and Kegan Paul.

Sellars, W. (1992a). "Berkeley and Descartes: Reflections on the Theory of Ideas," in J.F. Sicha (ed.), *Kant's Transcendental Metaphysics: Sellars' Cassirer Lectures Notes and Other Essays,* pp. 363–401.Atascadero, CA: Ridgeview Publishing Company.

Sellars, W. (1992b). "Kant's Transcendental Idealism," in J.F. Sicha (ed.), *Kant's Transcendental Metaphysics: Sellars' Cassirer Lectures Notes and other Essays,* pp. 403–417. Atascadero, CA: Ridgeview Publishing Company.

Sellars, W. (1997). *Empiricism and the Philosophy of Mind.* Cambridge, MA: Harvard University Press.

Sextus Empiricus. (1964). "Outlines of Pyrrhonism," In P. Hallie (ed.), S.G. Etheridge (trans.) *Sextus Empirius: Skepticism, Man and God: Selections from the Major Writings.* Middletown, CT: Wesleyan University Press.

Sharf, R. (2007). "How to Think with Chan *Gong'an,*" in C. Furth, J. Zeitlin and P. Hsiung (eds.), *Thinking with Cases: Specialist Knowledge in Chinese Cultural History,* pp. 205–243. Honolulu: University of Hawai'i Press.

Shear, J. (2004). "Mysticism and Scientific Naturalism," *Sophia* 41:*1,* pp. 83–99.

Shear, J. and R. Jevning. (1999). "Pure Consciousness: Scientific Exploration of Meditation Techniques," *Journal of Consciousness Studies* 6:(2–3), pp. 189–209.

Shiffer, S. (1972). *Meaning.* Oxford: Oxford University Press.

Shiffer, S. (1987). *Remnants of Meaning.* Cambridge, MA: MIT Press.

Shoemaker, S. (1968). "Self-Reference and Self-Awareness," *Journal of Philosophy* 65:*19,* pp. 555–567.

Shoemaker, S. (1994). "Self-Knowledge and 'Inner Sense'," *Philosophy and Phenomenological Research* 54:*2*, pp. 249–314.

Sider, T. (2001). *Four Dimensionalism: An Ontology of Persistence and Time*. Oxford: Oxford University Press.

Siderits, M. (2003). *Personal Identity and Buddhist Philosophy: Empty Persons*. Aldershot: Ashgate Publishing Ltd.

Siderits, M. (2007). *Buddhism as Philosophy*. Indianapolis: Hackett Publishing.

Siderits, M. (2011). "Is Everything Connected to Everything Else? What the Gopīs Know," in The Cowherds (2011), pp. 167–181.

Siderits, M., E. Thompson and D. Zahavi. (eds.) (2013). *Self, No Self? Perspectives from the Analytical, Phenomenological and Indian Traditions*. New York: Oxford University Press.

Siderits, M., T. Tillemans, and A. Chakrabarti (eds.). (2011). *Apoha: Buddhist Nominalism and Human Cognition*. New York: Columbia University Press.

Simmons, P. (2008). "Modes of Extension: Comments on Kit Fine's 'In Defence of Three Dimensionalism'," *Royal Institute of Philosophy Supplements* 83:*62*, pp. 17–21.

Simons, D.J. (2000a). "Attentional Capture and Inattentional Blindness," *Trends in Cognitive Sciences* 4:*4*, pp. 147–155.

Simons, D.J. (2000b). "Current Approaches to Change Blindness," *Visual Cognition* 7, pp. 1–15.

Simons, D.J. and M.S. Ambinder. (2005). "Change Blindness: Theory and Consequences," *Current Directions in Psychological Science* 14:*1*, pp. 44–48.

Skilton, A. (1997). *A Concise History of Buddhism*. Cambridge: Windhorse Publications.

Skow, B. (2009). "Relativity and the Moving Spotlight," *The Journal of Philosophy* 106: 666–678.

Sonam, R. (trans., ed.). (1994). *The Yogic Deeds of Bodhisattvas: Gyel-tsap on Āryadeva's Four Hundred*. Ithaca: Snow Lions Publications

Spelman, E. (1988). *Inessential Woman*. Boston: Beacon Press.

Steinkellner, E. (ed.) (1991). *Studies in the Buddhist Epistemological Tradition: Proceedings of the Second International Dharmakīrti Conference, Vienna, June* 11–16, *1989*. Vienna: Verlag der Österreichischen Akademi der Wissenschaften.

Stiles, W. (1959). "Color Vision: The Approach through Increment Threshold Sensitivity," *Proceedings of the National Academy of Sciences* 45:*1*, pp. 100–114.

Stoljar, D. (2006). *Ignorance and Imagination*. Oxford: Oxford University Press.

Stoltz, J. (2007). "Gettier and Factivity in Indo-Tibetan Epistemology," *Philosophical Quarterly* 57, pp. 394–415.

Strawson, G. (1997). "The Self," *Journal of Consciousness Studies* 4, pp. 405–428.

Strawson, G. (1999). "The Self," in S. Gallagher and J. Shear (eds.), *Models of the Self*, pp. 1–24. Exeter: Imprint Academic.

Strawson, G. (2009). *Selves: An Essay in Revisionary Metaphysics*. New York: Oxford University Press.

Strawson, G. (2011a). "The Minimal Self," in S. Gallagher (ed.), *Oxford Handbook of the Self*, pp. 253–278. New York: Oxford University Press.

Strawson, G. (2011b). *The Evident Connexion: Hume on Personal Identity*. New York: Oxford University Press.

Strawson, G. (2012). "We Live Beyond any Tale that We Happen to Enact," *Harvard Review of Philosophy* 18, pp. 73–90.

Strawson, G. (2013). "Real Naturalism v2." *Metodo. International Studies in Phenomenology and Philosophy*, 1(2), pp. 101–128.

Strawson, P. (1962). "Freedom and Resentment," *Proceedings of the British Academy* 48, pp. 1–25.

Stubenberg, L. (1998). *Consciousness and Qualia*. Philadelphia: John Benjamins Publishers.

Tanahashi, K. (1985). *Moon in a Dewdrop: Writings of Zen Master Dōgen*. San Francisco: North Point Press.

Thakchöe, S. (2007). *The Two Truths Debate: Tsongkhapa and Gorampa on the Middle Way*. Boston: Wisdom Publications.

Thakchöe, S. (2012a). "Candrakīrti's Theory of Perception: A Case for Non-Foundationalist Epistemology in Madhyamaka," *Acta Orientalia Vilnensia* 11, pp. 93–125.

Thakchöe, S. (2012b). "Prāsaṅgika's Semantic Nominalism: Reality is Linguistic Concept," *Journal of Indian Philosophy* 40, pp 427–452.

Thakchöe, S. (2013). "Prāsaṅgika Epistemology: A Reply to sTag tsang's Charge against Tsongkhapa's Use of *Pramāṇa* in Candrakīrti's Philosophy," *Journal of Indian Philosophy* 41, pp. 1–27.

Thompson, E. (2007). *Mind in Life: Biology, Phenomenology and the Sciences of the Mind*. Cambridge, MA: Harvard University Press.

Thompson, E. (forthcoming). "Neurophenomenology and Contemplative Experience," in P. Clayton (ed.), *The Oxford Handbook of Science and Religion*. New York: Oxford University Press.

Thompson, E., A. Lutz and D. Cosmelli. (2005). "Neurophenomenology: An Introduction for Neurophilosophers," in A. Brook and K. Akins (eds.), *Cognition and the Brain: The Philosophy and Neuroscience Movement*. Cambridge: Cambridge University Press, pp. 40–97.

Thompson, E. and F. Varela. (2003). "Neural Synchrony and the Unity of Mind: A Neurophenomenological Perspective," in A. Cleeremans (ed.), *The Unity of Consciousness*. New York: Oxford University Press., pp. 266–287.

Thompson, E. and D. Zahavi. (2007). "Philosophical Issues: Phenomenology," in P.D. Zalazo, M. Moscovitch and E. Thompson (eds.), *Cambridge Handbook of Consciousness*, pp. 67–88. New York: Cambridge University Press.

Thurman, R.A.F. (trans.) (1976). *The Holy Teaching of Vimalakīrti: A Mahāyāna Scripture*. Philadelphia: Pennsylvania State University Press.

Thurman, R.A.F. (1980). "Philosophical Nonegocentrism in Wittgenstein and Candrakīrti in Their Treatment of the Private Language Problem," *Philosophy East and West* 30:3, pp. 321–337.

Thurman, R.A.F. (1984). *The Central Philosophy of Tibet: A Study and Translation of Jey Tsong Khapa's* Essence of True Eloquence. Princeton: Princeton University Press.

Thurman, R.A.F. (1978). "Vajra Hermeneutics," *Journal of the American Academy of Religion* 46:1, pp. 19–39.

Tillemans, T. (1989). "Formal and Semantic Aspects of Tibetan Buddhist Debate Logic," *Journal of Indian Philosophy* 17, pp. 265–297.

Tillemans, T. (1999). *Logic, Language, Scripture.* Boston: Wisdom Publications.

Tillemans, T. (2008). "Reason, Irrationality and Akrasia (Weakness of the Will) in Buddhism: Reflections upon Śāntideva's Arguments with Himself," *Argumentation* 22:1, pp. 149–163.

Tillemans, T. (2011a). "*How do Mādhyamikas Think?: Notes on Jay Garfield, Graham Priest, and Paraconsistency*," in D'Amato, Garfield and Tillemans (2009), pp. 83–100.

Tillemans, T. (2011b). "How to Talk About Ineffable Things: Dignāga and Dharmakīrti on Apoha," in Siderits, Tillemans, & Arindam Chakrabarti (eds.) (2011), pp. 50–63.

Tsongkhapa. (1988). *bBu ma dgongs pa rab gsal (Illumination of the Purport of the Middle Way).* Sarnath: Gelugpa Student Welfare Committee.

Tsongkhapa. (1991a). *Instructions on the Profound Middle Path of the Prāsangika Madhyamaka Tradition (dBu ma thal 'gyur pa'i lugs kyi zab lam dbu ma'i lta khrid),* Collected Works, vol. Sha 578:3. Dharamsala: Paljor Press.

Tsongkhapa. (1991b). "*Kun gzhi dka' 'grel* (Eight Difficult Points)," Collected Works, vol. 15 (Ba), 8. Dharamsala: Paljor Press.

Tsongkhapa. (2000). *The Great Treatise on the Stages of the Path to Enlightenment (Lam Rim Chen Mo): Vol. 1.* The Lamrim Chenmo Translation Committee (trans.). Ithaca: Snow Lion Publications.

Tsongkhapa. (2002). *The Great Treatise on the Stages of the Path to Enlightenment (Lam Rim Chen Mo): Vol. 3.* The Lamrim Chenmo Translation Committee (trans.). Ithaca: Snow Lion Publications.

Tsongkhapa. (2004). *The Great Treatise on the Stages of the Path to Enlightenment (Lam Rim Chen Mo): Vol. 2.* The Lamrim Chenmo Translation Committee (trans.). Ithaca: Snow Lion Publications.

Tsongkhapa. (2006). *Ocean of Reasoning: A Great Commentary on Nāgārjuna's Mūlamadhyamakakārikā.* N. Samten and J. Garfield (trans.). New York: Oxford University Press.

Tsongkhapa. (2014). "In Praise of Dependent Origination," T. Jinpa (trans.). http://www.tibetanclassics.org/html-assets/In%20Praise%20of%20Dependent%20Origination.pdf.

Tye, A. (2009). *Consciousness Revisited.* Cambridge: MIT Press.

Tzohar, R. (2013). "Sthiramati's Critique of Signification and the Philosophical Role and Status of the Madhyāntavibhāga Language Use," Yogācāra Group Panel on Madhyāntavibhāga-bhāsya, American Academy of Religion Meeting, Baltimore.

van Fraassen, B.C. (1980). *The Scientific Image*. Oxford: Clarendon Press.

van Schaik, S. (2011). *Tibet: A History*. New Haven: Yale University Press.

Varela, F.J. (1996). "Neurophenomenology: A Methodological Remedy for the Hard Problem," *Journal of Consciousness Studies* 3, pp. 330–350.

Varela, F.J. (1999). "The Specious Present: A Neurophenomenology of Time Consciousness," in J. Petitot, F.J. Varela, B. Pachoud, and J.-M. Roy (eds.), *Naturalizing Phenomenology: Issues in Contemporary Phenomenology and Cognitive Science*, pp. 266–314. Stanford: Stanford University Press.

Varela, F.J. and J. Shear. (1999). *The View From Within: First-Person Approaches to the Study of Consciousness*. Thorverton: Imprint Academic.

Vasubandhu. (2002). "Treatise on the Three Natures (*Trisvabhāvanirdeśa*)," in J.L. Garfield (2002a), pp. 131–135.

Wallace, B.A. (2008). *Embracing Mind: The Common Ground of Science and Spirituality*. Boston: Shambhala Publications.

Wallace, B.A. (2009). *Contemplative Science: Where Buddhism and Neuroscience Converge*. New York: Columbia University Press.

Walser, J. (2005). *Nāgārjuna in Context: Mahāyāna Buddhism & Early Indian Culture*. New York: Columbia University Press.

Webster, W.R. (2006). "Human Zombies Are Metaphysically Impossible," *Synthese* 151:2, pp. 297–310.

Westerhoff, J. (2009). *Nāgārjuna's Madhyamaka: A Philosophical Introduction*. New York: Oxford University Press.

Westerhoff, J. (2010a). *The Dispeller of Disputes: Nāgārjuna's Vigrahavyavartani*. New York: Oxford University Press.

Westerhoff, J. (2010b). *Twelve Examples of Illusion*. New York: Oxford University Press.

Westerhoff, J. (2011). "The Merely Conventional Existence of the World," in The Cowherds (2011), pp. 189–212.

Williams, P. (2009). *Mahāyāna Buddhism: The Doctrinal Foundations*. 2nd ed. New York: Routledge.

Wittgenstein, L. (1969/1972). *On Certainty*. G.E.M. Anscombe & G.H. von Wright (eds.). New York: Harper's & Row.

Wittgenstein, L. (1961/1974). *Tractatus Logico-Philosophicus*. D.F. Pears and B.F. McGuinness (trans.). London, New York: Routledge and Kegan Paul.

Wittgenstein, L. (1953/2001). *Philosophical Investigations*. G.E.M. Anscombe (ed.) Malden: Blackwell Publishing.

Wood, T. (1991). *Mind Only:A Philosophical and Doctrinal Analysis of the Vijñānavāda*. Honolulu: University of Hawai'i Press.

Yagisawa, T. (2010). *Worlds and Individuals, Possible and Otherwise*. Oxford: Oxford University Press.

Yao, Z. (2005). *The Buddhist Theory of Self-Cognition*. New York: Routledge.

Zahavi, D. (2004). "Phenomenology and the Project of Naturalization," *Phenomenology and the Cognitive Sciences* 3:4, pp. 331–347.

Zahavi, D. (2005). *Subjectivity and Selfhood: Investigating the First-Person Perspective*. Cambridge, MA: MIT Press.

Zahavi, D. (2008). "Internalism, Externalism, and Transcendental Idealism," *Synthese* 160:3, pp. 355–374.

Zahavi, D. (2009). "Is the Self a Social Construct?" *Inquiry* 52:6, pp. 551–573.

Zelazo, P.D., M. Moscovitch, and E. Thompson (eds.). (2007). *The Cambridge Handbook of Consciousness*. New York: Cambridge University Press.

# INDEX


*Abhidhammatthavibhāvini* (see *Reality According to the Abhidhamma*)
Abhidharma 16, 18, 24, 28, 59–62, 79, 182, 194, 258, 287
  on emptiness 59–61
  and Madhyamaka 111
  Pāli Abhidharma 16, n.46
  Sanskrit Abhidharma 32, 46, 59
  on two truths 81–82
Academic skepticism 37
action selection 287
*Actualizing the Fundamental Point* 69
*Additapairyaya-sutta* (see *Fire sutta*)
*adhipati-pratyaya* (immediate condition) 30
affective state 96, 104, 125
agency 128, 280
aggregates (*skhandas*) 12, 106–108, 117, 126–127, 196
*ahaṃkāra* (self-construction) 117–118, 128–129, 302, n. 15
*ākara* 50, 133–134, 148, 158–159, 162, 221, 50, 95
*Alaṃbanāparikṣā svavṛtti* (see *Autocommentary to Examination of the Percept*)
*alambanā-pratyaya* (see supporting condition)
*ālaya-vijñāna* (see foundation consciousness)
Alexander, B. (see Ling, X.)
*ālika* 57
*Anatta-lakkhaṇa-sutta* (see *Discourse on the Characteristic of No-Self*)
*anātman* 97, 102
*anitya* 2
Anscombe, G.E.M. 95, n. 5
*Anthology of the Mahāyāna* 258
anti-realism 27, 31, 62–63, 65, 83, 87–88
*anumāna* 216
*anyapoha* 218–219
*apoha* 48–54, 160, 216, 218–219, 221–222, 225, 236
apperception 95, 103, 155, 184
*applicatio* 14
apprehension 239
  mode of apprehension 240
*arhat* 16, 239
Aristotle 14–15, 81, 96, 281
Armstrong, D. 92, n. 2
*artha* (see intentional object)
*arthakrīyā* 220, 236
*āryan* 233
āryas 233, 238
Asaṅga 20, 71, 114, 258
*Astahaṣrika-prajñāparamitā-sūtra* (*see Perfection of Wisdom sūtra in 8,000 verses*)
Atīśa 21
*ātman* 97, 104, 105, 117, 184
attachment 70
  and self 120
Aurobindo Ghosh 273, n. 13, 274, n. 14

authoritative cognition 145, 214–217, 222–226, 228–229, 232–238, 243
*Autocommentary to Examination of the Percept* 75, 134–135
*Autocommentary to Introduction to the Middle Way* 39–40, 193–195
*Avatamsika Sūtra* (see *Flower Garland Sūtra*)
aversion 70, 120
*avidya* (primal confusion) 2, 9, 28, 52, 68, 89, 114–115, 208, 225, 260, 302 306, n.50
Avramides, A. 325, n. 20
awakening 2, 11, 14, 18

B B principle 150
Baier, A. 119, n. 14
Baker, L. R. 209, n. 12
Bar-On, D. 147, n. 15
Being 257–258
*Being* (wu) 259
*Being and Time* 75
Berkeley, G. 38, 87, 159, 190–191, 195
Bhattacharyya, K. C. 95, n. 5, 96, n. 6
*Bhāvacakra* (wheel of life) 302
Bhāviveka 19, 244
blindsight 170–171
Block, N. 123, n. 1
Blumson, B. 256, n. 4
*bodhi* 2, 11, 14, 18
*Bodhicaryāvatāra* (see *How to Lead an Awakened Life*)
bodhicitta 18, 299–300, 307–308, 310
bodhisattva 18–19, 64, 231, 294, 315
*Bodhisattva Stages* 71
*Bodhisattvabhūmi* (see *Bodhisattva Stages*)
bracketing 176–177, 187, 189–203
Bradley, T. 38, 81
Brandom, R. 325, n. 5
*Brahmavihāras* 313
Buddha-nature 21
Buddhapālita 19, 66
*Buddhavacana* 17, 243

*caitta* 178
Cabezón, J. 158, n. 17
Candrakīrti
  and convention 39–40, 222–224, 225–228
  and conventional truth 46–47, 82–84, 155, 200, 202–203, 222, 230–236
  and epistemology 216, 222–224, 225–228, 230–236
  and non-egocentrism 39–40
  and emptiness 66–67
  and idealism 193–198
  and *pramāṇa* 222–224, 225–228
  and *Prāsaṅgika (reductio-wielders)* 19
  and *Pudgalavāda* 110–112
  and reflexive awareness 133, 137, 140–144, 148–149, 212
  and the self 106, 110–115, 205–207, 209
  and self-knowledge 133, 137 155, 169–170, 184, 197–198
  and the two truths 80, 82–84
  and Yogācāra 71, 130, 137, 140–144, 193–198
canon 17
care (*karuṇā)* 2, 11, 14, 18, 289, 295–297, 310–316, 313, n. 26, 317
Carpenter, A. 18, n. 9, 102, n. 11
Carruthers, P. 153–155, 184, n. 3
Cārvaka 97, 102
*catuṣkoti* (tetralemma)120, 204–205, 242–245, 246–248, 274–275, 257–260, 265
causation 25–26, 28, 29–31, 39, 47, 54, 93, 115, 142
  causal condition 29
  causal continuity 118
  causal dependence 26–28, 78
  and language 29

cessation 13, 16, 116
*cetanā* (intention) 105, 117, 120, 128, 128, n. 8, 198, 283, 287
Chalmers, D. 125, 131–132, 167–172
Chan 20–21, 173–174, 211
*chanda* (see action selection)
Chapman, T. 179
chariot simile 106, 108–109, 112–115, 196
Chi, R.S.Y., 244, n. 2
Chinese Buddhism 20–21
Churchland, P. 97, n. 7, 190, n. 8
Cittamātra (see Yogācāra)
Cogito 150
cognitive practice 233–234
cognitive science 72, 95, 142, 176, 183
coherentism 216, 230–236
*Commentary on Sixty Stanzas of Reasoning* 229
*Commentary on the Encyclopedia of Philosophy* 160, 215
*Commentary to the Ornament of Mahāyāna Sūtras* 268
comparative philosophy 3
compassion (see care)
conceptual imputation 27, 33, 35–36
conditions 28–29
  causal condition 29
  dominate condition 30
  immediate condition 30
  observed condition 29
Confucian philosophy 20, 97
consciousness, 185, 211
  access consciousness 122–125, 210
  creature consciousness (see subjective consciousness)
  and introspection 153–156
  Mipham on 85–87
  phenomenal consciousness 122–125, 210
  and qualia 156–162
  and reflexive awareness 135–152
  responsive consciousness 123–125
  and self 163–167
  and self-knowledge 171–174
  *skandha* 128, 130–131
  subjective consciousness 123–125
  unity of consciousness 102–105
  Yogācāra theory of 73–74
  Zombies 167–171
constitution 54, 59, 106–107, 169
consummate nature 73–74
contact (*sparsa*) 287
continua 45–48, 54, 60–61, 118, 129
convention
  Candrakīrti on 39–40, 196, 222–224, 225–228
  conventional falsehood 57, 226
  and emptiness 31–32, 39–40, 46, 65, 79–87
  and epistemology 225–227
  and ethics 120–121
  and identity 45
  and language 25, 39–40, 54, 57, 266–268, 271–272
  and personal identity 94, 102, 108–109, 111–113, 120–121, 128–129, 196
  Tsongkhapa on 39–40
  and *upāya* (skillful means) 57
conventional nature 227, 230, 232
conventional reality
  Candrakīrti on 46–47, 80, 82–84, 111–113, 155, 196, 200, 202–203, 222, 227, 230–236
  and dependent designation 26, 54, 64–65, 108–109, 111–113, 196
  and emptiness 31–32, 39–40, 46, 64–68, 79–87
  and epistemology 198, 226–240
  and essence 88–89
  and ethics 120–121
  *Heart Sūtra* on 80
  and hermeneutics 24, 26

conventional reality (*Cont.*)
Jizang on 257–258
and Mahāyāna 18–19,
Nāgārjuna on 64–65, 80, 82
as obscurational 46–47
Śāntarakṣita on 82–87, 200
Tsonkghapa on 39–40, 46–48, 155, 226–234, 267, 271–272
and skepticism 64–65
and supervenience 58–59
in Yogācāra 81, 87, 200
conventional truth 226–234
correspondence 250
Coseru, C. 159, n. 19, 172, n. 21, 178, 186, n. 4, 215, n. 1
*Critique of Pure Reason* 38–39, 99, 95, 99, 103–104, 116–117, 191, 197–198, 208

dancing girl 103
Daoism 20–21, 97
*Dasheng xuanlun* (see *Profound Meaning of Mahāyāna*)
De Beauvoir, S. 98, 176
deception 232, 239–240, 243, 249, 265, 271
and conventional truth 232, 239–240
inference as deceptive 243
and introspection 134–136, 200–203
language as deceptive 249–254, 265–266, 271
*bden pa* (see *satya*)
Deguchi, Y. 260–261, n. 6
Dennett, D. 101, 167, 172–173
dependence 34–35, 37, 196, 269
and conceptual imputation 33–40
causal dependence 27–32
mereological dependence 27, 32–33
dependent designation 26, 54, 65, 108–109, 111–113, 196
dependent nature 73–74, 81–82, 199–200
dependent origination 24–40, 64–65, 252, 279, 281
and emptiness 64–65
and ethics 279
and language 252
Nāgārjuna on 64–65, 252
Tsongkhapa on 26
Derrida, J. 257
*Descent into Lanka Sūtra* 20, 71, 143, n.268
Dewey, J. 236, n. 16
*Dhammacakkapavatana-sutta* (see *Discourse Setting in Motion the Wheel of Doctrine*)
*dharma* 16, 18, 32, 46, 58–61, 79, 111, 314
as trope 16
as substantially existent 18, 32, 46, 58–61,
and the two truths, 58–61, 79
as empty 111
as doctrine 314
Dharmakīrti 20, 49–51, 71, 137, 139, 146–148, 160, 164, 215, 219–220,
On *apoha* 50–51
role in Buddhist epistemology 20
doctrine of *apoha* 49–51, 215–220
on phenomenal properties 160
on *pramāṇa* 215–220
on reflexive awareness 137, 139, 146–148
on subjectivity 164
on universals 50–51
and Yogācāra 71
Dharmottara 160
diachronic identity 91–92, 94, 96, 99, 102
*Diamond Cutter sūtra* 65
Dignāga 20, 49, 50, 71, 75, 133–139, 145–146, 157, 209, 212, 224, 186, n.4
and Buddhist epistemology 20
and doctrine of *apoha* 49–51
on perception 75, 133–139
on phenomenal properties 157
as phenomenologist 209

on reflexive awareness 145–146, 186, n. 4, 212
on self-knowledge 137–138
and Yogācāra 71
*Discourse of Vimalakīrti* 18, 20, 63–64, 68, 70, 255–266, 258, 260
*Discourse on the Characteristic of No-Self* 105
*Discourse Setting in Motion the Wheel of Doctrine* 6, 27, 101, n.2
*Discourse Unraveling the Thought* 20, 71, 72–75, 77, 187, 268–269, 329
divine states (see *Brahmavihāras*)
divinities 35
*dmigs rkyen* (see supporting condition)
Dōgen 69–71, 115–116, 155, 212–213,
on language 261–265
on the self 215–216
on subjectivity 212–213
on the two truths 70–71
*don* (see intentional object)
*don dam bden pa*
doubt 198–199
doxography 19–20, 158
*dran pa* (see mindfulness)
*dravyasāt* (substantial existence) 18, 46, 59, 62
Dreyfus, G. 159, n. 19, 215, n. 1, 301, n. 20
*'du shes* (see *saṃjñā*)
dualism 96, 192
Duckworth, D. 134, n. 14, 272, n. 11
*dukkha* (suffering) 2, 6–7, 10, 13, 16, 18, 126, 240, 281–283, 286, 301
cessation of, 16
and consciousness 26
of change 8
and ethics 18, 281–282, 286
Ferlinghetti on 6
as fundamental commitment 2
of pervasive conditioning 8
pervasiveness of 6–7
and primal confusion 10, 13
*'dun pa* (see action selection)
Dunne, J. 215, n. 1

Eckel, M. 134, n. 14
ego-identity 116–117, 120
egoism 10, 13, 290, 301, 310–312
eightfold path 2
elephant simile 187–192, 205–206
eliminativism 60, 102, 111, 97, n.7
*Elucidation of Epistemology* 148
embodiment 96, 203–204
emptiness
Abhidharma conception of 59–61
and appearance 202, 232
Candrakīrti on 66–67
with respect to characteristic 74, 269
and conventional truth 64–68, 240
Dōgen on, 69–71
and convention 31–32, 39–40, 46, 65, 79–87
and dependent origination 24
Fazang on 76–79
*Heart Sūtra* on 63
Hua Yan doctrine 76–79
And impermanence 59
and ineffability 245–246
Jizang on 257–260
and language 252–253
Madhyamaka doctrine 18–19, 62–71
Mipham on 202
Nāgārjuna on 31, 64–68, 167–168, 251–253
And the object of negation 56, 232
of other 22
and paradox 81, 245–246
with respect to production 74, 279
and subject-object duality 192–193, 205
*Sūtra Unraveling the Thought* on 72–75
And three naturelessness 72–75
Tsongkhapa on 31–32, 58, n. 1, 67
Vasubandhu on 75, 192–193
Yogācāra doctrine 71–76

*Encyclopedia of Epistemology* 49, 138, 145
*Encyclopedia of Ontology* 102
engagement 14
entailment 217
*Entangled Vines* 260
epistemic warrant (see *pramāṇa*)
*Epitome of Philosophy* 160
epochē 190, 193
equanimity 289–290
*Essay on the Three Means of Valid Cognition* 224
essence 2, 18, 97–98
*Essence of Eloquence* 267, 270
essentialism 98–99
*Examination of the Percept* 32, n. 8, 75, 134, 159,
experience 70, 131, 132, 151, 157, 168, 175, 182, 191, 193, 203, 211
expressibility 245–246, 248, 254
expressibility paradox 254
expressivism 147, n. 15
externality 74, 81, 134, 188, 205
extrinsic nature 67

fallibilism 234, 236–237
*fāngbiàn* 272
Fazang 21, 75–79
fear 301–303
Feltz, A. 287, n. 5
Ferlinghetti, L. 6
fiction 58, 108, 210–211, 248–254
*Fire Sutta* 12
*Flower Garland Sūtra* 20, 76, 268, n. 9
*for-me-ness* 165–166
foundation consciousness 114, 117, 129–130, 161, 183, 188, 192
foundationalism 216, 224, 234–235
four noble truths 2, 279–281, 289, 315, 381, n. 14,
four-dimensionalism 52–53, 88
Franco, E. 215, n. 1
Freud, S. 126, 150
*Fundamental Verses on the Middle Way* 19, 31–32, 41, 64, 66–67, 70, 80, 82, 204, 223, 227, 230, 244, 247, 251, 314

Gadamer, H-G. 325, n. 20
dgag bya (see object of negation)
Ganeri, J. 100, 102, 102, n. 11, 330, n. 6
Gangeśa 102
Geluk tradition 3, 22, 83, 136, 148, 151
*Genjōkōan* (see *Actualizing the Fundamental Point*)
Gennaro, R. 156
Gettier, E. 99–100, n. 10
Gibson, J. 158
Gold, J. 268–270
Gopnik, A. 45, n. 13
Gorampa (Go rams pa bsod nams seng ge) 22, 136, 148, 155
*Great Discourse on Mindfulness* 305
*Great Exposition of the Stages of the Path* 81, n. 5
Great Vehicle (see Mahāyāna)
Gregory, P. 158, n. 17
Guererro, L. 236, n. 16, 221, n. 6
Gungthang (Gun thang dkon mchog bstan pa'i sgron me) 86, n. 10, 134, 191
Gyeltsab (rGyal tshab dar ma rin chen) 22, 83, 83, n. 7, 86, 203,

Hansen, C. 233, n. 4, 273, n. 12
Harman, G. 125, n. 5
Hattori, M. 215, n. 1
Haugeland, J. 291–292, n. 8
Hayes, R. 215, n. 1
*Heart of Wisdom Sūtra* 18, 63, 77, 80
hedonic tone 185, 287
Hegel, G. 81

Heidegger, M. 9, 66–67, 75, 98, 126, 174, 176–177, 187, 195, 198, 211–212, 257, 125, n. 4
Heim, M. 8, n. 5, 46, n. 14, 128, n. 8, 291, n. 7
hermeneutics 14–15, 24, 26, 273, 292–293
*hetu* 28–29
*hetu-pratyaya* 29
higher-order cognition 103–104, 147
higher-order perception 135–136, 139, 145, 149, 151, 156
higher-order state 136–137, 140, 143, 145, 147, 151, 208–209
higher-order thought 135–136, 139–140, 149, 152, 156
Hinayāna 16
Hopkins, J. 158, n. 17
*How to Lead an Awakened Life* 119, 279, 299, 303, 305–310
Hu, R. (see Alexander, B.)
Hua yan 20–21, 67, 76, 79
Huiyuan 224–225
Huizao 225
Hume, D. 317, n.119
  on abstract ideas 50–51
  on causation 25–26, 29
  on ethics, 119, n. 14, 317
  on identity over time 45, 92
  on the self 94, 107
  and skepticism 37–38
  on substance 195
Husserl, E. 99, 136, 139, 144, 146, 162, 164, 175–176, 187, 190, 197, 209, 211, 130, n. 10
Hutto, D. 101, 291–292, n. 8
Huxley, A. 323, n. 2

idealism
  British idealism 38, 159–160, 190–191
  Candrakīrti on 193–198
  German idealism 38
  Kant's refutation, 190–191
  Yogācāra 20, 27, 33–34, 72–76, 82–83, 203
identity
  and construction 117
  and convention 94, 102, 108–109, 111–113, 120–121, 128–129, 196
  diachronic 39, 54, 91–97, 99, 102
  and existence 36
  personal 91–97, 99, 102, 107–109, 111–113, 115–117, 120–121, 128–129, 196
  synchronic 91, 94–96, 97–101
*Illumination of the Ascertained Object* 148
illusion 10–11, 34, 48, 50, n. 15. 57, 65, 85, 87, n. 11, 89, 103, n. 12, 114, 166, 173, 226, 233, 238–239, 246, 268, 273, 302, 309, 314,
imagined nature 72–73, 181, n. 2, 188, 192, 199
immediate condition 20
impermanence 2, 8, 10, 24, 40–48,
  and 3D-4D debate 52–54
  and emptiness 59
  gross 41–42, 60
  and identity 40–42
  and self 43–45, 104
  and *dukkha* 8, 10
  Sarvastavādin theory of 42, n. 11
  subtle 41–42, 60
"In Praise of Dependent Origination" (*rTen 'brel pa legs bshad snying po*) 31
inattentional blindness 170, n.181
Indigo Girls on primal confusion, 9
ineffability 245–246, 254–266
inference 216–222, 236
inherent existence 228–229, 232, 238, 240
inner sense 177, 191, 193

*Instructions on the Profound Middle Path of the Prāsaṅgika Madhyamaka Tradition (dBu ma thal 'gyur pa'i lugs kyi zab lam dbu ma'i lta khrid*0 26
intensional semantics 251
intention (*cetanā*) 105, 117, 120, 128, 128, n. 8, 198, 283, 287
intentional object 134–135, 192
interdependence 2, 8, 48, 26, 71, 76, 142, 280
intrinsic existence 32
intrinsic identity 18, 24, 71, 75, 111
intrinsic nature 2, 31, 62, 66, 67–68, 142, 202
*Introduction to the Middle Way* 39, 53, 54, 106, 110–111, 134–135, 202, 226–227, 231–234, 234, n. 15, 279, 286, 313, n. 26, 327,
introspection 208, 210
  and consciousness 122–126
  fallibility of 85, 154–156, 170–173, 177–179, 181–182, 183–184, 201
  as higher order thought 151–152
  Kant on 95
  as mediated 95, 177–179
  Mipham on 201
  and mental sense faculty 151
  and neurophenomenology 208, 210
  Śāntarakṣita on 85, 103
  Thompson on 208, 210
  Tsongkhapa on 133, 151–152, 169–170, 184

James, W. 236, n. 16
Jamyang Shepa ('Jam dbyangs bzhad pa ngag dbang brtson 'grus) 22
Jangya (lCang bya) 22
Japan 21
*Jātaka* 279
Jenkins, S. 289, n. 6, 299, n. 11, 301, n. 13
*Jewel Rosary of Advice to the King* 17, 279
*Jin Shi Zi Zhang* (see *Treatise on the Golden Lion*)
*'jig rten bden pa* 58
Jinpa, T. 81, n. 5
Jizang 257–260, 265
Jonang (*Jo nang*) 22

Kagyu (*'bkad brgyud*) tradition 22
Kalupahana, D. 236, n. 16
Kamalaśīla 71
Kania, A. 256, n. 4
Kant, I.,
  on introspection 95
  on phenomena and noumena 38–39
  *Refutation of Idealism* 197–198, 208
  *Schematism* 99
  subjectivity 10, 103–104, 116–117
  transcendental unity of apperception 95, 99, 103–104, 116–117
*karma* 189, 284–285
*karuṇā* (see care)
Katsura, S. 215, n. 1
*Kattō* (See *Entangled Vines*)
Kegon 21
Kellner, B, 158, n. 18, 159, n. 19, 215, n. 1, 221, n. 5
*khanda* 12
Khaydrup (mKhas grub dge legs dpal bzang) 22
*A King Requests Saindhava* 265
*Kleśas* (dysfunctional cognitive states) 290, 305
*kliśṭamanas* (see distorted consciousness)
knowledge 145–152, 198, 214–216, 225–241
  Candrakīrti on 230–234
  coherentism 234–236
  and convention 225–234
  fallibilism 236–237
  and illusion 238–239

Nāgārjuna on 234–236
and ontology 237–238
pragmatism 236–237
and *pramāṇa* 214–216
self-knowledge 145–152, 198
Tsongkhapa on 230–234
and the two truths 239–241
Kriegel, U. 138–139, 149, 165–166, 178
Kumārila 102
*kun brtags* (see imagined nature)
*kun 'dro* (see *sarvaga*)
*kun gzhi* (see foundation consciousness)
*kun rdzob* [(see *samvṛti*)

*lakṣana-niḥsvabhāvataḥ* (see emptiness with respect to characteristic)
*Lam rim chen mo* (see *Great Exposition of the Stages of the Path*)
language
and causation 29
and conception 249–250
and convention 25, 39–40, 54, 57, 120, 266–268, 271–272
Dōgen on 261–265
and introspection 126, 153
inexpressibility 68, 254–266
Jizang on 257–260
as metaphor 268–270
Nāgārjuna on 251–254, 267
and paradox 68, 254–266
and propositional content 250–254
and tantra 273–277
Tsongkhapa on 245, 267, 270–271
and universals 250–251, 274
and use 266–273, 275–276
and the *Vimalakīrti-nirdeśa* 255–256, 258, 260
Wittgenstein on 275–276
and Yogācāra 268–270
*Lankāvatāra sūtra* (see *Descent into Lanka Sūtra*)
law of the excluded middle 204
*lebenswelt* 35, 39, 87, 180, 186, 205
*lectio* 14
*Legs bshad snying po* (see *Essence of Eloquence)*
Leibniz, G. 92
Levine, J. 157
Lewis, D. 89, 152
Lin, C-K, 224, n. 11
Ling, X. (see Hu, R.)
*Liuzu Tanjing* (see *Platform Sūtra of the Sixth Patriarch*)
logic 20, 243–249
categorical logic 242–244
catuṣkoṭi 243–249
formal logic 242–243
modal logic 88
paraconsistent logic 248
*lokavyavahāra-satya* 57
*Lotus Sūtra* 20, 21
*Lucid Exposition* 66, 84, 110, 202, 223, 226
Lusthaus, D. 134, n. 13, 187, n. 5

Madhyamaka 3, 18–19, 61–68
and Abhidharma 111
and anti-realism 65
and consciousness 130
on conventional truth 82–83, 85
on dependent origination 27, 29–32, 35
on emptiness 18–19, 46, 66–68, 74–76
epistemology 216, 233–237, 239–240
on intrinsic nature 61–64
logic 248–249, 271
and modality 87–89
and realism 65, 111
Śāntarakṣita on 201–202
and self 110–115, 120
*sūtras* 18–19
on the two truths 46, 64–65, 80–81
and Yogācāra 22, 77, 86–87, 199–200, 202, n.83

*Madhyamakālaṃkāra* (see *Ornament of the Middle Way*)
*Madhyamakāvatāra* (see *Introduction to the Middle Way*)
*Madhyamakāvatārabhāṣya* (see *Autocommentary to Introduction to the Middle Way*)
*Mahāsatipaṭṭāna-sutta* (see *Great Discourse on Mindfulness*)
Mahāyāna 16–18, 20, 24, 30–32, 39, 59, 79, 294, 313, 268, n. 9
*Mahāyāna Mahāparinirvāṇa-sūtra* (see *Sūtra on the Occasion of the Entry of the Buddha into Final Nirvāṇa*)
*Mahāyānasūtrālaṃkāra* (see *Ornament to the Māhāyana sutras*)
*Mahāyāna-saṃgraha* (see *Anthology of the Mahāyāna*)
*manas-vijñāna* 103, 191
Makeham, J. 134, n. 14
Mañjuśrī 64
*mantra* 274
McClintock, S. 158, n. 18, 159, n. 19, 221, n. 5
materialism 60, 102, 152
Matilal, B. 244, n. 2
meditation 21–22, 140, 183–184, 155, n. 16
memory 93, 105, 116, 136–137, 140–141
mereological dependence 27, 32–33
Merleau-Ponty, M. 176, 211
metaphor 268–270
*mettā* 2, 11, 14, 289
Meyer-Dunn semantics 242
Meyers, K. 128, n. 8
Middle Way (see Madhyamaka)
*Milindapañha* (see *Questions of King Milinda*)
mindfulness 127, 303–304
minimalism 99–101, 110–111, 115, 118–119
Mipham (Mi pham 'jam dbyangs rnam rgyal rgyam tso)
  on consciousness 155–157
  on introspection 201, 206–207
  on Madhyamaka 200–202
  and nonsectarianism 23, 71
  on reflexive awareness 139
  on Śāntarakṣita 83–86, 146, 200–202
  on Yogācāra 83–86
Mitchell, J. 171
monasticism 16, 23
*mu* 204, 246, 259
*muditā* 2, 11, 14, 289–290, 295
*Mūlamadhyamakakārikā* (see *Fundamental Verses on the Middle Way*)
mutual dependence 226–227
Myth of the Given 35, 75, 85, 204

Nāgārjuna 223, 227, 244, 314
  and anti-realism 87–88
  and the catuṣkoṭi 204–205
  on causation 26, 30–33
  and coherentism 234–236
  on conventional reality 64–65, 80, 82
  on emptiness 31, 64–68, 167–168, 251–253
  on epistemology 234–236
  on impermanence 41
  on intrinsic nature 67–68
  on knowledge 234–236
  on language 251–254, 267
  and the Mahāyāna 17, 19
  on paradox 80–81
  and skepticism 65–66
  on the two truths 59–61, 64–65, 80–81, 82

Nāgasena 42–44, 106–109
Nagel, T. 131, 178
Nālandā University 21–22, 82
*rnam pa* (see *ākara*)
Nattier, J. 63, n. 2
negation 14, 219, 246, 252, 253, 259
net of Indra 76, 79
neurophenomenology 176, 192, 208,
*Ngas don rab gsal* (see *Illumination of the Ascertained Object*)
Ngawang Dendar (Ngag dbang bstan dar lha ram pa) 134–135
Ngog Loden Sherab (rNgog lo ts'a ba blo ldan shes rab) 22
*nibbāna* 12–13, 16
*Nicomachean Ethics* 14–15
Nida-Rümelin, M. 157
Nietzsche, F. 98
nihilism 46–48, 63, 71, 105, 114
*nirodha* 12
*nirvāṇa* 2, 11–14, 40, 247
*niścaya* (see determination)
*niácaya-pratyaya* 160
Nishida, K. 115, 116
nominalism 26, 51, 217, 240
non-being 13, 257, 259
non-duality 205, 255, 261,
  and ethics 10–11, 290–291, 295, 315
  and hermeneutics 332–333
  and language 274–275, 276–277
  subject-object 10–11, 74–75, 80–81, 166–167, 188–213
  and the two truths 63–65, 70, 80–81, 315
non-egocentrism 40
non-sectarianism 23
noumena 39
numerical identity 92–93
Nyāya 102, 104, 112, 216, 223–224, 234–235, 242, 244, 251–252
*Nyāyabindu* (see *Epitome of Philosophy*)
Nyingma (*sNying ma*) tradition 22

object of negation 56, 59, 61–62, 66, 71, 75, 111, 115, 129, n. 9, 130,
*On Certainty* 47, 142, 198, 223
*On the Basis of Morality* 10
*On the Phenomenology of Internal Time Consciousness* 9
oral lineage 22
ordination lineage 21
*Ornament of Mahāyāna Sūtras* 268
*Ornament of the Middle Way* 82–83, 144, 199, 200
*Ōsakusendaba* (see *A King Requests Saindhava*)
outer sense 177, 193
*Outlines of Pyrrhonism* 37

pain 7
Pāli 16–17
  Abhidharma 16, 46, n. 14
  Buddhism 16
  canon 15, 25, 105
  suttas 16, 244, 268, n. 9
  tradition 17
Panchen Chokyi Nyima (Thub bstan chos kyi nyi ma) 22
*parabhāva* 61, 67
paracompleteness 248
paraconsistent logic 68, 81, 248
paradox 65–70, 80–81, 204, 245–246, 254–256
*Paramārthasamutgtāta* 71
*paramartha-satya* (see ultimate truth)
*paratantra* (see dependent nature)
Parfit, D. 45, n. 13, 93–94
*parikalpita* (see imagined nature)
*pariniṣpanna* (see consummate nature)

*Path of Purification* (see *Visuddhimagga*)
perception
and consciousness 132–135
and *dukkha* 13
and experience 122
and illusion 86, 180–181
as a *pramāṇa* 216, 218, 236
and qualia 156–162
and reflexive awareness 136–144
as a *skhanda* 127, 130
Tsongkhapa on 151–152
Perdue, D. 244, n. 2
*Perfection of Wisdom Sūtra in 8,000 verses* 18, 65–66
*Perfection of Wisdom sūtras* 18, 59, 61, 65, 77, 194, 244, 269
personal identity
and convention 94, 102, 108–109, 111–113, 120–121, 128–129, 196
diachronic 91–92, 94, 96, 99, 102
ego-identity 116–117, 120
personalist 109
pervasion (*vyapti*) 217
pessimistic induction 237
phenomenal concept 132–133, 155, 157
phenomenal properties 133, 136, 156–157, 160, 162
phenomenology 175–179
deep phenomenlogy 179–180, 183
and emptiness 35, 72–76
moral phenomenology 279, 294–317
and ontology 199
and self-consciousness 162–167, 172–174, 212–213
surface phenomenology 179–184, 188
Tracy Chapman on 179
and the three natures 72–76, 186–206
Vasubandhu's 87, 155, 186–193, 205–206, 210
and Yogācāra 72–76, 186–209
*Philosophical Investigations* 33, 75, 112, 126, 178, 198, 201, 250, 254, 257, 267
*Platform Sūtra of the Sixth Patriarch* 20
Plato 96
Possible worlds 88
Powers, J. 134, n. 14
pragmatism 234, 236–237, 246
*Prajñāparamitā sūtras* (see *Perfection of Wisdom sutras*)
*Prajñāparamitā-Hṛdāya sutra* (see *Heart of Wisdom Sūtra*)
*prajñāptisāt* 18, 46, 59
*pramāṇa* 145, 214–217, 232–238,
and *apoha* 222
Candrakīrti on 222–234
Huiyan on 224–225
conventional pramāṇa 226–234
Nyāya theory 222–223
ultimate pramāṇa 233
*Pramāṇasammucāya* (see *Encyclopedia of Epistemology*)
Pramāṇavāda 20, 215, 223
*prameya* 215–216, 224–225, 235, 237–238
*Prapañca* 89
*prāsaṅgika* (see *reductio-wielders*)
*pratītya-samutpāda* 2, 279
*pratijñā* 215, 250, 267
*pratyakṣa* 216
*pratyaya* 28–29
*pratyekabuddhas* 231
*preta* 35
primal confusion 9–11
Candrakīrti on 114–115
as origin of *dukkha* 2, 11, 28, 52
and ethics 306
Indigo girls on 6
and introspection 208
and intuitions 89
and *pramāṇa* 50, n. 15

as superimposition 9–11, 52, 68
primitive identity 96–97
primordial awakening 21
*Profound Meaning of Mahāyāna* 257
protension 102
Pudgalavāda 109–111
*puruṣārthas* 220, 222, 236
Pyrrhonian skepticism 37

qualia 122–123, 152, 156–162, 169, 206–207
qualitative consciousness (see phenomenal consciousness)
qualitative state 167–168, 169
*Questions of King Milinda* 42–44, 46, 47, 53–54, 106–109, 112
Quine, W.V. 36, 50, 96, 190

*rang rgyud pa* (see *those who advance their own argument*)
Ratnakīrti 49, 51, 221–222
*Ratnāvalī* (see *Jewel Rosary of Advice to the King*)
realism 63, 85, 87, 203
Geluk 151
Madhyamaka 65, 111
about the self 119
*Reality According to the Abhidhamma* 60
rebirth 18
reduction 58, 60
mereological reduction 59
ontological reduction 59
phenomenological reduction 199
*reductio-wielders* 19, 58, n. 1
reflexive awareness, 135–149, 186, n. 4
Candrakīrti on 133, 137, 140–144, 148–149, 212
and consciousness 135–144
memory argument 140–142
and self-knowledge 135–152
and subjectivity 136–144
Tsongkhapa on 136, 148–152
*reg pa* (see contact)
reification 13, 46–48, 70, 116, 118, 208, 211
*Reply to Objections* 234–236, 251–254
representation 50, 95, 133–134, 148, 158–159, 162
responsiveness 123
retention 102
Ri-meh (*Ris-med,* non-sectarianism) 23, 71
"rock" problem 142
Routley, R. 242
*rūpa* (matter) 12, 127

*śabda* (testimony, scriptural authority) 216, 225
*Saddharma Puṇḍarīka Sūtra* (see *Lotus Sūtra*)
Saddhatissa, H, 291, n. 7
Sakya tradition 22, 136
Sakya Chokden (Sha skya mchog ldan) 22, 136
Sakya Pandita (Chos rje sa skya pan di ta kun dga' rgyal mtshan) 22, 147, 148, 267
*samanantara-pratyaya* 30
*Saṃdhinirmocana sutra* (see *Discourse Unraveling the Thought*)
*saṃjñā* 127, 127 n. 7, 287
*sammuti* 46, n. 14
*samprajaña* 127, 304
*saṃsāra* 28, 254
*samskāra* 12, 59
*saṃveda* 127
*samvṛti* 39, 46, n. 14, 57, 84, 166, 277
*samvṛti-satya* 57
San Lun 257
Sanskrit 17, 22

Śāntarakṣita
on conventional reality 82–87, 200
on introspection 201, 203
on reflexive awareness 136, 144, 212
on the self 103–105
synthesis of Madhyamaka and Yogācāra 82–87, 83, n. 7, 89, 199–203
and transmission to Tibet 21
on the two truths 82–87
on unity of consciousness 103–104, 111
and Yogācāra as phenomenology 71, 82–87, 199–203
Śāntideva 119, 140–142, 303, 307–310, 315
Sarnath 279
Sartre, J-P. 147, 176
*sarvaga* (continuously operative) 287
Sarvastivāda 42, n. 11
*satya* 56–57, 228
Sautrāntika 158–159, 164
schemata 116
Schopenhauer, A. 10, 38, 181
Schwitzgebel, E. 178
scriptural authority (*śabda)* 216, 225, 236
Seal, B. 3
self
and aggregates 106
basis of designation 48
Candrakīrti on 106, 110–115, 205–207, 209
and consciousness 166, 186, 205–206, 211–213
Dōgen on 69–71
and ethics 120
and experiential integration 104
and identity 91–93, 95–96
and illusion 115, 118, 166
and intentionality 117–118
and impermanence 104
Madhyamaka conceptions of 109–116
Milindapaña on 105–109
Orthodox Indian views 102–104
Pāli account of 105–106
self-knowledge 145–152, 198
mere self 48
narrative self 101
physical basis 100–101
Śāntarakṣita on 103–105
Tsongkhapa on 48
Uddyokatara on 102–103
Western positions 91–101
self-awareness 142, 212
self-consciousness 99, 162–163, 166, 174, 176, 185
self-grasping 13, 111, 114, 117–118, 130
self-knowledge 193, 201–202
Candrakīrti on 133, 137 155, 169–170, 184, 197–198
Dignāga on 137–138
Kriegel on 138–139
and consciousness 171–174
higher-order models 152–156
Mitchell on 171
and reflexivity 135–146
and self-luminosity 147–152
self-luminosity 135–136, 146–147
Sellars, W. 75, 85, 90, 99–100, n. 10, 126, 133, 136, 142, 198, 325, n. 20
sensation 127, 206
sentience 144
sevenfold analysis (Candrakīrti's) 112–113, 197
Sextus Empiricus 37
Sharf, R. 266, n. 7
*shes bzhin* (see mindfulness)
Shoemaker, S. 147, n. 15
Siderits, M. 3, 18, 32, 59, 60, 62, n. 8300
silence 243, 254–266
*skandha* 12, 106, 117, 126–127

and consciousness 128, 130–131
and *khanda* 12
five *skandhas* 12, 106, 196
skepticism 65–66
skillful means (*upāya*) 57–58, 272, 297
*skye ba ngo on yid med pa* (see emptiness with respect to production)
*smṛti* (see mindfulness)
sortal 53–54
*sous erasure* 257–258
*sparsa* (see contact)
specific identity 92–93
Spelman, E. 98, n. 9
spontaneity 21, 70–71, 145, 174, 261, 267, 288, 289, 309, 317
śrāvaka 231
Śrāvakayāna 16–18, 42, 268, n. 9
*srid 'khor* (see *bhāvacakra*)
Steinkellner, E. 215, n. 1
Sthiramati 34, 71, 267–268
Stoltz, A. 330, n. 6
Strawson, G. 178
structuralism 67
Stubenberg, L. 142–143
subjectivity 35, 206–213
and consciousness 123–126
Dōgen on 213
higher order theories of 152–156
expert 70–71, 174
Merleau-Ponty on 211–212
Nishida on 115
and reflexivity 136–144
and the self 95, 99, 119–120, 162–167
and self-luminosity 146–152
transformation of 70–71
and qualia 156–162, 206–207
and unity of consciousness 102–104
and "what it is like" 206–209
Yogācāra accounts of 186–206, 209–210
Zen accounts of 211
and zombies 170–171
subject-object duality 75, 115, 160, 167, 192–193, 200, 205, 208, 213
substantial existence (see *dravyasāt*)
suffering (*dukkha*) 2, 6–7, 10, 13, 16, 18, 39, 126, 179, 240, 282–283, 286, 301
cessation of, 16
and consciousness 26
of change 8
and ethics 18, 281–282, 286
as fundamental commitment 2
of pervasive conditioning 8
pervasiveness of 6–7
and primal confusion 10, 13
Sumaṅgala 60
*śūnya* 2
*śūnyatā* 18
supporting condition 29, 77
*sūtra* 6, 18, 20
and *sutta* 6
Mahāyāna *sutras* 17
*Sūtra on the Occasion of the Entry of the Buddha into Final Nirvāṇa* 319
*sutta* 6, 17, 57
and *sūtra* 6
Pāli Suttas 16, 244, n. 268
*svabhāva* 2, 61–67, 98, 251
*svaprakaśa* (self-illumination) 143
*svasaṃvedanā* (reflexive awareness) 127, 136
*svatantrika* (see *those who advance their own argument*)

Takṣaśilā 22
Tanaka, K. 238, n. 11
tantra 273–277
*Tattvasaṃgraha* (see *Encyclopedia of Ontology*)
Tendai 21
tetralemma (*catuṣkoti*) 120, 204–205, 242–245, 246–248, 257–260, 265, 274–275

*tha snyad* (conventional, nominal) 57, 238
*tha snyad bden pa* (nominal or conventional truth) 58
*thab mkhas* (*upāya*, skilful means) 272–273
Thakchöe, S. 81, n. 5, 134, n. 14
*thal 'gyur pa* (see *reductio-wielders*)
Theravāda 16, 289, 291
*Thirty Stanzas* 34, 71, 258
Thompson, E. 35, n. 9, 100, 117–118, 130, n. 10, 164, 172, n. 21, 175–176, 208, 211–212
*those who advance their own argument* 19, n.58
*Three Dialogues Between Hylas and Philonous* 38, 159
Three Treatise Shool (*Sanlun*) 257
Three-dimensionalism 52–53, 88
Three-natures 72–74, 77–78, 186, 188
Three-naturelessnesses 72–75, 78
Thurman, R. 224, n. 10, 273–277
Tiantai 20–21
Tibet 21–23
Tibetan schools 21–22
Tillemans, T. 244, n. 2
*Transcendental Aesthetic* 191
transcendental subject 104
translation 4, 5, 21–22, 56, 289, 322, 330–333
*Treatise of Human Nature* 107
*Treatise on the Golden Lion* 77
*Treatise on the Three Natures* 71, 187, 193, 202,
*Trimsikakārikā* (see *Thirty Stanzas*)
*Trisvabhāva* (see three natures)
*Trisvabhāvanirdeśa* (see *Treatise on the Three Natures*)
tropes (*dharmas* as) 16
Tropes of Anasedemus 34, 37
truth 47, 56, 88, 201, 226, 228, 238–239, 269
*Tshad ma rnam 'grel* (see *Elucidation of Epistemology*)
*tshad ma* (*pramāṇa*) 214, 215
*mtshan nyid ngo bo nyid med pa* (see emptiness with respect to characteristic)

Tsongkhapa (Tsong kha pa)
  And convention 39–40,
  on conventional reality 39–40, 46–48, 155, 226–234, 267, 271–272
  on conventional truth 226–234
  on dependent origination 26
  on doxography 19–20
  on emptiness 31–32, 58, n. 1, 67
  and the Geluk school 22
  on ignorance or primal confusion 9
  on introspection 133, 151–152, 169–170, 184
  on karma 284
  on knowledge 230–234
  on language 245, 267, 270–271
  on the object of negation 71
  on reflexive awareness 136, 148–152
  on the self 48
  on transformation 13
  on the two truths 81, n. 5
  and Wittgenstein 39–40, 133
  on Yogācāra 130
*tshor ba* (see hedonic tone)
*Twenty Stanzas* 34, 71
*Twenty Verses* 32, 75
*Twilight of the Idols* 98
two realities (see two truths)
two truths 56–59, 112, 120, 195, 202, 239–240, 258
  Abhidharma conception 79–80
  Candrakīrti on truths 80, 82–84
  Dōgen on 70–71
  fourfold two truths 258
  and knowledge 239–241
  in Madhyamaka 46, 64–65, 80–81
  in Mahāyāna 18–19, 79–87
  Nāgārjuna on 59–61, 64–65, 80–81, 82

and paradox 80–81
Śāntarakṣita on 82–87
Tsongkhapa on 81, n. 5
In Yogācāra 81–82
Tzohar, R. 268–270

Uddyotakara 102–104
ultimate existence 47, 59, 61, 79, 232, 245
ultimate nature 227, 231, 232
ultimate non-existence 245
ultimate pramāṇa 238
ultimate reality 19, 46, 63, 81, 121, 206, 314
ultimate truth 18, 58
as emptiness 80
and ethics 315
as identical to conventional truth 80, 88, 227–228, 239–240
as ineffable 255–266
as literal truth 24, 58
unconscious 115
universals
and *apoha* 48–54, 221–222
and continua 51–54
Dharmakīrti on 50–51
Dignāga on 49–50
Huizhao on 225
and inference 217
and meaning 250–251, 274
meaning universal 274
Ratnakīrti on 221–222
term universal 274
*upadāna-niḥsvabhāvataḥ* (see production)
*upamāna* (inference) 216, 229, 236
*upāya* (see skillful means)
*upekkhā* (see equanimity)
*upekṣā* (see equanimity)

Vaibhāśika 133, 158, 159
*Vajrachedika* (see *Diamond Cutter*)
*Vasanas* (predispositions) 219, 222
Varela, F. 35, n. 9
Vasubandhu
on emptiness 75, 192–193
idealism 34, 75
phenomenology 87, 155, 186–193, 205–206, 210
and Yogācāra 20, 71
*vedanā* 12, 127, 185, 287
Vedānta 80
*Vigrahavyāvārtanī* (see *Reply to Objections*)
*vijñāna* 12, 127–130, 185
*Vijnānavāda* 20, 71
*Vijñaptimātra* 20, 71
Vikramśīla 22
Vimalakīrti 64, 260
*Vimalakīrti-nirdeśa-sūtra* (see *Discourse of Vimalakīrti*)
*Vimśatikā* (see *Twenty Verses*)
Vinaya 15–16
visual field 180–181, 188
*Visuddhimagga* (see *Path of Purification*)
*vyapti* 217
*vyāvahāra* 39, 227, 238

Walser, J. 19, n. 10
Westerhoff, J. 87, n. 11, 238, n. 17, 251, n. 3
"what it is like" 206–207
without-thinking 173
Wittgenstein, L. n. 58, n.99–100
on analogy 223
and Candrakīrti 39–40
on causality 31
on convention 37–38, 112
on conventionalism 39–40, 47, 99–100, n,. 10, 142, 257
on epistemology 47, 142
on language as a tool 58, n. 1, 250, 254, 257, 267, 275–276
on mereological dependence 33
on nominalism 51–52

Wittgenstein, L. n. (*Cont.*)
  on self-knowledge 75, 126, 133, 178, 198, 201
  on subjectivity 10
  and Tsongkhapa 39–40, 133

*yid dbang shes* (see *manas-vijñāna*, introspective consciousness)
Yogācāra 71–76,
  Candrakīrti on 71, 130, 137, 140–144, 193–198
  conventional reality 81, 87, 200
  and Madhyamaka 22, 77, 86–87, 189, 199–200, 202, n.83
  and consciousness 129, 173–174
  and dependent orgination 27, 33
  on emptiness 72–76
  idealism 20, 85, 201
  on language 268–270
  Mipham on 85
  and metaphysics 72
  and perception 160–161
  and phenomenology 20, 85, 87–89, 186–193, 203, 209
  and reflexive awareness 136–144
  and subjectivity 186–206, 209–210
  and three natures 72–74
  and three naturelessnesses 72–75
  on the two truths 81–82
  Tsongkhapa on 130
*yongs su grub pa* (*parinispanna*, see consummate nature)
*Yuktiṣaṣṭikāvṛtti* (see *Commentary on Sixty Stanzas of Reasoning*)

Zahavi, D. 130, n. 10, 162–165, 178
Zen 21, 69, 173–174, 204, 211–212
gzhan dbang (see dependent nature)
gzhan stong 22
zombies 122, 125, 132, 133, 167–171 206